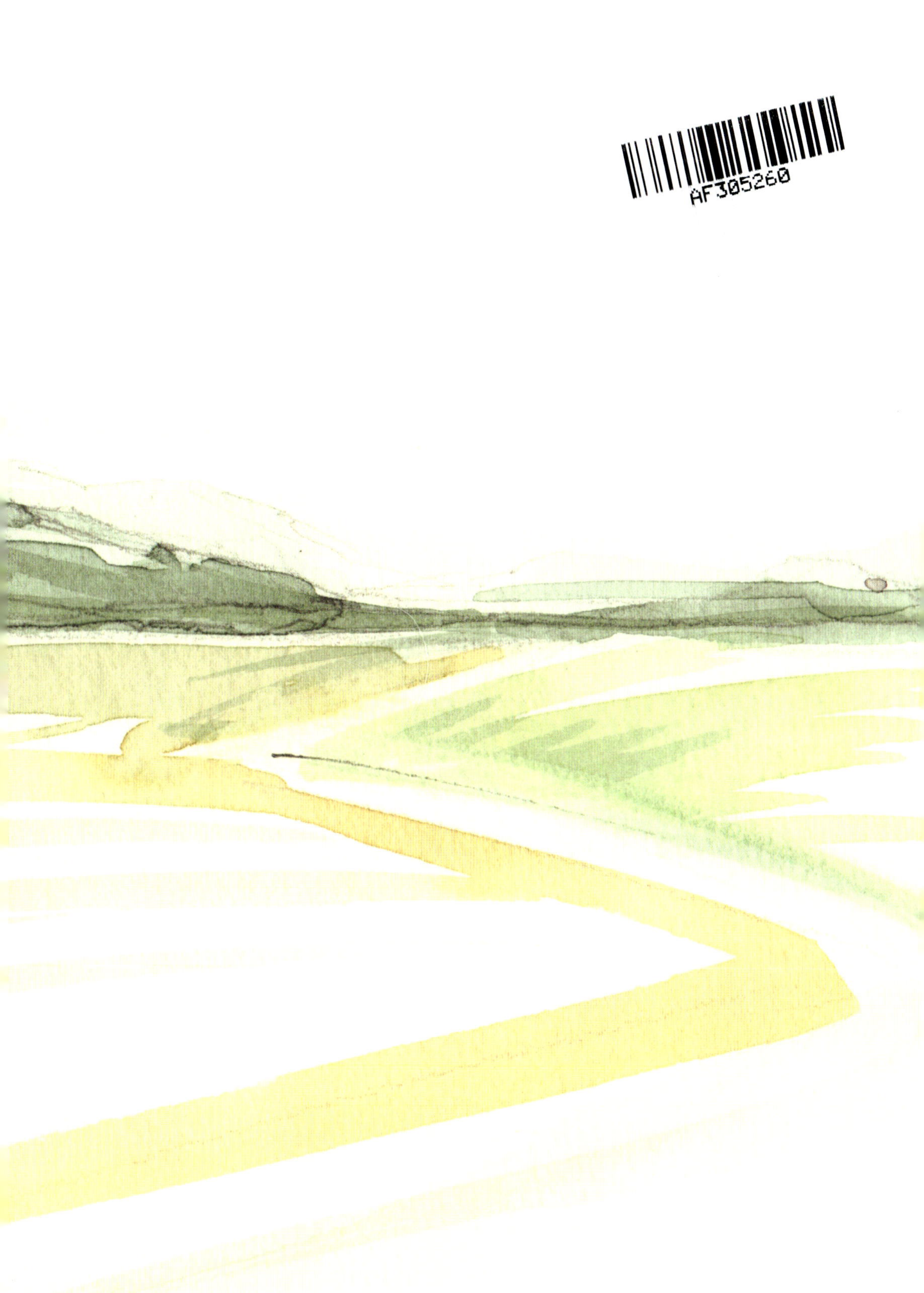

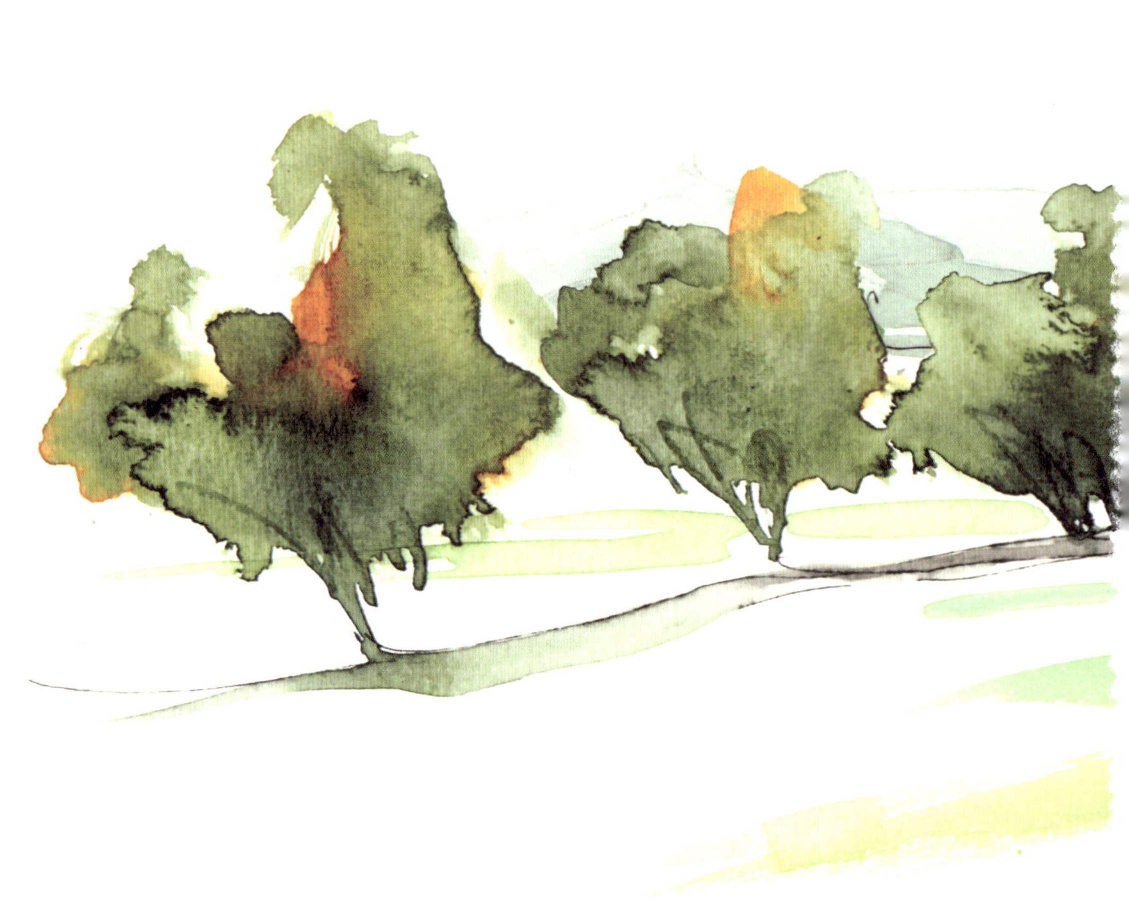

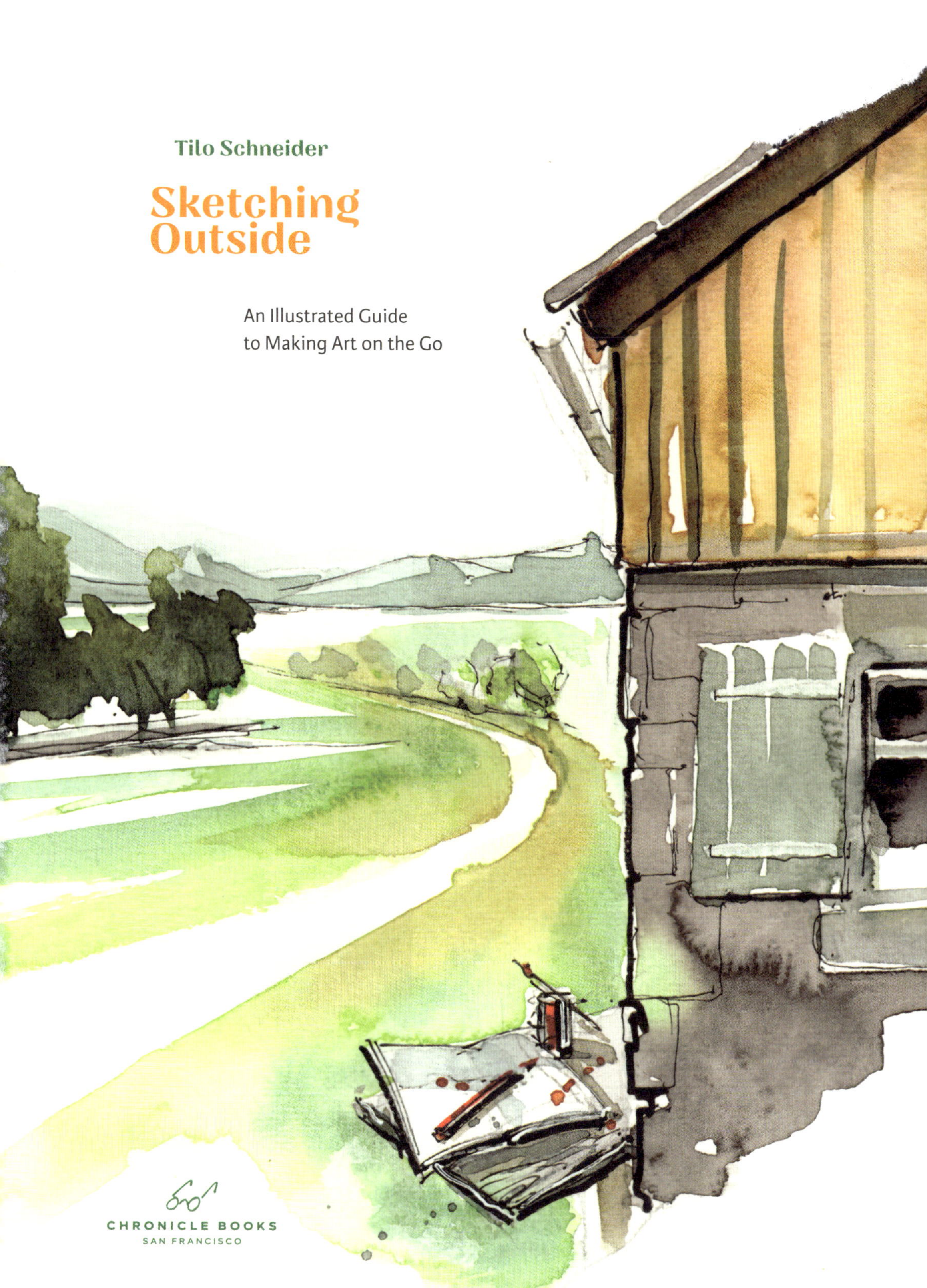
Tilo Schneider

Sketching
Outside

An Illustrated Guide
to Making Art on the Go

CHRONICLE BOOKS
SAN FRANCISCO

Foreword

This book takes you outdoors to draw, observe, and move around in the natural world. When it gets too cramped indoors for ideas, vision, and creativity, it's time to pack a pencil and paper and head out for a short walk, a daylong hike, or that long-awaited sketching tour.

As a designer and travel illustrator, I like the word "sketching," with its connotations of the unfinished, the draft, the attempted rendering. It aptly sums up what's fascinating about drawing, whether indoors or outdoors: to just do it and see what happens.

You don't have to be a brilliant artist to succeed on this pathway. My book encourages you to shape your own creative outdoor experiences with open eyes, few materials, and a little practice. Without any fear of the blank page, whether you're a beginner or an experienced artist.

This book was created outdoors, en plein air. Not only did I produce almost all the pictures, sketches, and watercolor drawings outside, but I also wrote most of the text, location notes, and practical instructions in all kinds of natural settings—in wind and weather, with an unobstructed view.

I have the privilege of living close to nature in my favorite landscape: the foothills of the Alps. This is where I return after my workshops and painting trips. But no matter where you live, step outside your front door to see all the new artistic landscapes you can discover!

—*Tilo Schneider,* Bernau am Chiemsee, 2023

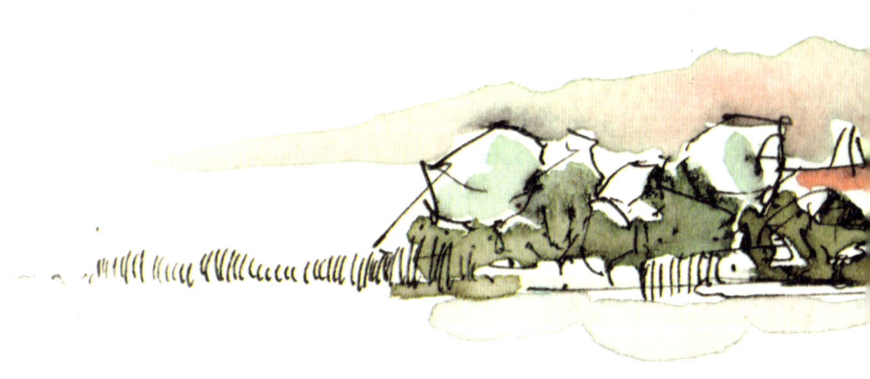

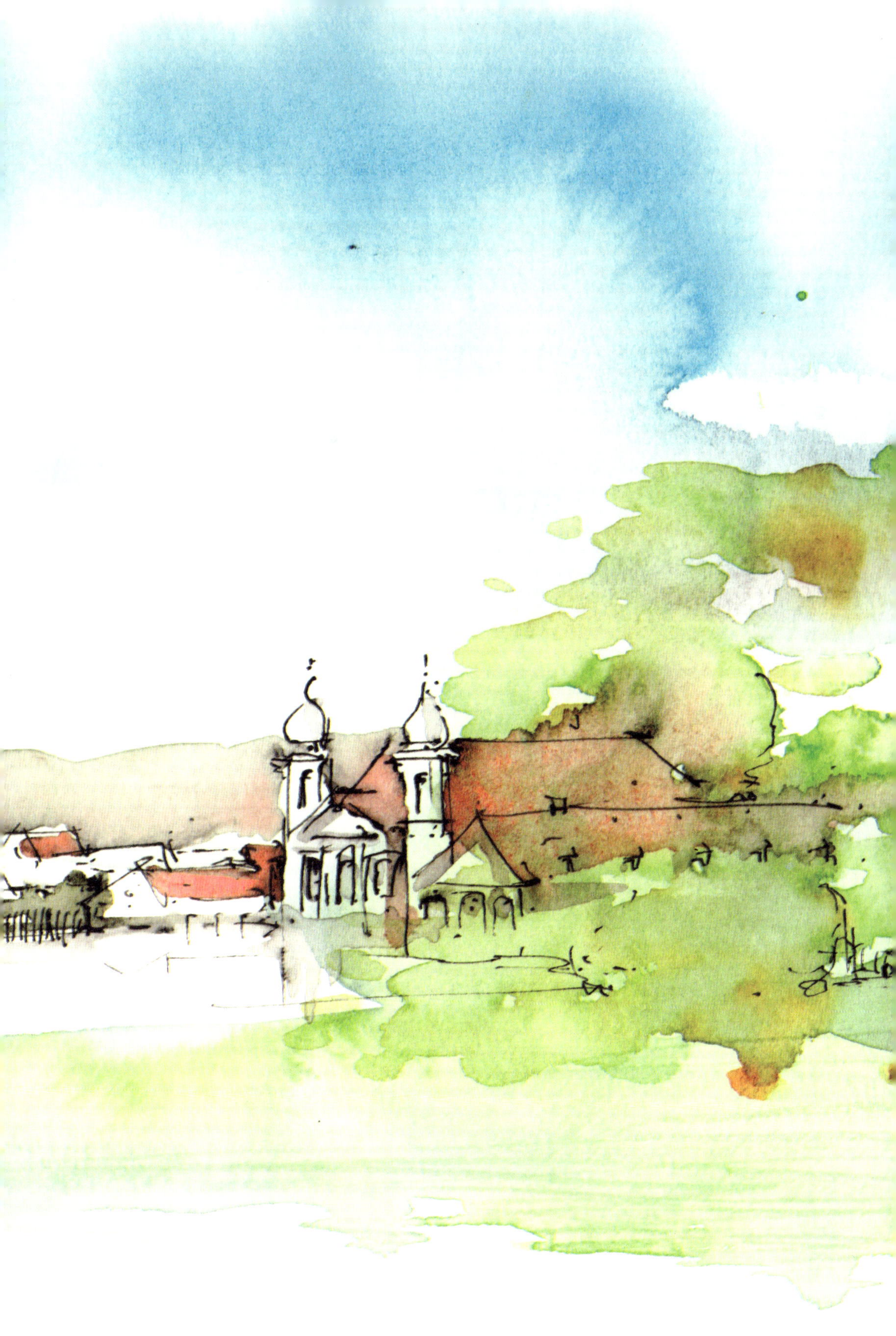

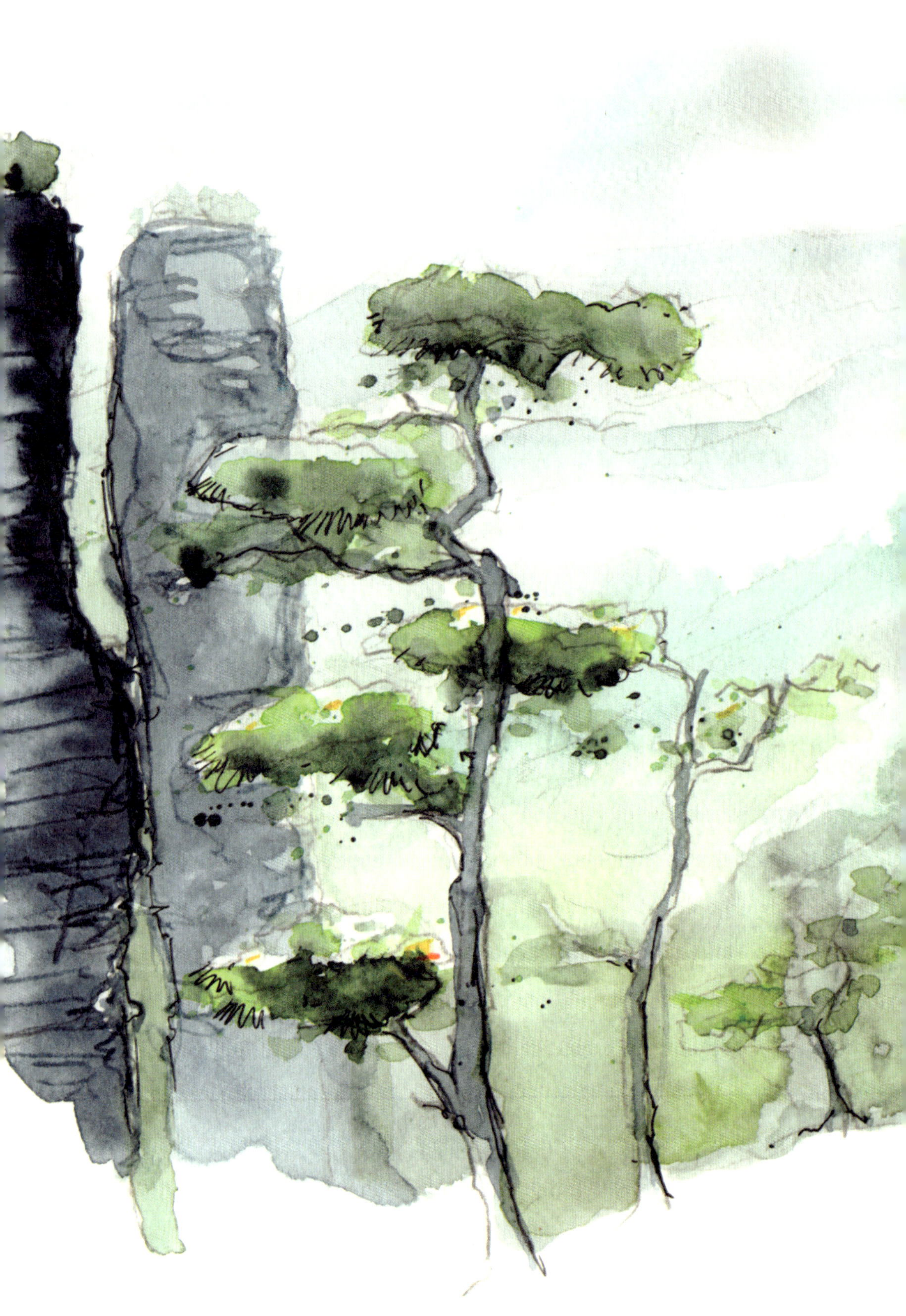

Why You Should Read This Book

The first time you open this book, you won't be outdoors. Maybe you'll be in a bookstore, in an office, at a desk, or at home on the sofa. You probably do most of your creative work indoors in familiar, sheltered surroundings where everything is within reach and your internet connection is stable. So why should you sketch outdoors?

I want to take you outside for two reasons. For one, with just a few things in your bag, you can sketch—by hand—nature, landscapes, mountains, the weather, and much more. These are authentic outdoor experiences that no smartphone can capture for you.

The second benefit is that you'll return indoors a changed person. Mindful observations while walking outdoors, experiencing your surroundings visually and physically, changing horizons, shapes, and colors are all excellent stimulants for creativity. They give us fresh ideas and pictures that we can take with us and further build on.

En Plein Air

You may be wondering: Is sketching outdoors a new trending pastime? Is it an excuse to get away or a form of self-care? It's certainly more than that and certainly not new. Attempts to escape the acceleration of the era are as old as the Industrial Revolution. In the early nineteenth century, rambling in the great outdoors was all the rage. Artists, too, felt compelled to pack a pencil and paper in their backpacks to explore new pathways: from the romanticism of William Turner to classical modernism and from Caspar David Friedrich's jaunts in picturesque rocky landscapes to Lyonel Feininger's hiking sketches of the Harz Mountains.

Traveling architects like Karl Friedrich Schinkel also captured their impressions in drawings and paintings. The German architect Bruno Taut drew inspiration from 1930s Japan and recorded his travel experiences and ideas in a sketchbook.

Equip Yourself Wisely

I want to remove as many barriers as possible to getting you started. Typically, a book about drawing begins with a long list of necessary materials and tools. You can find my recommendations at the end of this book. They're not set in stone. You may want to add some of them to the list of products you already use. Consider the topics on the following pages an invitation to experiment.

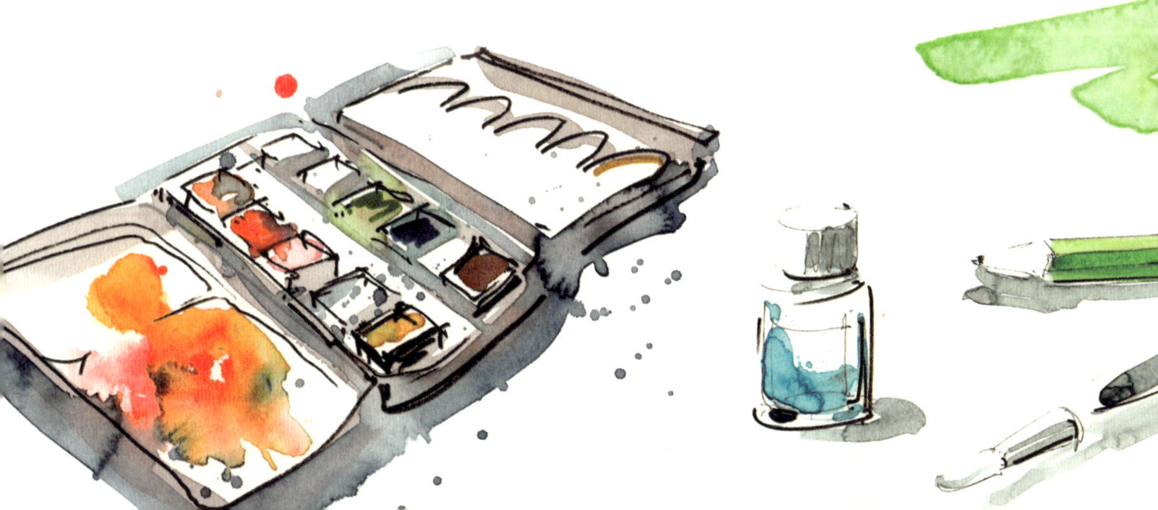

How to Use This Book

You can read the book in one sitting or pick out individual chapters. I prepared a pathway for you through the major and minor themes of outdoor sketching. You don't need to follow it in the order presented here; each chapter contains practical exercises for exploring on your own.

Take this book with you outdoors. Don't put it on the bookshelf with your other art books until you've gotten down to work.

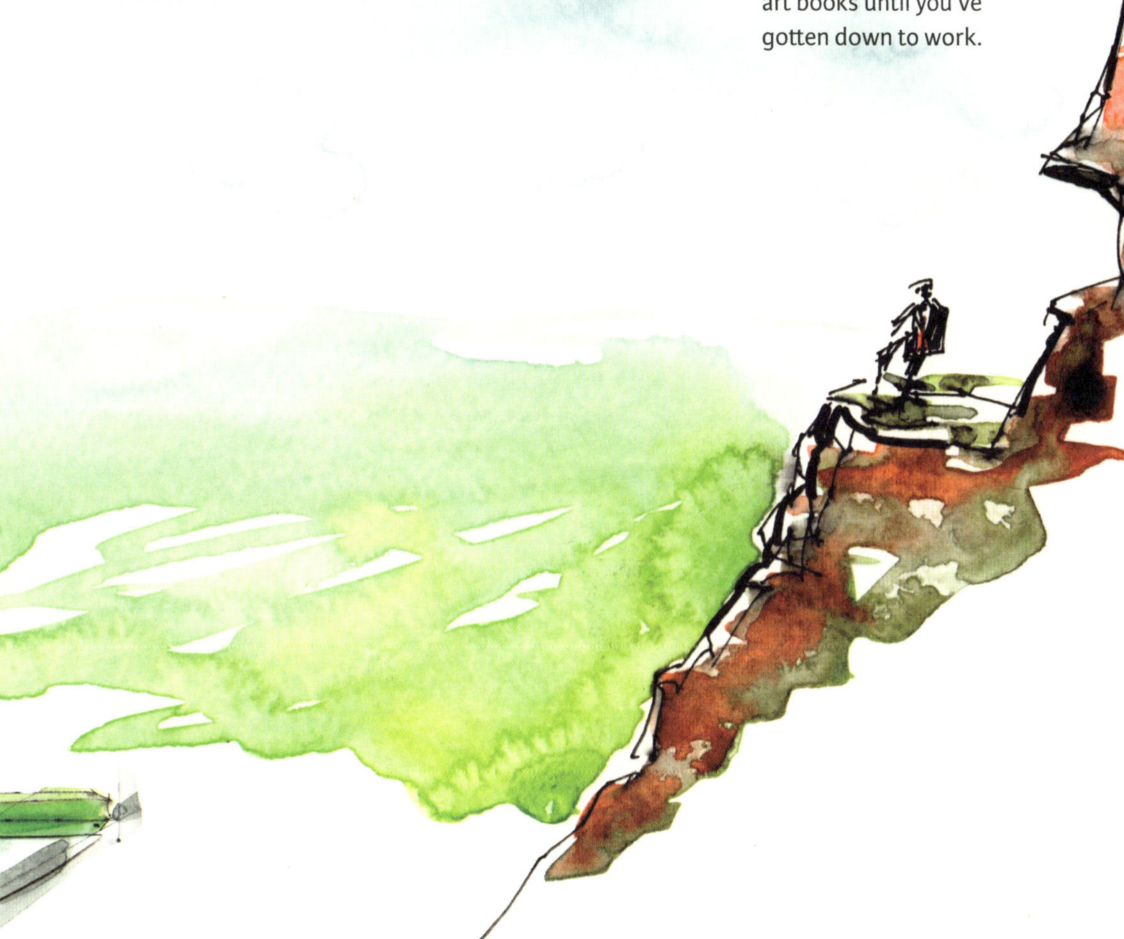

A Diary, Travel Companion, Place for Ideas, and Creative Playground

Your sketchbook is your own private business; it's not meant for a target audience, and it doesn't serve a readership. Knowing this frees you from placing excessive expectations on your own creativity. No one will judge you; anything goes.

So, you might ask, is this art for art's sake pure self-indulgence? An artist's sketchbook is many things: a visual diary, a travel journal, and a playground for creative ideas. I use mine to capture ideas for drafts while traveling. A few years ago, I took a very inspiring trip to Japan. While traveling the country, I got a lot of ideas for a client project and quickly scribbled them down. The sketchbook from that trip effectively combined drawings and travel impressions.

Most Importantly, a Book

There are many ways that sketchbooks differ from sketchpads. First, you can't tear out single pages. You can't use the paper from a sketchbook to later exhibit and sell your work. All the other differences are advantages. Sketchbooks are compact and easy to carry and don't need an underlying support, and the bound pages don't get lost easily, but they will reliably end up on a shelf, labeled with the year and place.

Most importantly, sketchbooks are *books*. A sketchbook is a tactile, sensory, aesthetic experience. The more travel entries, patina, and traces of daily use, the better!

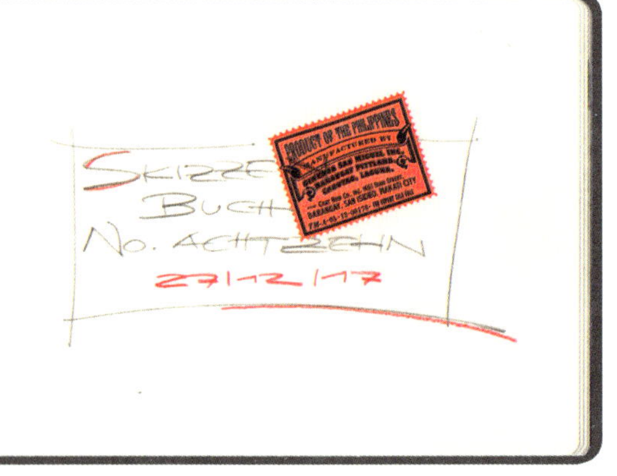

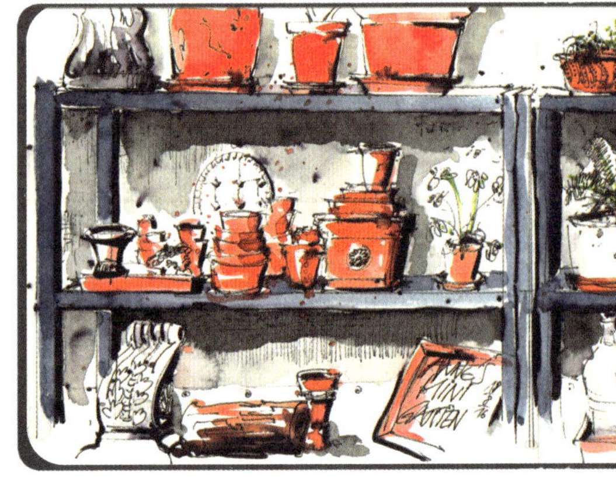

Tip: Horizontal subjects like landscapes call for horizontal sketchbooks (for sketching vertical forms such as architecture, simply turn them around). Compact books in vertical format make it easier to draw undisturbed in busy places and fit comfortably in your hand.

Every illustrator has their own ritual for initiating a new sketchbook. I usually label and collage the first inside page. I begin with a date, a number, a few lines, some color, and pasted found objects.

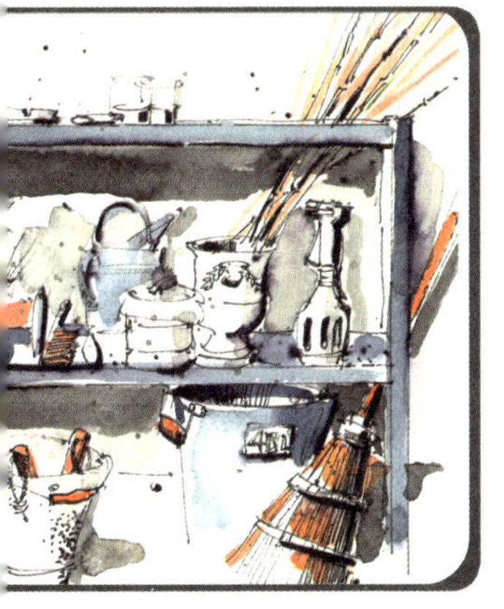

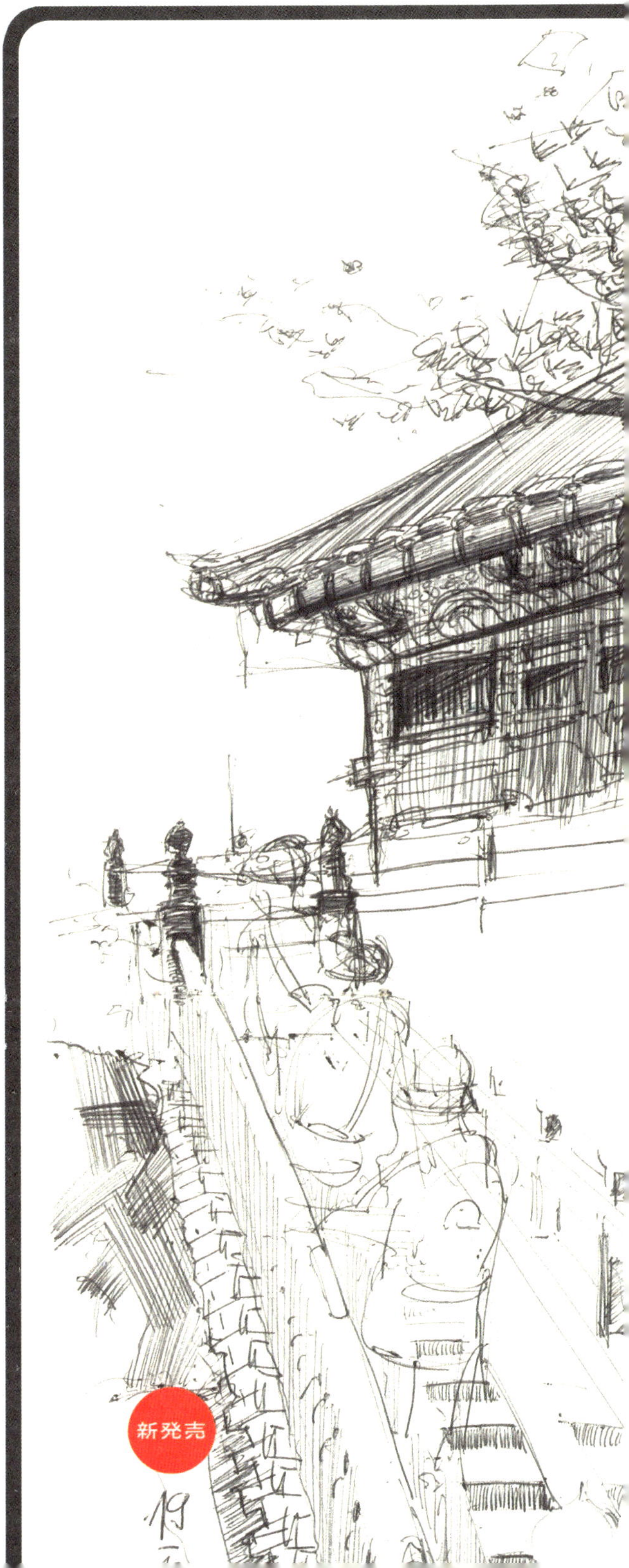

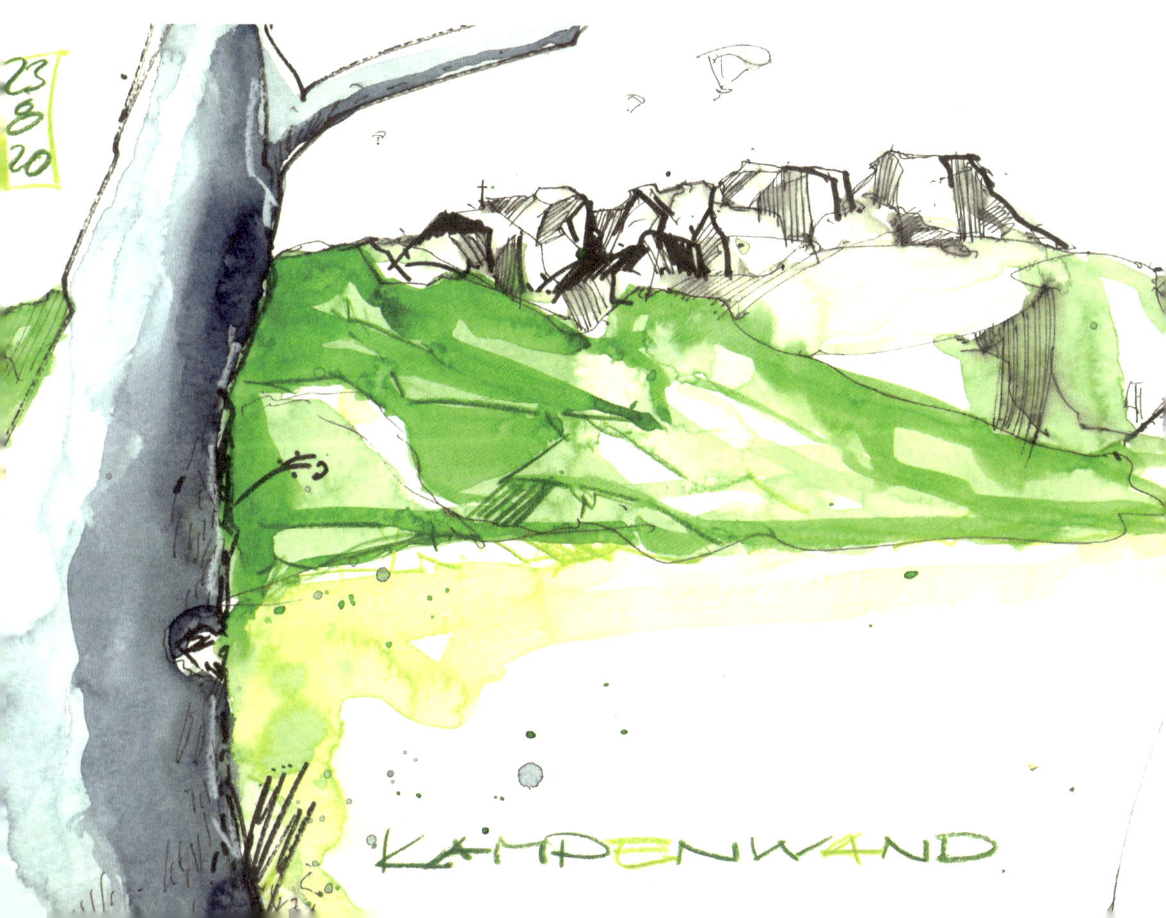
23
8
20
KAMPENWAND.

From the City into the Natural World

Maybe you're already an outdoor sketch artist. Thanks to social media, a global creative community of urban sketchers has formed in recent years. They're creative enthusiasts who escape their living rooms and sit on street corners with their sketchbooks, defying the unpredictability of a drawing in the here and now. Outside, in the city bustle, in a café, on the subway.

But let's go a step further for even more powerful sketching: out into the natural world. Changing light and weather conditions, imposing landscapes, and surprising encounters along the way make outdoor sketching an experience with a lasting impact. After just a few yards and a few stops to sketch along the way, a new world of your very own opens up both in your sketchbook and within yourself.

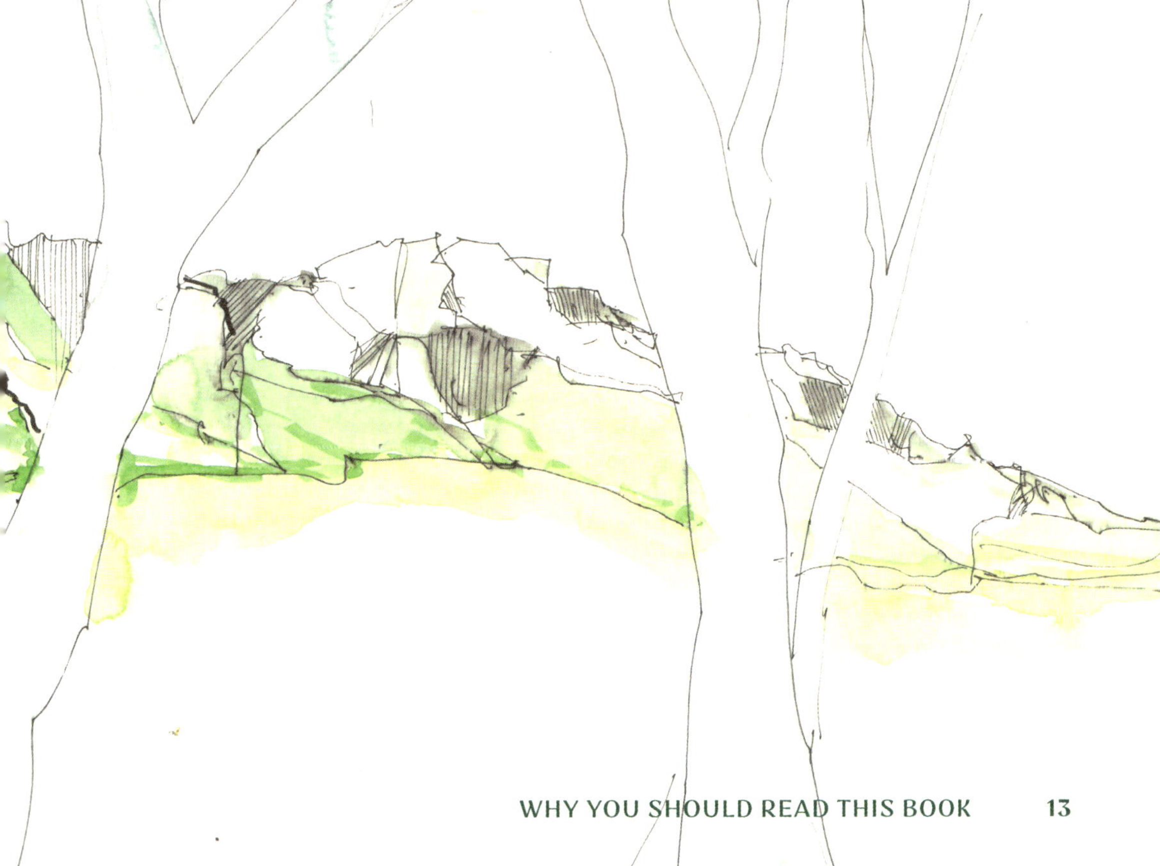

Go Out and Get Started

Do you feel like packing your painting things and going outdoors yet? It's not enough to read drawing guides. Only personal experience with your own sketchbook will give you the sense of a stimulating, meaningful, and lasting creative activity. There are plenty of good reasons to get started. Three of them are unbeatable:

Right on Your Doorstep

You don't have to plan a trip to sketch outdoors. Just swap your desk and computer for sturdy shoes and a sketchbook. The nearest hillside and minimal drawing materials are all you need. You're on foot, heightening your awareness, having personal (visual) experiences that are direct and immediate.

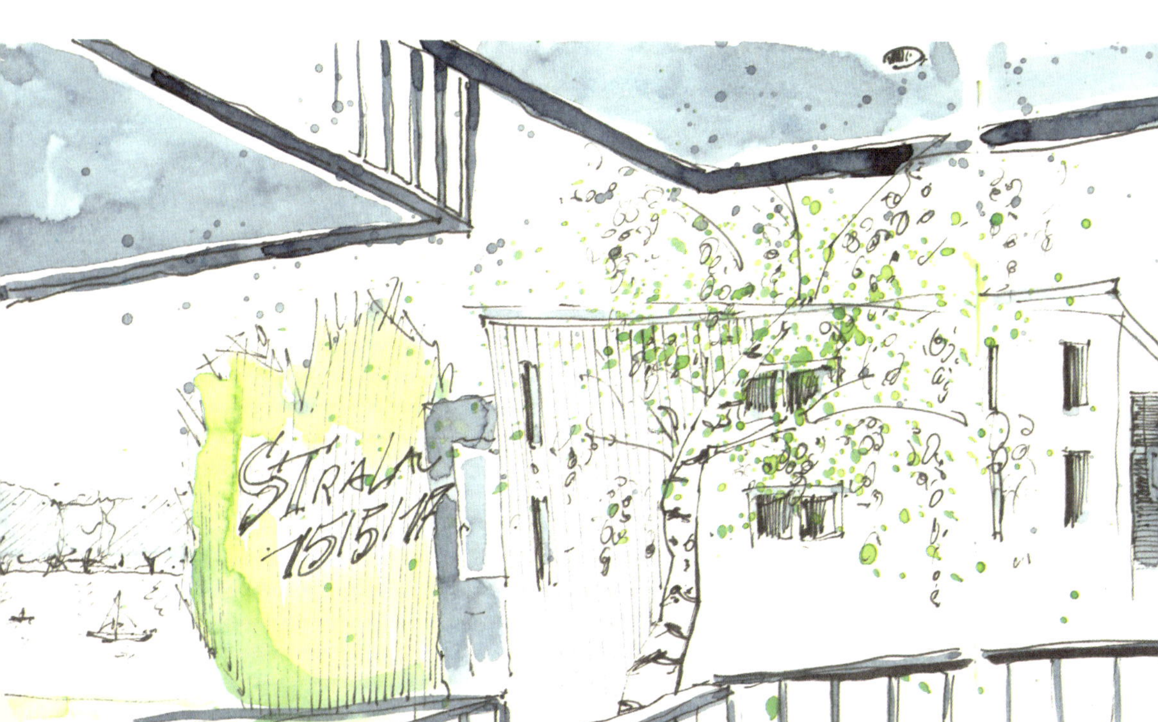

By Hand

Drawing is an authentic, manual, creative experience. What your hand produces is guided and influenced by your eye, head, and gut. Sketching and scribbling are creative methods that have long become established in the world of work. Pictures, styles, and ideas evolve and grow as you create. Even a digital brush on a tablet captures your individual handwriting.

Serendipity

Drawing means relinquishing control and being open to surprises. It's like when you're using a lot of water to work with watercolors: You can plan all you want, but you can't predict the result. When sketching outdoors, more surprises come into play: a ray of light breaking through the clouds, a raindrop falling on the paper, or the wind blowing the pages around. Random encounters with people and animals also take your sketches in new directions.

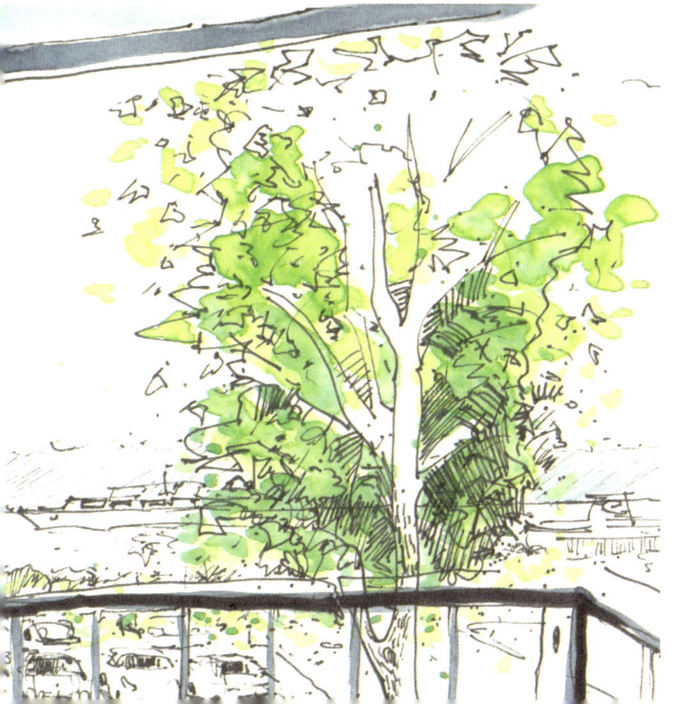

First ² Steps

You're ready to go! But are you really? You know the feeling: You're out with a brand-new sketchbook and you come across a great subject. But it can be so overstimulating that you don't know how or where to start your drawing. A breathtaking landscape, boats rocking on the water, towering clouds in the sky; shapes, colors, and details are gathered in the foreground, middle ground, and background, all clamoring to be captured in your sketch. You don't want to leave any of it out, yet it's overwhelming.

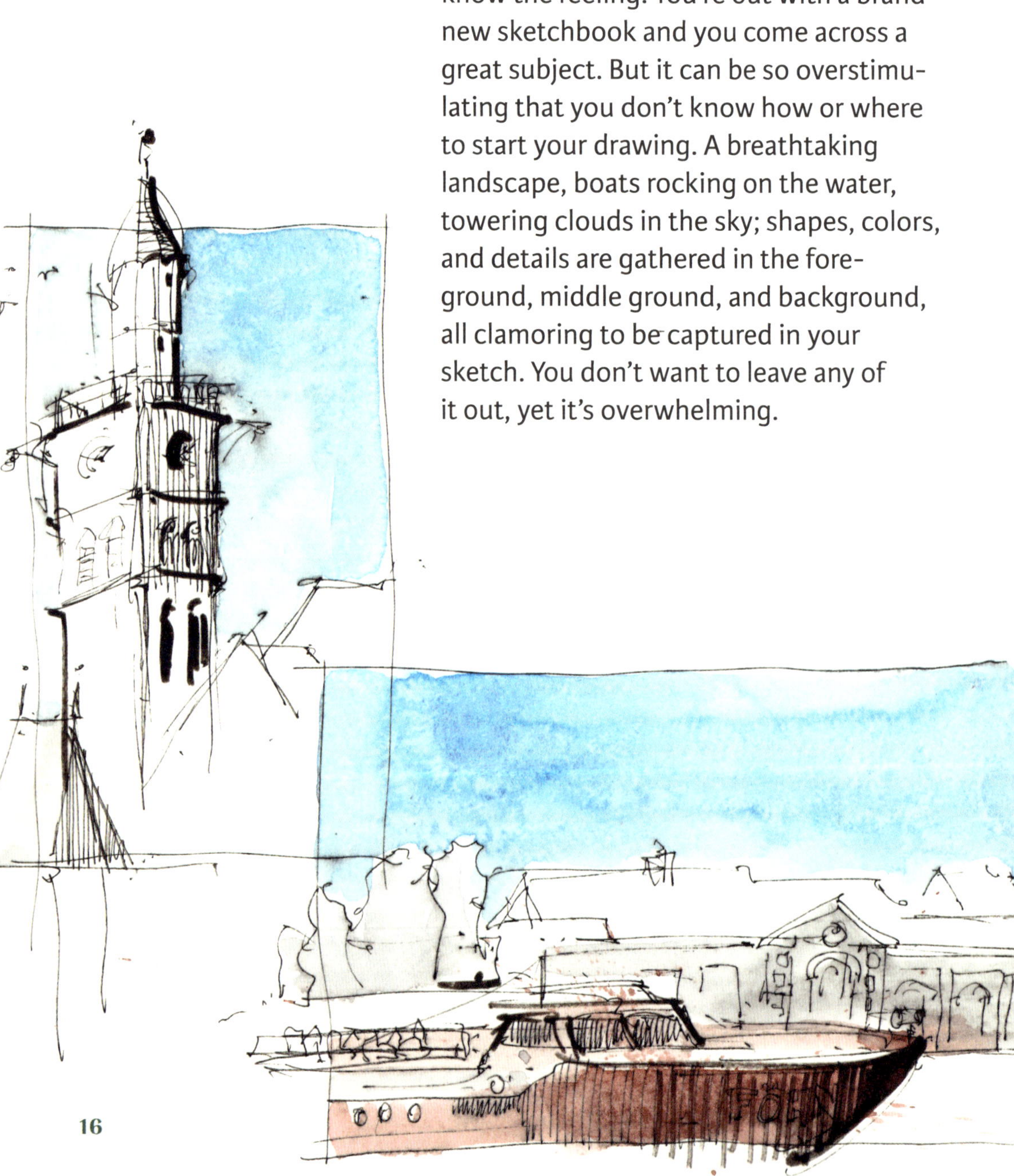

Give your mind and hand time to warm up.
On the following pages, you'll learn methods
and exercises that make it much easier to get
started. Just as an athlete never goes into
a race without warming up, no professional
artist or experienced travel illustrator
starts cold.

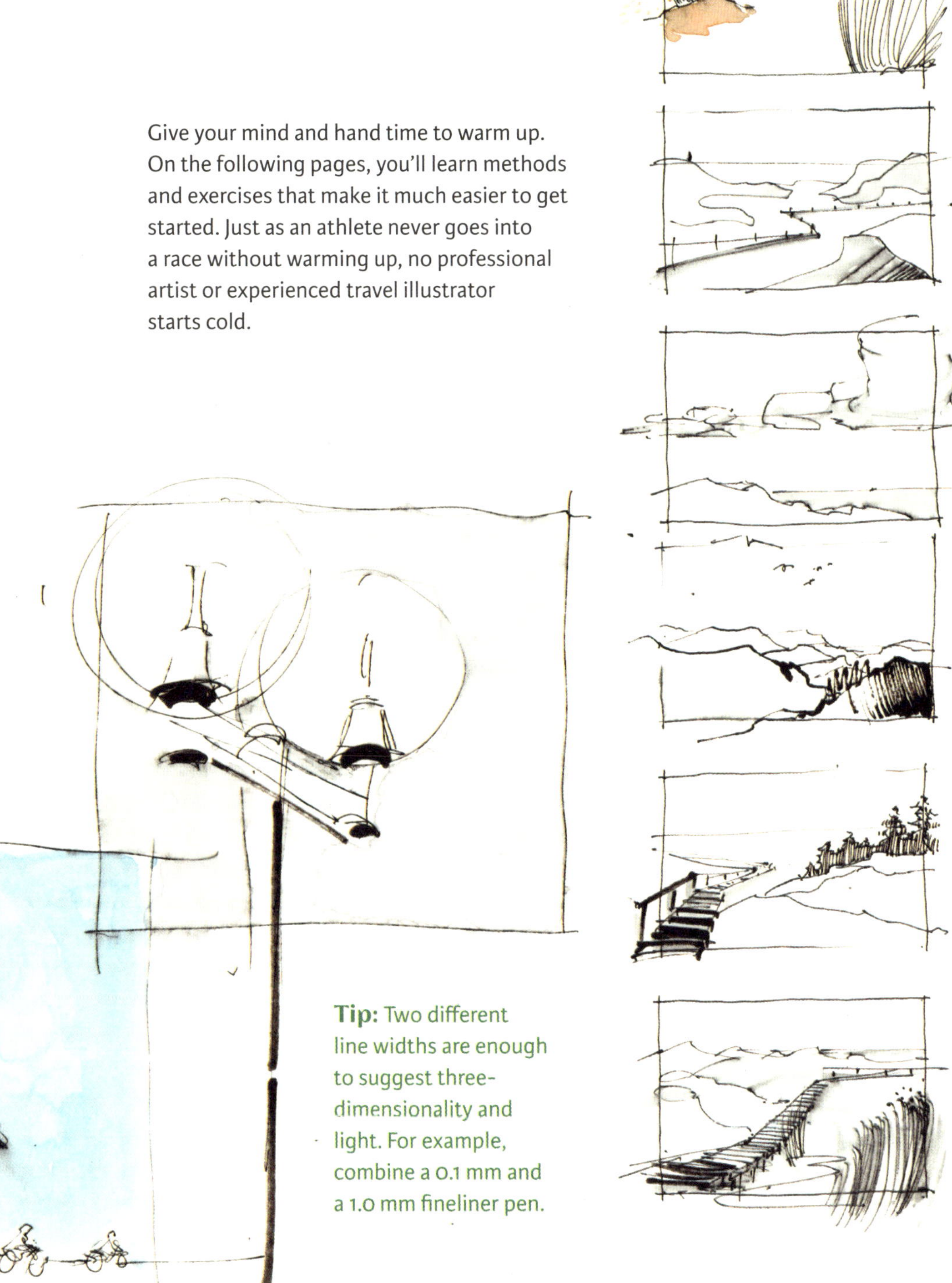

Tip: Two different
line widths are enough
to suggest three-
dimensionality and
light. For example,
combine a 0.1 mm and
a 1.0 mm fineliner pen.

Start with Miniatures

Just as you can't possibly grasp everything—a subject, a scene, an event—in depth at first glance, you can't possibly capture everything equally. That's why I recommend starting with miniatures. Draw a few empty picture frames on the page and gradually fill them with little sketches. The small size sharpens your eye for the essentials because there's no room for unnecessary details. Even the "big picture" can be captured in miniature.

Greater Creative Freedom

Now compose a picture from single impressions. In this way, you avoid having to go to great lengths to reproduce a complex subject or a small-scale scene in too much detail. Instead, leave it to the viewer's imagination to piece together and complete the picture. The miniature snapshots also give you more creative freedom: No one will hold you accountable if you move the newspaper vendor to the left, enlarge a tree, or turn a parked car into bicycles.

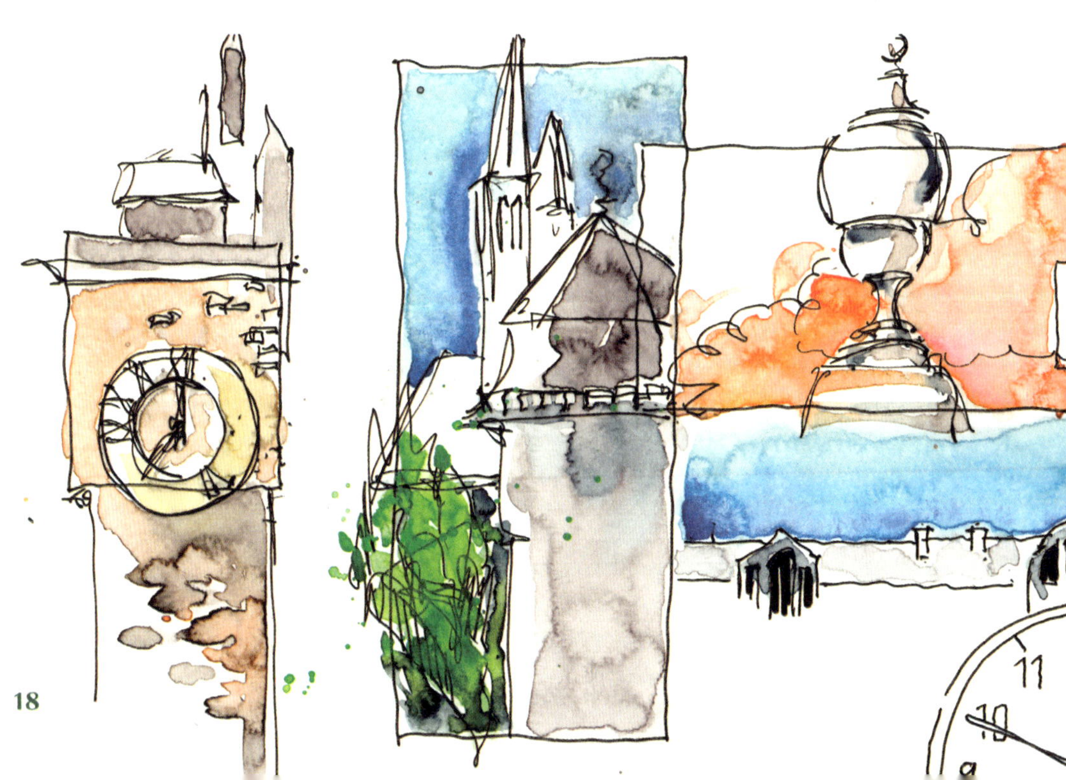

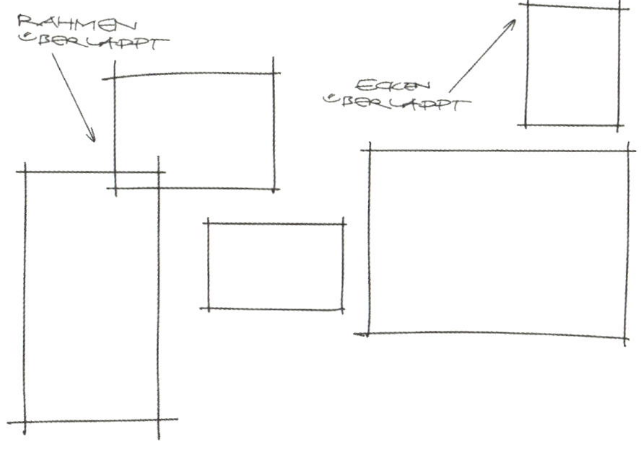

Tip: Find out how to color and further design frames on page 62.

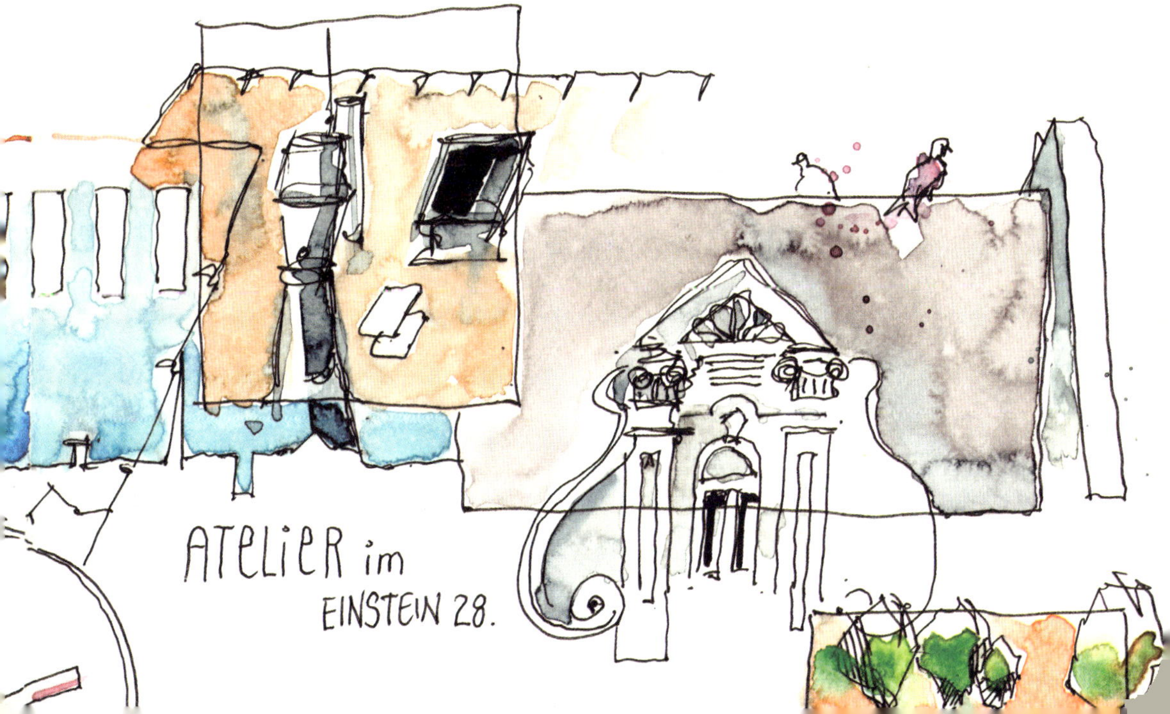

Exercise: Big Impressions in a Small Format

Are miniatures just preliminary sketches for a final work of art? No—as the following exercise shows:

1. Position three to five vertical and horizontal frames freely on a page.
2. Vary the sizes, overlapping the edges if you like.
3. Then send your eyes on a tracking shot through the entire subject and capture what seems important to you.
4. Try collecting, arranging, and composing additional subjects. Strong miniatures can say a lot.

Outsmart Yourself—Take the Hard Way

Drawing freehand makes most of us feel insecure. Especially if we rarely draw or haven't for a long time. Many have replaced pen and paper with a computer screen and mouse and use highly efficient digital applications to create perfect-looking visual standards to which we—both illustrators and viewers—have long become accustomed. Compare this to the mistakes and inaccuracies that are common in hand-drawn sketches, as well as personal style, artistic freedom, and uniqueness.

The Appeal of Imperfection

Yet architects, interior designers, and landscape planners tell me analog images are making a comeback. They often win over customers, clients, or business partners with spontaneous sketches at the building site, a little watercolor in a design, or a mood board scribbled by hand. That's why I ask the participants in my architecture workshops which of the works by famous architects exhibited in museums are more admired: the detailed floor plan, the photorealistic CAD (computer-aided design) rendering, or the freehand sketch made on a hotel napkin? What stays in our collective memory is the imperfect: the rough drafts that leave room for interpretation.

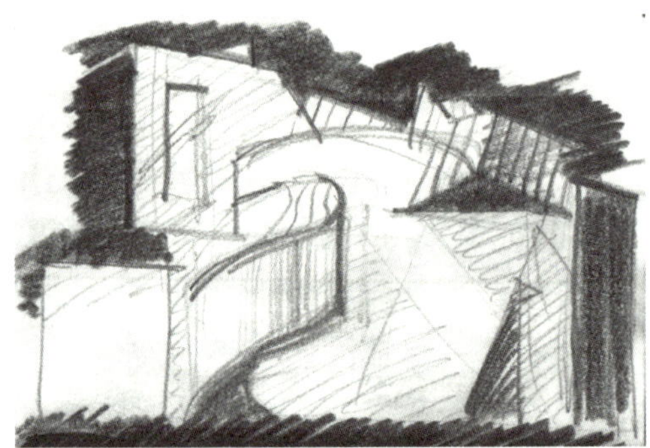

I made this quick sketch of the Vitra Design Museum as a student sitting on the grass in Weil am Rhein, Germany.

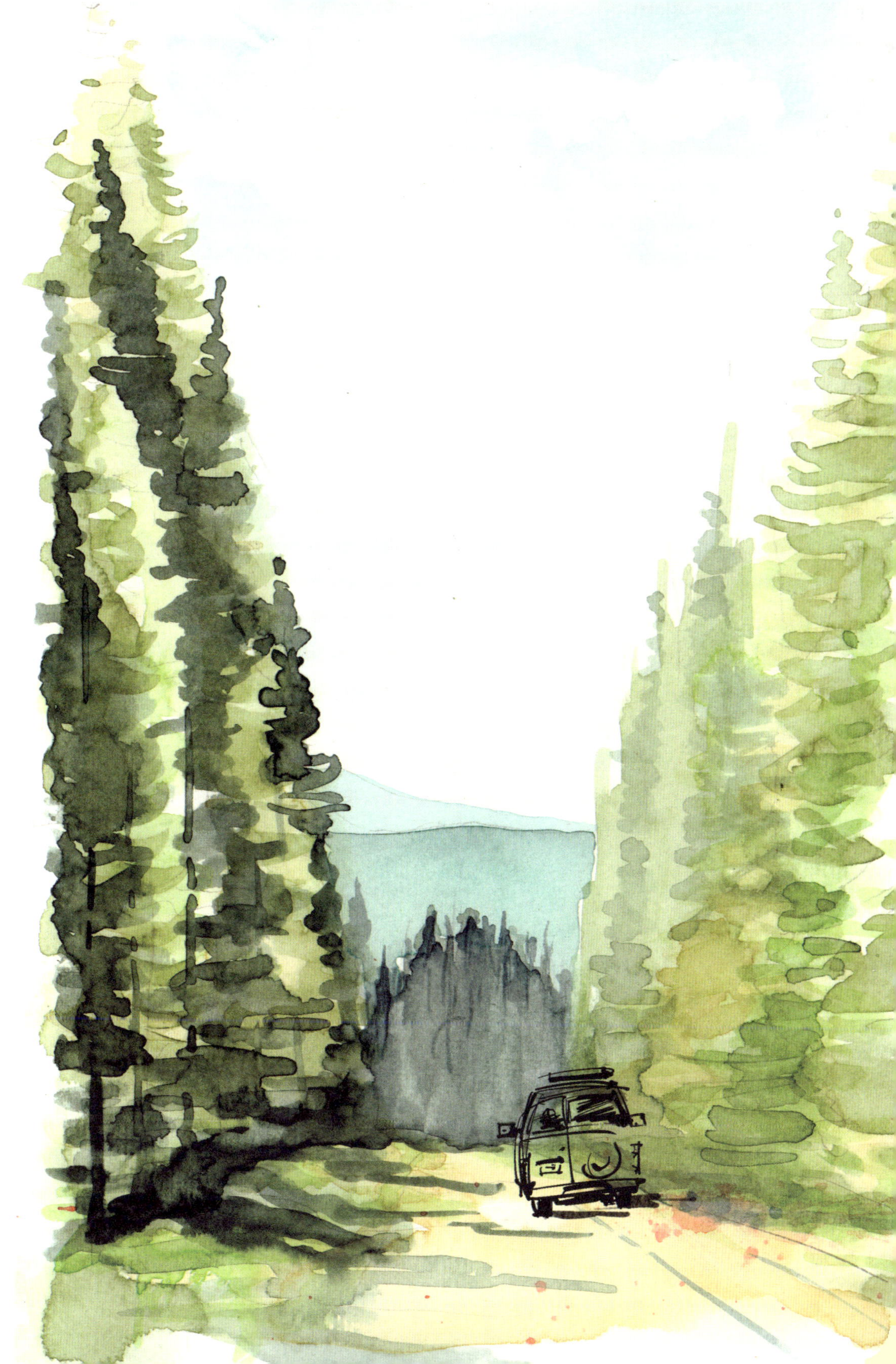

Effective Methods to Push Past Insecurities

Allow for Imperfections

Dare to create imperfect and unfinished freehand sketches. Dust off your painting tools and start with a simple subject: wind turbines on the horizon, a tree in the park, the house across the street.

Or go a step further and outsmart yourself the next time you sketch by completely changing your method and taking a risk. Choose an outdoor subject that challenges you, one that's likely to push you to the limits of your drawing skills: a multilayered landscape, a complex urban panorama, an animal that you encounter. The more complex the subject, the more you learn and gain in skill—I promise!

Exercise: Drawing with Your Other Hand

Sticking with the example of the landscape, pick up your drawing tool with the "wrong" hand: a right-hander with the left, a left-hander with the right. You're entering a new territory! Your line will be uneven. The proportions will be uncertain, imprecise. Entire elements of the picture won't end up in the "right" place. Be kind to yourself. Enjoy the freedom to make mistakes (blame them on your "wrong" hand). Gradually leave the comfort zone of your drawing habits and surprise yourself and others with a completely new, fresh style.

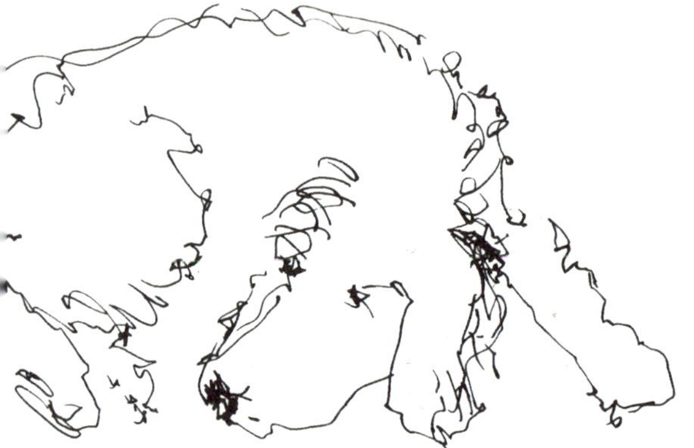

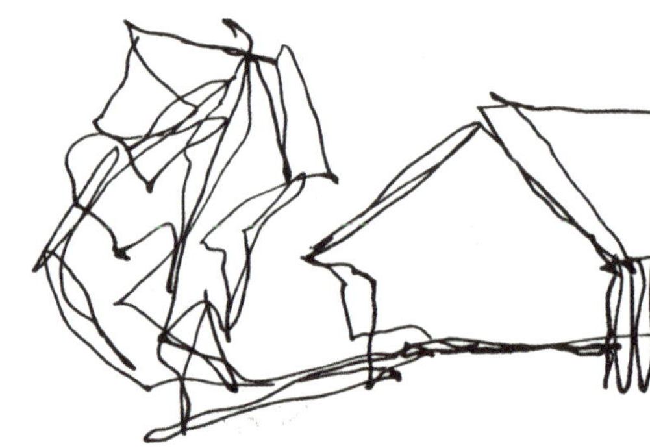

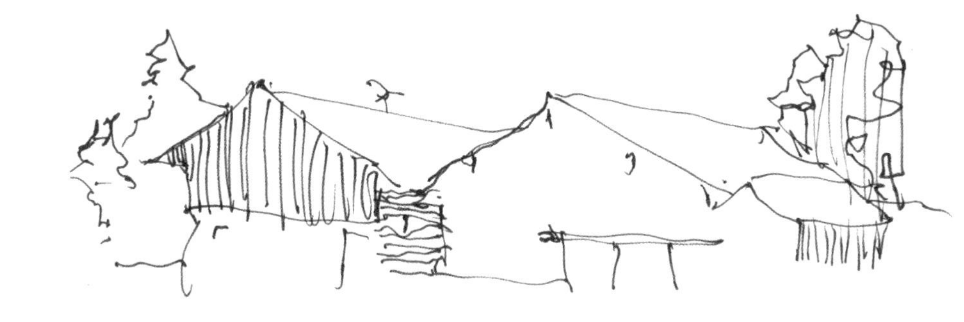

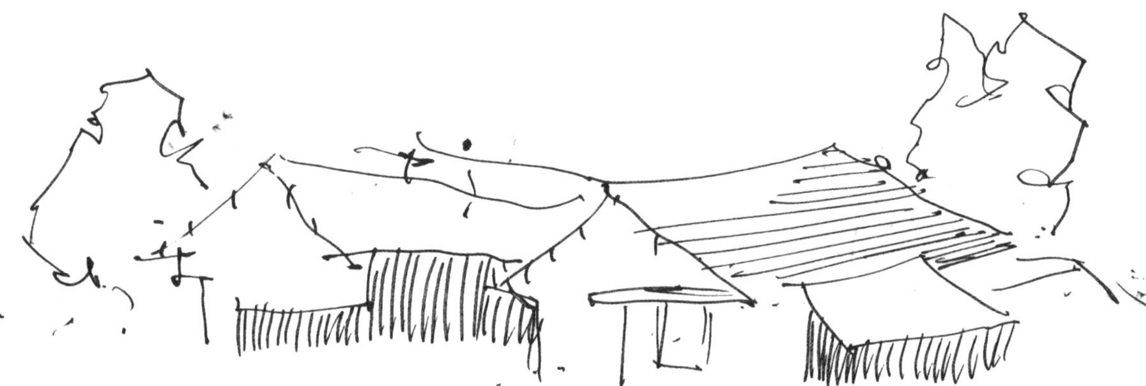

Not "wrong"—just different: The sketches of these barns were created with a quick change of method. Right hand, left hand, then one-line drawing. More suggestions for changing your style are on the next spread.

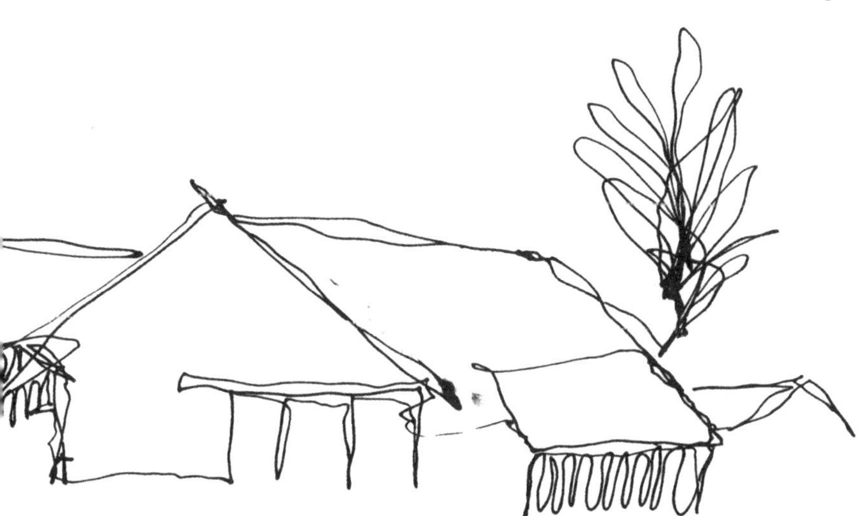

One-Line Drawing

My preferred technique for simplifying complex subjects is to draw them using one continuous line. Without lifting the pencil, move it loosely across the paper. For details, shadows, and contours, move back along your line to the desired point. Allow your hand to follow paths twice; no lifting it from the page or stopping until your one-line work is complete. When you reach the final point, put the pencil down and look back on a few wonderfully contemplative minutes of drawing. And possibly a picture that you didn't expect.

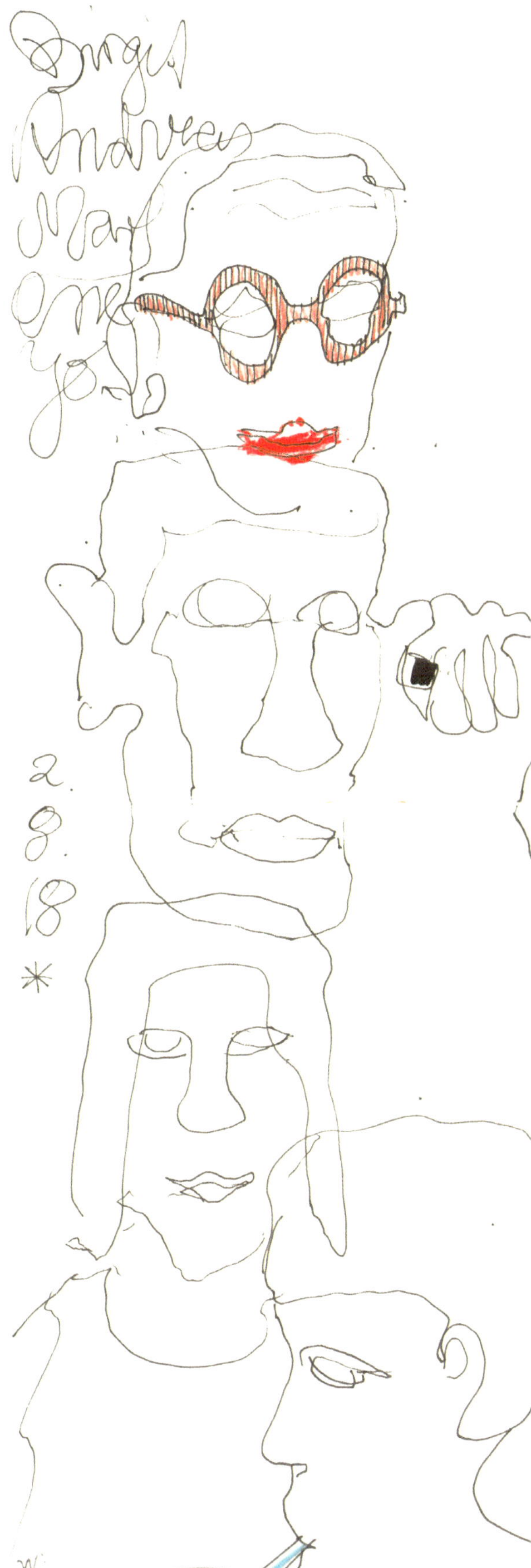

Drawing Blind and Against the Clock

Two other methods to combat insecurity are blind drawing and time-limited drawing. For the former, you close your eyes while you put your subject on paper. For the latter, you give yourself a maximum of twenty seconds for the entire sketch. You'll be amazed by the results. Try out these challenges to find which one helps you loosen up your line. You don't need to stand on your head, draw in the dark, or with two fingers. What counts is your willingness to embrace new methods, techniques, and styles—to free yourself from your own and other people's demands for perfection.

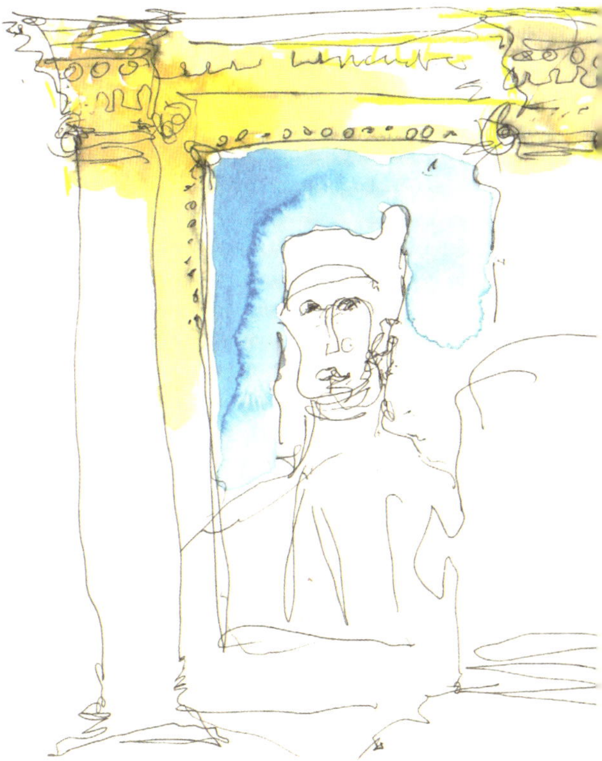

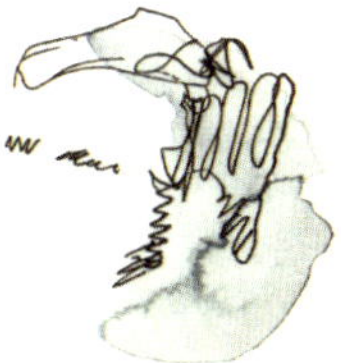

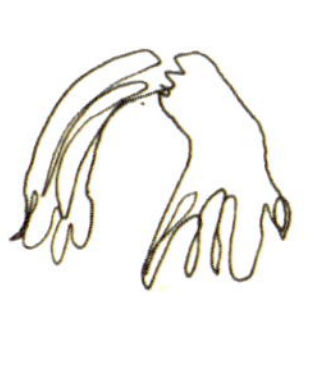

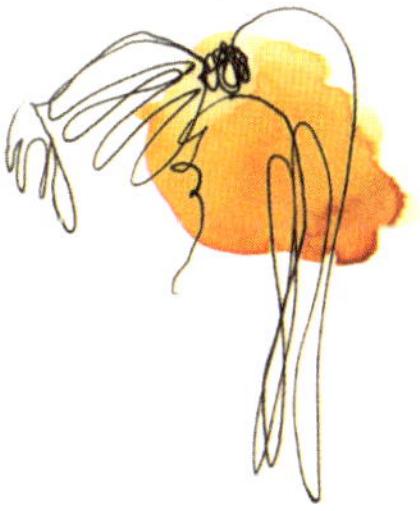

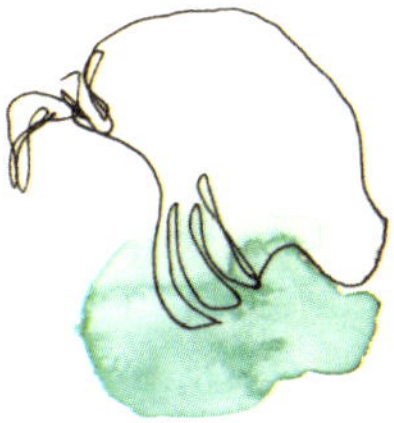

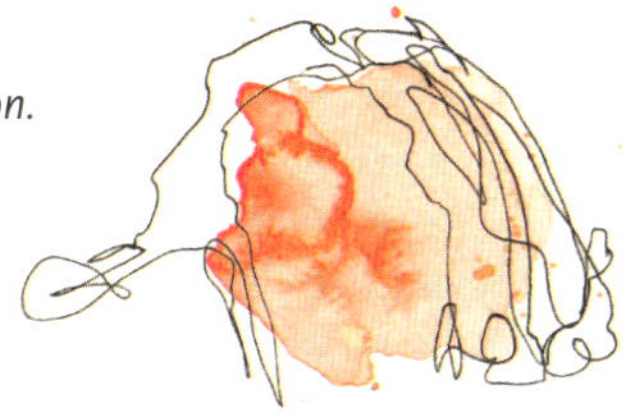

Flash portraits: Reduced to one line, limited to the hairstyle. I leave the faces to the viewer's imagination.

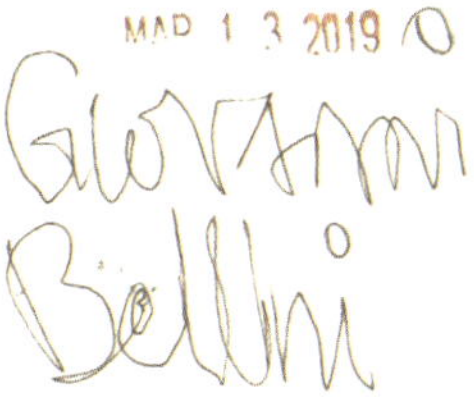

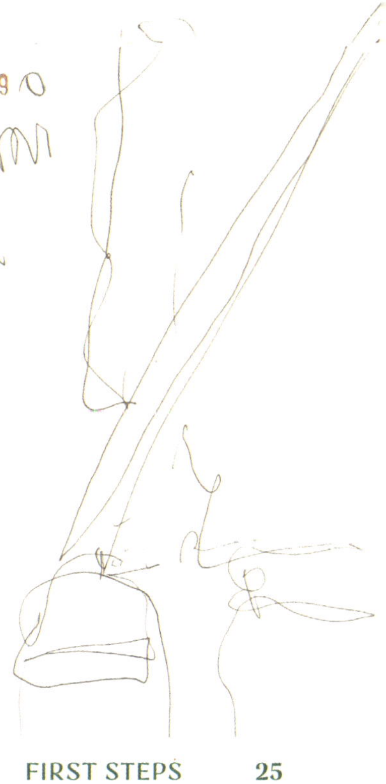

Landscapes

When you go outdoors (perhaps after trying my warm-up exercises), you'll enter a world of visual impressions, but also a path with artistic challenges. Landscapes are a huge source of subjects.

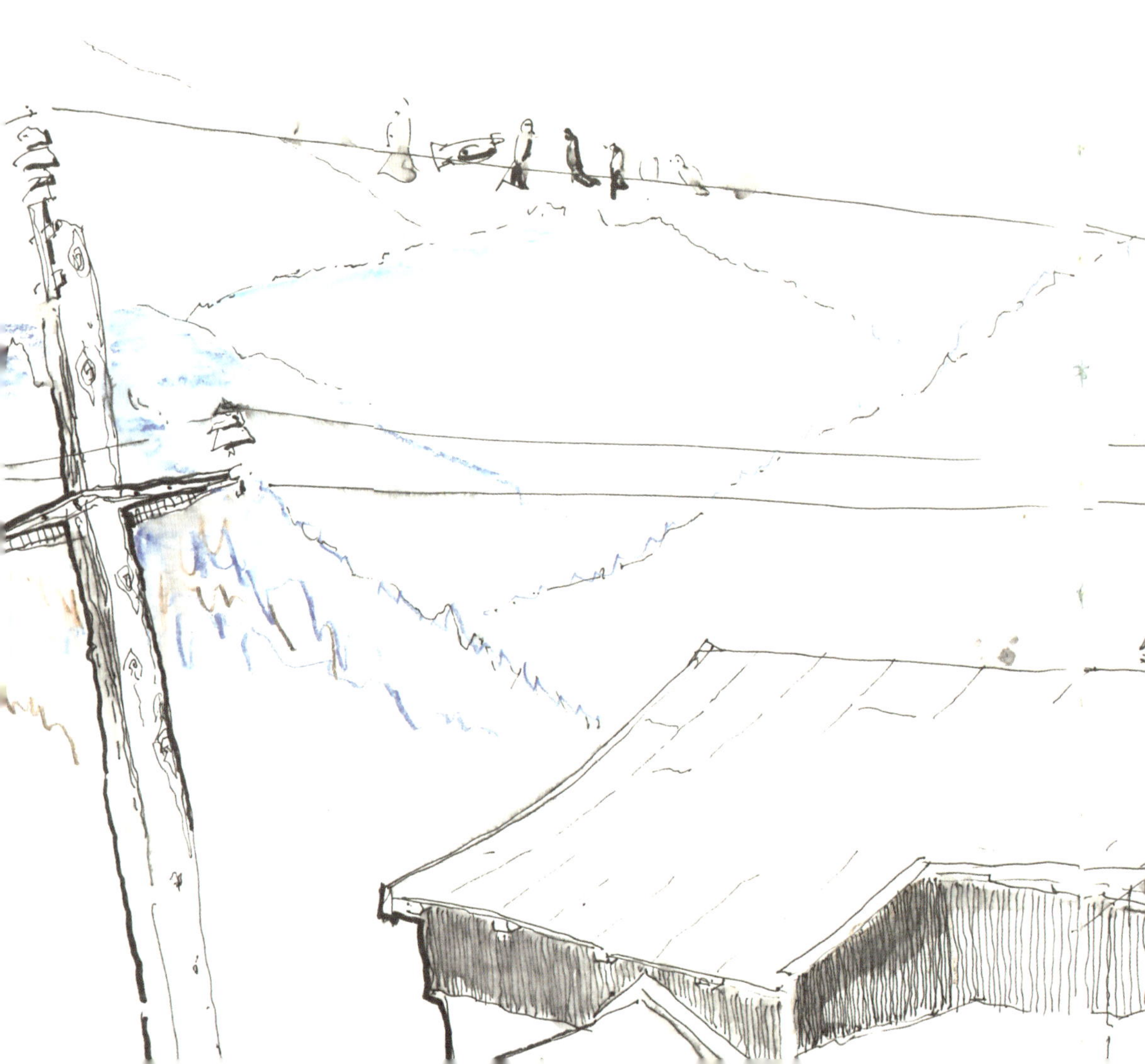

Your Pathway

Our relationship with landscapes is very personal. Each of us prefers a different environment to travel in, a different backdrop to illustrate—whether forest, sea, mountain, beach, river, coast, village, or cityscape. What may seem uninviting to one person may be beautiful to another.

To explore a landscape, you need to move around in it. Take your time. My most productive drawing tours are on foot. Bicycles, trains, and cars will help you cover greater distances or move from one landscape to another more quickly if you want. No matter how and where you go, the landscape is always already there: a walk-in picture, a stage for great outdoor spectacles, a frame for your travel stories.

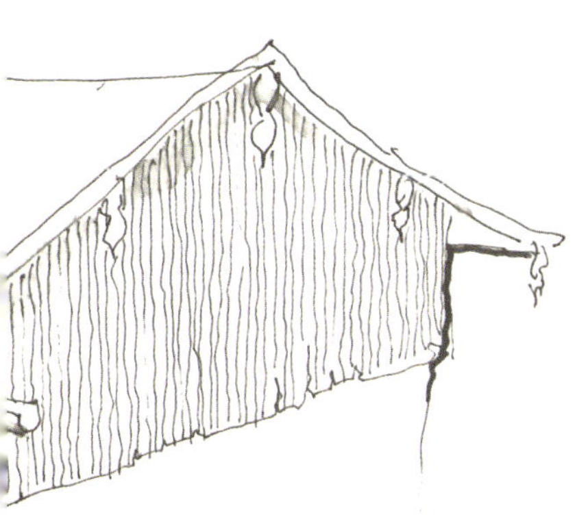

What Defines a Landscape

When sketching, I pay attention to three aspects that are important when depicting a landscape:

Topography

The topography describes the shape of the terrain. The lines and fields you draw combine to form a picture; the geographic location of your drawing becomes visible (see the following double-page spread). In this chapter, I'll take four detours to show you examples of how each landscape reveals its unique qualities.

Composition

On the small pages of a sketchbook, panoramic landscapes can lose their intensity. A skillful composition will prevent this. I'll explain from page 36 on how to methodically use the position of the horizon, perspective, weight, light, and shadow.

Three-Dimensionality

There are methods you can use to create three-dimensionality. Starting on page 72, you can find out how to deliberately experiment with the size and position of elements and how to use atmospheric and color perspective effectively to create depth in the landscape.

Topography

The landscape is like a stage. On a tableau visible from afar, backdrops are staggered in the depth of the space: coastal strips and sea, forest edges and meadow areas, chains of hills and mountain ridges. Surfaces push themselves in front of and behind each other, overlap, and crowd into view. A fascinating network of lines emerges—flowing gently, undulating, or rising steeply.

Every type of landscape has its own repertoire of topographical lines. A dune landscape has rounded, rippling lines, while mountains form angular and jagged ones. A river valley winds through the plains, while a hilly landscape is characterized by contours that rise and fall. The modulation of the lines and strokes in your drawing help you to "locate" your subject. On the opposite page, I'll show you how to create a landscape sketch one step at a time.

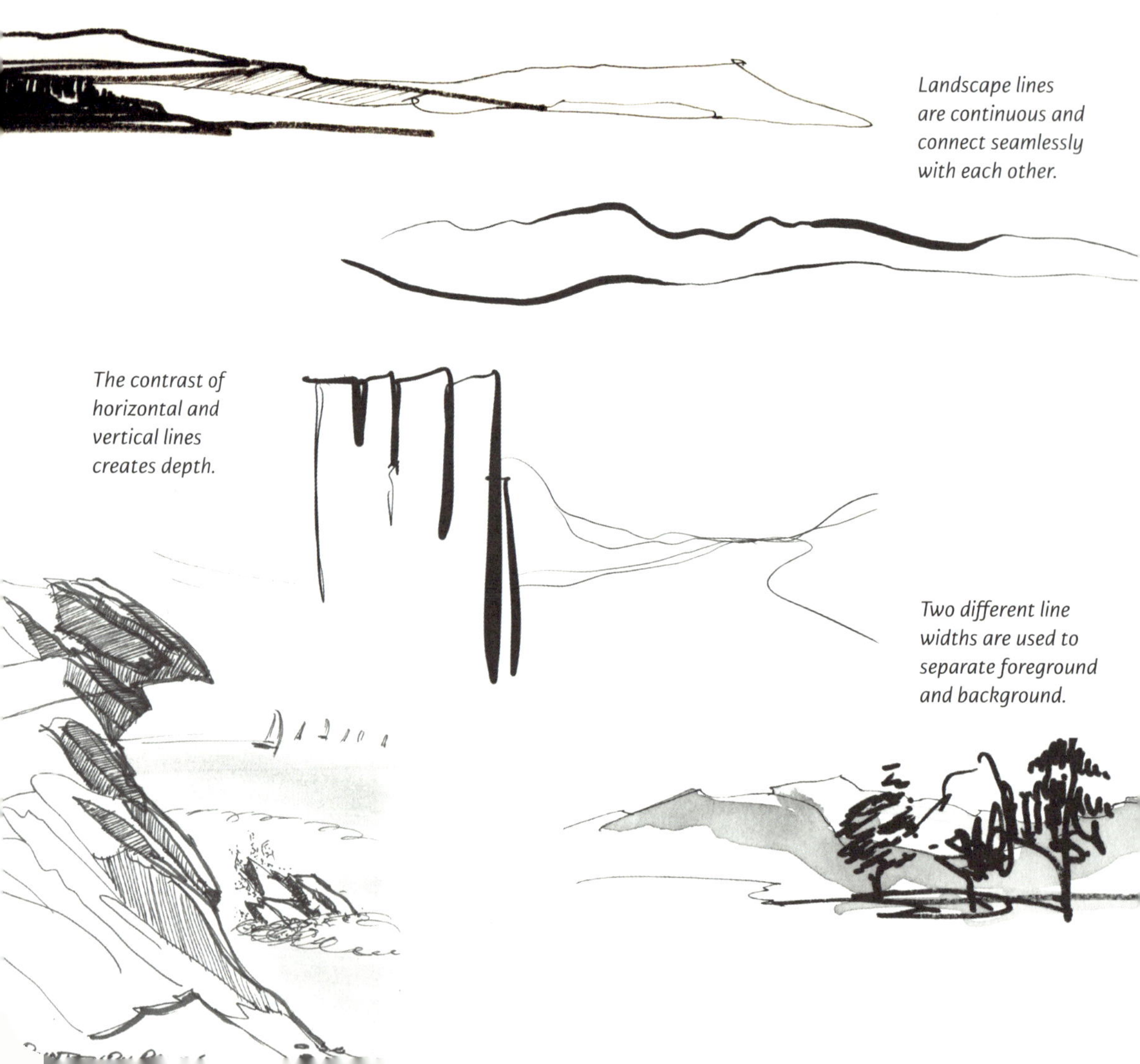

Landscape lines are continuous and connect seamlessly with each other.

The contrast of horizontal and vertical lines creates depth.

Two different line widths are used to separate foreground and background.

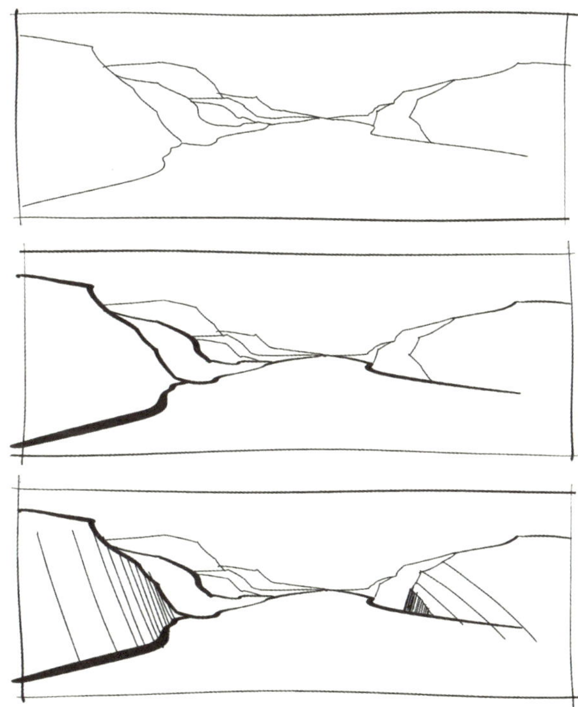

Exercise: Landscape and Line

You can try this exercise anytime, whether you're at home or out in a landscape. All you need is a pencil or fineliner. To create lines with a varied thickness, I recommend using an ink pen or a brush pen.

Use a horizontal layout for your sketch to emphasize the expanse of the landscape. The nice thing about this exercise is that it works just as well at the seaside as it does in the mountains.

1. Draw quick, flowing lines on the paper that become denser toward the background.
2. Contour lines overlap, touch, connect, and rarely end abruptly in the middle of the picture.
3. Avoid unnatural monotony by creating a varied pattern of lines.
4. Repeat the exercise using lines with increasing and decreasing thicknesses.
5. Vary the line weight by changing how hard you press your pen on the paper, with strong lines in the foreground and delicate lines in the background.

Detour: Coast and Sea

Going to the seaside to sketch sounds like a vacation: relaxing, breathing the fresh sea air, taking in a broad horizon, lots of blue hues, sand in your paint box, your sketchbook pages fluttering in the wind. But are there enough worthwhile subjects to draw? Haven't flat beaches, endless horizons, and glowing sunsets been drawn and painted enough? Let's take a closer look at what the coastal landscape is all about.

You Never Step in the Same Ocean Twice

The sheer scale is impressive: 221,000 miles of coastline around the world are testament to the diversity of this landscape. Sandy beaches, rocky coves, cliffs, dunes, and mudflats. Whether it's the fresh North Sea wind tousling your hair, the salt of the Atlantic on your tongue, or a sun-drenched day on the Mediterranean, there's something for every artistic taste. Put your favorite places down on paper!

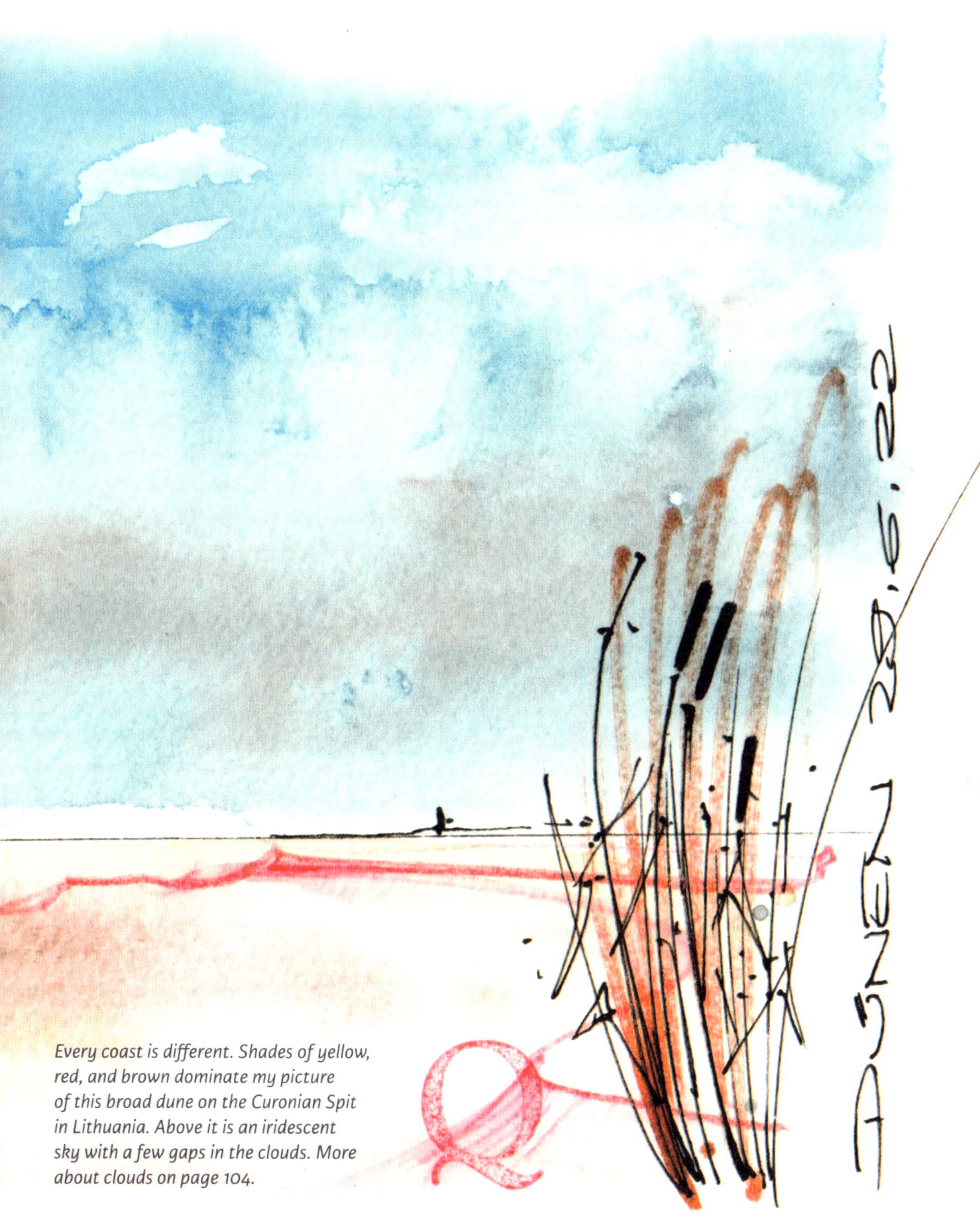

Every coast is different. Shades of yellow, red, and brown dominate my picture of this broad dune on the Curonian Spit in Lithuania. Above it is an iridescent sky with a few gaps in the clouds. More about clouds on page 104.

Water Isn't Blue

It's the sky—with a little help from the clouds and the position of the sun—that determines the color of the sea. In addition to well-known sky blue, other colors are reflected in a variety of ways. When you color your sketch, think of it as a snapshot—not as a photo-realistic image. It's much more fun to make your own color choices.

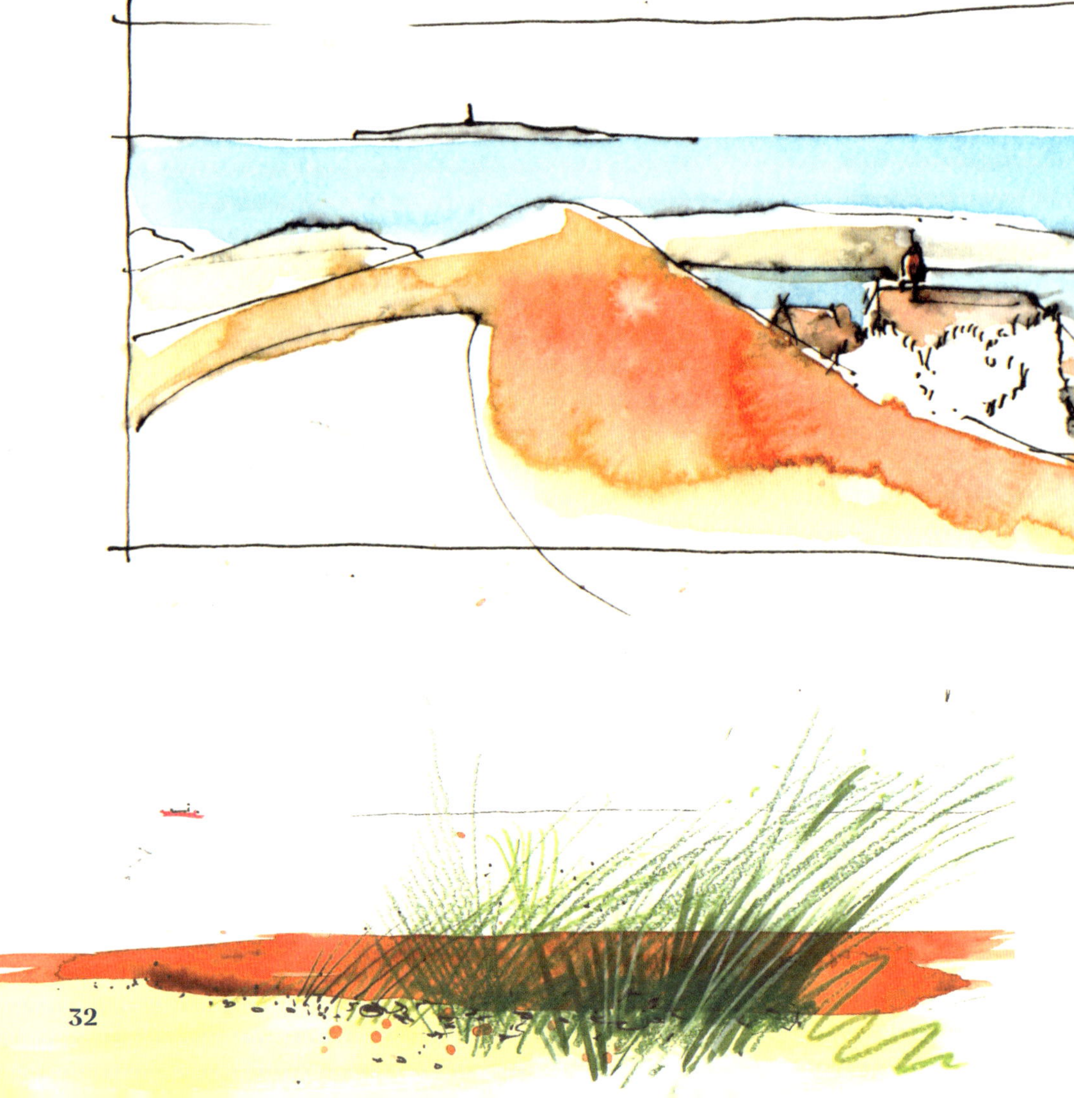

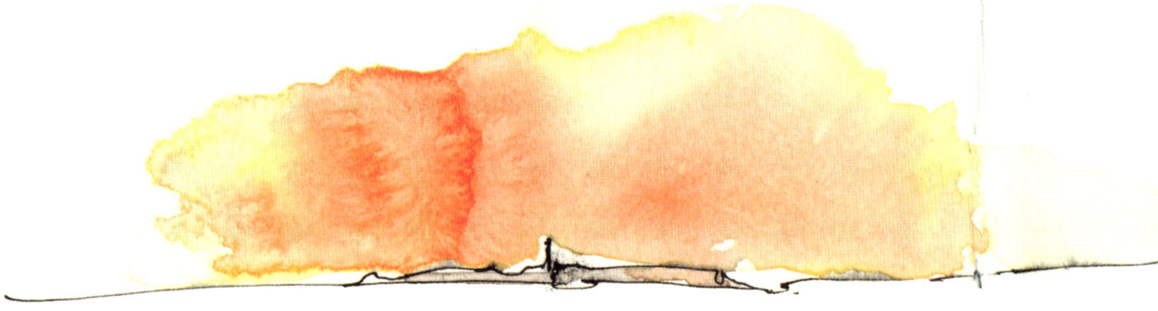

The sky and water separate on the horizon. Often, I decide to color only one of the two surfaces so as not to overload the drawing. In this picture, I left the sea white to draw attention to the golden sky over the German island of Sylt.

Tip: You can learn how to paint magnificent skies in the weather chapter starting on page 84. There's more information about trees and vegetation starting on page 111.

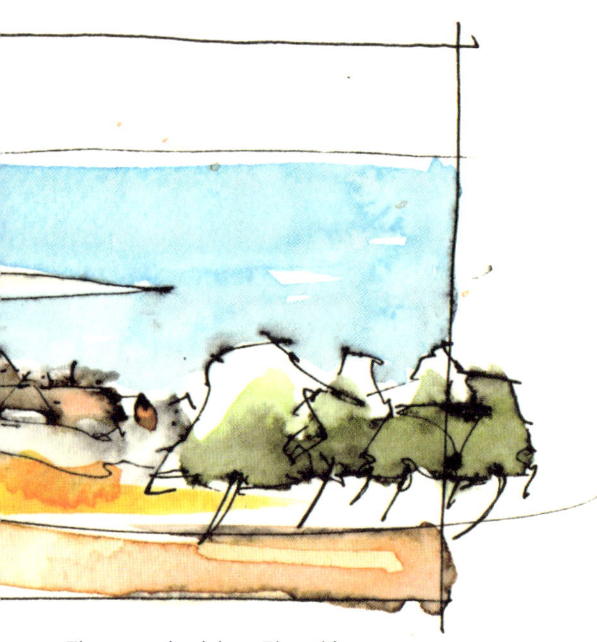

Three-part backdrop: The subject is divided into staggered foreground, middle ground, and background sections, creating a sense of depth in a very small space.

A Typical Coastal Scene

Our idea of the sea—and thus our sketchbook—incorporates a host of maritime symbols. Looking back, they will evoke our memories: seaside structures like piers and lighthouses, aggressive seagulls, gnarled trees bent over by the wind, boats and fishing nets, driftwood, and people out for a stroll. If possible, add familiar details to your drawings of a day at the seaside while avoiding the pitfalls of kitsch and cliché.

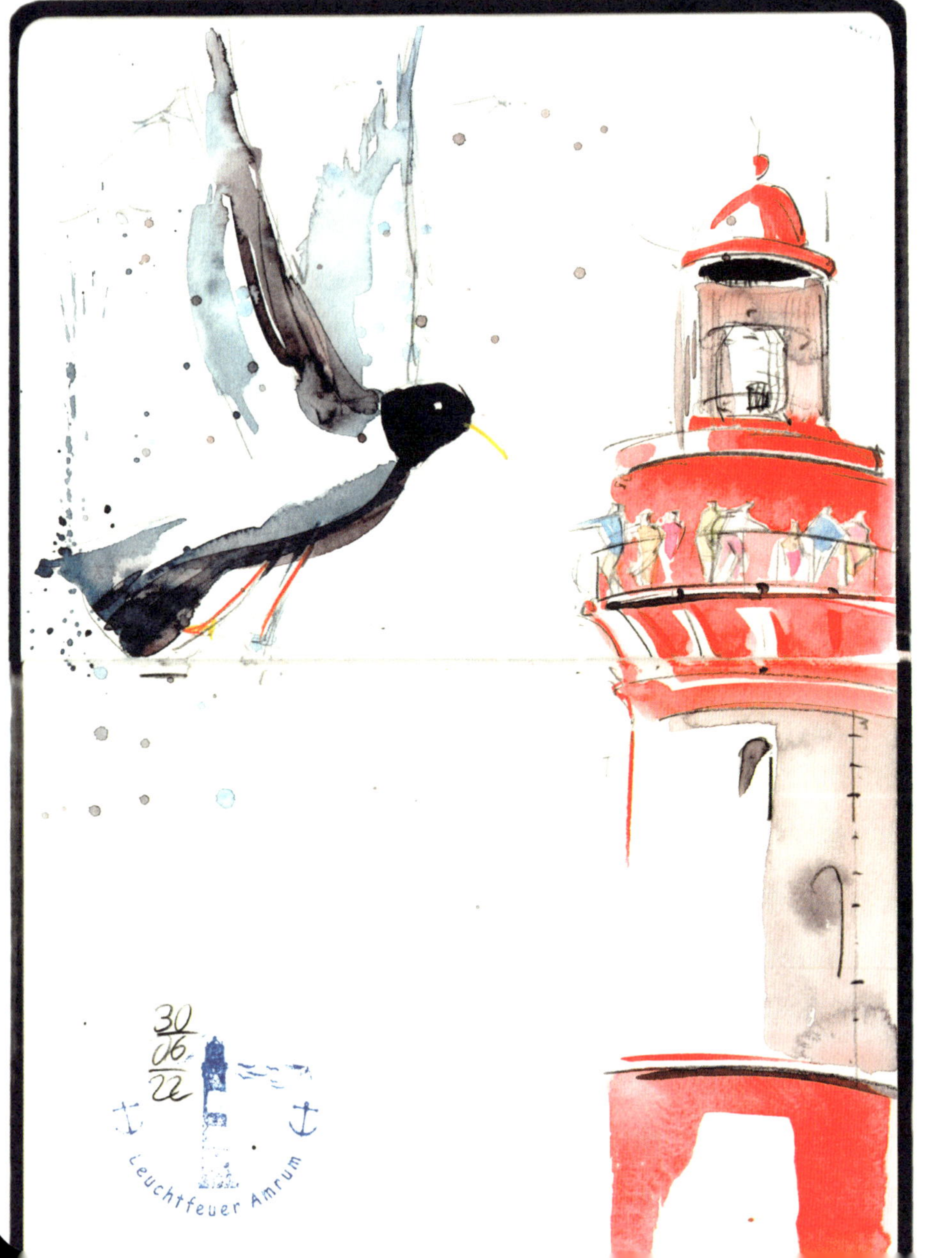

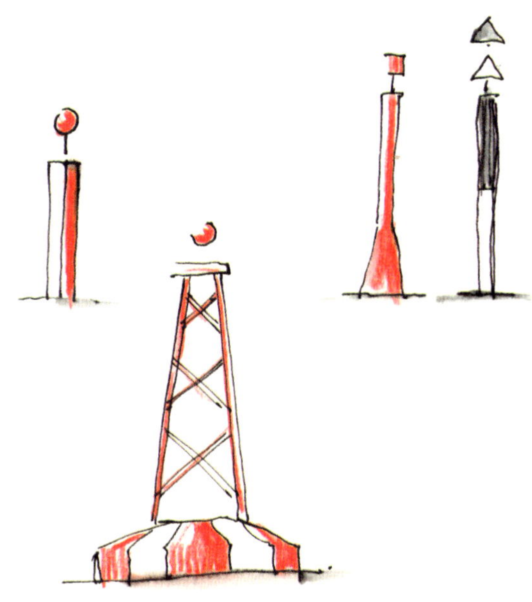

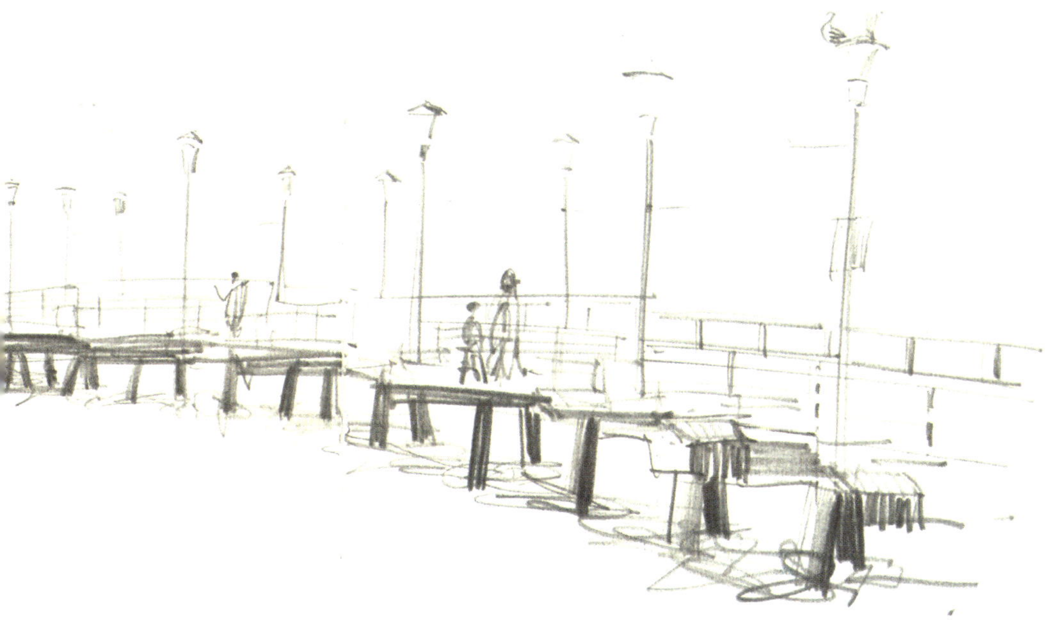

Composition

The space on your sketchbook page is limited. How can you capture an expansive landscape in such a small space? I admit, it's not an easy undertaking—especially if you packed a small sketchbook to draw comfortably on the go.

My solution: It's the composition that matters, not the size of the paper. Good composition ensures clarity and order, gives the image depth, and leaves a strong impression on the viewer. You can find the basics of successful picture composition on the following pages.

Set the Picture Horizon

In simple terms, the line of the horizon in the picture is determined by your position as a viewer; in other words, your eye level— whether you're lying on the beach, sitting on the grass, or standing on a hill. If you change your position, the position of this line—the picture horizon—changes, too.

The picture horizon is an abstract line that may be obscured by mountains, trees, or houses. And it may not necessarily correspond to the natural horizon where the sky meets the water and land. Play around with this imaginary line and compose your picture freely. A low viewing position means an image horizon at the bottom and lots of sky in the subject. A higher position puts the image horizon at the top, with lots of landscape in the foreground.

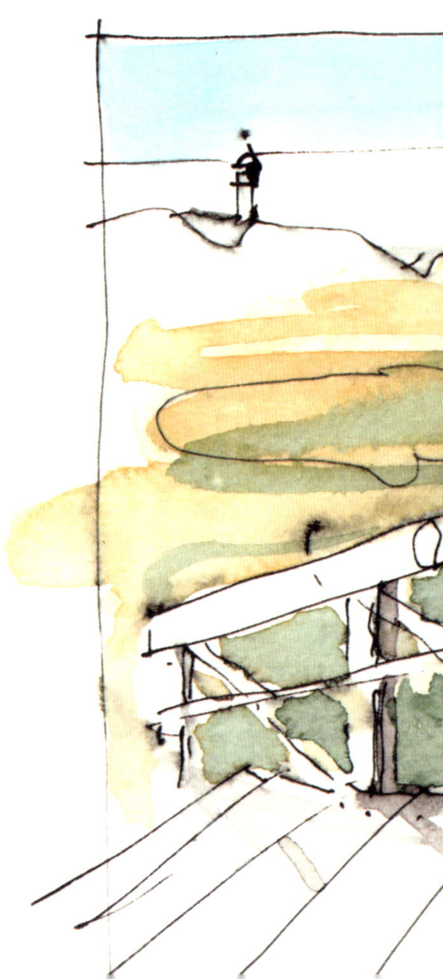

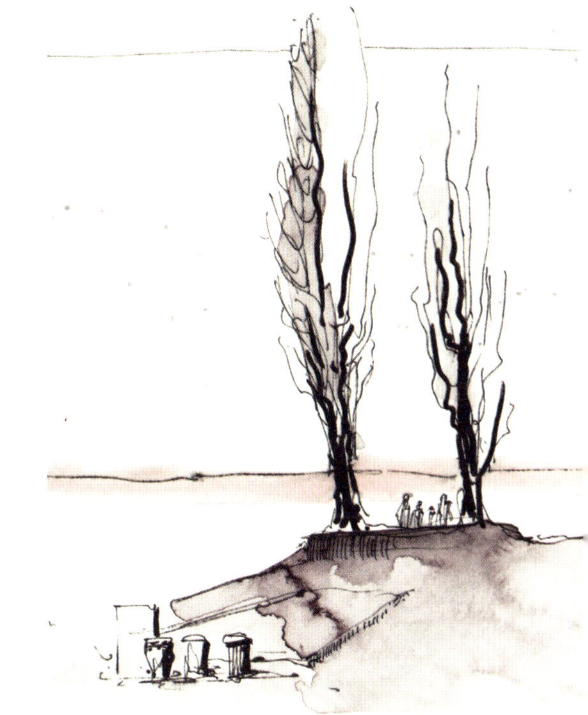

Picture horizon below: Plenty
of sky above Lake Constance,
Germany. Here, the clouds
and sky can still be filled in.

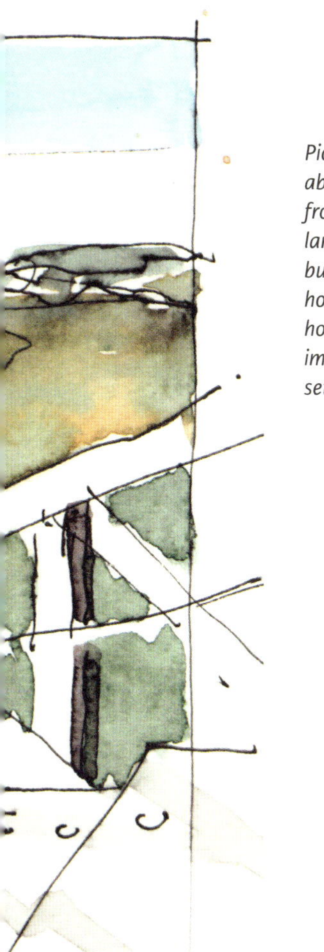

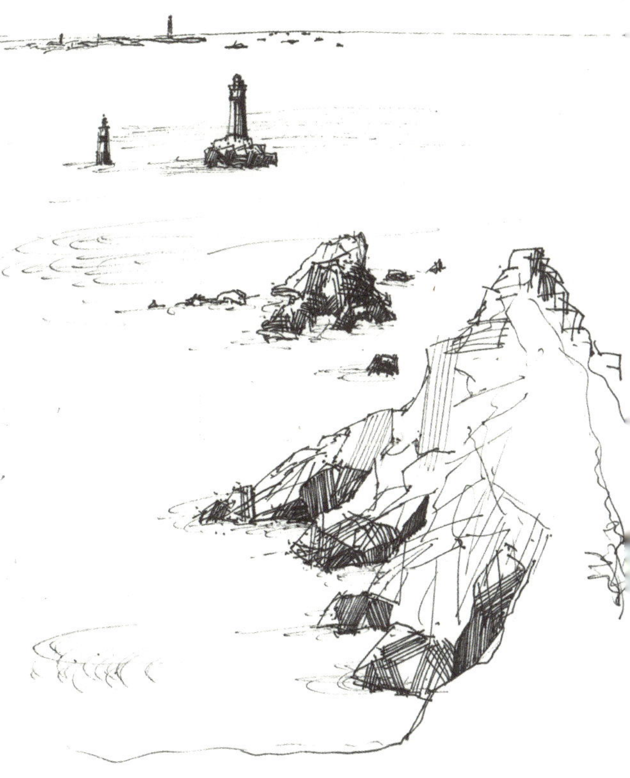

Picture horizon
above: With a view
from above, the dune
landscape slowly
builds up to the
horizon. The light-
house in the left
image is intriguingly
set off to the side.

Vanishing Point and Vanishing Lines

The use of perspective creates depth. In the example of a small Sardinian town (opposite page), you can see how the edges of roofs and roadsides converge. These lines, which create the illusion of depth, are called vanishing lines. They meet at one or more vanishing points on the horizon of the picture.

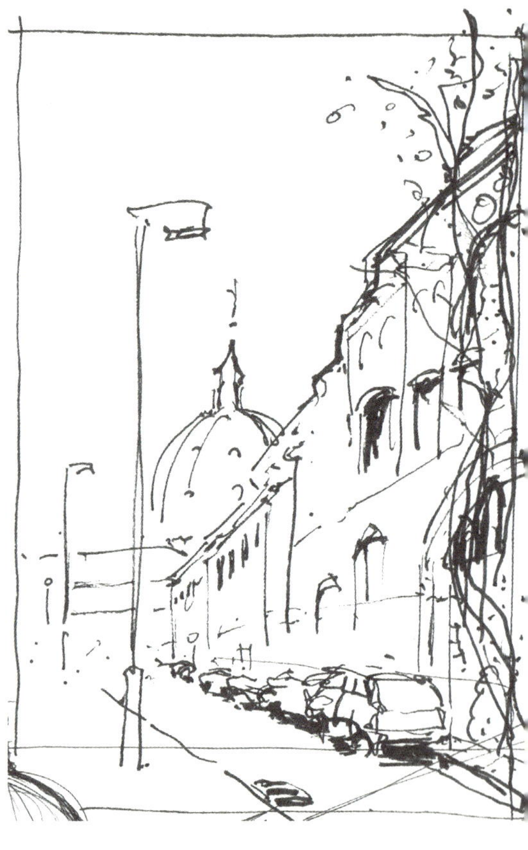

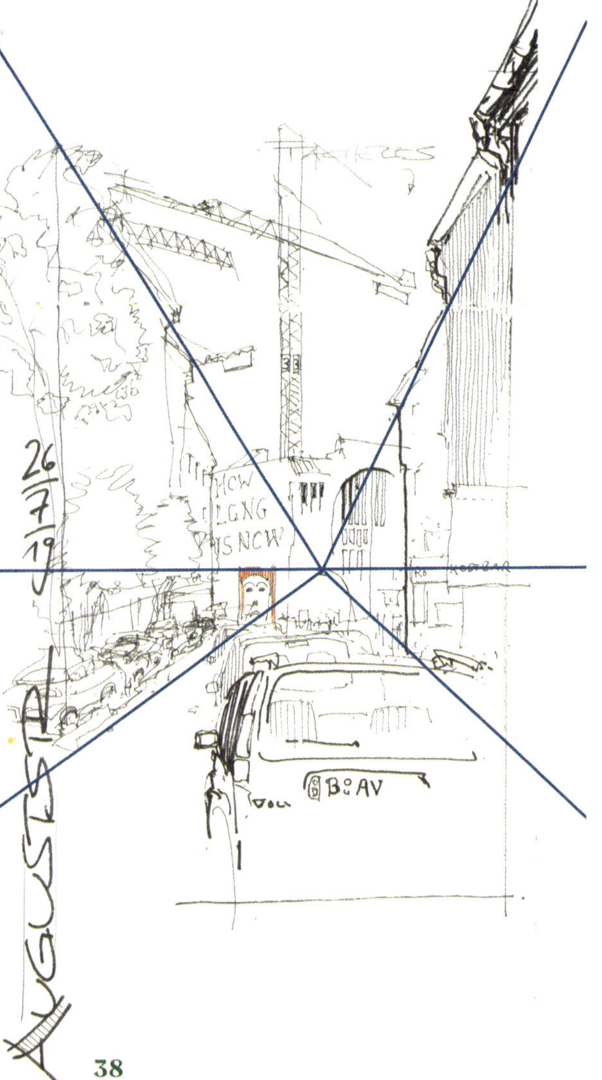

Central perspective: The easiest way to create depth is with a direct frontal viewpoint with a central vanishing point.

Corner perspective:
By leaving the frontal
position, you add more
vanishing points.

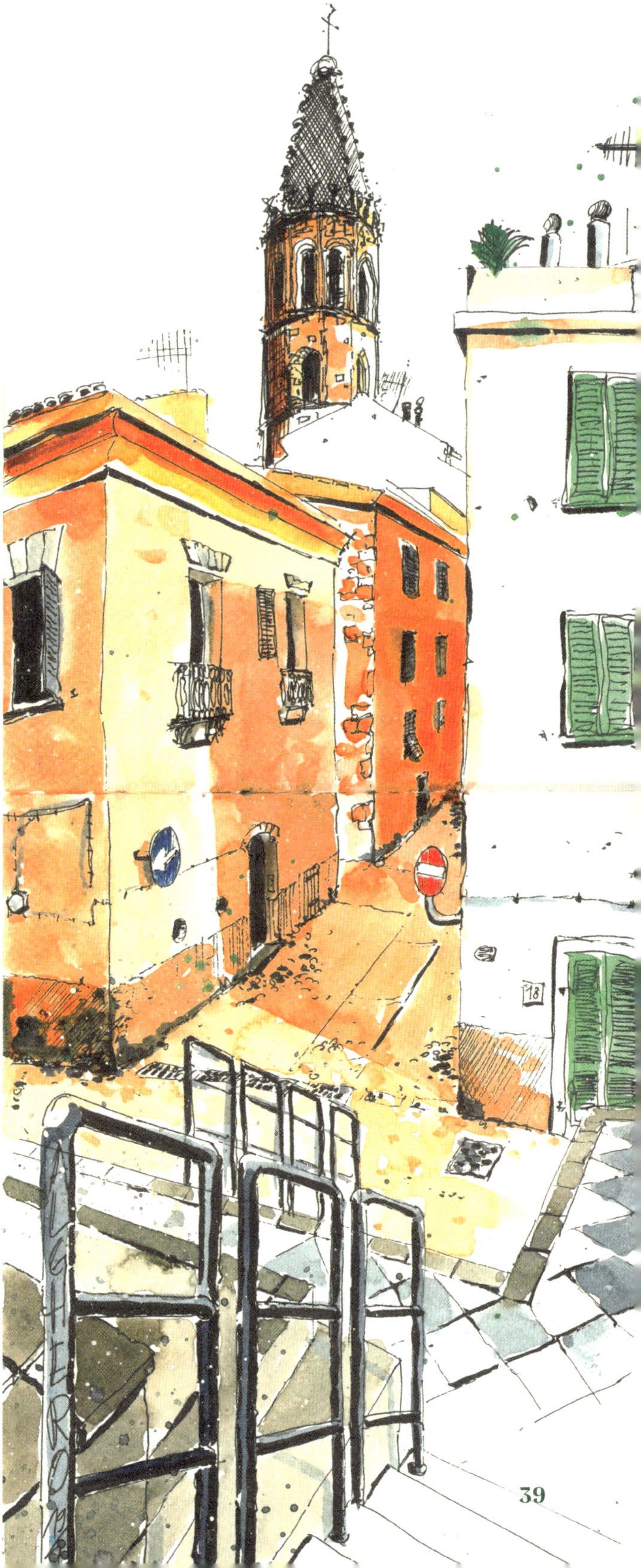

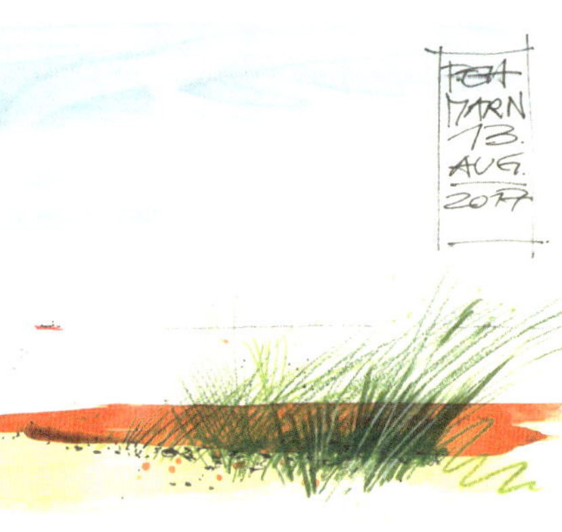

39

Avoid Monotony

Landscapes are not the product of computer-generated design. They're full of unevenness, asymmetries, and surprises. Create your pictures based on nature's model. And should nature ever fail you as a teacher, you can help her along with a few tweaks.

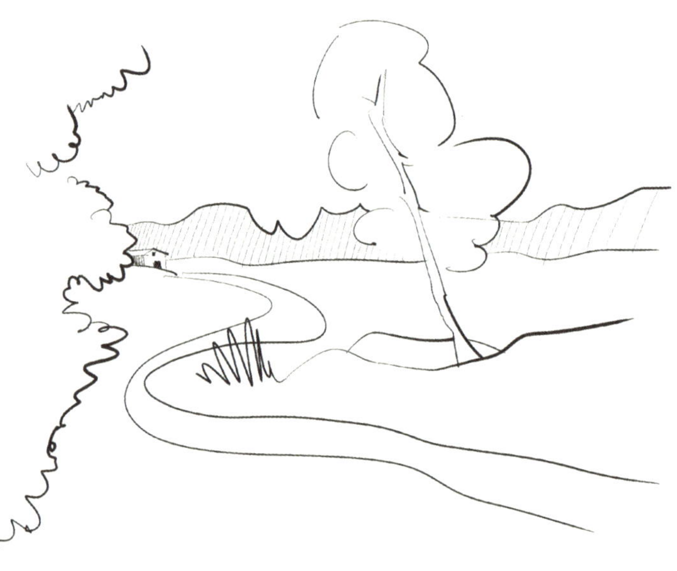

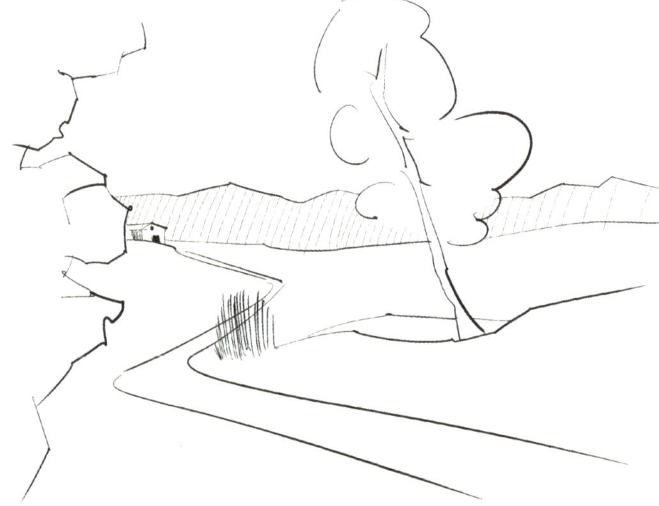

*Set counterpoints:
Nature's repertoire of lines includes a whole host of curves and straight lines. A picture comes alive through the contrast between the two. If your subject threatens to drift into monotony due to all the arches and curves, contrast curved lines with straight ones. If necessary, deviate from the original—as I did with this dirt road.*

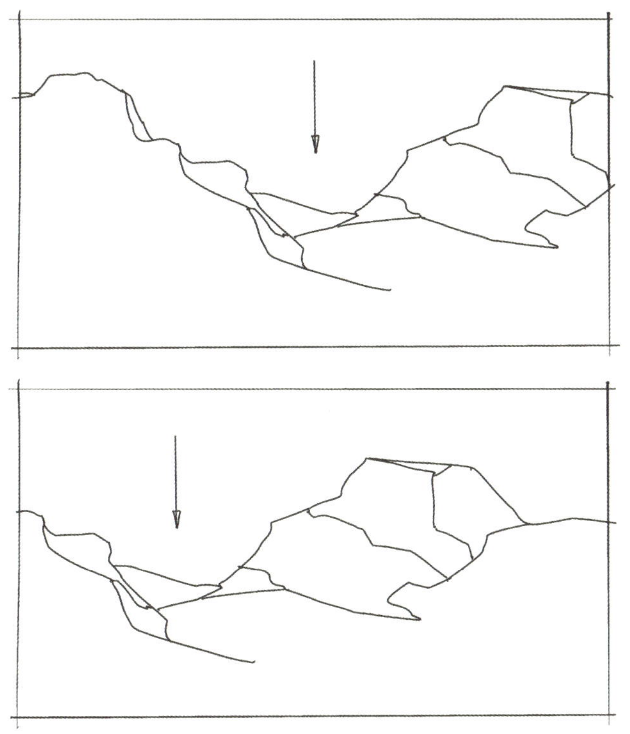

Shift the vanishing point:
A sketch with a center vanishing point can be uninteresting. Shapes on the left half of the picture are mirrored on the right half, which seems uninspired. If you move the vanishing point of your sketch toward the edge of the picture, the composition will be more appealing. To try this out, make your sketch larger to begin with, so that you can later determine the best way to frame it.

Tip: Hold both hands in front of the subject like a movie director to frame it and adjust your image detail.

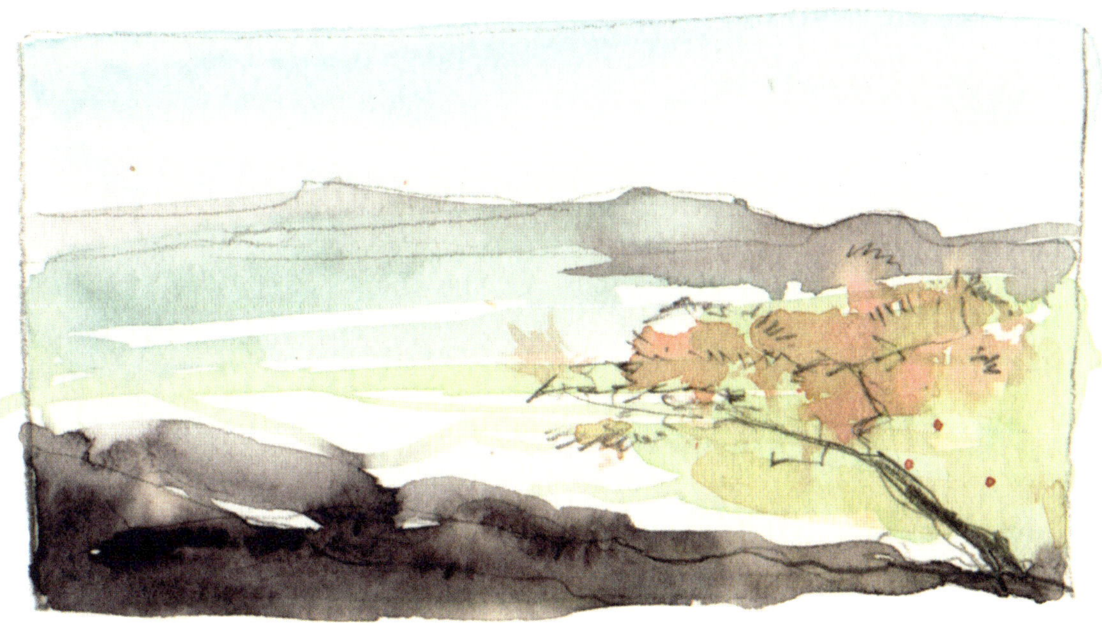

Find Your Focus

Beginners tend to clutter their drawings with too much stuff. Either they're enthusiastic about great subjects—"Wow, all the houses in this piazza are beautiful; I can't leave out the fountain; that tree is fabulous and the clouds over the rooftops just have to be in the picture."

Or the artist can't decide what's important and what should be left out—"I want to remember it all, so I'd rather not leave anything out."

Don't Get Bogged Down

What is your drawing about? Try to place only one point of focus in the picture. This can be an object, a building, a mountain peak, a tree, or a figure. How do you draw attention to it? Place the object prominently in the foreground or choose an interesting detail from it. Work in more detail at this point, strengthen the line, contrast light and dark, and use color for emphasis.

Of course, secondary elements are also allowed in the picture—things we discover at second glance (like the vehicle below: bumper, door handle, fuel cap). But be careful. Make sure that the hierarchy is clear. Don't let supporting actors steal the show from the main character.

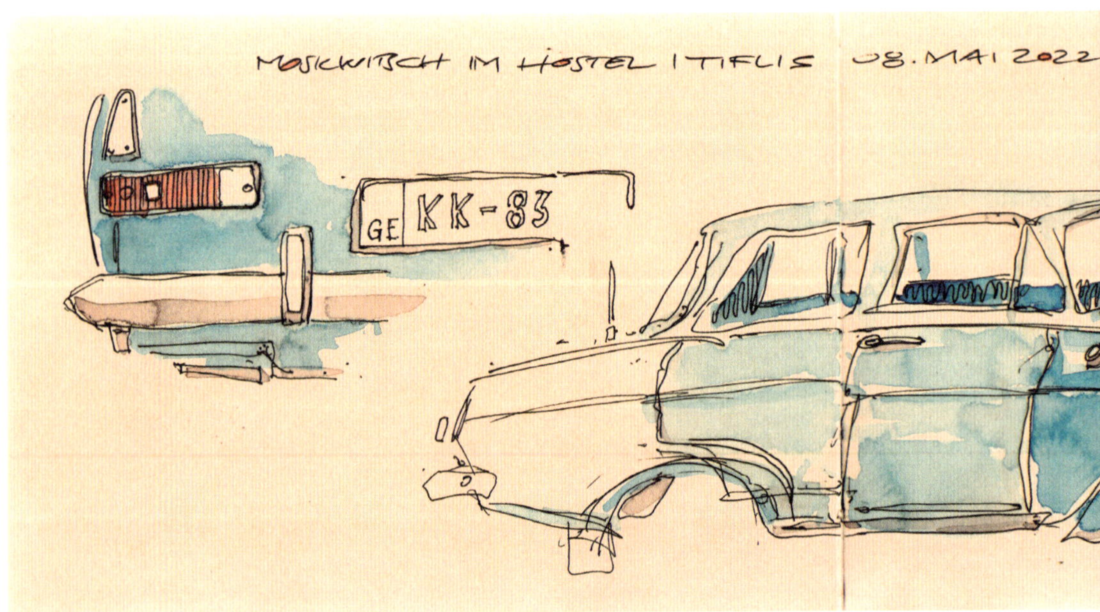

I was interested
in the ornate
dome of this
Orthodox church
in Tbilisi, Georgia.
I deliberately
omitted further
facade details
below it.

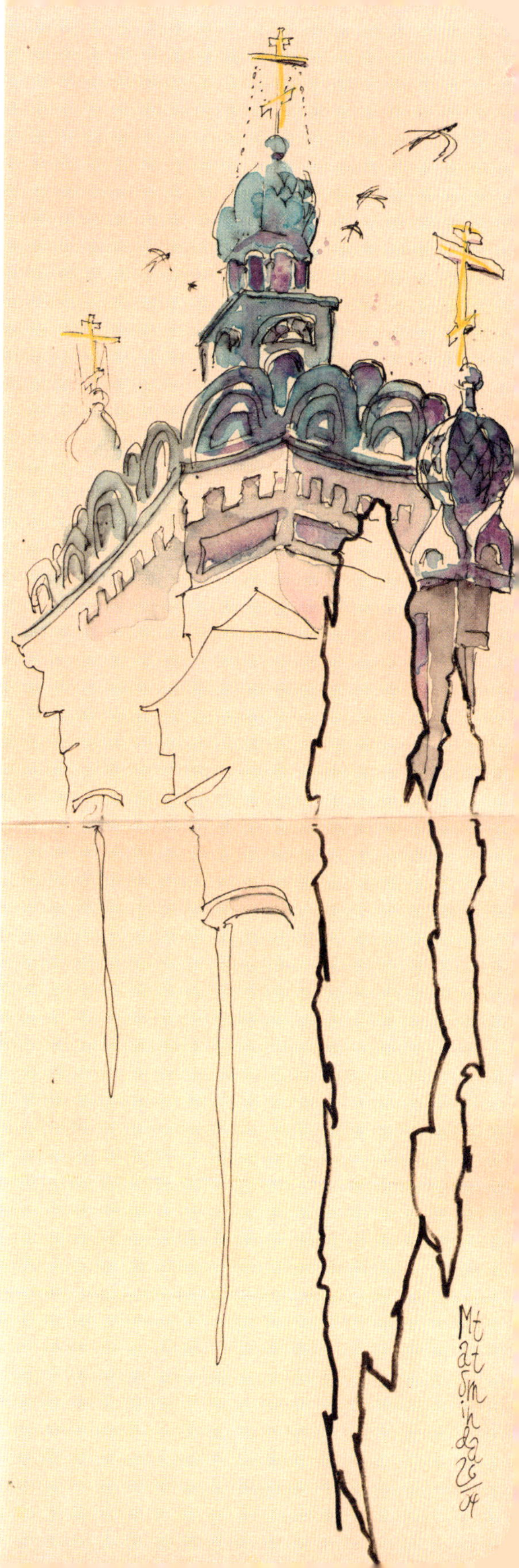

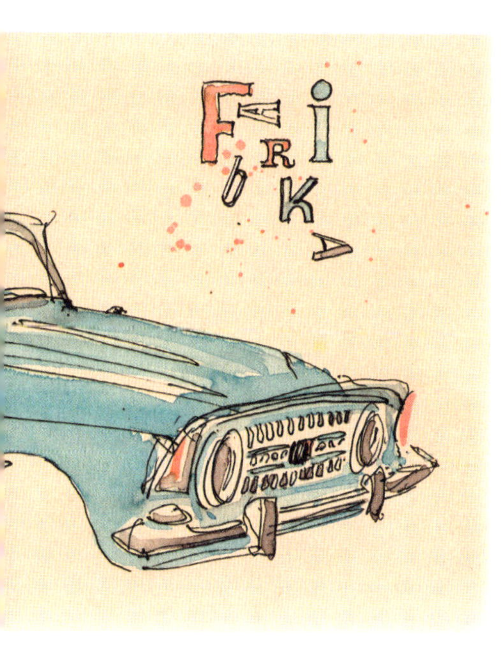

A Guided View

English speakers usually read the newspaper—and pictures—from top left to bottom right. We then linger briefly at the bottom before turning the page. You can guide the viewers of your sketch through the picture in different directions. Ascending and descending diagonals, perspective lines, or staggered elements should guide their gaze to the place in the picture that is most important to you. Sometimes a single image tells a whole story as our gaze wanders through it.

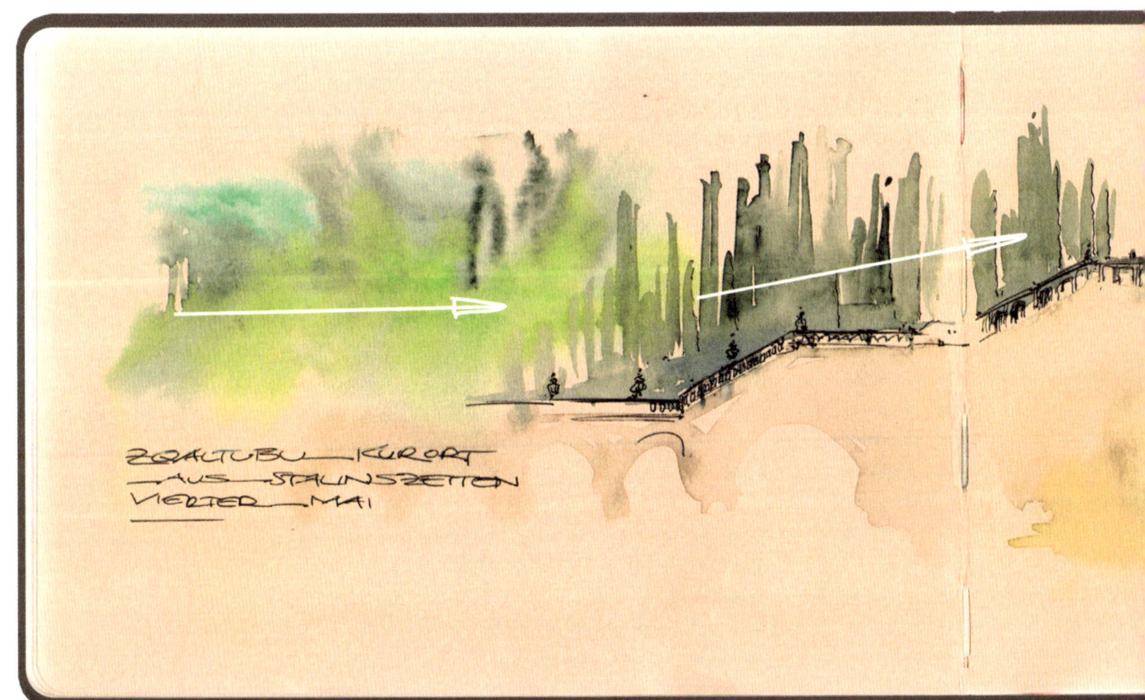

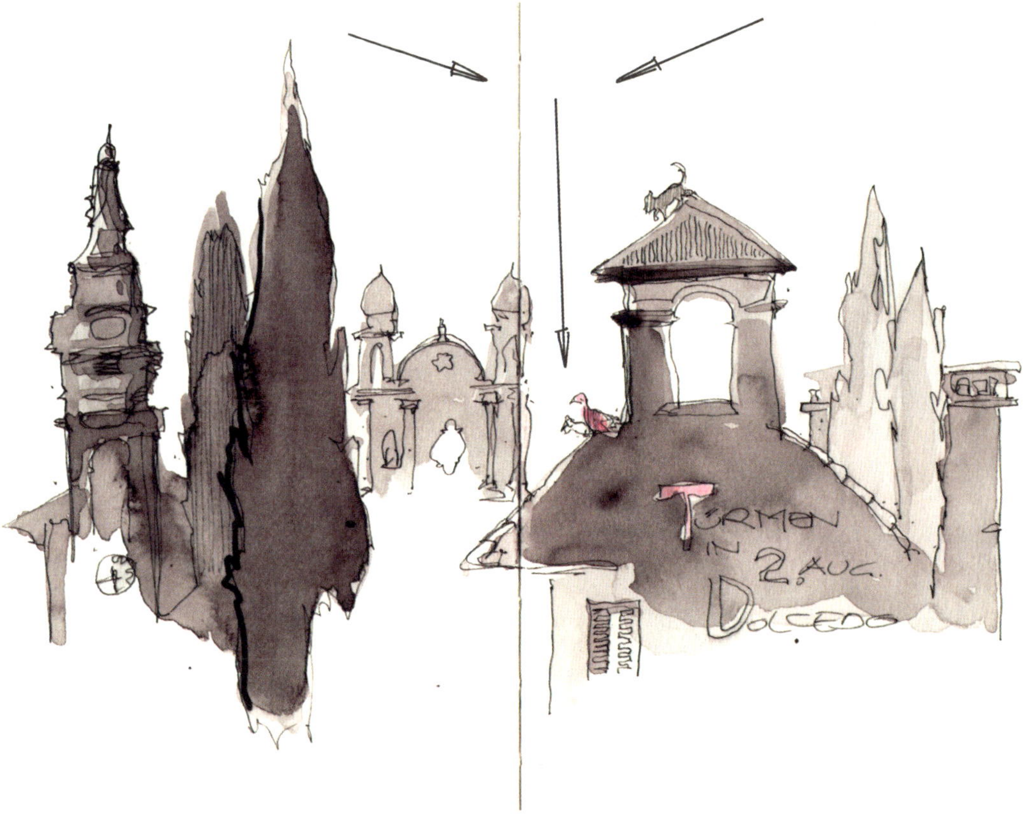

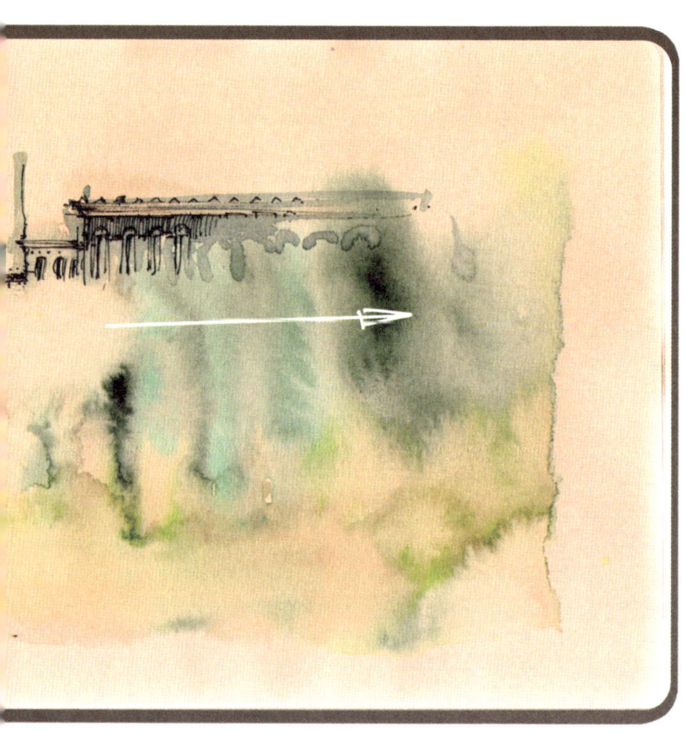

Georgia sketchbook: A glimpse into the past. What inspired me for the picture of this luxurious Stalinist-era sanatorium was the flight of steps set into the park landscape. I wanted the viewer to feel what it's like to stroll up the gently rising steps. The contrast between flowing watercolor and finely chiseled fineliner strokes further emphasizes the mystique of the place.

(For watercolor techniques, see page 98).

Weights in the Picture

When you go hiking with a heavy backpack on your back, you bend forward to maintain your balance. When you sit down close to one side of a cable car, it tilts. If someone sits down on the other side, it's balanced again. A drawing also has weight distribution.

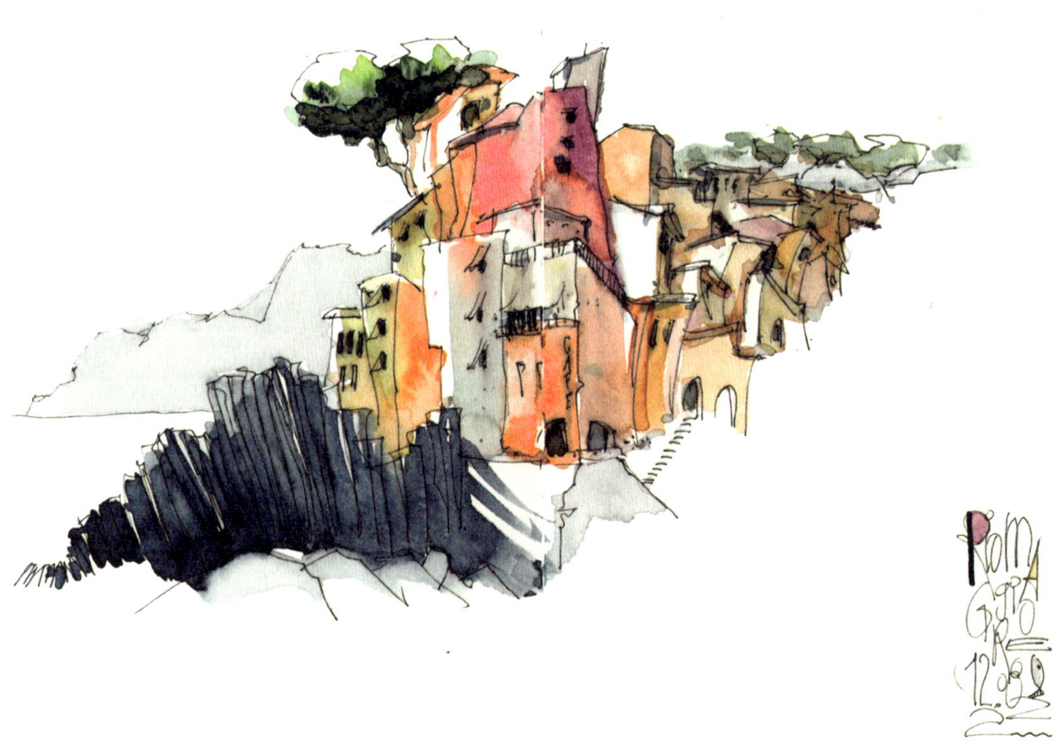

Tip: The final ingredient to add balance can be a label, place, or date.

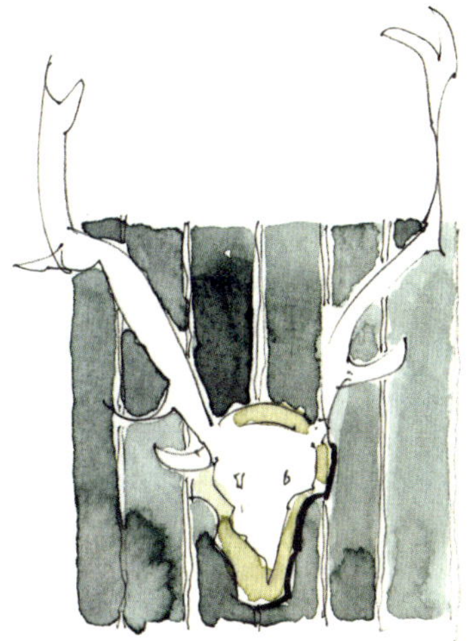

Achieving Balance

Every element in a picture is given weight through its size, contour, arrangement, or color. If the mixture of all the elements gets out of balance, the picture seems to tip over. If converging lines, dominant objects, or dark areas threaten to throw your composition off track, you can easily counteract this. Move or add new elements to the picture. Don't cling too closely to the real subject; take the design of the picture into your own hands.

Symmetrical subjects (top) have an inherent sense of balance. In an asymmetrical composition (bottom), I distribute the weights accordingly: a "heavy" element in the foreground on the right with a dark sky on the left as a counterweight.

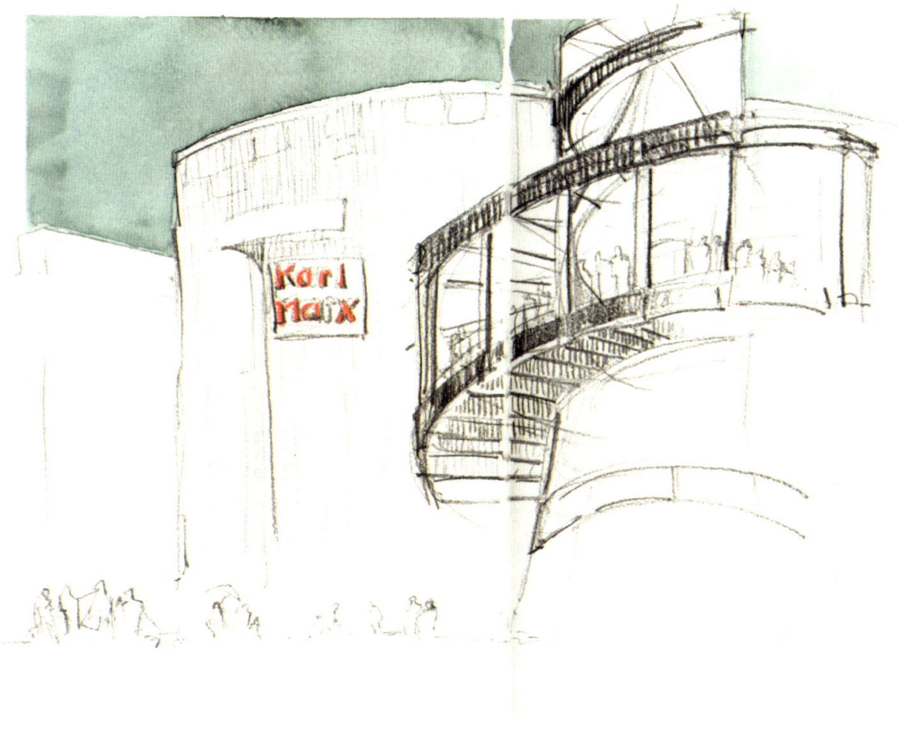

Detour: Lakes and Rivers

Water is inspiring; rivers and lakes, too, as well as the sea. Deep valleys, gently meandering watercourses, and hidden coves invite you to draw while walking by a lake, resting by a stream, or riding a ferry heading to the opposite shore.

Your creative possibilities are as varied as the subjects: sketching and painting with pen and brush, with a lot or a little water, in warm or cold weather.

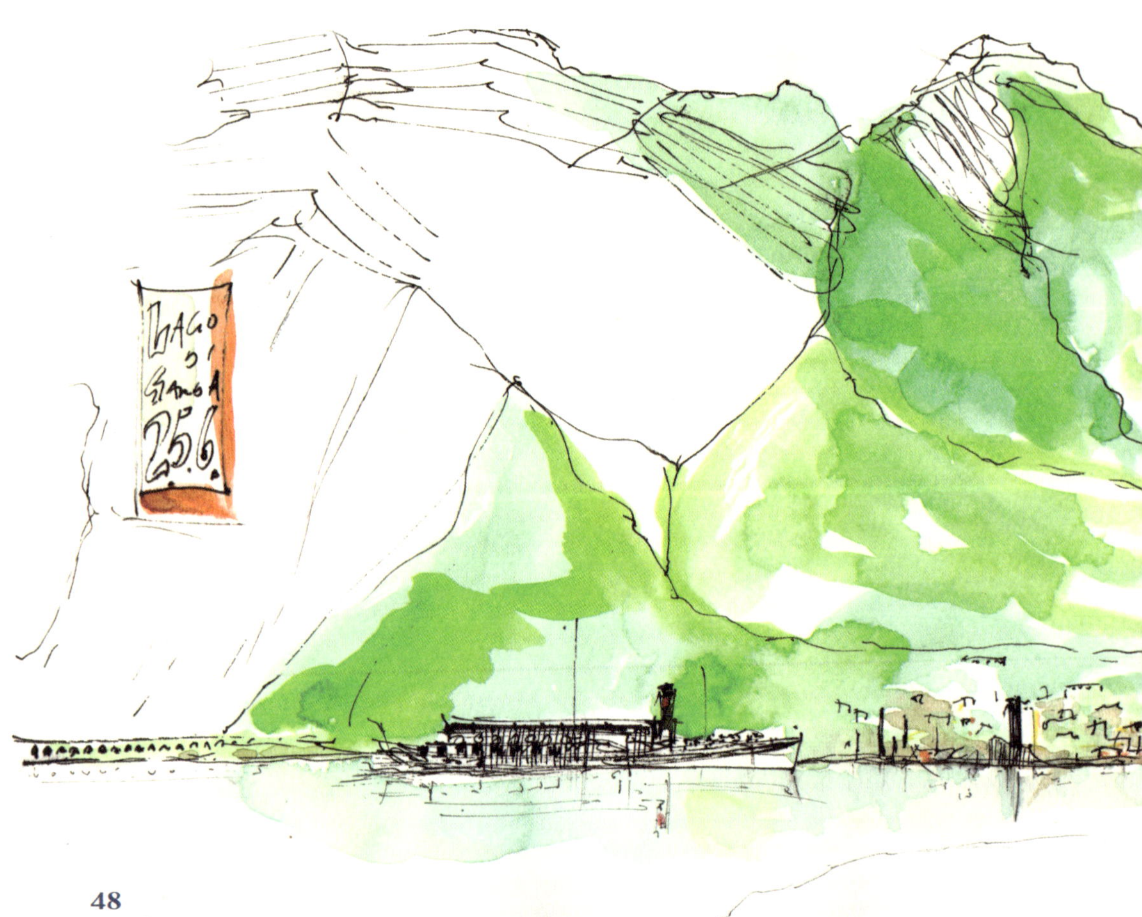

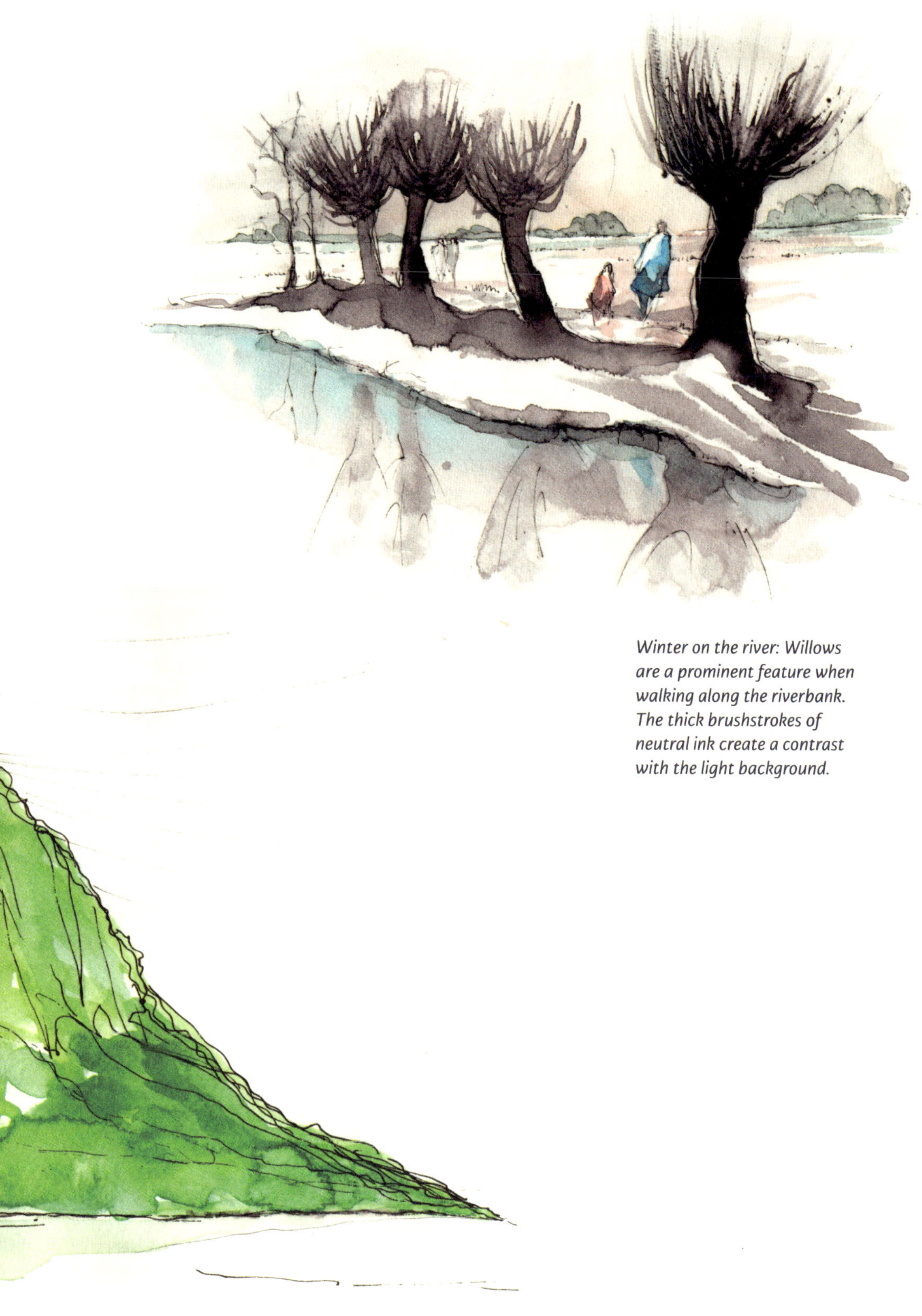

Winter on the river: Willows are a prominent feature when walking along the riverbank. The thick brushstrokes of neutral ink create a contrast with the light background.

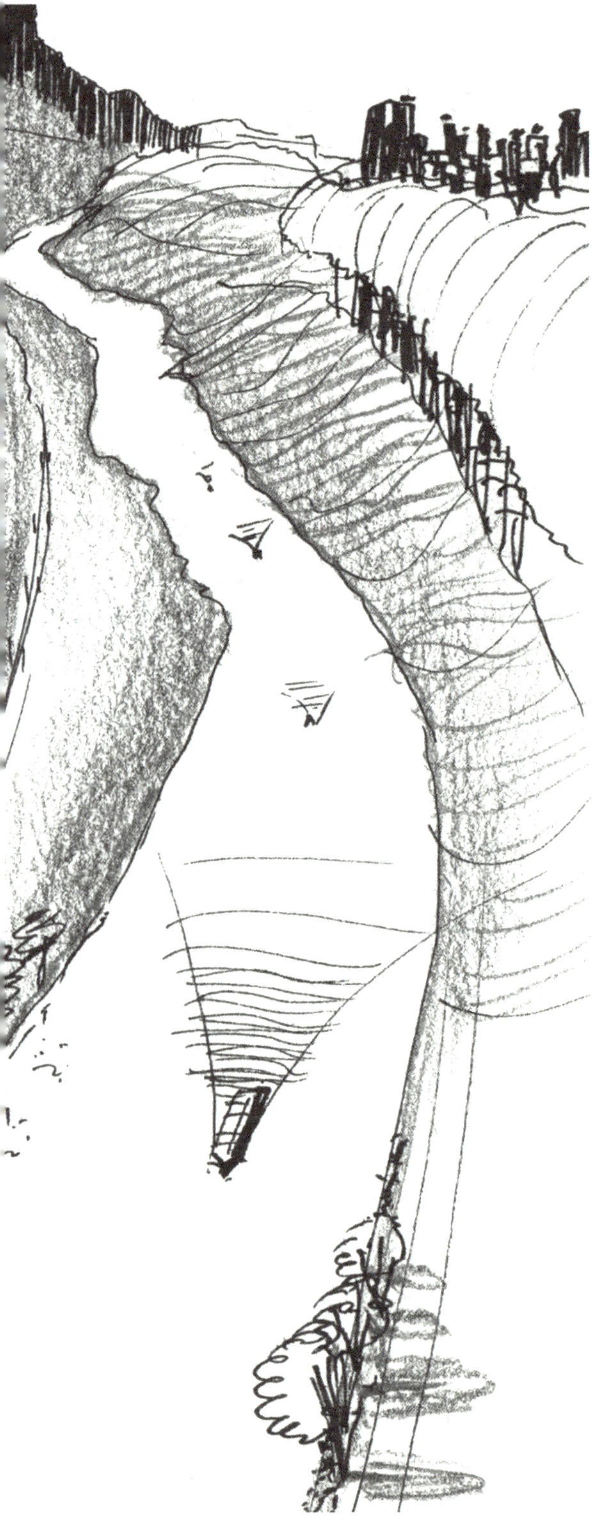

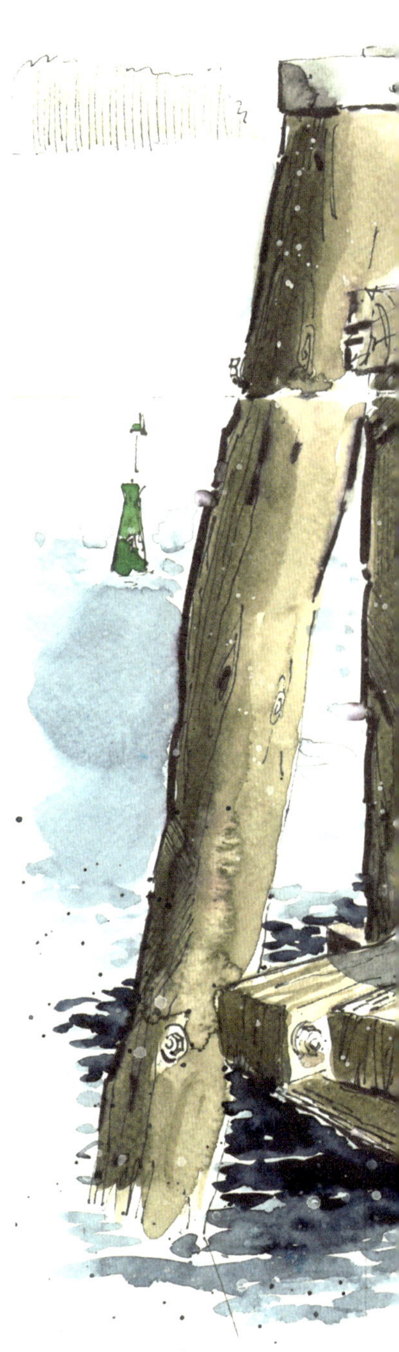

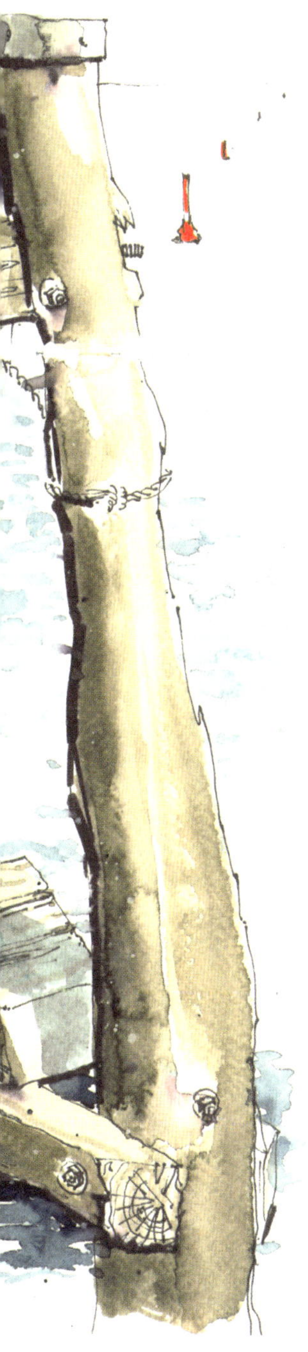

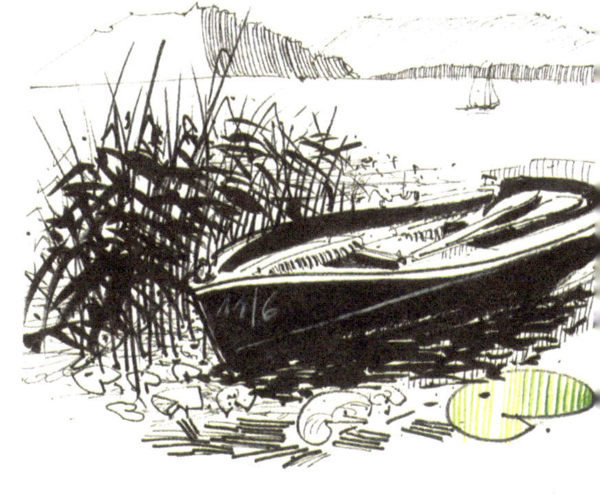

The Elbe: Cargo ships move slowly upstream. The layer of sand through which the river winds in the Elbe Sandstone Mountains was once three thousand feet high. I captured this unique landscape in black and white with fiber-tip pen and pencil.

Seeing colors with your head and heart: Our imagination fills in the colors of the fishing boat in the water. A single water lily leaf as an accent helps set this process in motion.

Upstream or downstream? When it gets narrow on the river, fairway buoys point the way. Red marks the right boundary in the direction of flow. The contrast of the green buoy as a complementary color livens up the picture.

You can find out more about the effect of colors when sketching outdoors starting on page 130.

In Its Own Element

Whether it's the water of a lake or the clouds above, watercolors, used effectively on watercolor paper, automatically create the impression of "wetness." The wetter, the better. For the watercolor sketch of Lake Constance, I moistened the paper beforehand. Simply apply clear water to parts of the image, add watercolor paint to the wet areas, and spread it quickly with the brush. Even if you have little control over the result, the mixture of color gradients and drying edges is delightful and surprising. You can find more watercolor techniques starting on page 98.

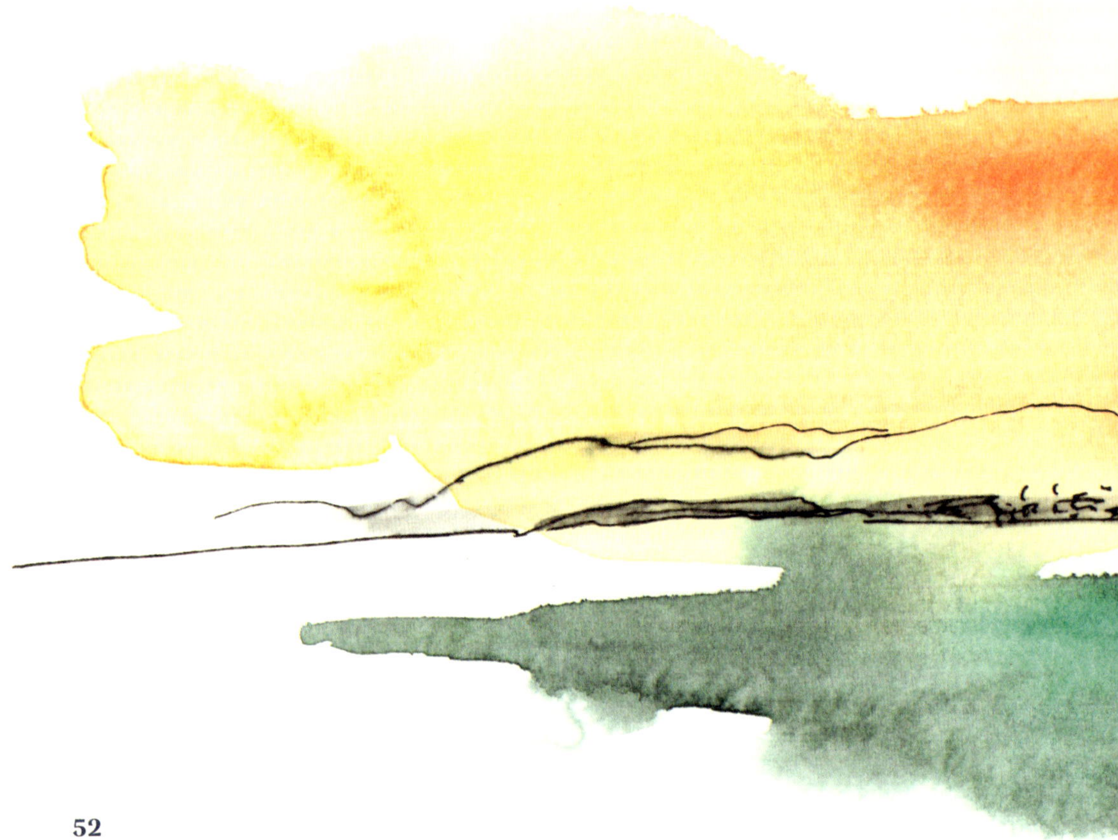

Tip: Avoid precisely "coloring in" line draw-ings. Apply color generously; the yellow background connects the landscape and sky in this topographical sketch. Add a few details—dots and dashes create the illusion of a village on the opposite bank.

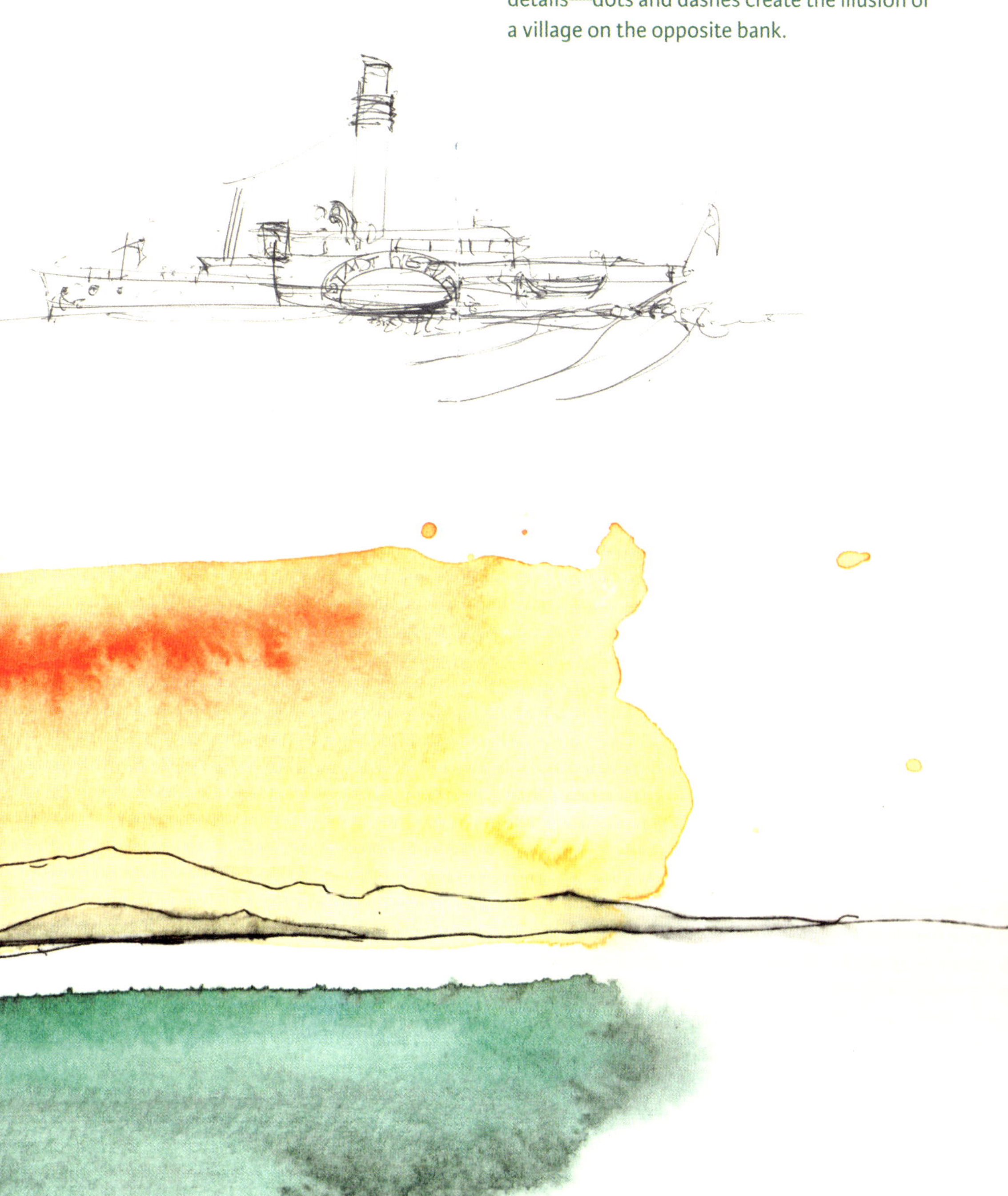

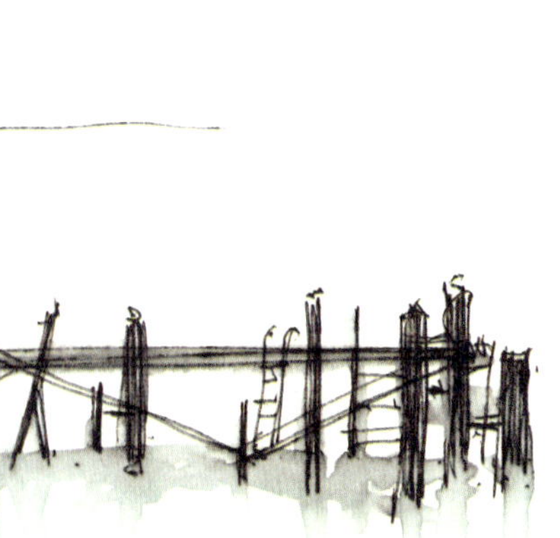

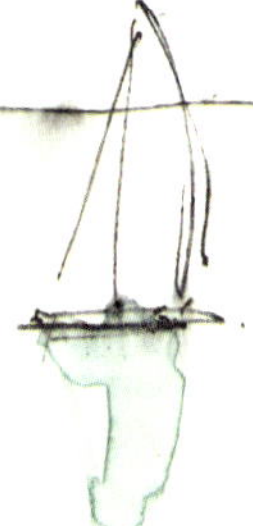

Reflections in Water

When I teach, my classes often end up standing by a body of water, and it doesn't take long for the question to arise: How do I paint water—a material that's colorless by nature? Or: Why does my boat on the lake look like it's frozen in place?

Water reflects incoming light. Objects or entire landscapes are mirrored on its surface. Wind, waves, and currents disturb these reflections. It also makes a difference whether this occurs near the shore or at a greater distance.

Angle of Incidence Equals Angle of Reflection

Objects that hit the water surface at a 90-degree angle are reflected vertically into the image. Here it is sufficient to extend the "original" downward. Sloping shapes are also "folded" downward—at the same angle at which they hit the water surface.

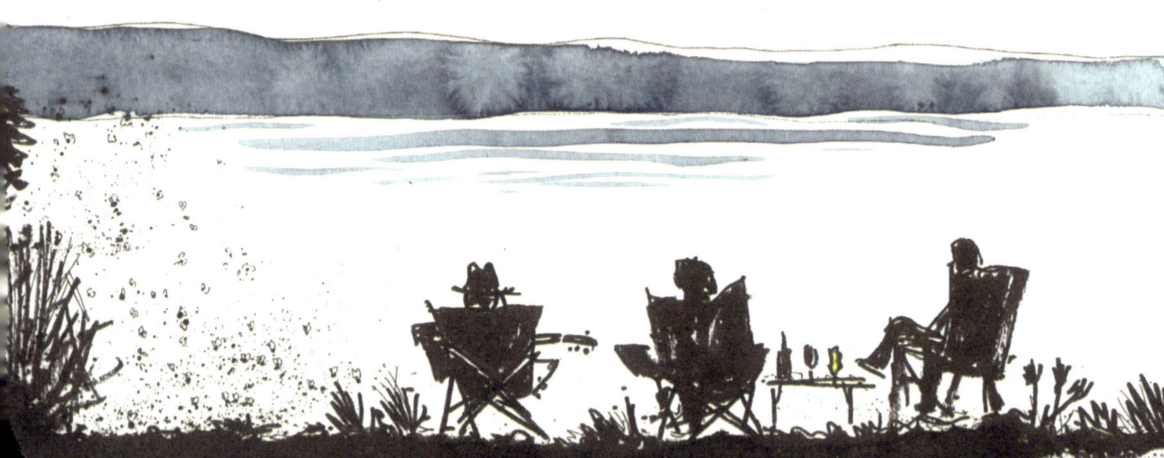

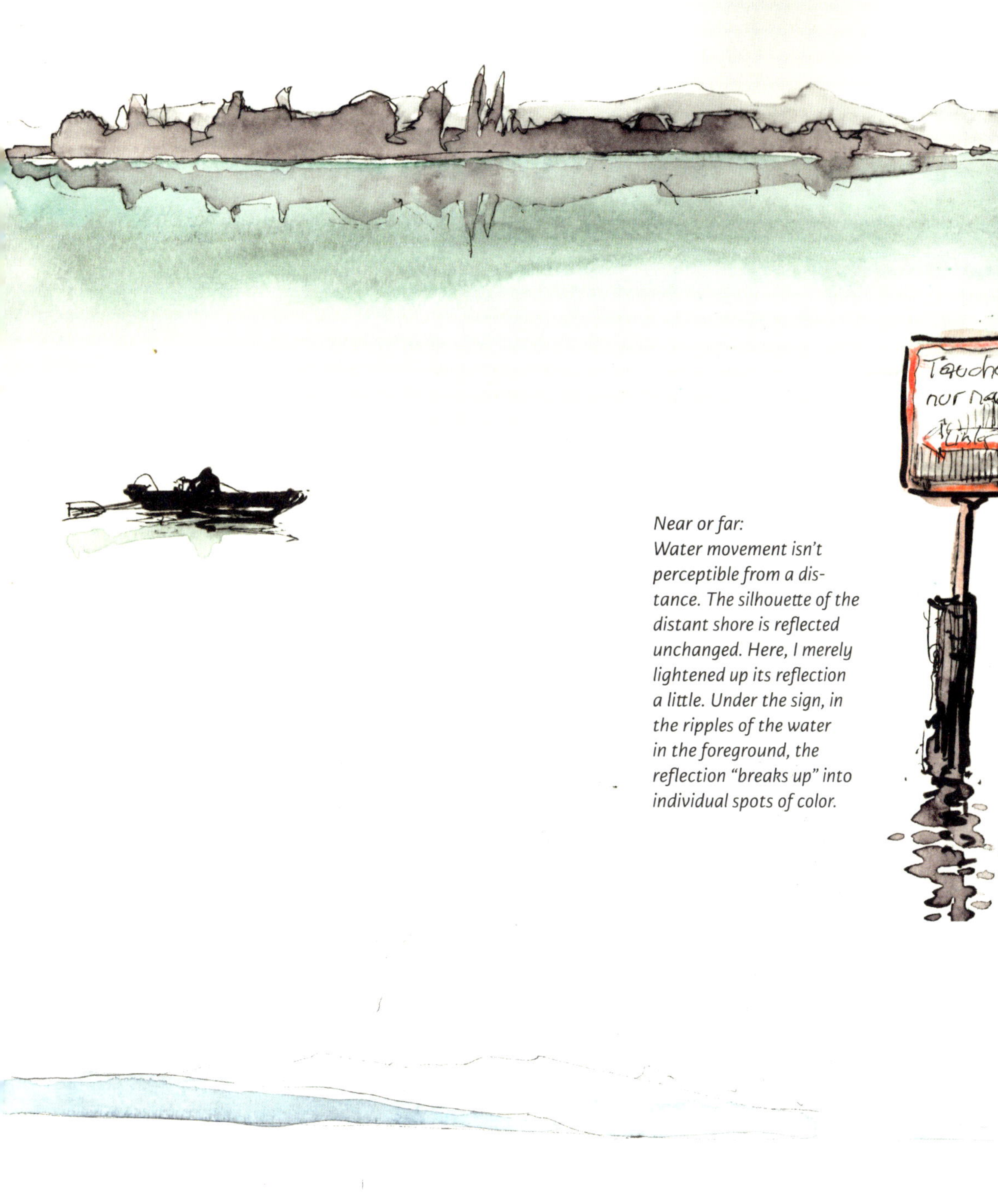

Near or far:
Water movement isn't
perceptible from a dis-
tance. The silhouette of the
distant shore is reflected
unchanged. Here, I merely
lightened up its reflection
a little. Under the sign, in
the ripples of the water
in the foreground, the
reflection "breaks up" into
individual spots of color.

Light and shadow contribute significantly to the picture's message: short shadows at midday, flat sidelight in winter, dramatic backlight with perspective shadows in the evening.

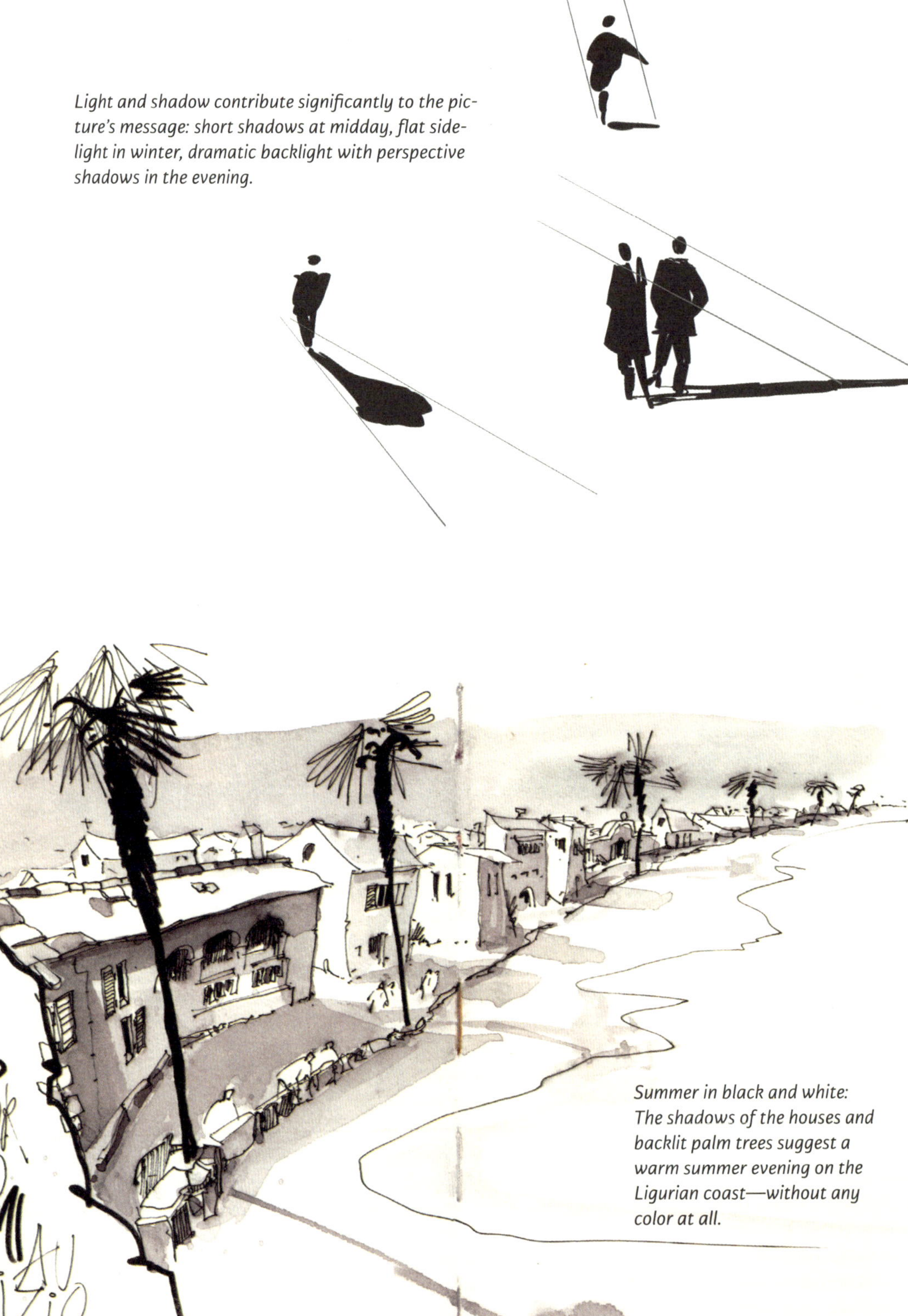

Summer in black and white: The shadows of the houses and backlit palm trees suggest a warm summer evening on the Ligurian coast—without any color at all.

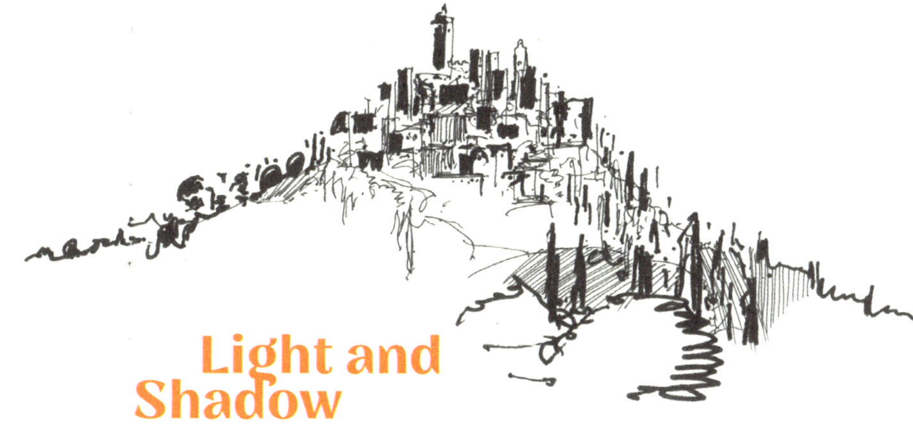

Light and Shadow

Nature and light are inextricably linked. Geographic location, time of day, season, weather—every moment outdoors and every place reveals a different kind of light. And different shadows. There are far more nuances to light than the ubiquitous sunset by the sea or the nocturnal play of shadows cast by the light of a streetlamp.

Ground Contact

Shadows don't just influence the mood of your picture, they also ensure ground contact. Trees, vehicles, and objects will float around on the page if they're not anchored to the ground by shadows. The projected shadow doesn't have to be geometrically correct; sometimes a simple line is enough.

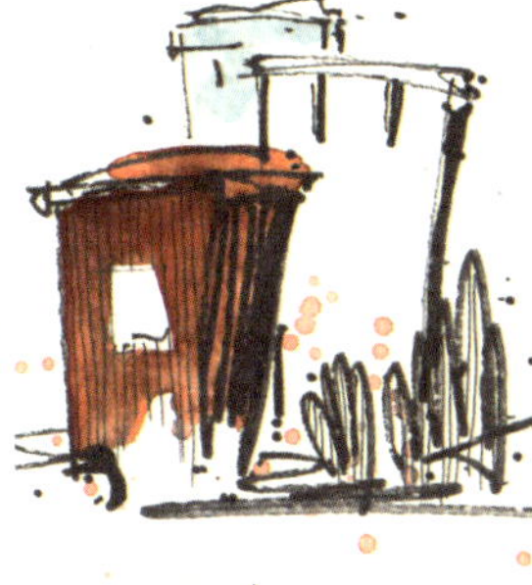

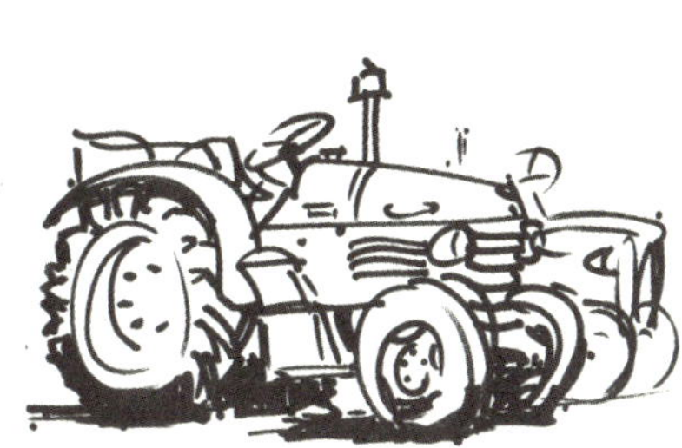

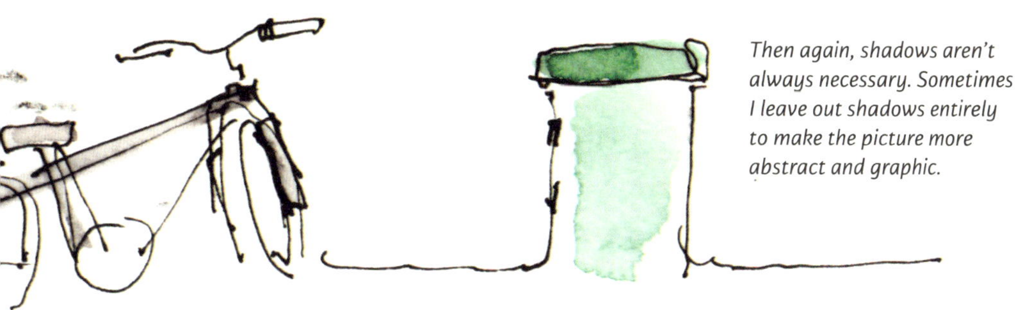

Then again, shadows aren't always necessary. Sometimes I leave out shadows entirely to make the picture more abstract and graphic.

The White of the Paper

A new, blank page in a sketchbook consists of 100 percent light. By
that I mean the white of the paper. Only your drawing on the paper
takes something away from this whiteness. It's a shame when
nothing of the light of the surface remains; when, in the heat of
the moment, the whole surface is filled with watercolors, without
deliberately leaving some white in certain places.

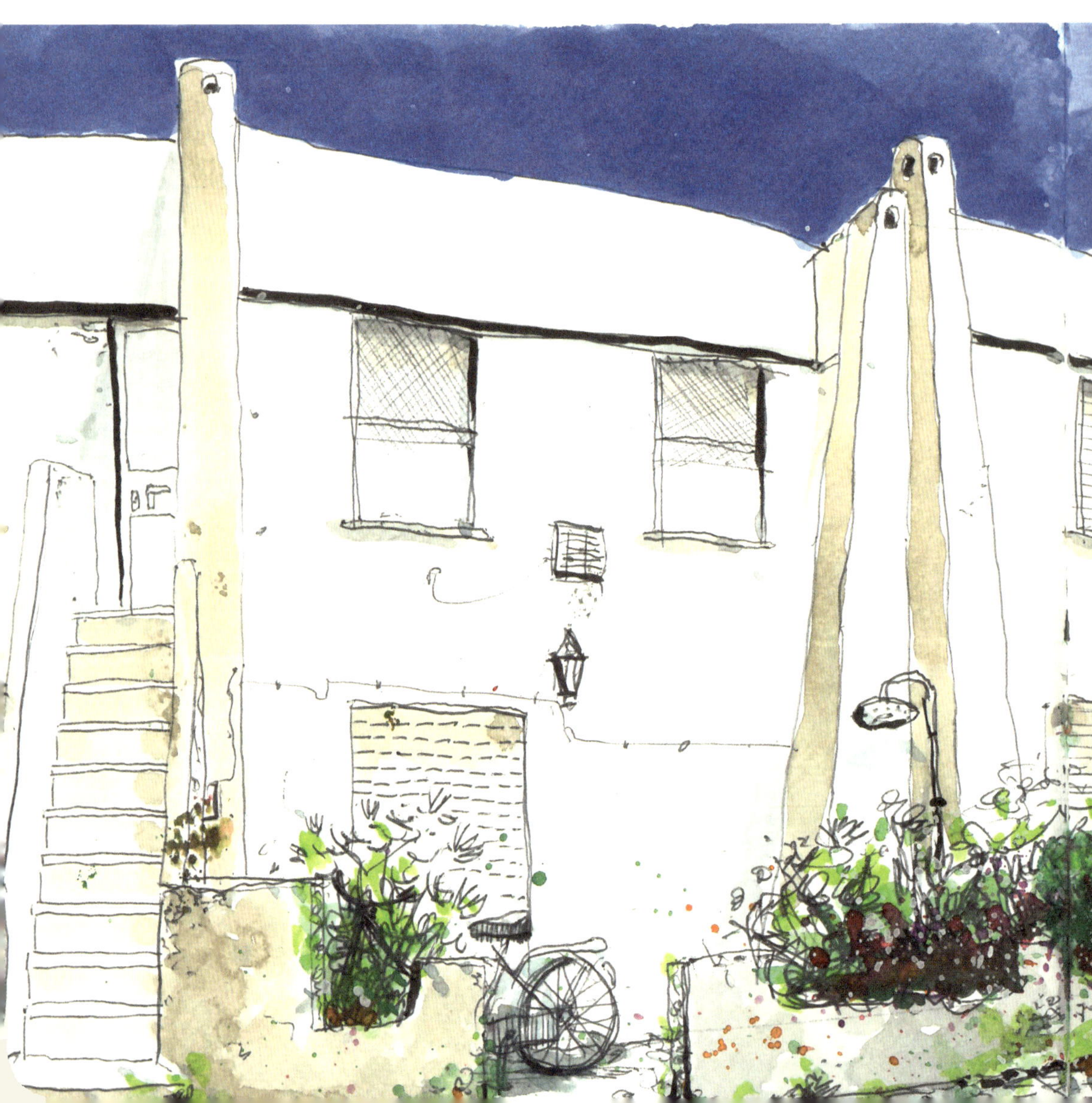

This drawing was made in Sardinia. After spending the morning at the beach, I fled the sun and heat. I sat down on a bench under a tree. I enjoyed the midday calm of the siesta. I listened to the silence and looked at the empty square in front of me. Not a soul in sight; even dogs and cats had disappeared. I absorbed this emptiness into myself. I let myself be inspired by it and captured it in my sketchbook. My advice: Leave at least 30 percent of the paper blank in each drawing. Can you see how much midday sun there is in this picture?

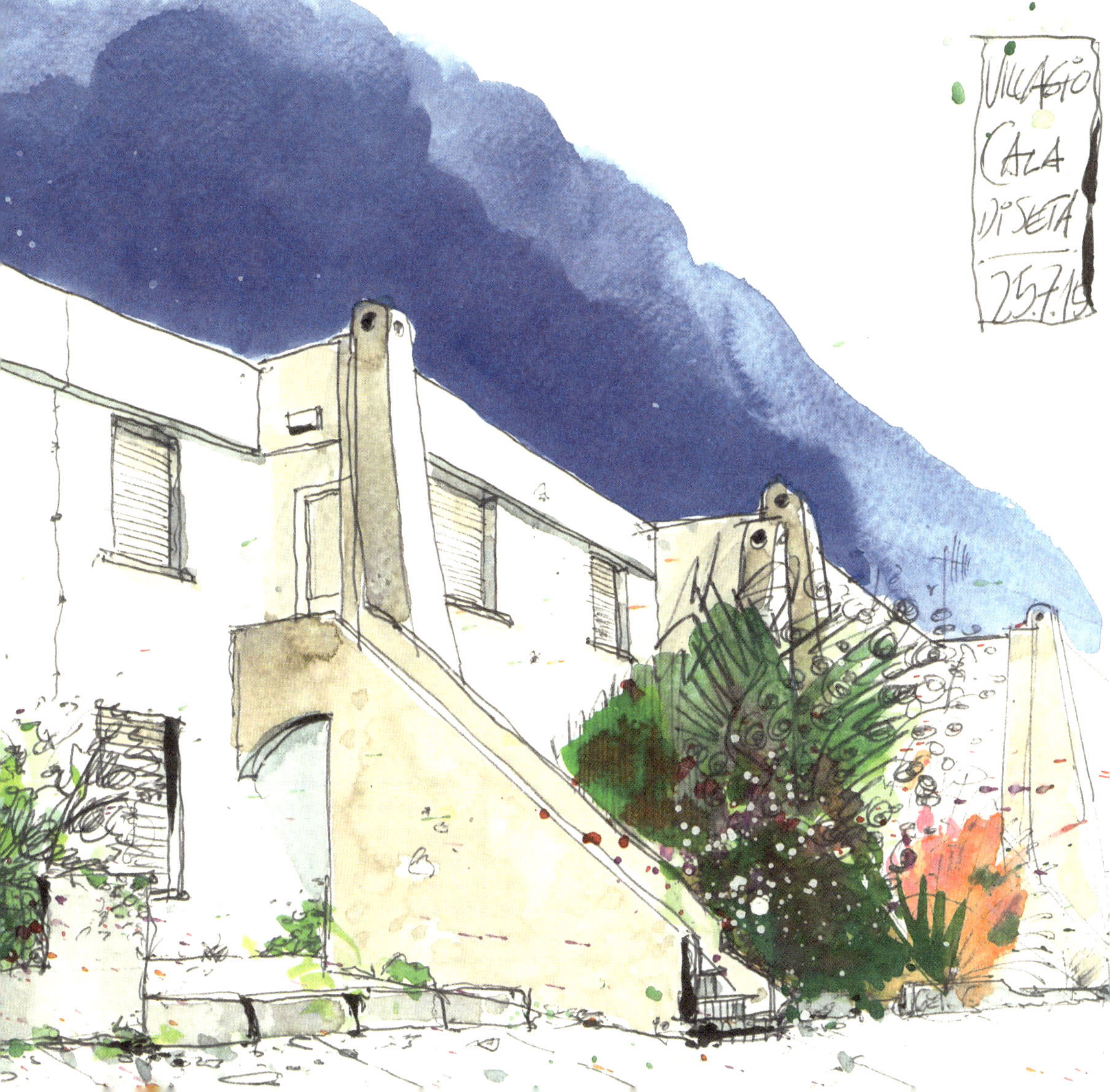

Crop or Isolate?

Again, the real question is: What message are you trying to convey with your picture? Full disclosure or mere suggestion? Restraint or tension?

Compositions with one or more isolated forms emphasize these and radiate a certain calm. The viewer can concentrate on the subject. Only what's important can be seen in the picture. The less, the better.

Compositions with cropped forms, on the other hand, have their own appeal. Your picture, the story of your picture, does not end at the edge of the paper. The landscape continues in the mind of the observer. The cropped house takes on an unknown charm. The cat chases an invisible mouse.

No matter who or what you crop out, do it deliberately. Don't just suggest the edge of the image, but define it clearly. Don't divide an object exactly in the middle; it looks contrived. Choose a section that invites you to imagine the shape or scene outside of the image.

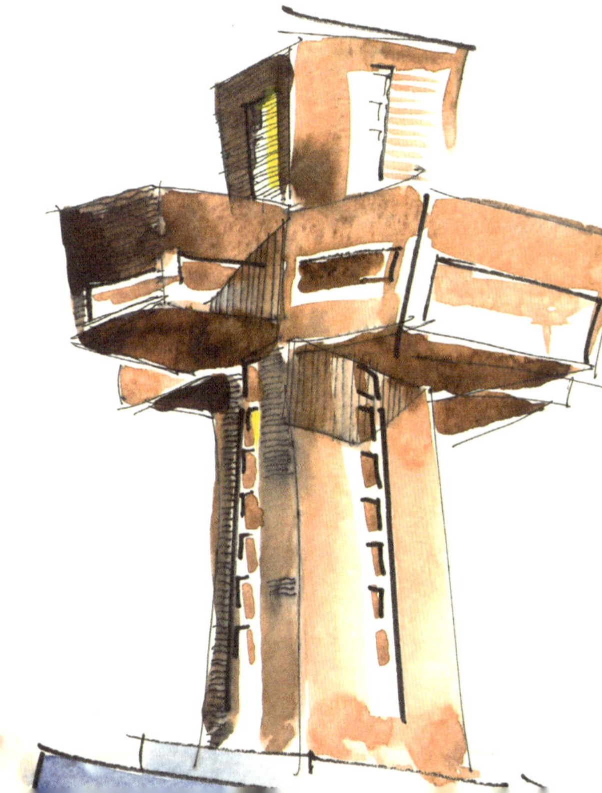

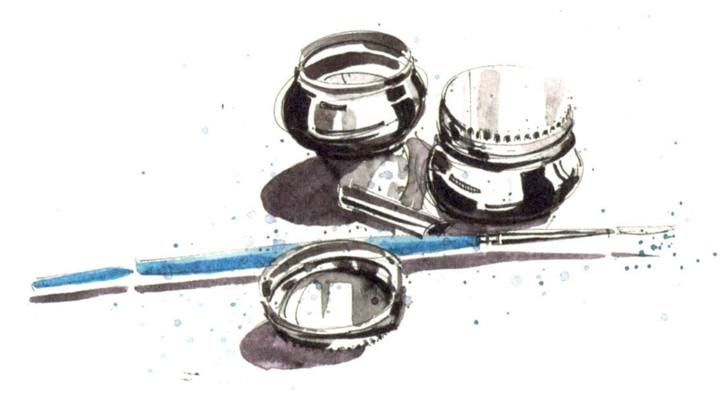

Wildbad Kreuth, Germany: The maypole and the landscape are cropped. This makes them grow far beyond the edge of the picture. I increased the effect even more by using diagonal elements to break up the familiar order of vertical lines.

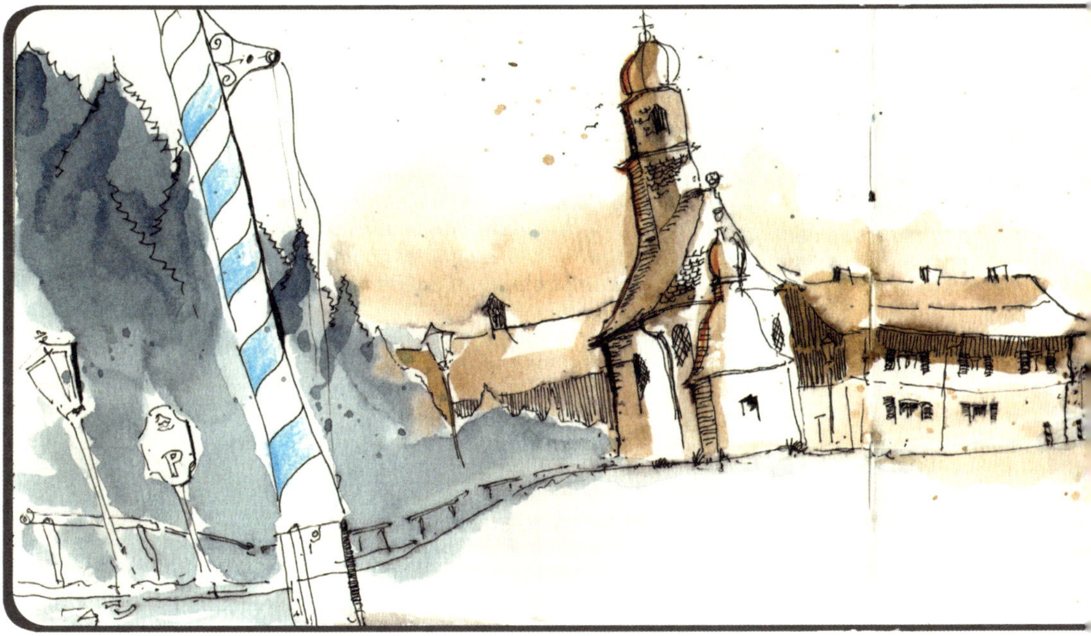

Frame It!

Just as the edges of your sketchbook delimit and "frame" your subjects, you can also use frames creatively within a page. In my warm-up exercise (Start with Miniatures, page 19), you already learned how to sketch in picture frames. What else can picture frames do?

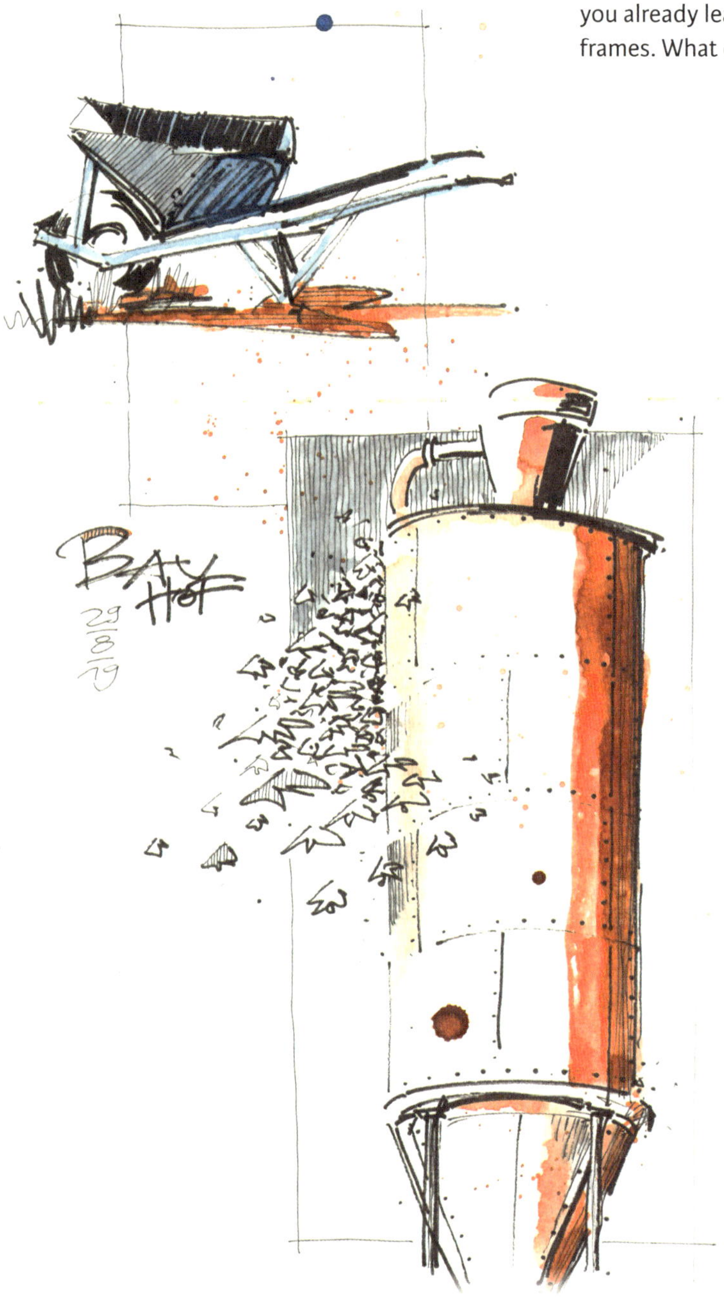

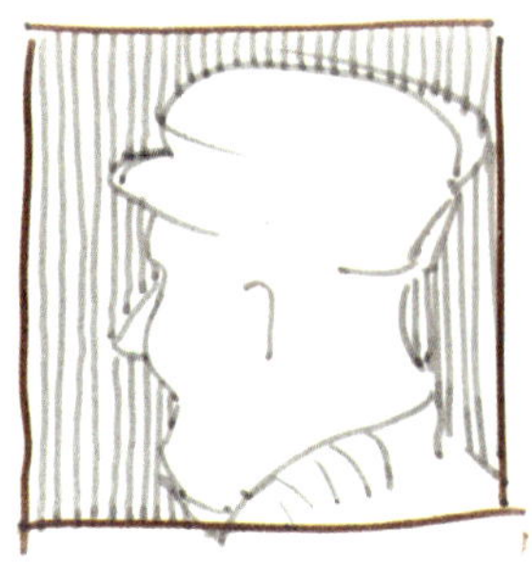

Tip: Fill the area inside the frame around your subject with hatching or watercolor—not for decorative reasons, but to reinforce your message. The contrast between light and dark, and the interplay of color surfaces, will further enhance the impact of your subject.

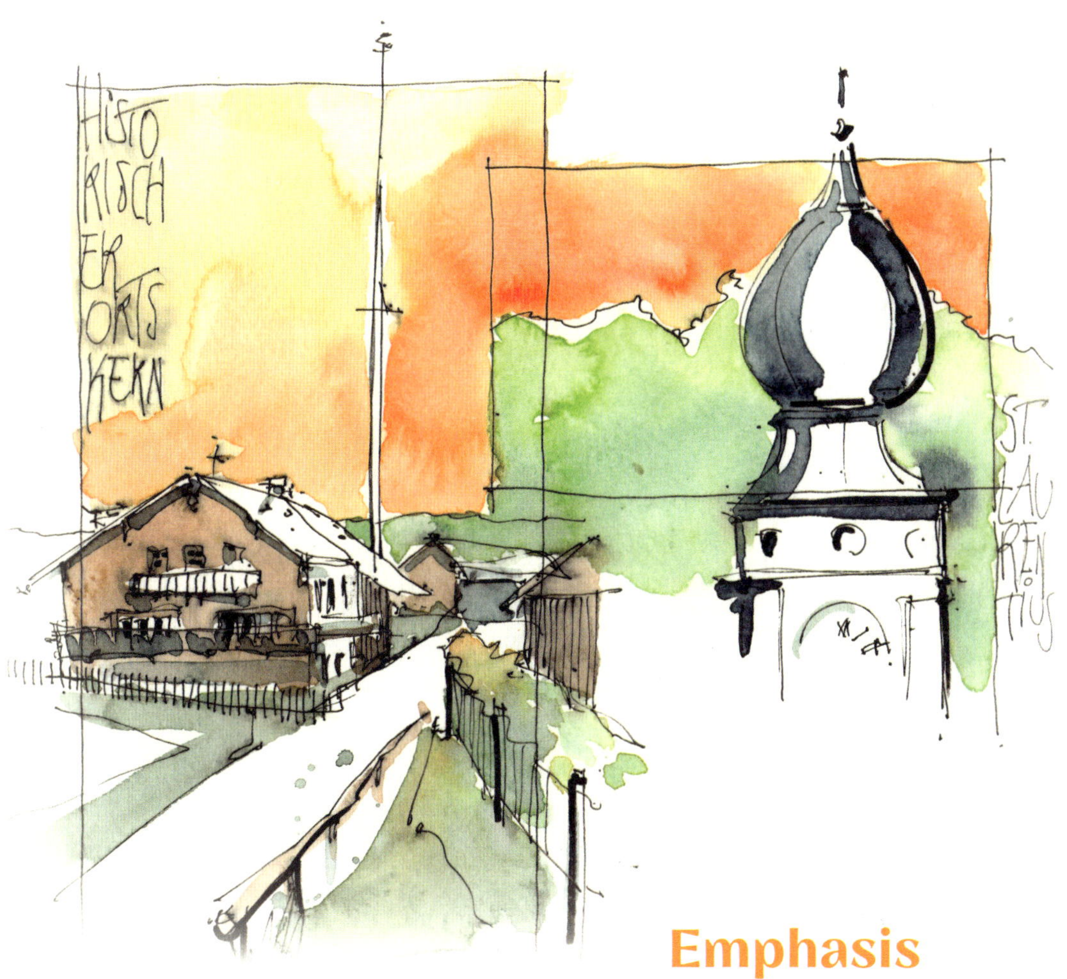

Emphasis

Do you want to draw attention to part of your drawing? Or stabilize irregular shapes? Or set them off in contrast against a clear, geometric surface? Simply draw a frame—four quick lines that overlap slightly at the corners—with a fineliner or pencil. Whether you create the frame first or let it develop together with the subject will become clear as you sketch.

Deliberately let individual elements of the picture go outside the lines; after all, the frame is meant to create order, not constrict. Stretched, horizontal frames are suitable for landscapes. Vertical frames emphasize vertical forms.

Tape a Frame

If I want to create frames without drawing a border line, I use masking tape to cover the edges. Another advantage of this is that I can test the shape and effect of the frame first and adjust it to my subject.

Exercise: Taping

Try this yourself with some good-quality masking tape from the hardware store:

1. Tear off the tape in the desired lengths from the roll.
2. If you're afraid of damaging your paper, first stick it to another surface. Each time you peel it off, the adhesive decreases.
3. Stick the tape on your paper, overlapping the pieces at the corners.
4. Apply watercolor paint to the interior area.
5. Peel off the tape—done.

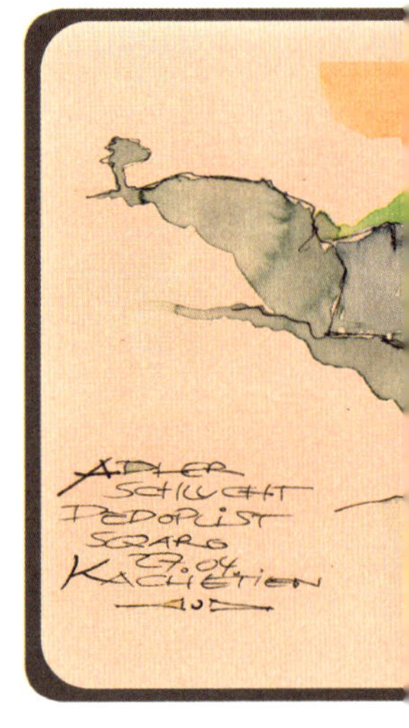

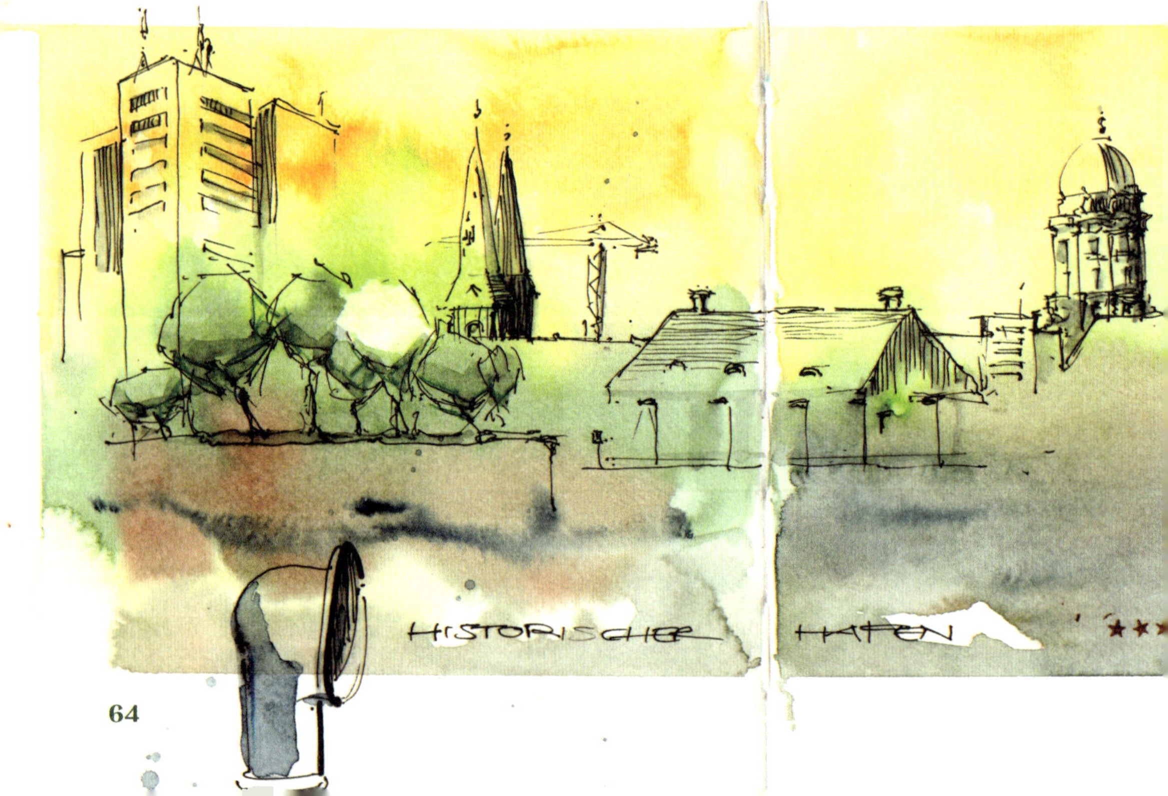

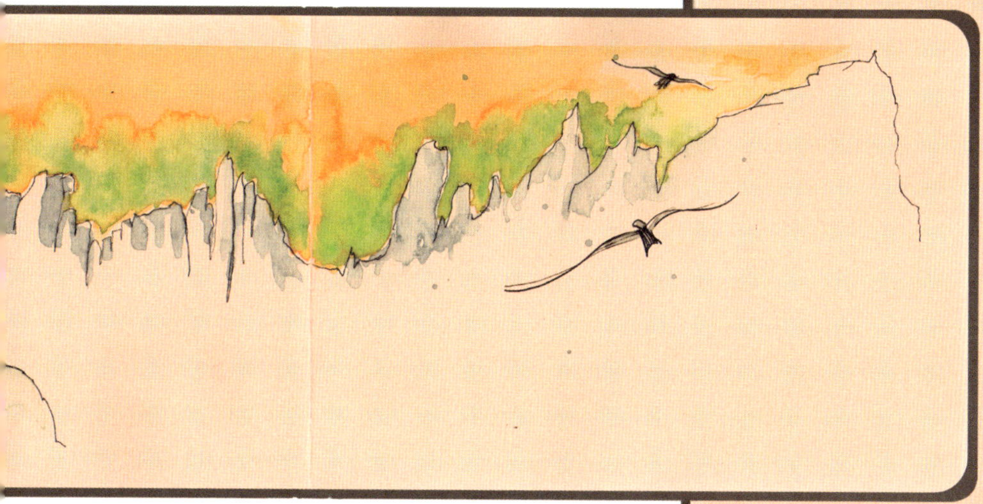

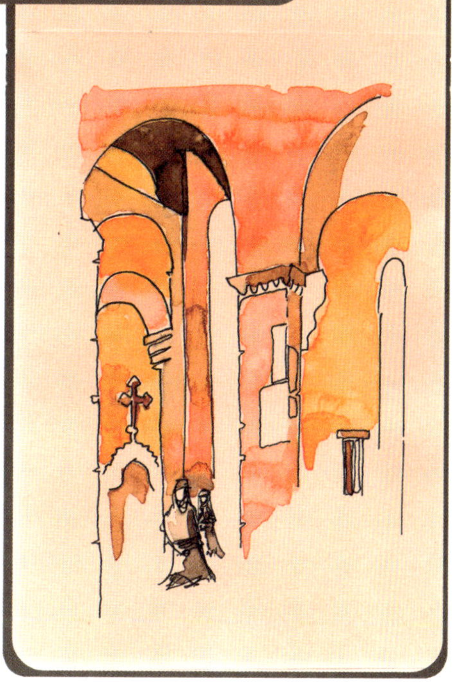

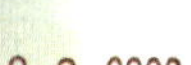

Special case: This sketchbook contains both pages
with isolated subjects and
pages with cropped subjects.
To maintain a consistent
aesthetic, I covered the
edges of the latter with tape.
Thus, these are also
"isolated"—no lines touching
on the pages when I leaf
through my travel journal.

Detour: Foothills

Up to the hills. Expand your view, raise your horizons. Since the beginning of time and for many different reasons, people—painters, poets, mountaineers, soldiers, surveyors, and foresters—have sought out places that offer them a view of the landscape. As have all those who hike through these areas.

No matter what heights you are drawn to when sketching, enjoy the view from above. Take a careful look at the landscape below, then reach for your pencil and sketchbook.

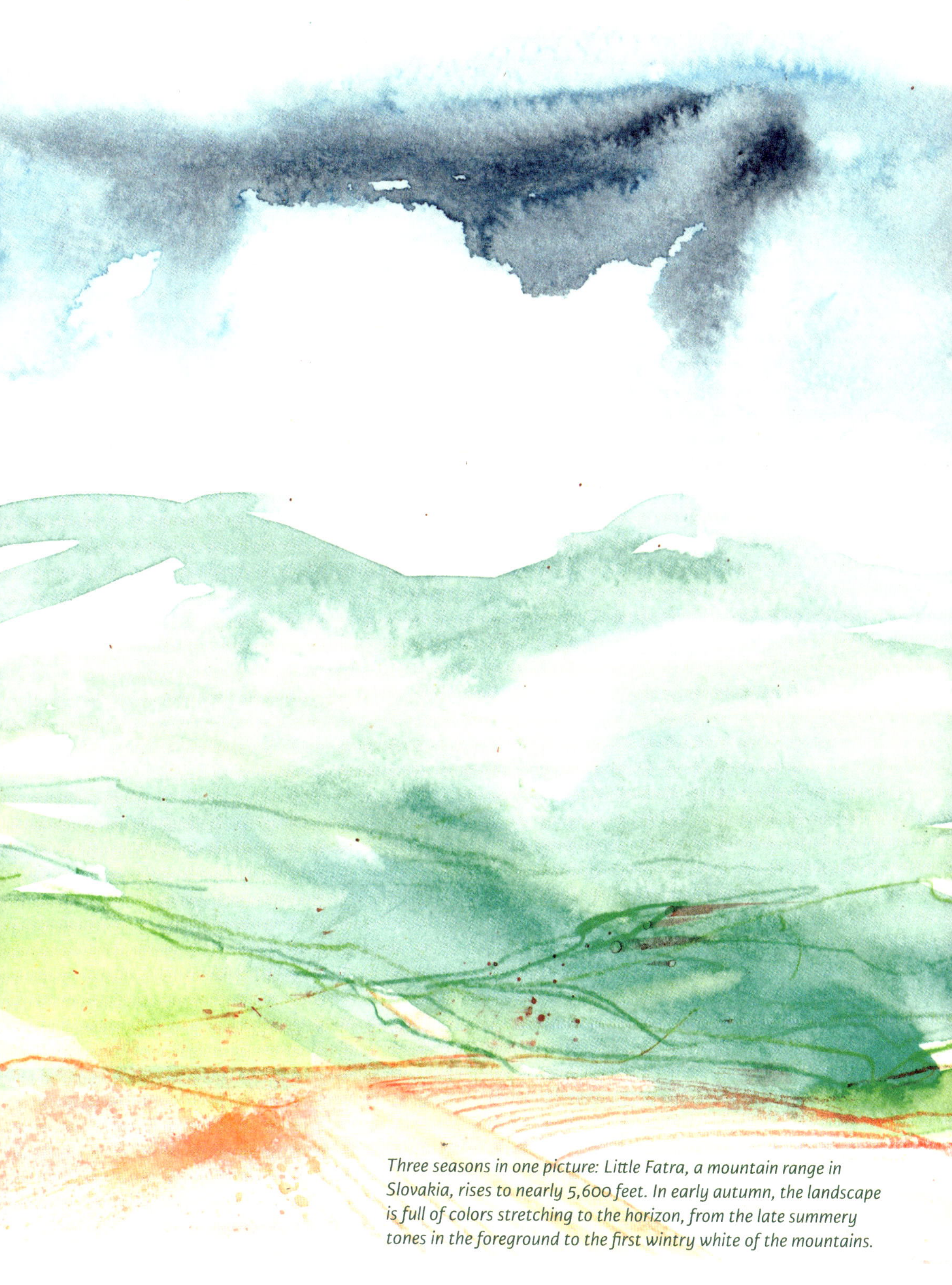

Three seasons in one picture: Little Fatra, a mountain range in Slovakia, rises to nearly 5,600 feet. In early autumn, the landscape is full of colors stretching to the horizon, from the late summery tones in the foreground to the first wintry white of the mountains.

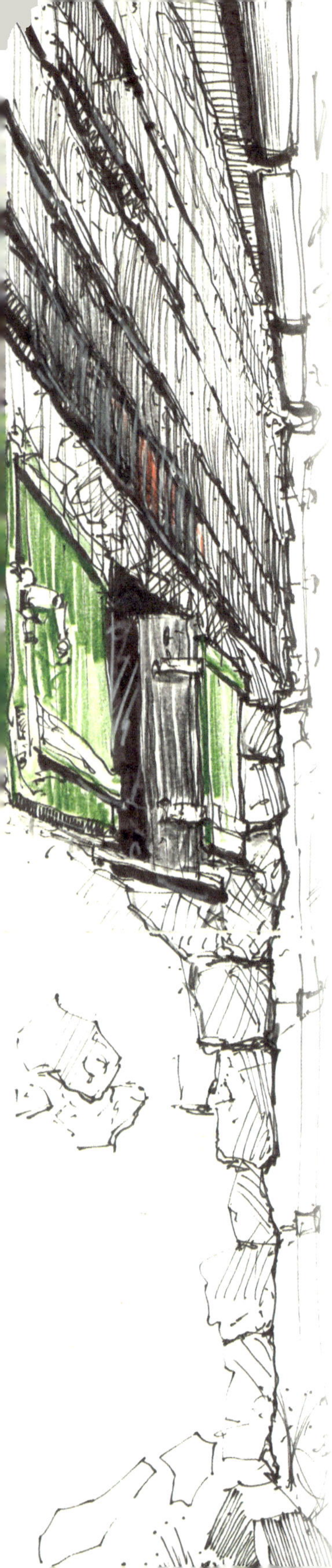

Form and Structure

Topographically interesting subjects aren't just found in the Alps. Even the peaks of low mountain ranges have unique shapes that are interesting to draw. Their geometry varies greatly: pyramid peaks, table mountains, volcanic cones, and many more shapes. Each mountaintop has its own characteristics, so it's worth taking a closer look when drawing.

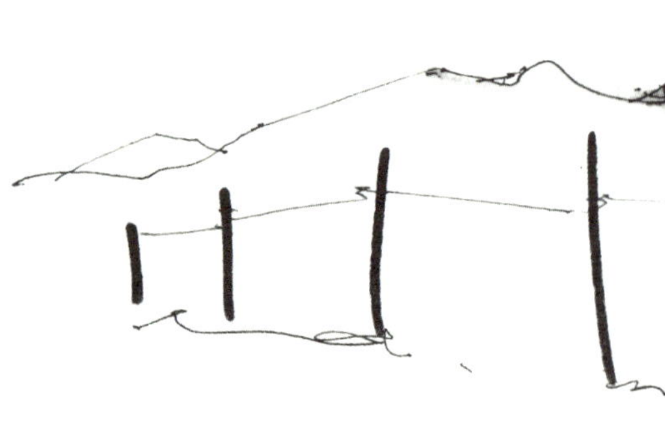

With the wall behind me: From a sheltered spot on this bench, I captured the view of the mountains. The strong perspective of the wall and fence intensifies the three-dimensional impression.

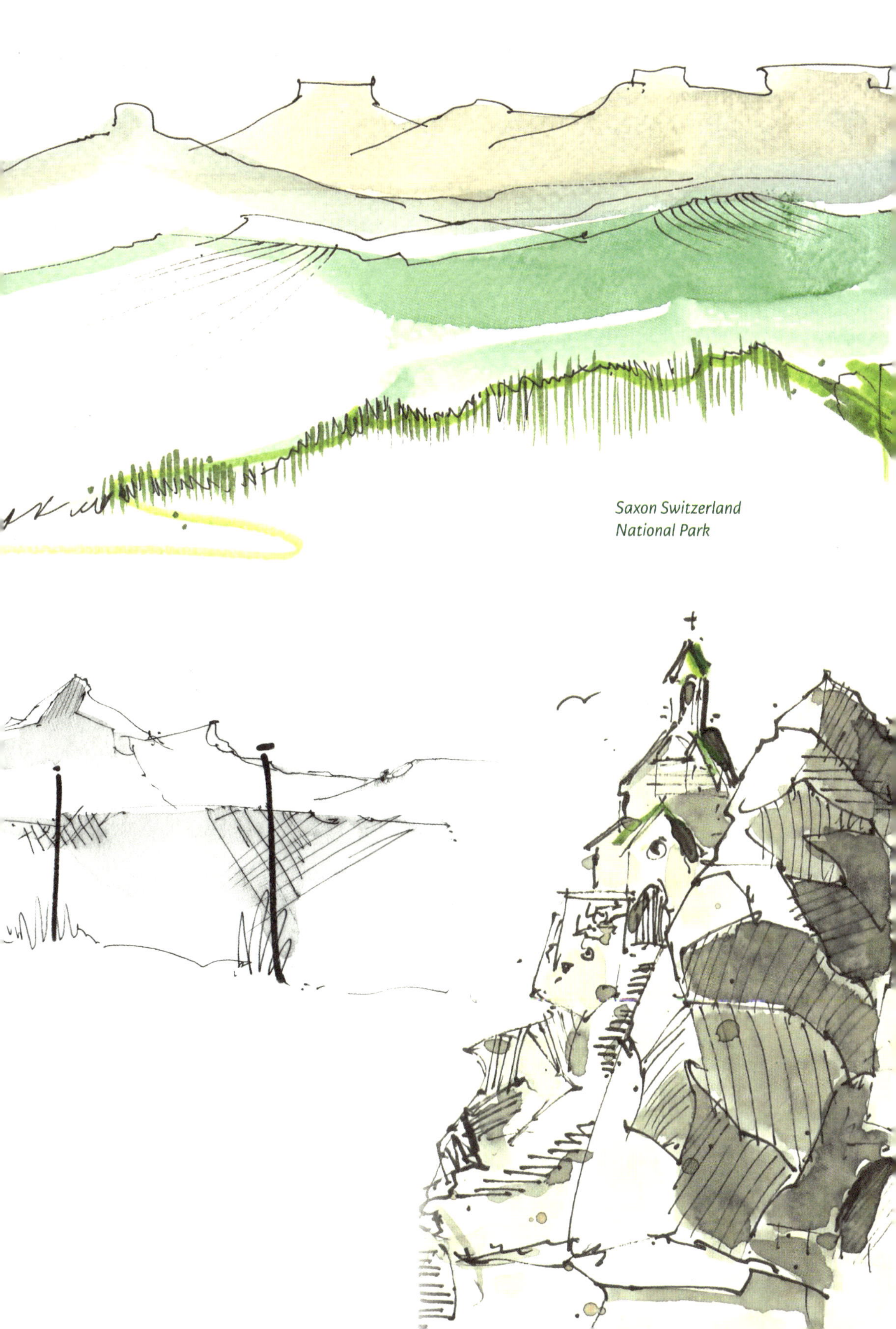
Saxon Switzerland
National Park

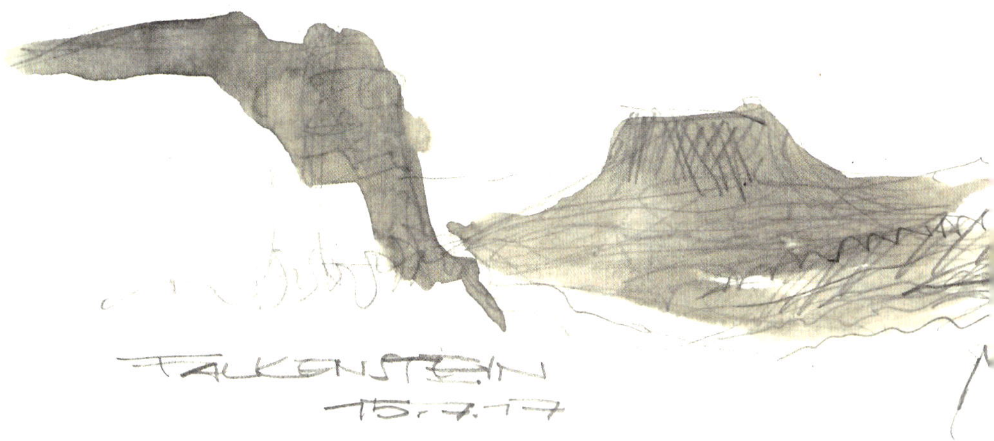

Nature's building material: Mountains look different depending on the type of rock they are composed of. The pencil sketch of this sandstone peak depicts its soft, porous materiality. The topic of materiality will also accompany us in my next detour, to the mountains, on page 79.

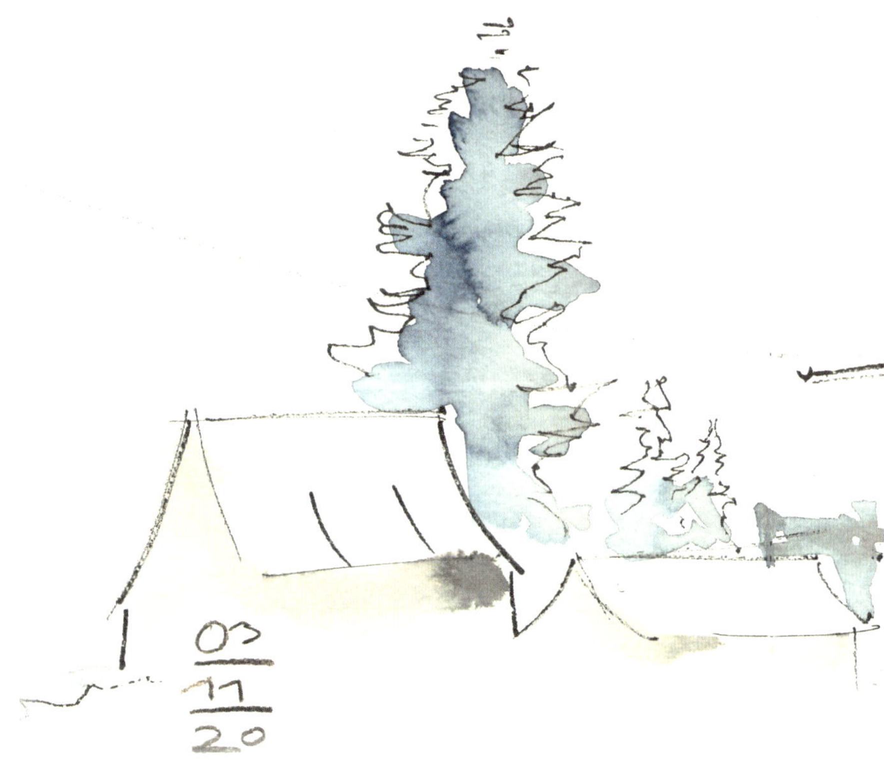

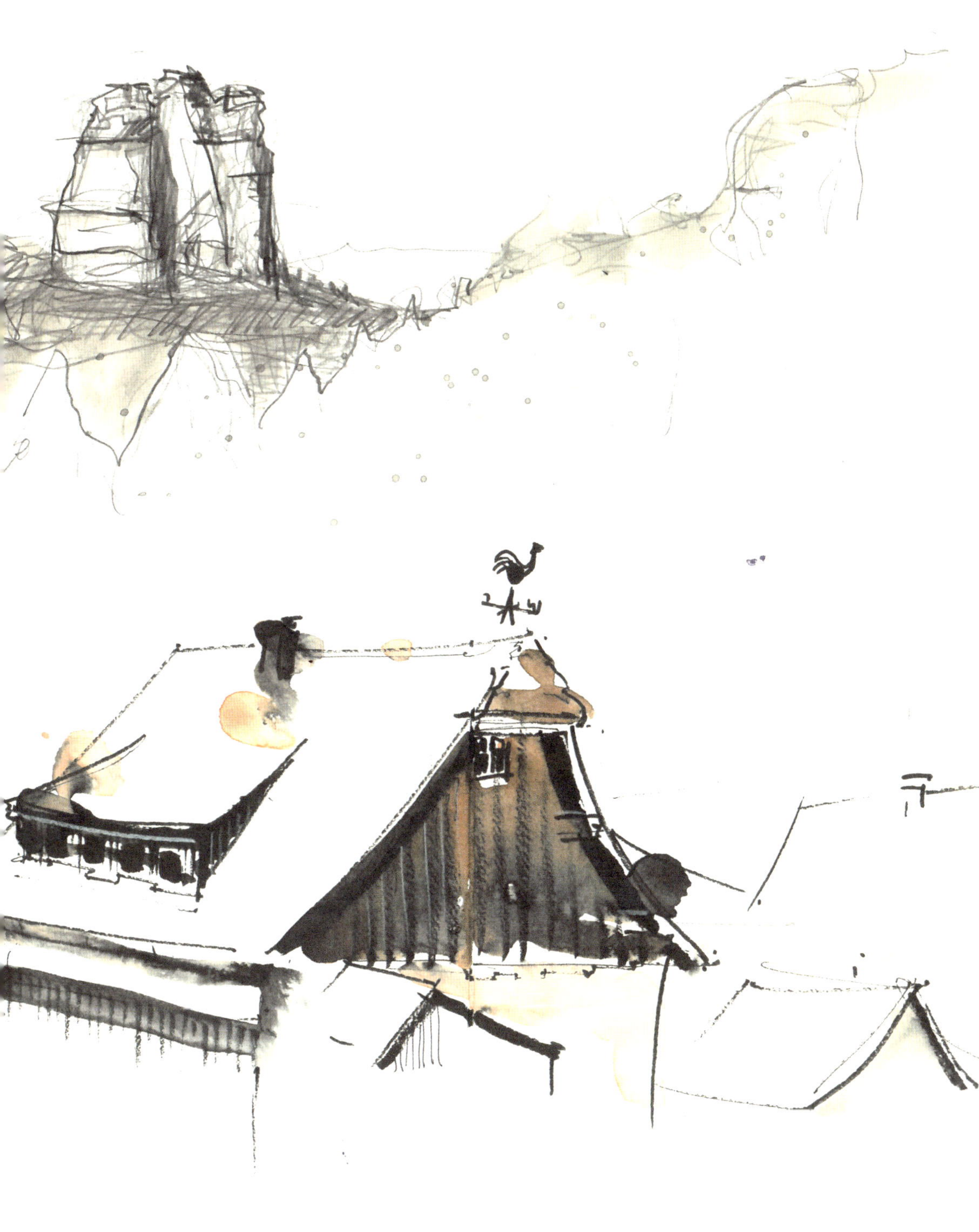

Three-Dimensionality

We already dealt with questions of three-dimensionality in the composition section—"horizon" and "vanishing point" are the keywords. But don't exert too much effort constructing three-dimensional perspectives geometrically. Rules and theory are necessary, but they usually spoil the fun of drawing.

On the following pages, I'll present some proven methods that, when used thoughtfully, add depth to your sketches in no time.

Size, Position, Overlap, and Foreshortening

Large shapes appear closer than small ones. If you also position the small object slightly higher, the impression of three-dimensional depth increases. An even simpler method is to overlap objects in a picture. This "pushing" of objects in front of and behind each other is guaranteed to create a three-dimensional impression—as with the trees that are only hinted at in front of the apse.

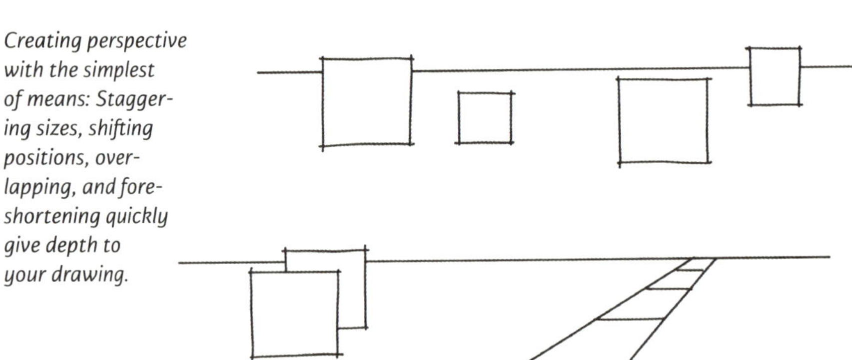

Creating perspective with the simplest of means: Staggering sizes, shifting positions, overlapping, and foreshortening quickly give depth to your drawing.

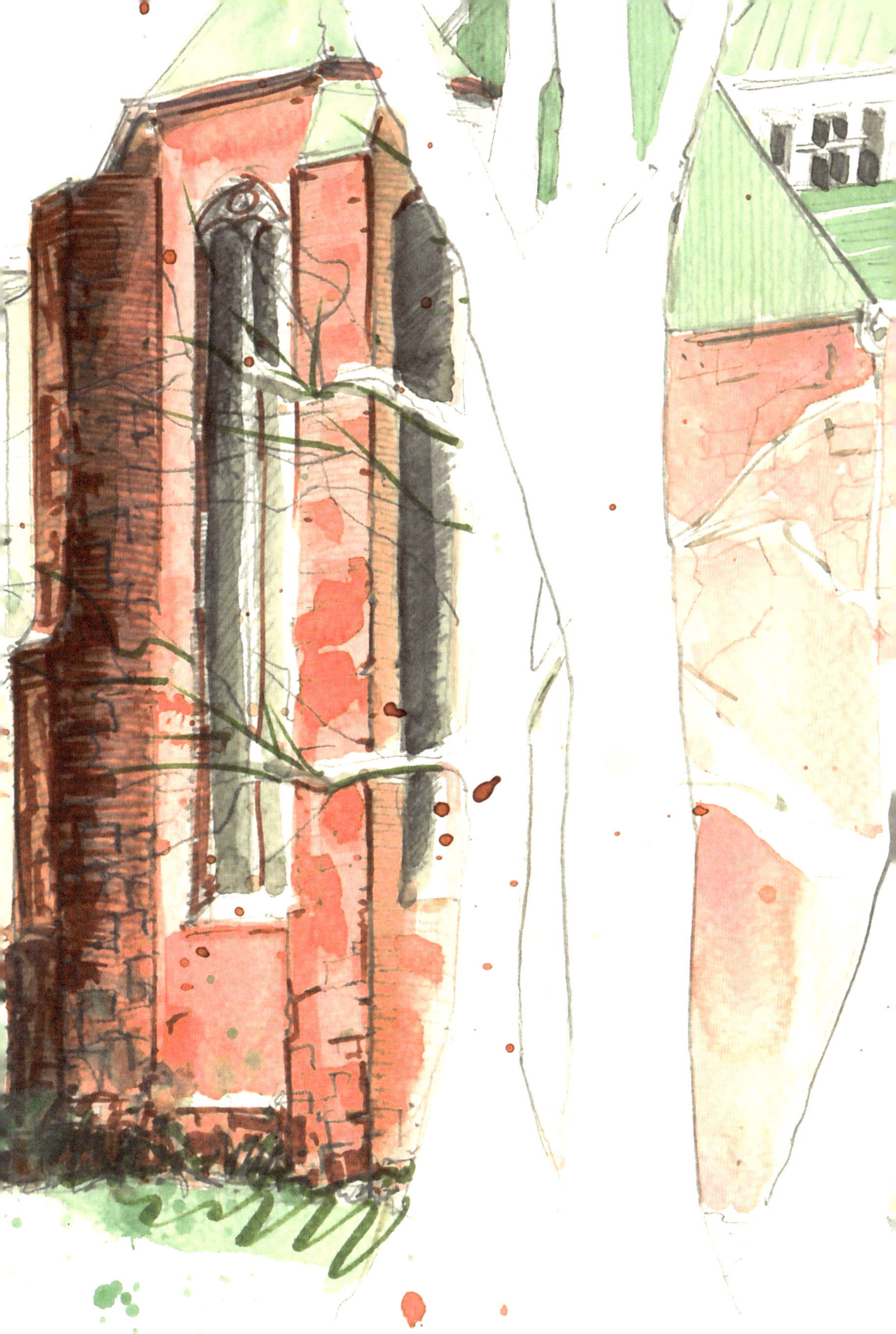

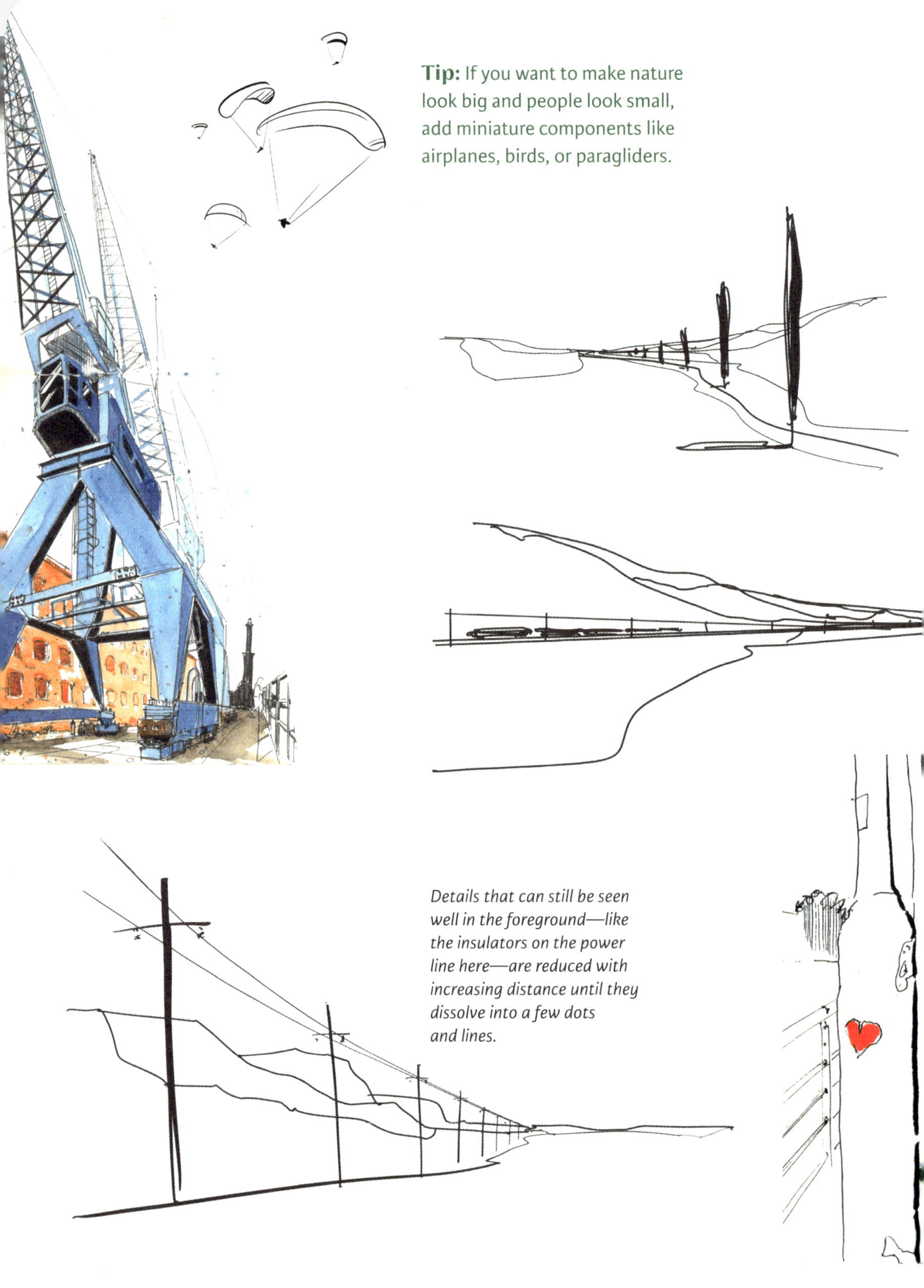

Tip: If you want to make nature look big and people look small, add miniature components like airplanes, birds, or paragliders.

Details that can still be seen well in the foreground—like the insulators on the power line here—are reduced with increasing distance until they dissolve into a few dots and lines.

The Depth Effect

Deliberate use of foreshortening creates depth in the smallest of spaces. Don't worry about a perspective-correct layout. My trick is to incorporate a few repeating elements: lanterns, railings, curbs, road markings—done. Arranged in a row with strong foreshortening, they create a lot of depth.

Landscape and Picture Depth

The same applies on a large scale to a landscape panorama: The more perspective elements, the greater the three-dimensional effect. Overhead power lines, tree-lined avenues, a train racing by are all reliable ingredients for a three-dimensional composition.

Perspective on the river: Rhythmically staggered lampposts and rapidly foreshortened metal plates on board and on land draw the viewer into the depths of the image.

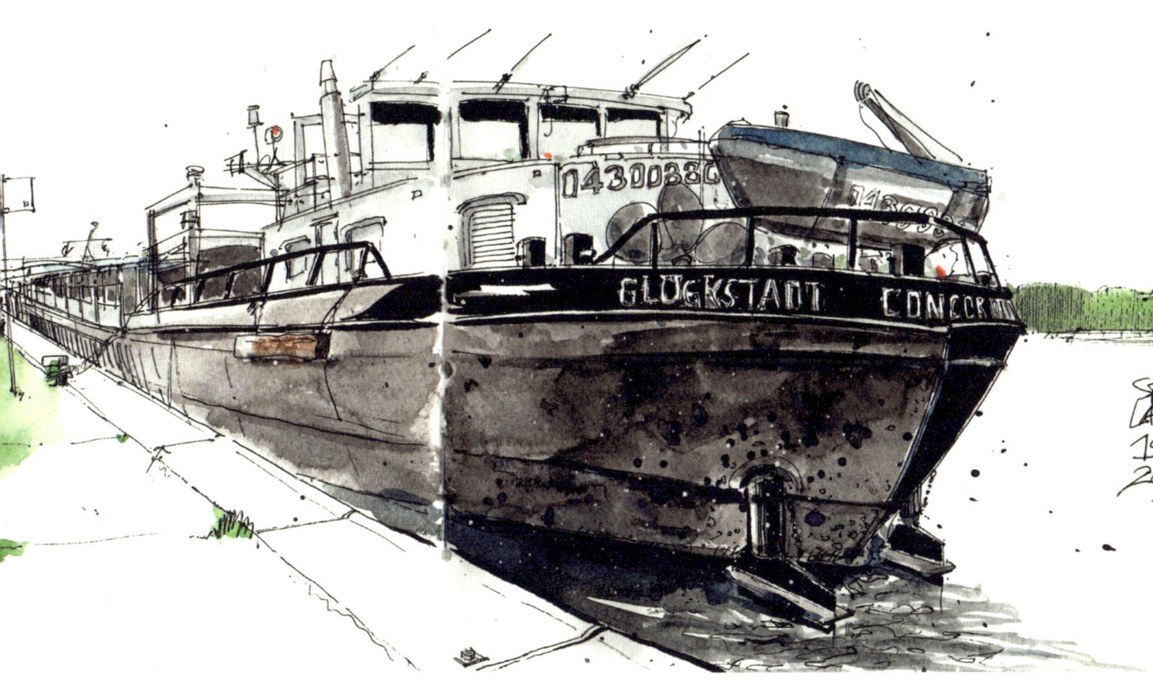

Atmospheric and Color Perspective

The way colors behave in the landscape is also important for the depth effect of your pictures. When the green of the forest and meadow and the yellow and brown of the fields fade with increasing distance, when the contours of the landscape lose their sharpness and even dissolve on the horizon, two phenomena are at work that we can take advantage of when drawing.

Atmospheric Perspective

Atmospheric perspective refers to the three-dimensional effect caused by haze and dust in the air. When you are depicting a landscape, this means sharply defined shapes and contrasting light and dark in the foreground, with blurring and decreasing contrast in the background.

If one giant dressed in white and one dressed in black were to set off toward the horizon, they would be barely distinguishable in the distance—both would appear dressed in a uniform gray.

Color Perspective

Our atmosphere acts as a color filter: warm tones—yellow, orange, red, and brown—are "swallowed" with increasing distance. Cool, muted colors ranging from green to blue remain, albeit in a faded, lighter hue. Our sense of spatial depth follows this pattern: Warm colors represent proximity; cool colors represent distance. The rules of color perspective aren't absolute. You may choose to break them for narrative reasons. But they make the visual space of your drawings comprehensible.

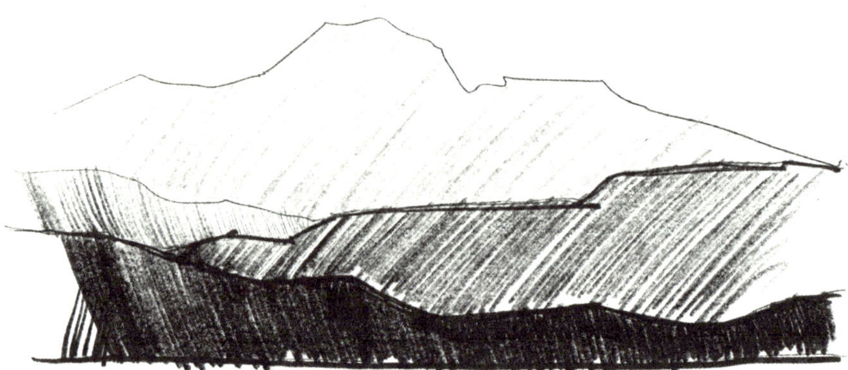

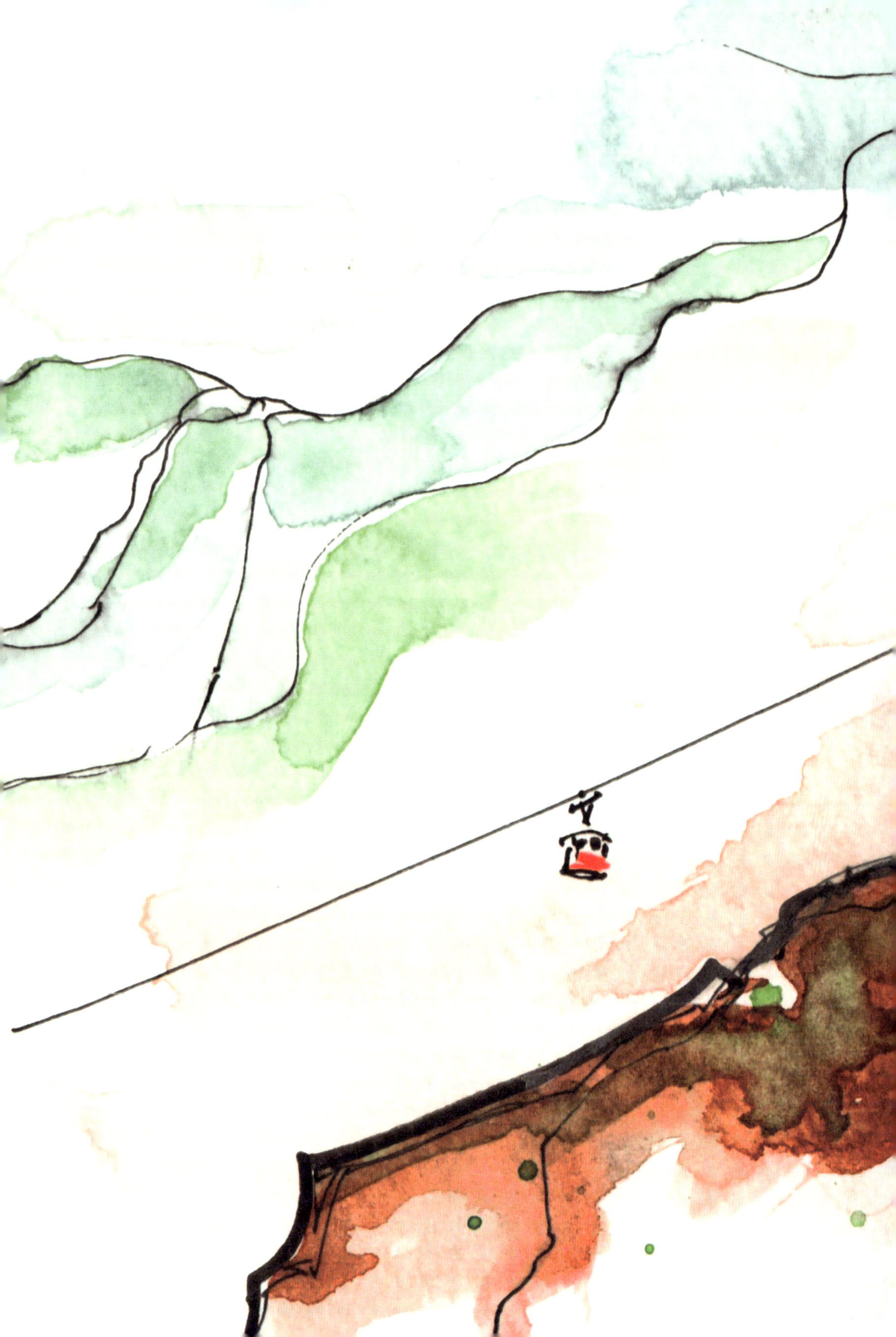

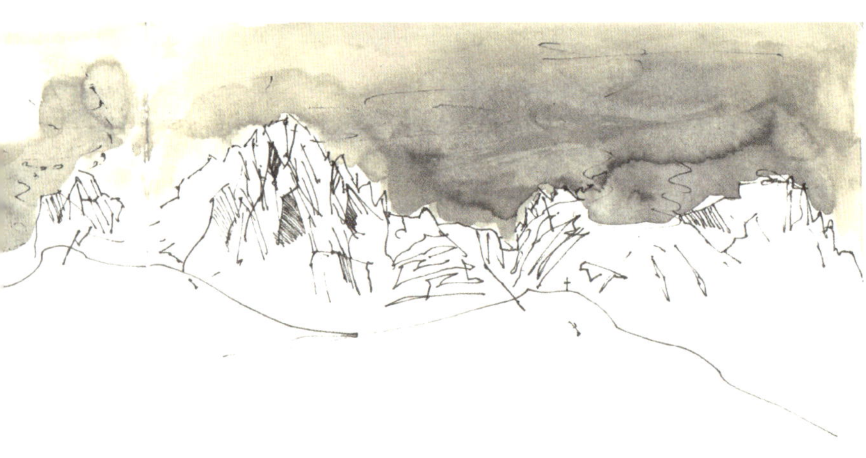

1997m
WILDER.KAISER

* KASBEK * 5047 METER

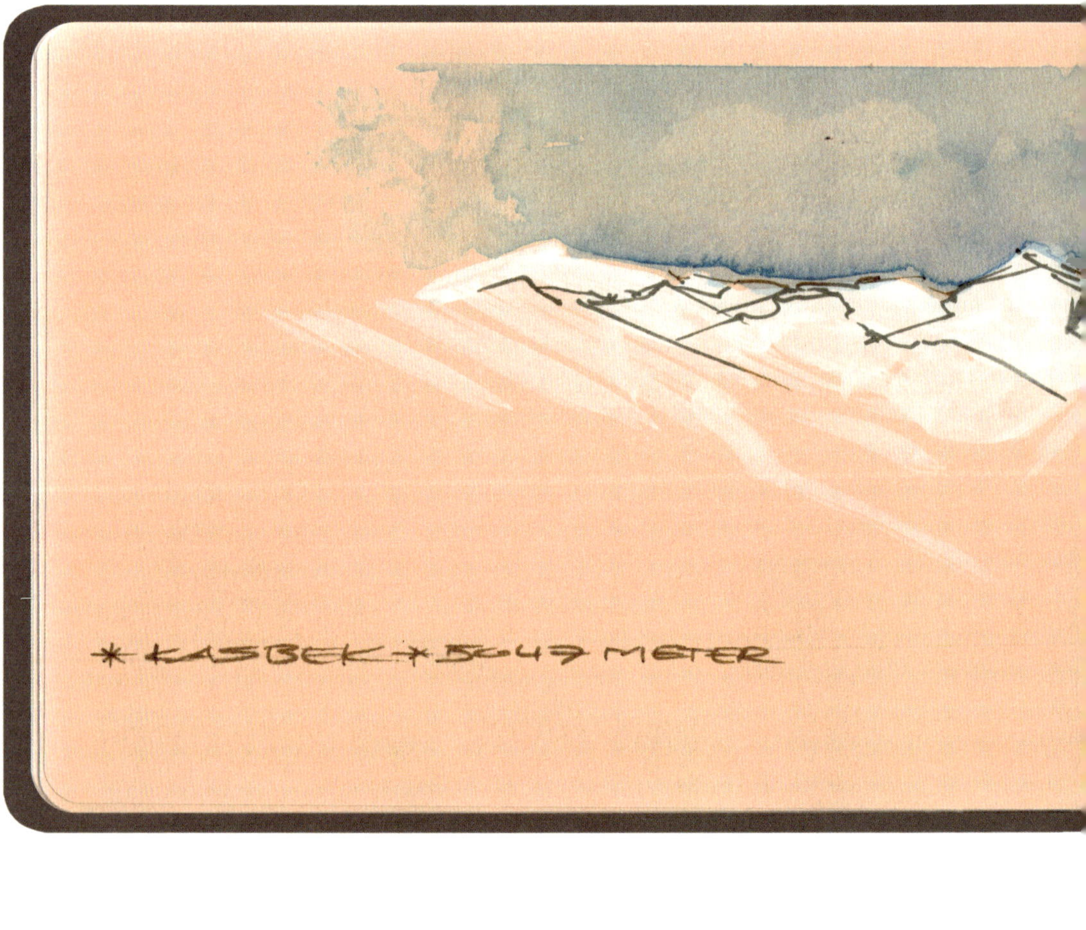

Detour: Mountains

Sketching in the mountains trains you in the art of simplicity. The subjects become sparser, almost monochrome: gray rock faces, green grassy summits, shimmering white scree fields. At the same time, the scenery appears more overwhelming and dramatic: Jagged peaks, icy heights, and sharp mountain silhouettes compete for your attention. All this needs to be captured with minimalist lines, clear contours, and just a few colors—snapshots of your elation upon reaching the summit.

A sketchbook of the mountains bears witness to visual mindfulness and reduction. When you leaf through it at home, it takes you back outdoors, where you see only what's truly worth seeing.

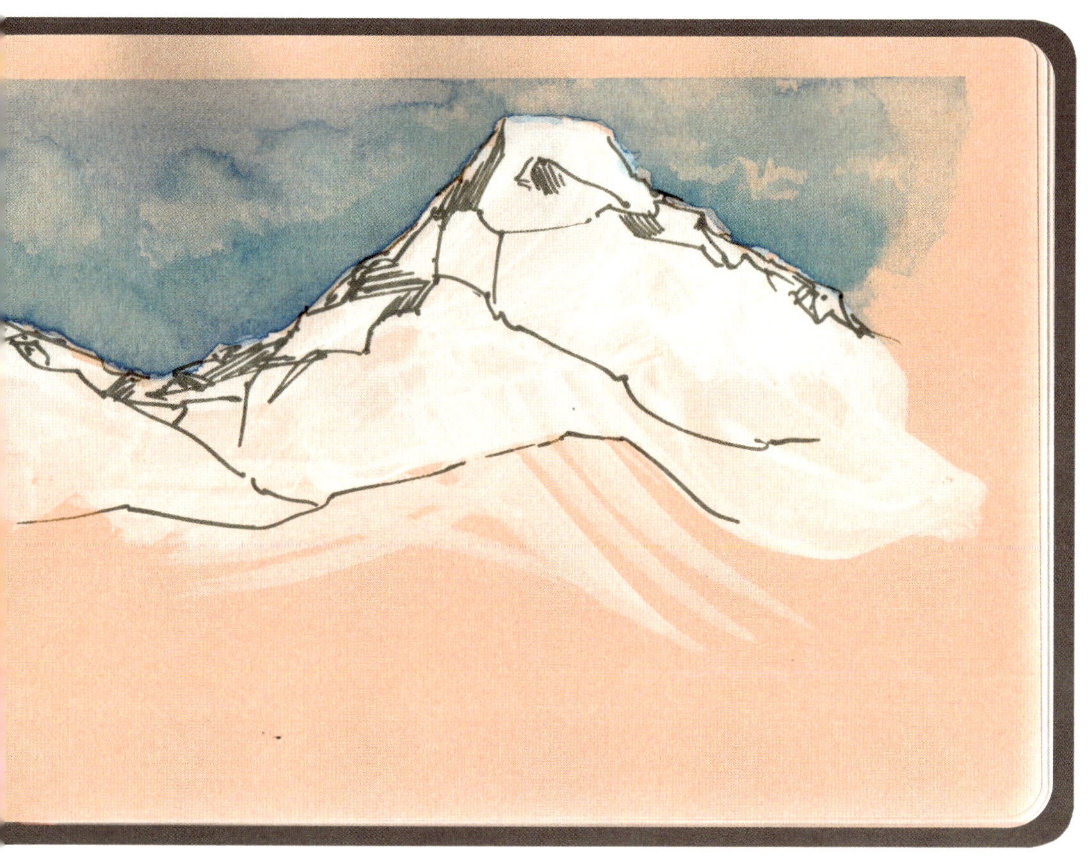

Prominence and Dominance

In the section on composition, I talked about guiding the eye and the focus of the image. Perhaps you're taken with a mountain peak and give it a prominent place on your drawing paper.

But what makes a mountain a mountain? Let's start with some geography. As noted on every hiking map, the elevation above sea level plays a role. But how your favorite summit relates to other mountains in the area is more crucial for the composition of your sketch.

To help, let me explain two technical alpine terms. "Prominence" gives us an impression of the independence of a mountain. It refers to the difference in altitude between the summit and the nearest valley or saddle, from which a still higher mountain rises.

"Dominance," on the other hand, measures the radius around a summit to the next highest mountain (in other words, the area in which it towers above its surroundings). You can use both to your advantage.

However high you go when drawing and whichever view awaits you at the top, capture the magnificence of the mountains in your sketchbook!

Tip: If the weather puts a damper on your plans, read about how to sketch mountains on a tablet from the comfort of your home on page 238.

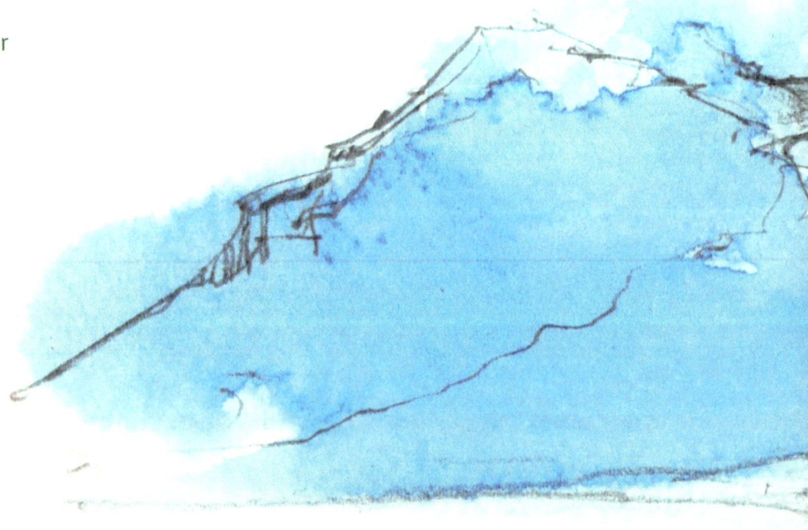

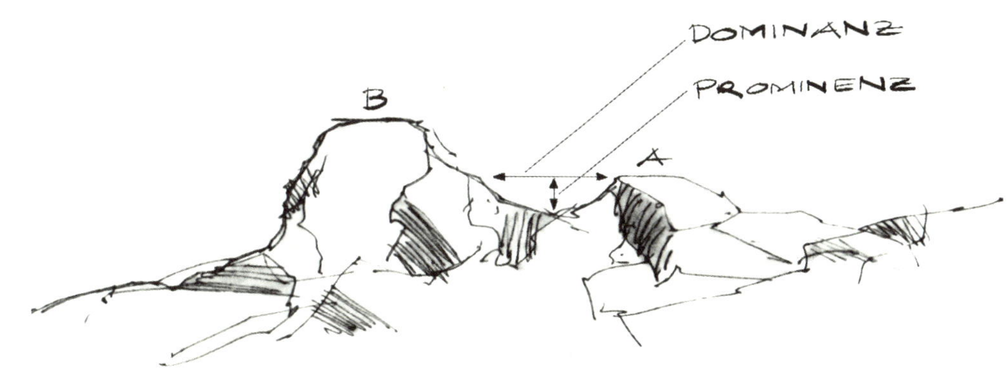

I made a quick pencil sketch of the profile of the Wilder Kaiser in Tyrol, Austria. The main and secondary summits are emphasized with hatching.

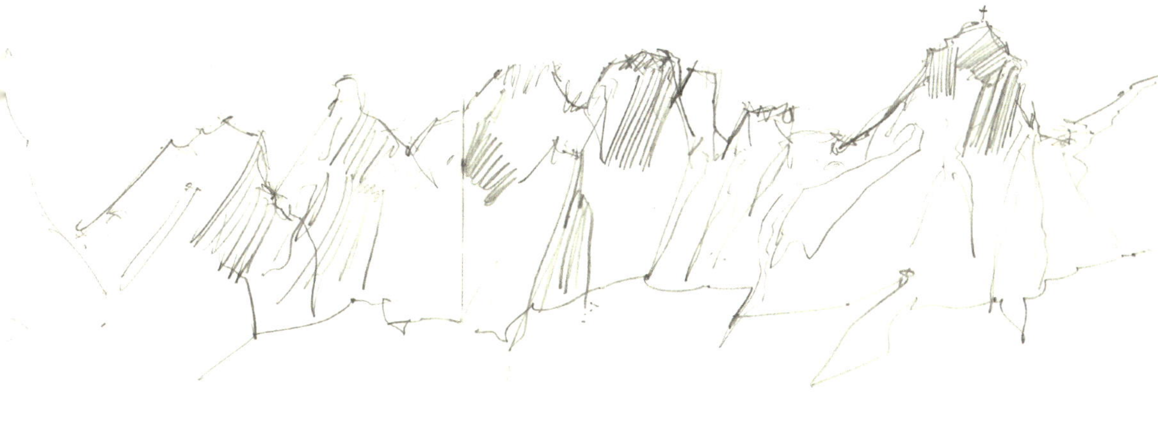

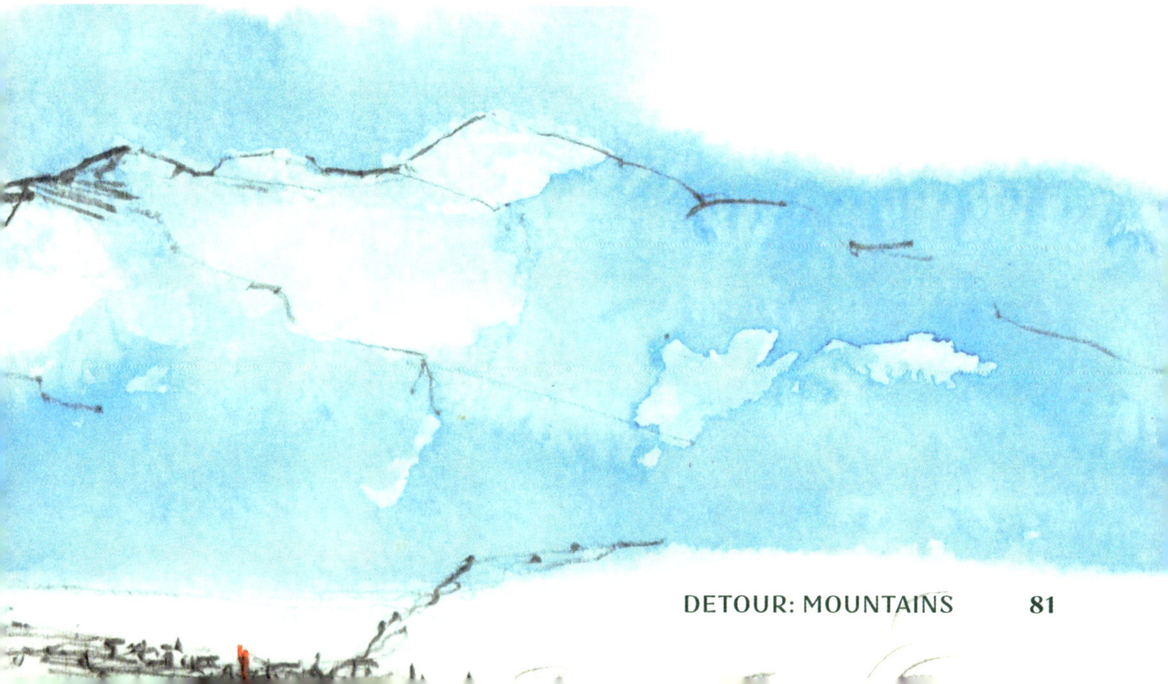

Not All Rock Is the Same

The shape of mountains is partly determined by the type of rock they are made of. Granite, limestone, sandstone—various minerals have combined to form rocks that give our mountains their appearance and sometimes even their name, like the Dolomites.

Geology alone won't fill a sketchbook, but it may sharpen your eye for mountain subjects. Different structures, surfaces, colors, and shapes as well as the effects of light, weather, and erosion are always interesting from an artistic perspective.

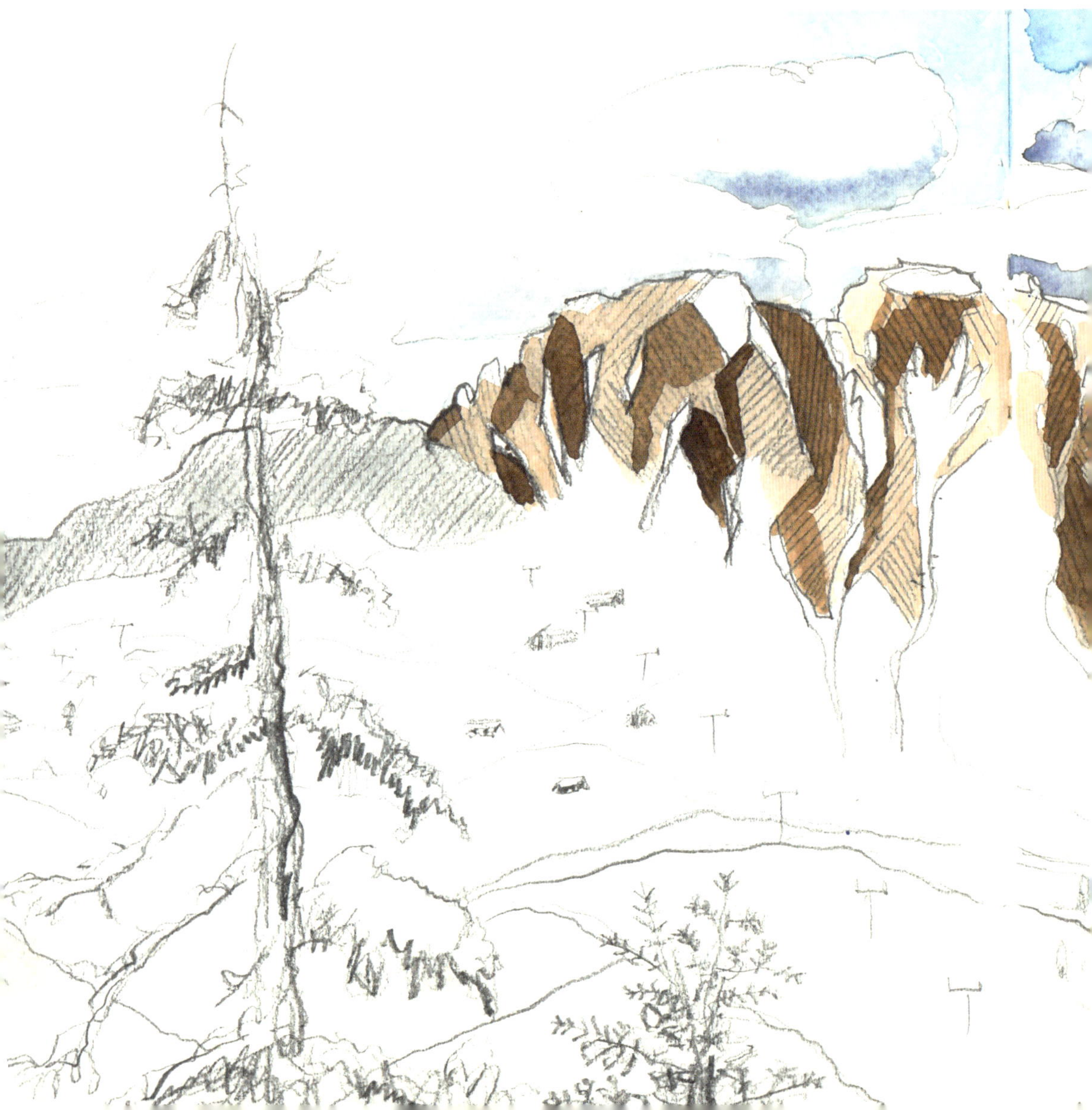

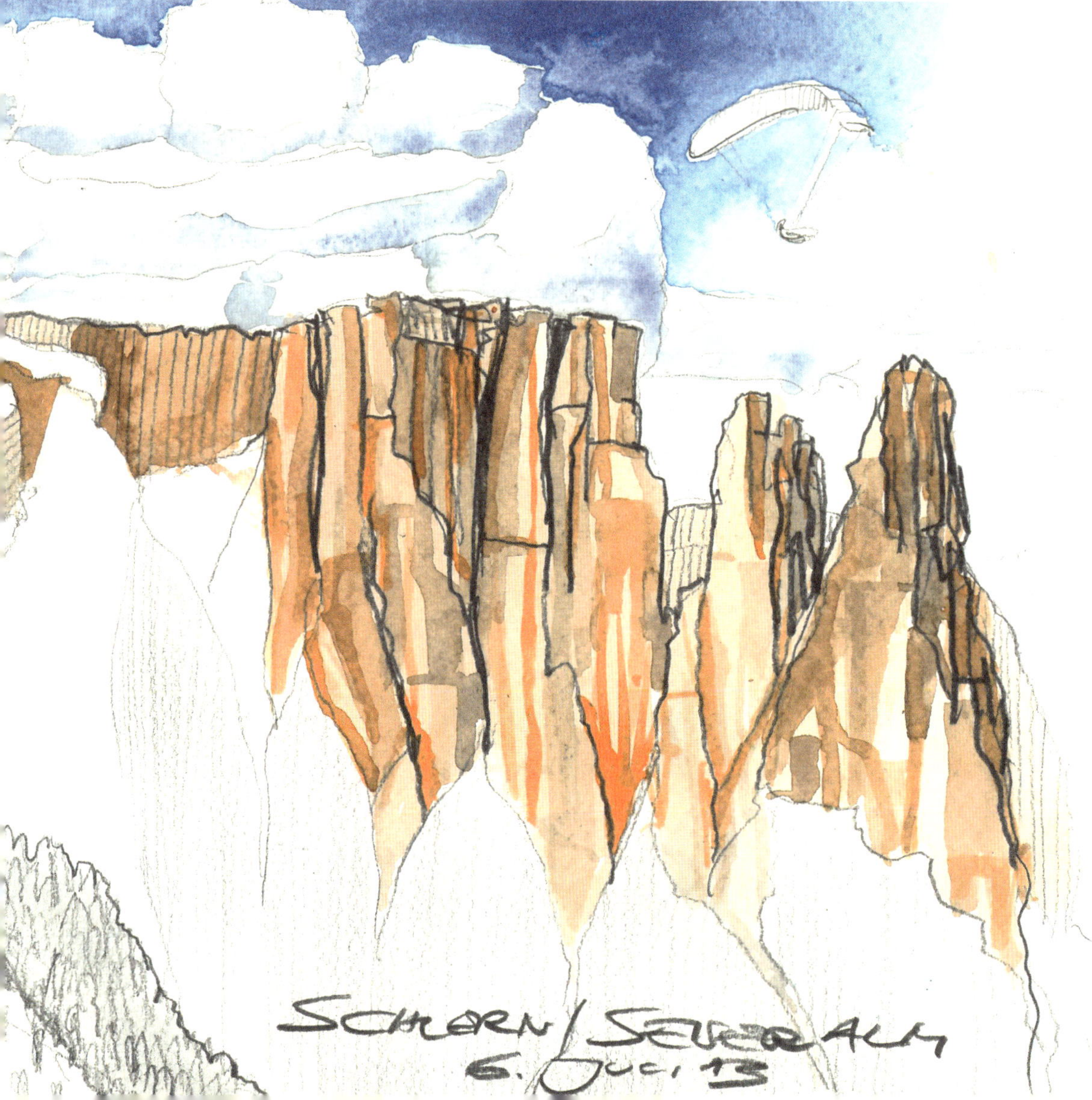

The Schlern in South Tyrol, Italy: a plateau, towers, and sloping rock faces. Striking shapes in dolomite rock, painted in watercolor. The warm brown tones bring the mountain range a little closer to the viewer.

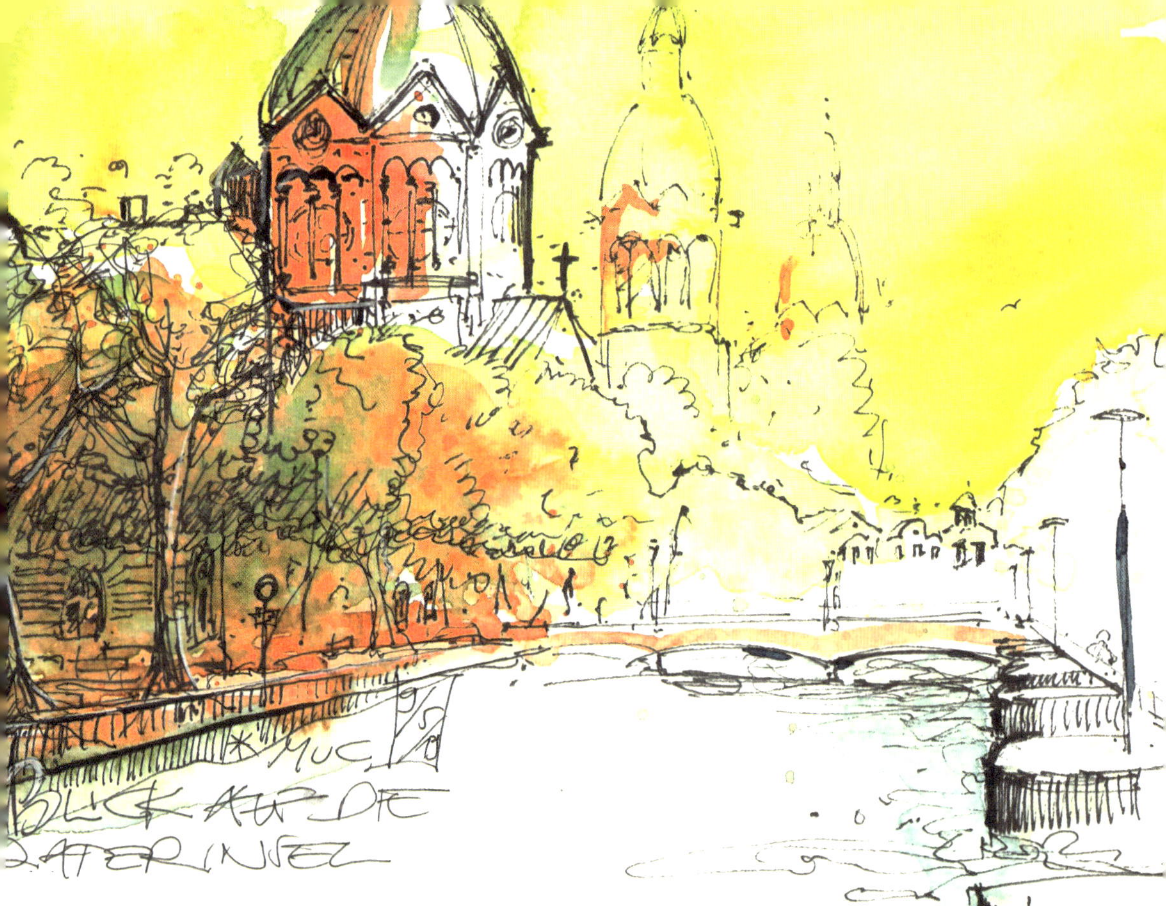

Weather 4 Conditions

Landscape and the weather are closely connected. Both can surprise you. If a landscape is described in your trip planner as "varied," it sounds promising enough, but if the weather is forecast to be "changeable," you may start having doubts about going at all. I think this is when things start to get interesting from a drawing point of view. Wind, clouds, precipitation, and changes in light and temperature promise more interesting subjects than bright blue skies and sunshine.

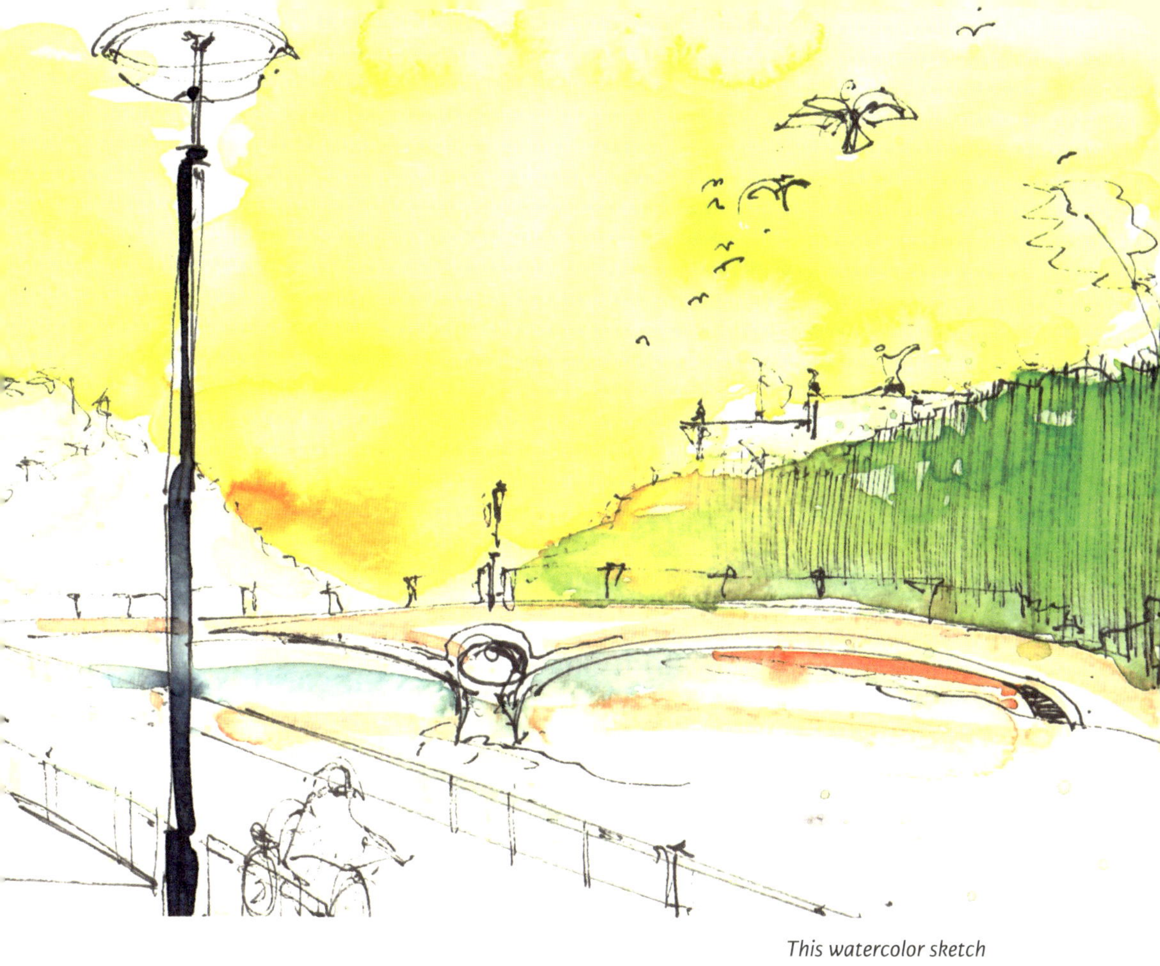

*This watercolor sketch
of the Isar River and
Munich's Praterinsel
reflects a subjective color
mood without a typical
blue and white sky.*

This chapter covers suitable techniques and
the right tools for sketching the weather.
You'll also find suggestions for adjusting your
equipment to the weather and season. One
detour is dedicated solely to clouds.

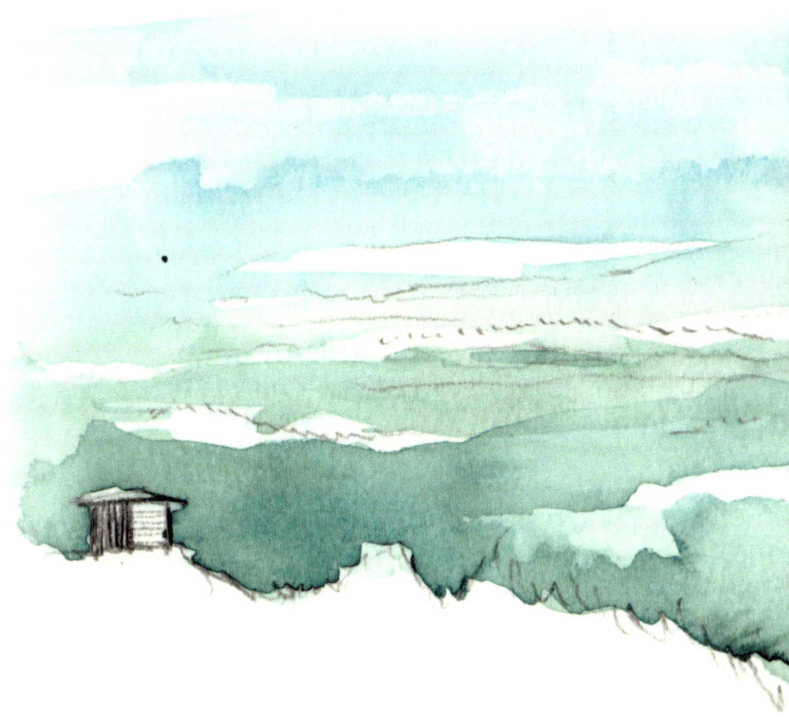

Detour:
Drawing the Weather

Who doesn't like to draw when the weather is nice? It's so tempting: warm air, a sunny spot, lightweight clothing, and your painting gear. Not to mention, of course, blue skies. But be careful! Picture-perfect weather can tempt you to produce clichéd images. While others capture dreamlike summer days in their near-identical photos, I prefer to seek out artistic variety and go my own way.

Look back on the history of art and you'll see how generations of painters effectively used the drama and visual power of the weather in their pictures of natural scenes. They employed various painting techniques for this in the studio and in the great outdoors.

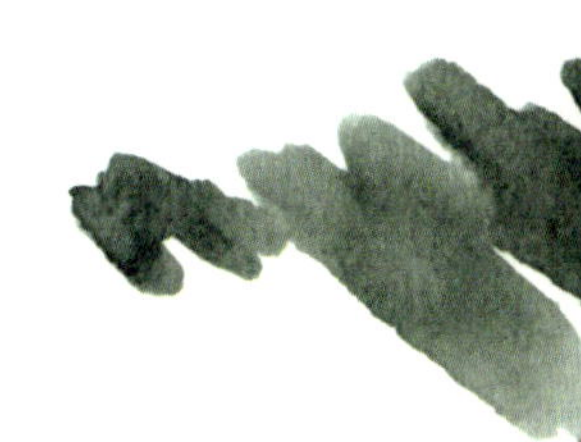

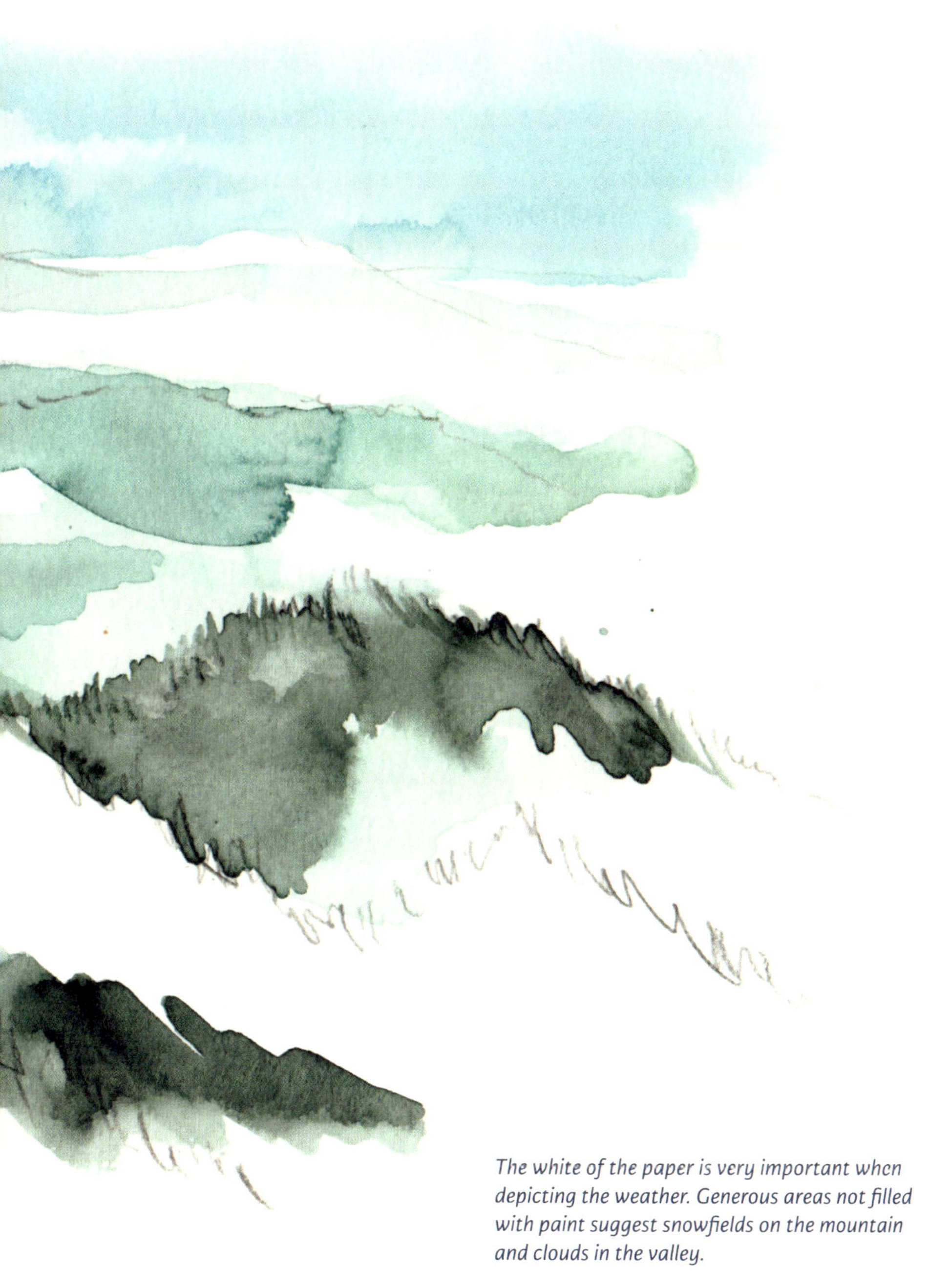

The white of the paper is very important when depicting the weather. Generous areas not filled with paint suggest snowfields on the mountain and clouds in the valley.

Rain

Even though high humidity and paper don't go well together, I don't let it stop me from sketching outdoors on rainy days. Watercolor is, of course, the appropriate medium. Fiber-tip pens also create "wet effects." Sometimes it's unintentional, but it can be useful when your fineliner stroke dissolves on contact with water or when a supposedly waterproof marker bleeds uncontrollably.

Tip: Items on wet surfaces reflect vertically. Their mirror image is upside down and blurred, with a watercolor effect (see Reflections in Water on page 54).

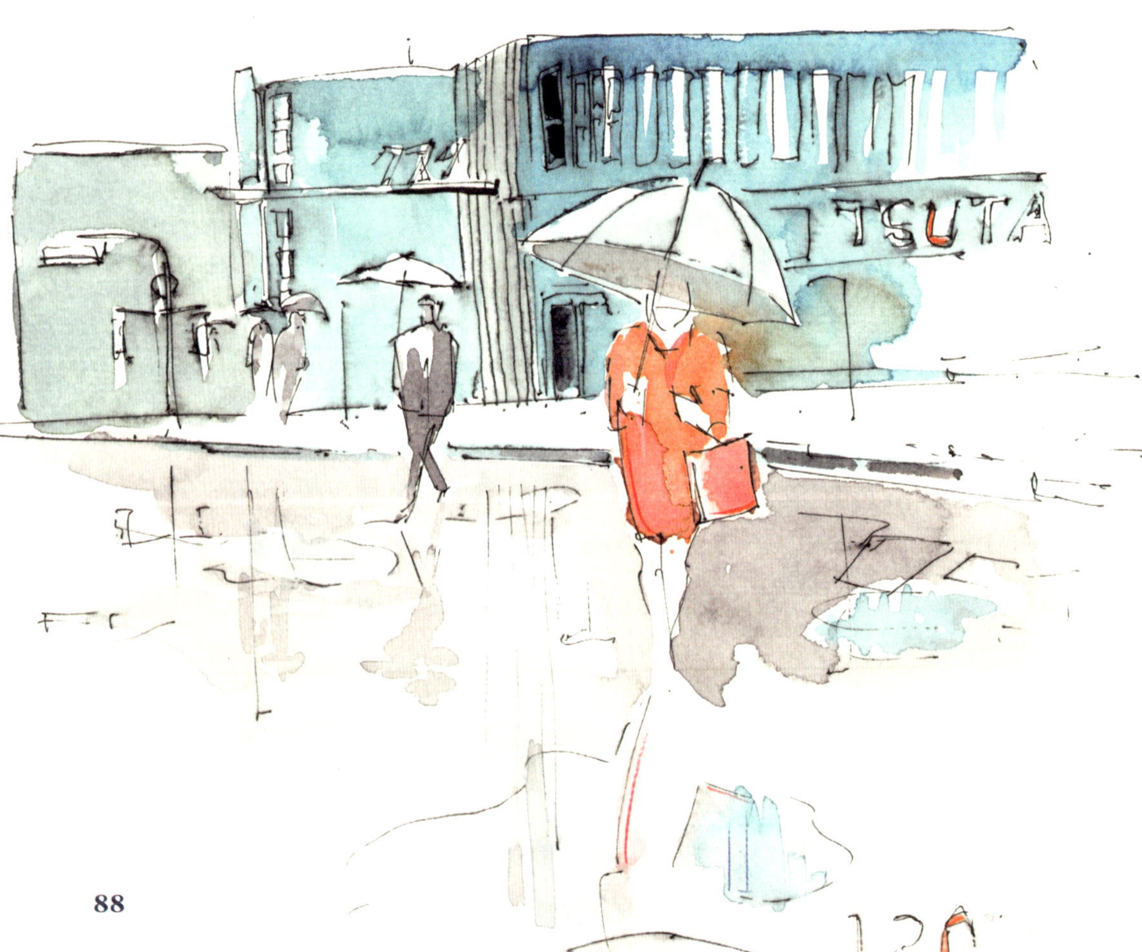

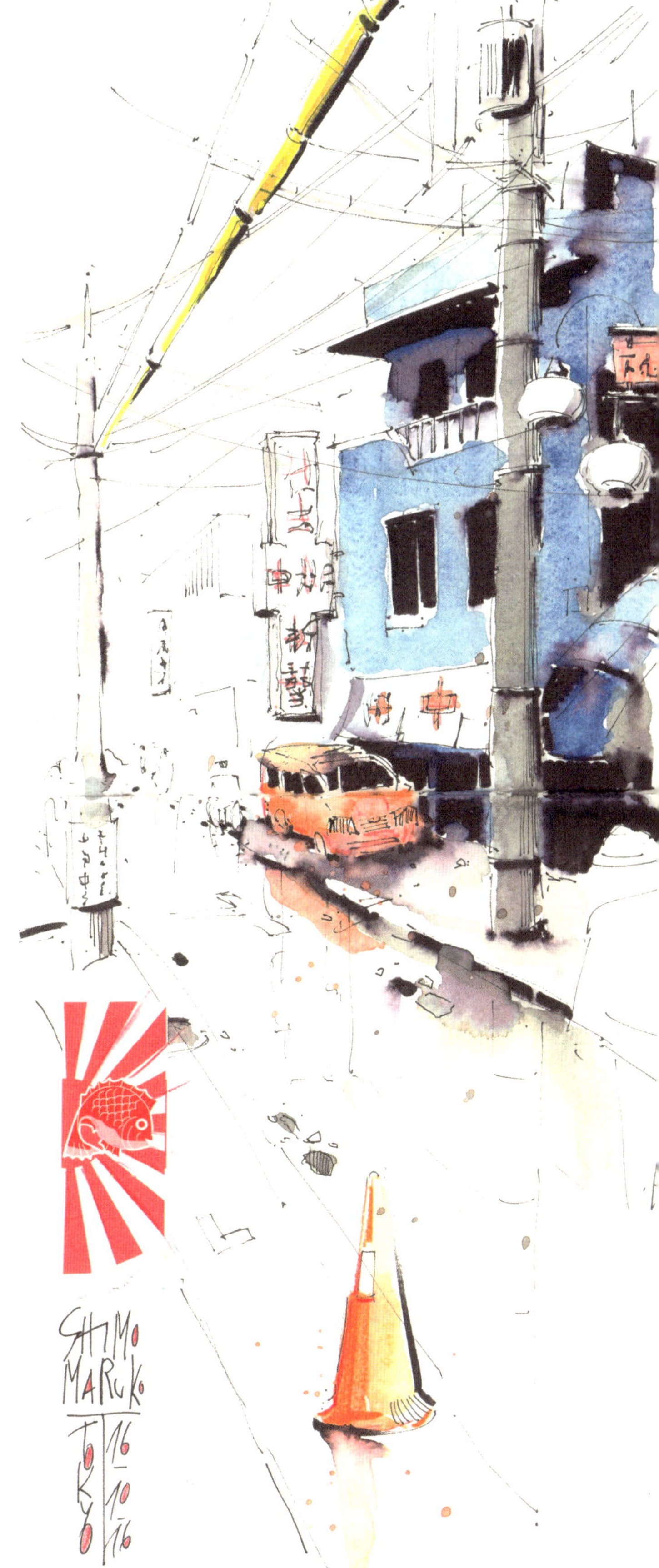

Jotted down while traveling in Tokyo: Metropolis of millions in autumn. It's raining. It has been raining all night. The long rivulets pouring down from the cloudy sky conjure up a curtain of water in the dull morning light and deep puddles on sidewalks and streets. The view from the hotel window: blurry. Not very inviting. And yet I am drawn outside into the rain to draw. It's still early. The streets aren't very busy. I squeeze under a small awning. I internalize what I see in front of me. The asphalt glistens with the wet. A tangle of cables, like a spiderweb. In the distance, a fading neon sign. I quickly sketch, protected from the rain, and later in the hotel I color the wettest parts.

My tip: Wonderful pictures come from the fine contrast between dry lines and wet colors.

Fog

Foggy weather is accompanied by a unique visual aura. Rising wafts of mist suddenly obscure the view. Contours lose their sharpness, colors their brightness. As if hidden by a wafer-thin curtain, your subject's backdrop partially disintegrates or disappears altogether. Then sections of the landscape are unexpectedly revealed.

I had this experience in the Berchtesgaden Alps in Germany. When the visual impact of the landscape is limited by the weather, I reduce my stylistic devices. For example, I limit my colors to a cool indigo blue and cardinal purple. Using the wash technique on dampened paper, I create soft transitions (see Watercolor Techniques on page 98). Omissions in the colored areas and topographical lines reinforce the impression of a landscape shrouded in fog.

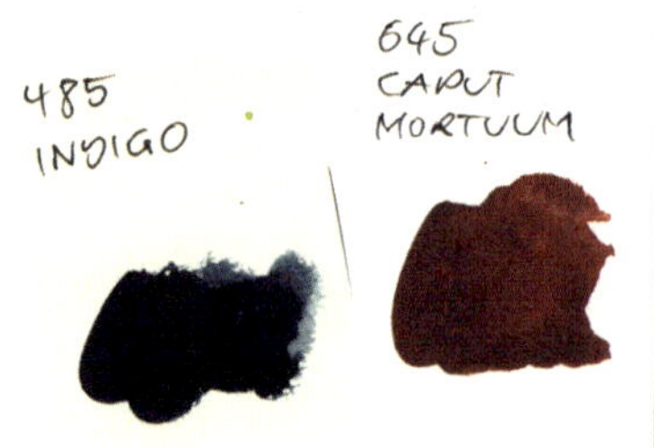

Weather—reduced to two colors: warm in the foreground, cool in the background.

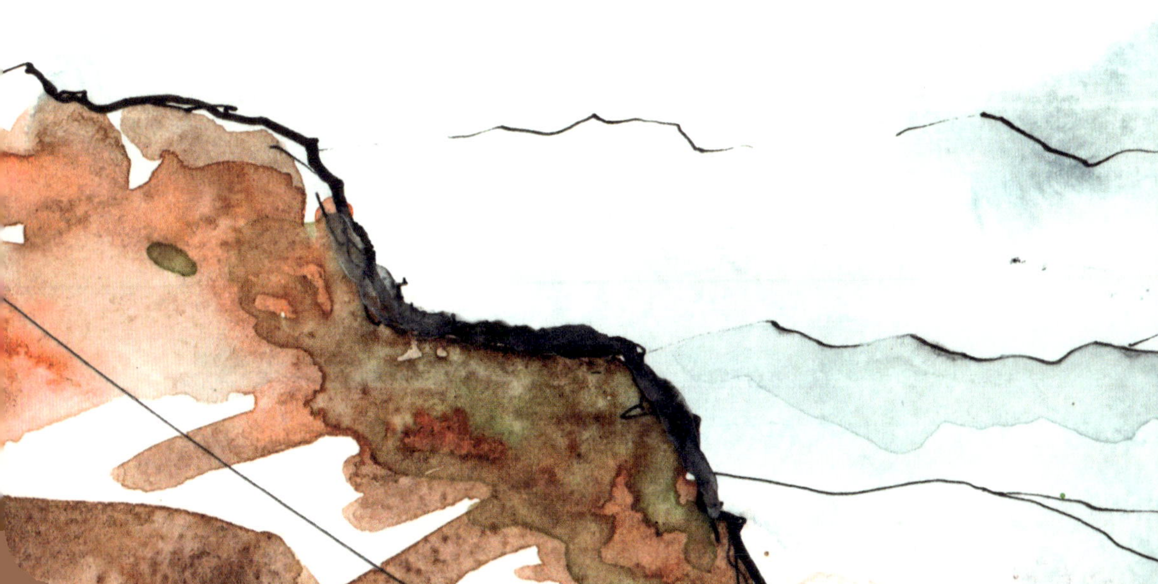

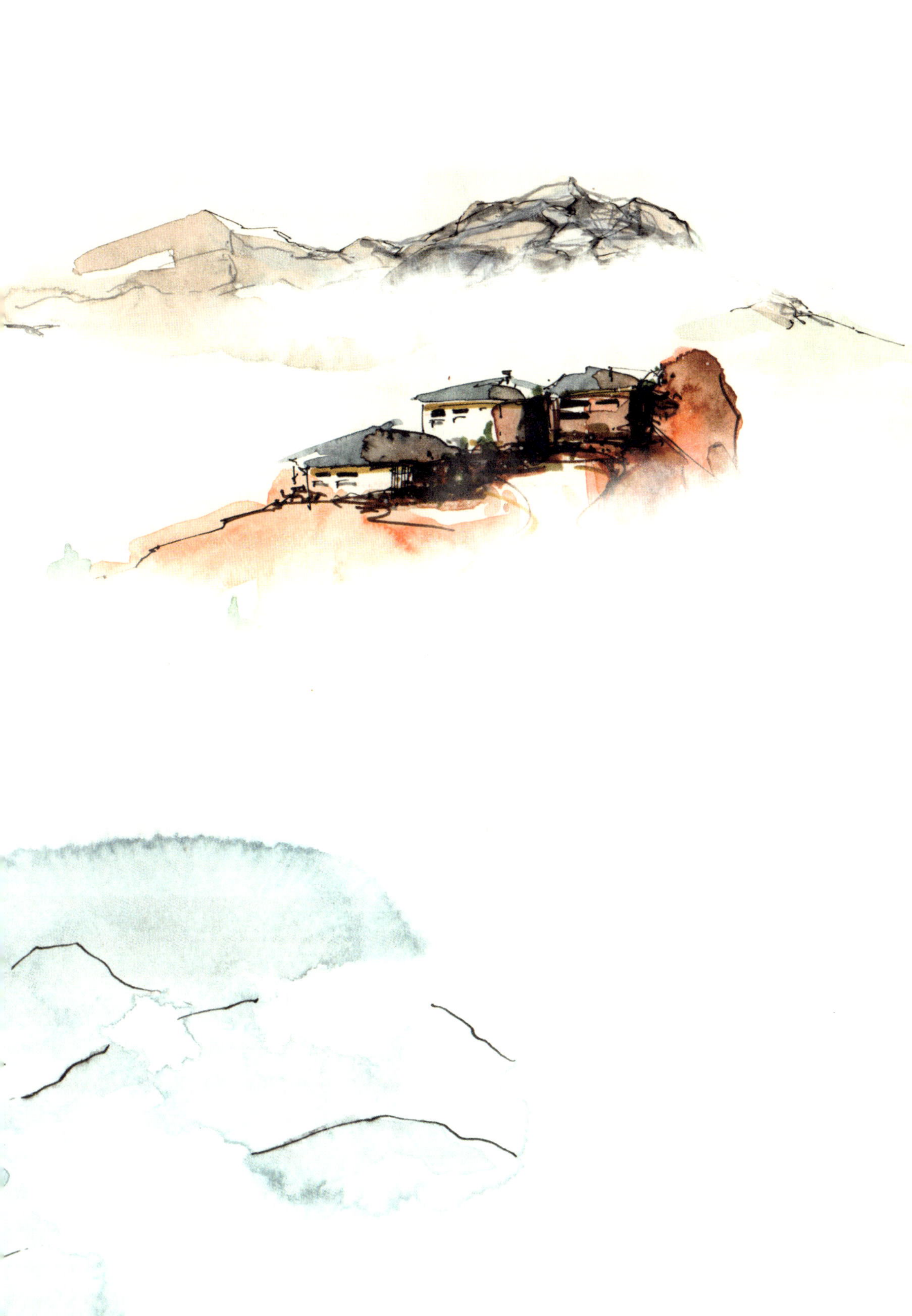

Snow

A frigid, snowy winter evokes clammy fingers and frozen toes, not ideal drawing conditions. Isn't it better to put away your painting supplies for a few months and stay at home? Passionate sketchers don't hibernate, they share tips for overcoming the challenges of the cold season: gloves without fingertips, for example, or schnapps in your paint cup to prevent your water and brush from freezing.

Apart from the technical challenges, what's interesting about the subject of a snowy landscape? Above all, I associate snow with silence. When forests, meadows, paths, streets, squares, and cities are covered in thick white, sound is absorbed and everything becomes quieter. Perhaps even in our drawings.

Sketchbooks with tinted paper are a good alternative for depicting snow. You can apply opaque white with a pencil or brush on the brown, gray, or blue background. Snowy surfaces stand out clearly against the midtone of the paper. Line drawings in dark-colored areas and hatching create a sense of three-dimensionality in the opposite direction.

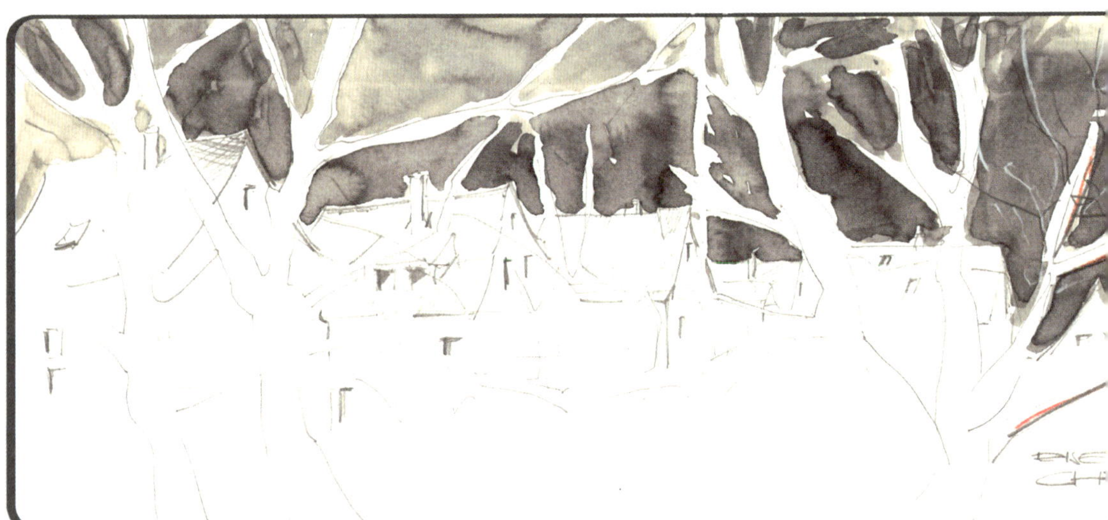

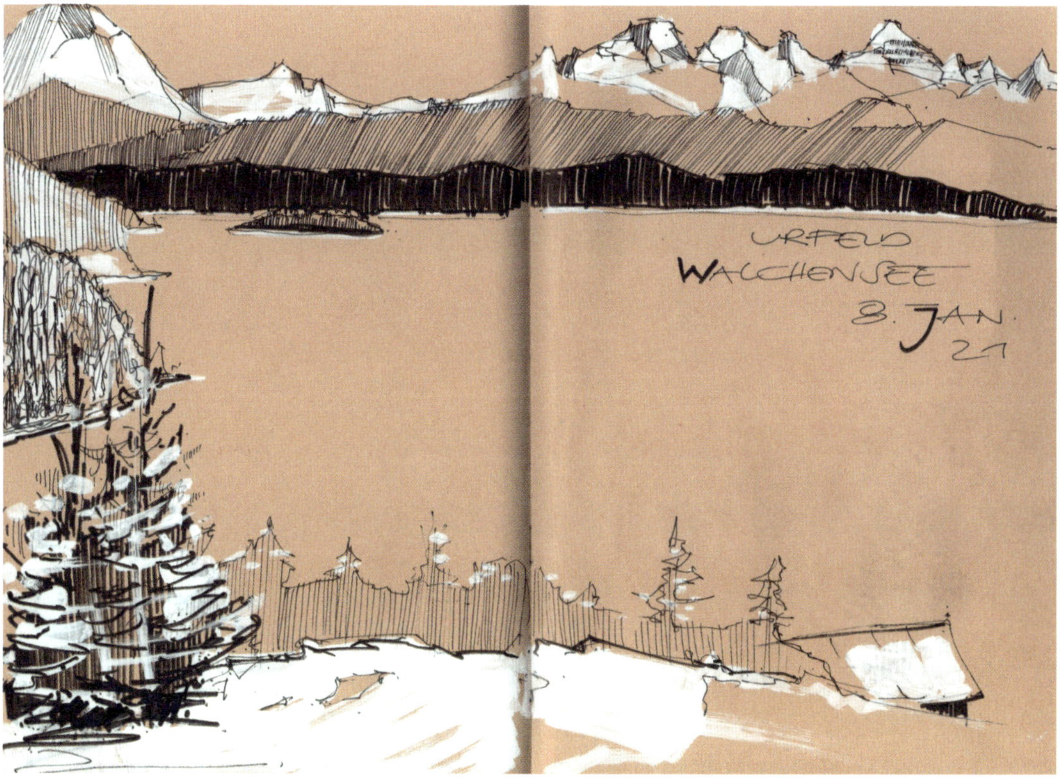

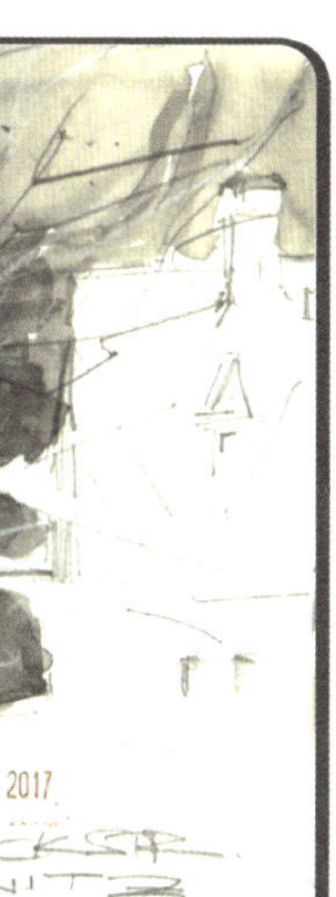

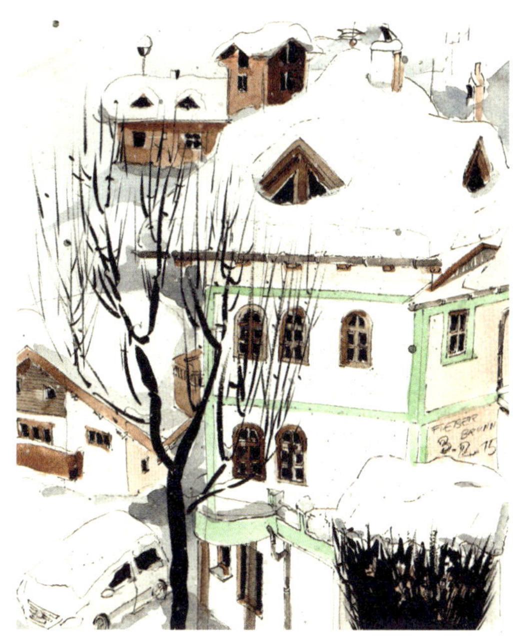

Snow is already present in the image with the white of the paper. In contrast to dark sections, as in this housing estate on the left, the impression of snow is created by skillful use of white paper.

Haze and Smog

The air is not always as clear as on a cold winter's day.
Haze, fog, and clouds—but also smog, air pollution, and
other environmental influences—can cloud the atmosphere. Compared to an aesthetically bland blue sky,
"hazy" air is far more interesting. At first glance, smoky
industrial areas, exhaust-filled street canyons, and
stuffy city centers aren't enticing spots for drawing.
But take a second look and try sketching there.

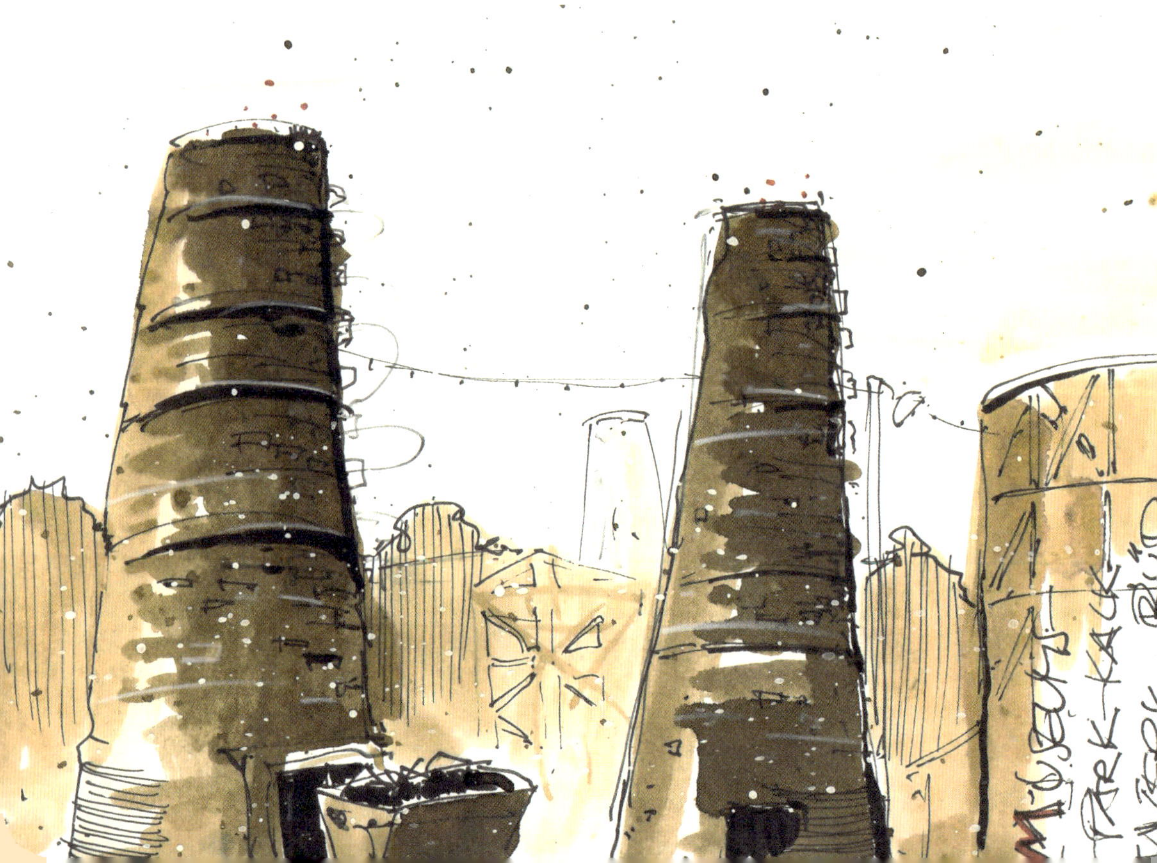

*Instead of watercolor, sepia ink provides
the appropriate tone for this industrial
plant. A few splashes of ink and opaque
white enhance the impression of a
dirty atmosphere.*

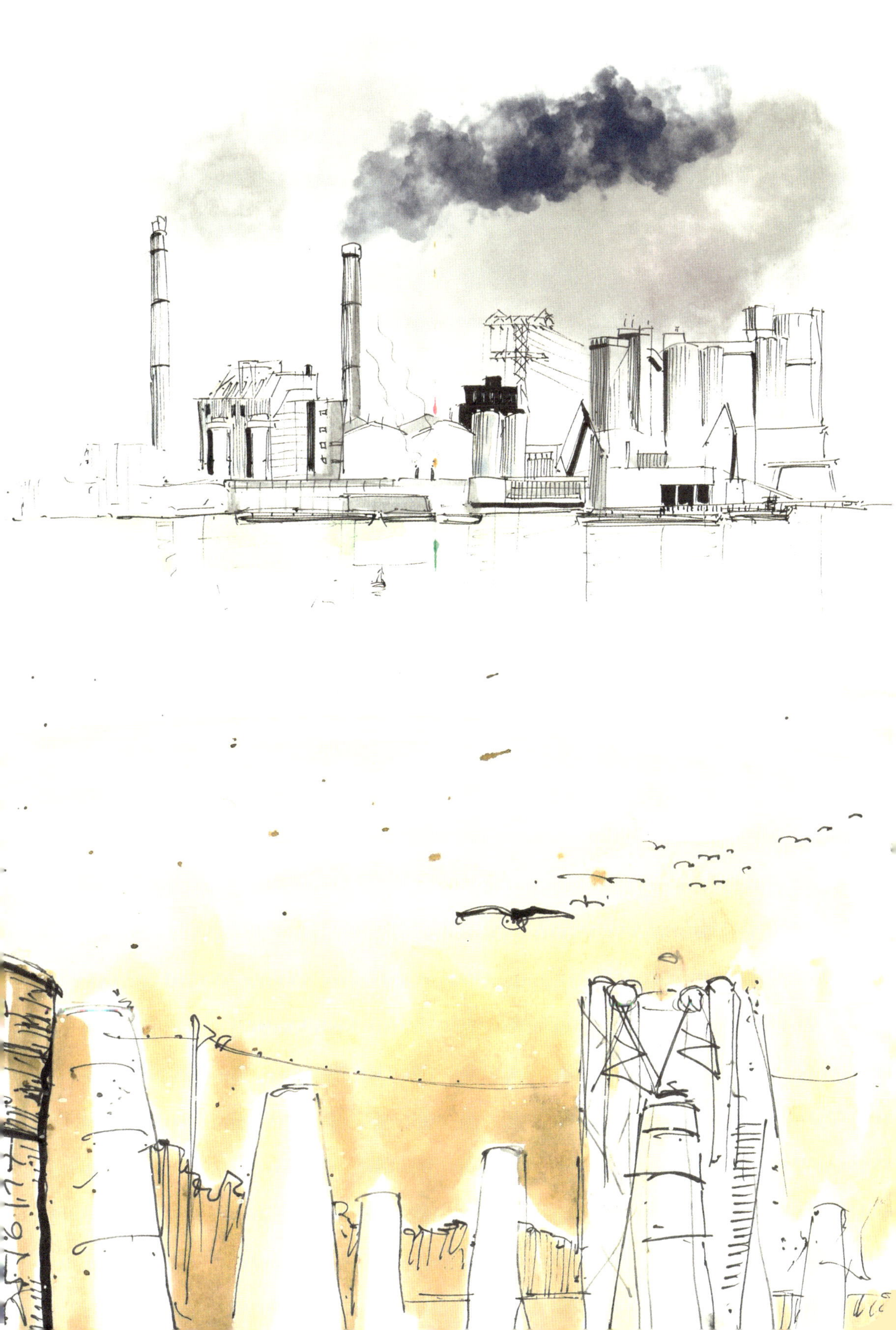

Drawing Tools: From Specialty to All-Purpose

Pencils, pens, and fiber-tip pens take up hardly any space in your bag. But that doesn't mean you should take all of them with you: Minimalism is good—not only to save space, but to deliberately narrow down the range of techniques at your disposal on your sketching excursion. For example, I like to use fountain pens with angled nibs for sketching. They allow me to modulate between fine and broad lines, depending on how I hold them in my hand. They're sometimes all I need to work with on a given day.

There's also potential for frugality when it comes to choosing colored pencils, markers, and watercolors. Let's say you're outdoors on a cold winter's day. The color palette of the landscape is limited, as expected. I suggest that you adapt to the situation and pack only one or two colors.

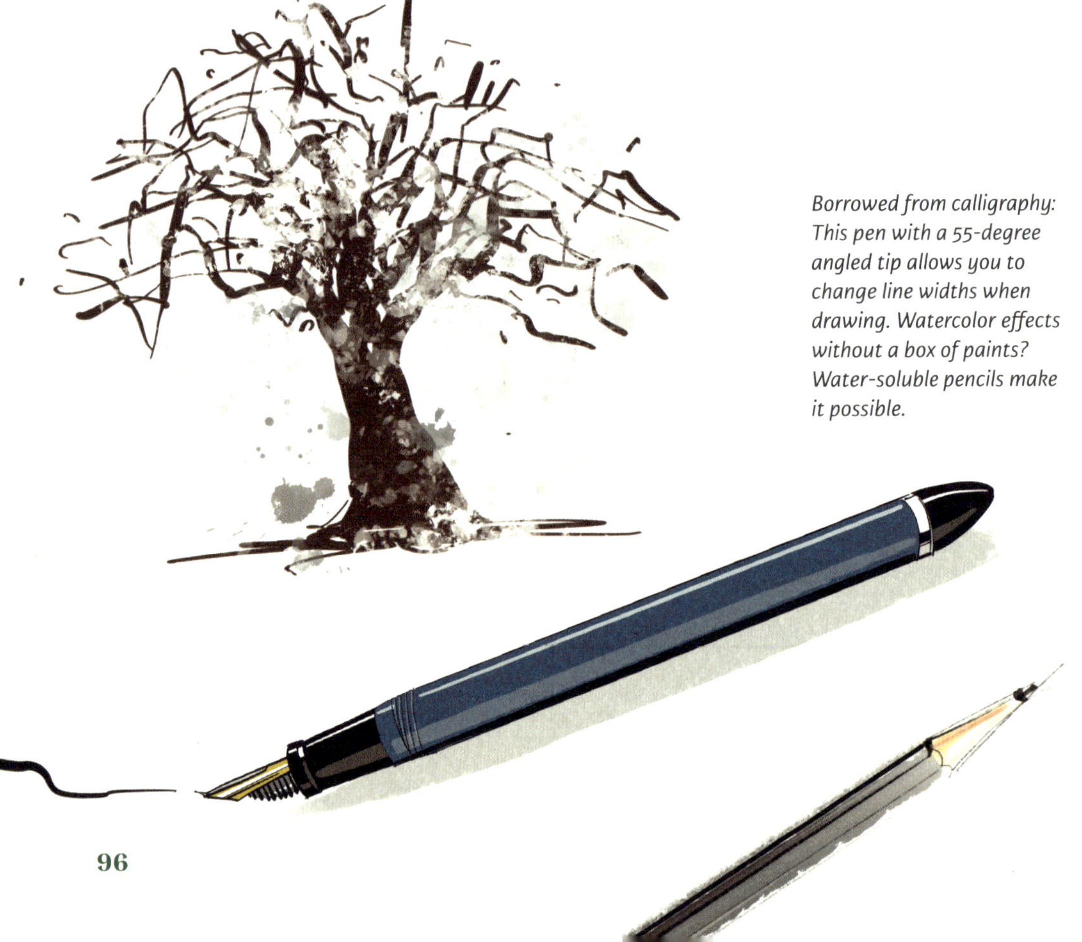

Borrowed from calligraphy: This pen with a 55-degree angled tip allows you to change line widths when drawing. Watercolor effects without a box of paints? Water-soluble pencils make it possible.

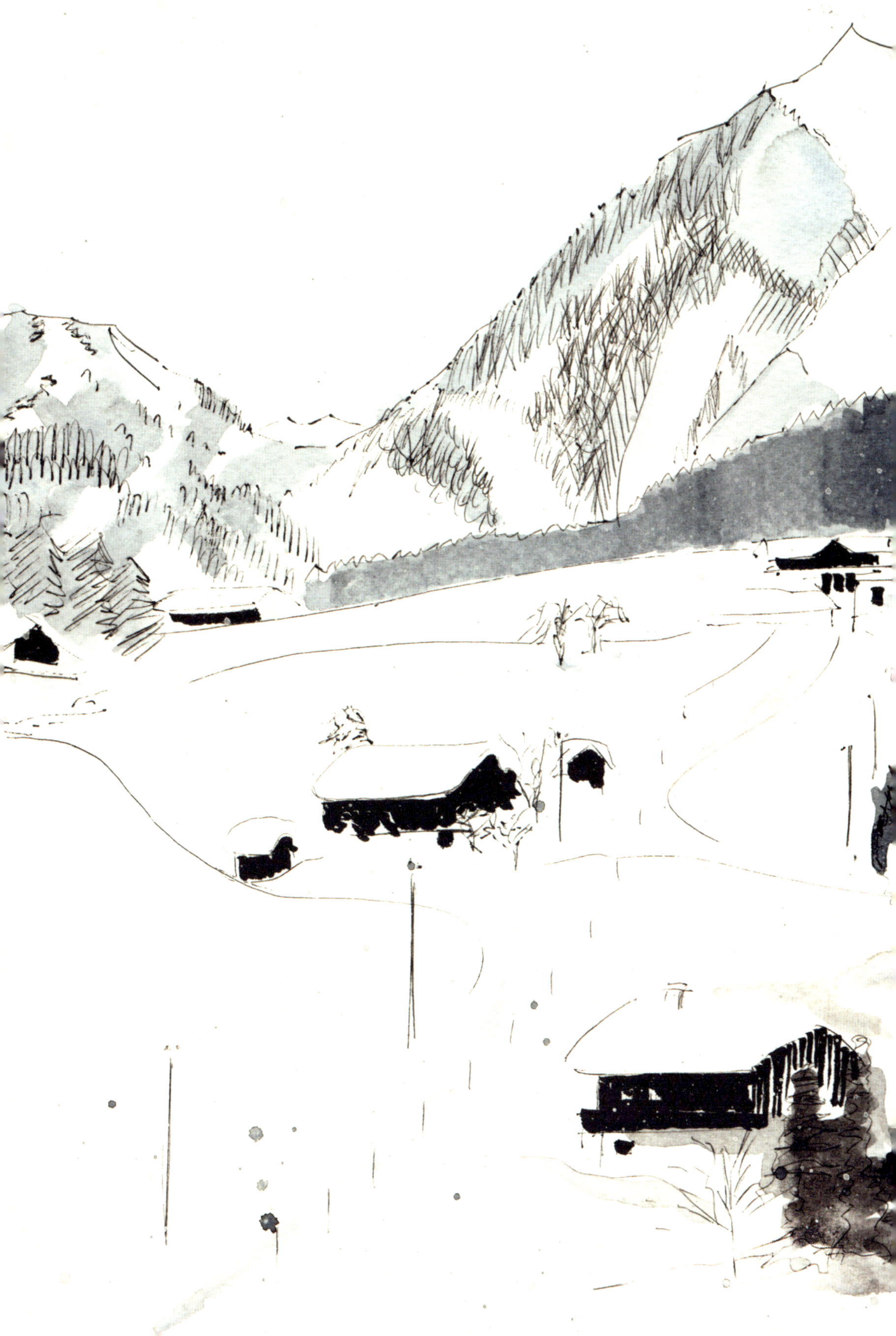

Watercolor Techniques: Adding Color Quickly

Sometimes a few colored strokes with a pen are enough to capture a very specific atmosphere in the picture. Special weather effects, on the other hand—rain-slicked streets, storm clouds, fog-shrouded mountain ridges—practically cry out for watercolors. They're not only a suitable painting medium but are what made outdoor painting practicable in the first place: in a compact box, without tubes, without solvents.

Four Techniques, Endless Possibilities

Depending on the ratio of pigment and water, the results on the paper vary—from grainy, rough effects to soft, blurred gradients. There are basically four methods for using watercolor effectively: granulating, glazing, washing, and wet-on-wet.

In and around all these techniques lie endless possibilities. Beginners often don't use enough water and are disappointed by their first attempts with watercolors. For the experienced artist, on the other hand, watercolor techniques may seem too "quaint" and thus unsophisticated. My advice to everyone: Open the tap and let the paints and water flow!

Tip: Using brushes that are too small makes it more difficult to get started with watercolor painting. High-quality watercolor brushes in sizes 8–10 and up guarantee a generous stroke.

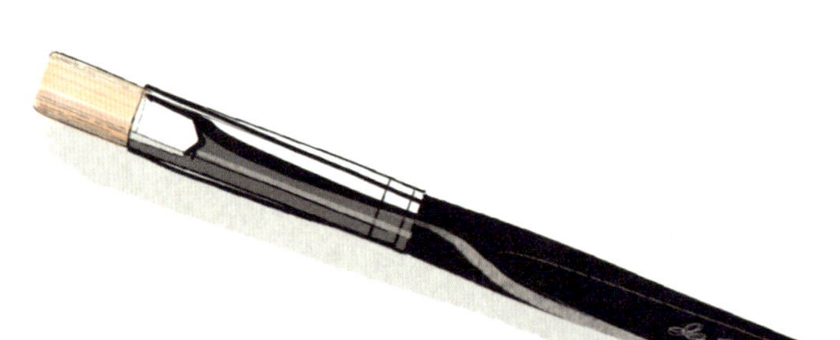

Granulating

Granulating is almost like drawing—a dry brushstroke on paper. This technique creates a rough application of paint, suitable for detailed areas of your image like stones, grass, meadows in the foreground, or certain cloud structures.

Glazing

Glazing is the process of applying layers of paint on top of one another after they dry. With each additional layer, the color becomes darker. If you apply different colors on top of one another, the result is determined by the principle of optical color mixing: blue over yellow produces green.

Wash Painting

As an experienced artist, you're probably skeptical about leaving things to chance. But how wonderful it is to watch watercolors flow into each other on paper! It's almost like watching the weather: Clouds merge, the colors of the sky overlap and mix, and contrasts of light and dark polarize the landscape, sometimes in a matter of seconds.

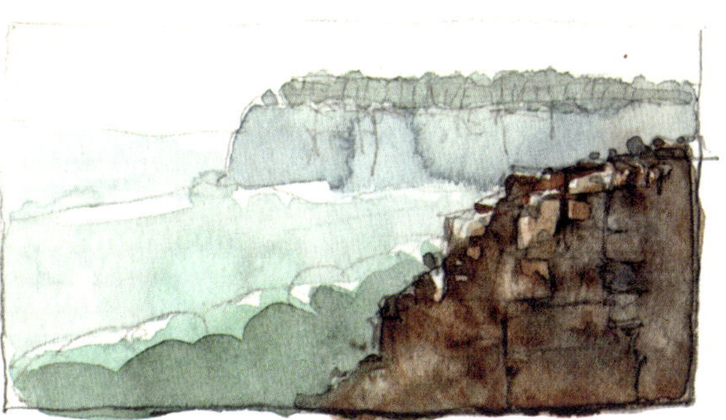

Tip: Watercolors lose some brightness and intensity as they dry. Add a few bold strokes with a pen or marker, and your drawing will come back to life.

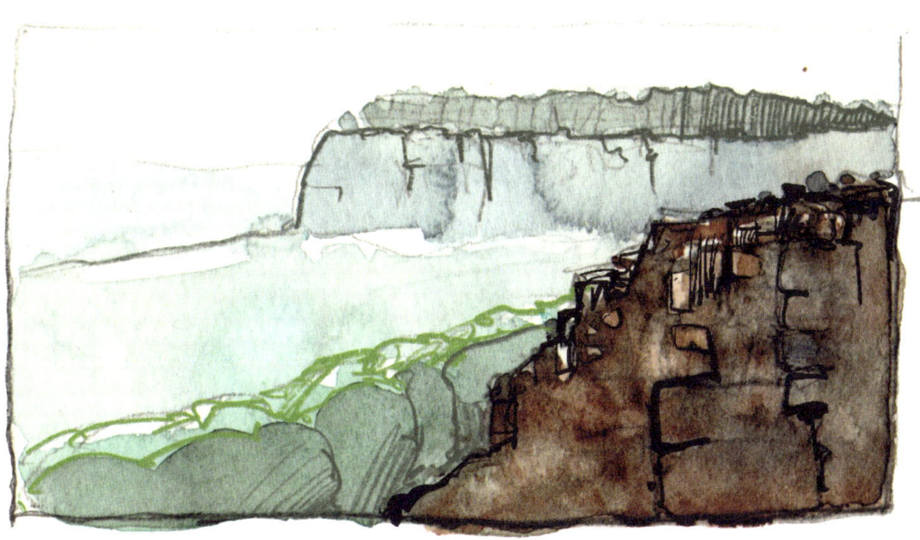

Relinquish Control

What amazes you when
observing nature may make
you feel uncertain when
sketching in watercolor.
Washing—mixing colors
while they're still wet—
means relinquishing control.
It also means embracing
surprising effects and
allowing the paint itself
to influence the outcome.
Try it out!

Wash Exercise

1. Make a preliminary
   sketch with a fineliner
   pen; I chose a few
   drinking glasses
   because they suit
   "liquid" watercolor
   painting.
2. Place a pool of paint
   with plenty of water
   in the sketch for each
   glass; start with a
   light color.
3. Add a second color or
   undiluted pigment of
   the first color as a
   shadow; allow it to run.
4. Remove excess liquid
   with a brush or paper
   towel.
5. Never completely fill
   in the preliminary
   sketch; paint over
   the lines from time
   to time.
6. Add reflections
   typical of glass with
   a black marker; dab
   the color of the
   drink onto the rim
   of the glass and
   add a few splashes.
   Cheers!

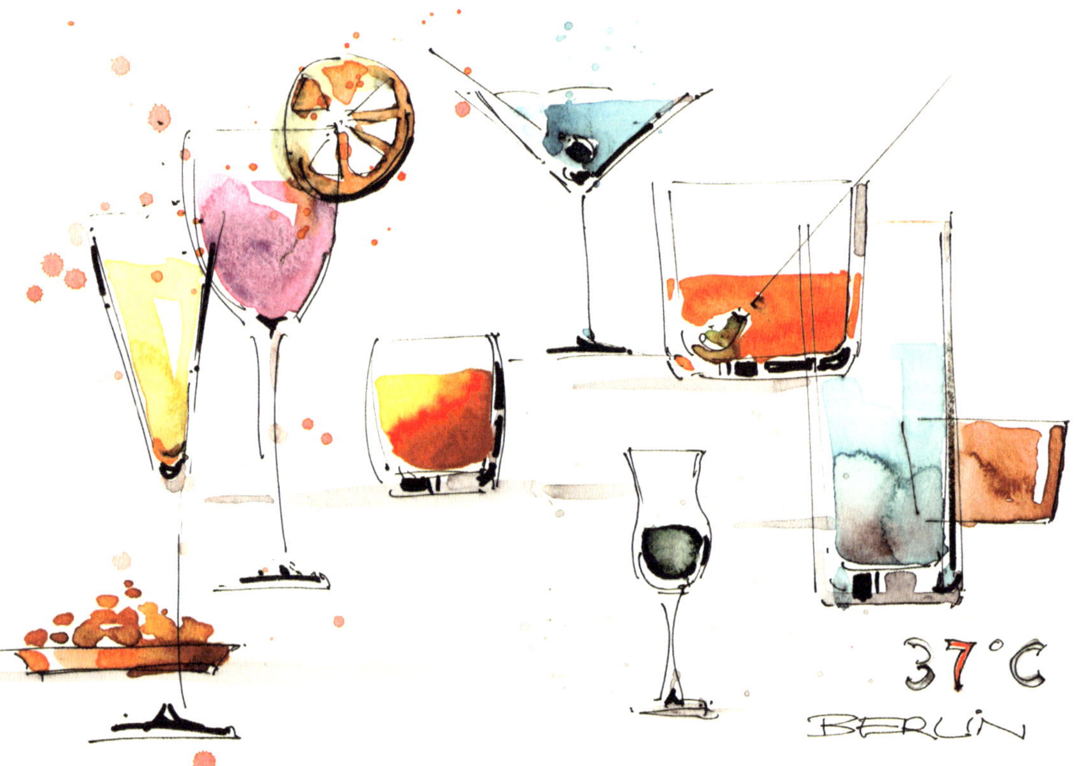

Wet-on-Wet

In the previous exercise, you opened yourself to chance: very good. Now we're going to use even more water and see what happens.

Are you impatient? You may not want to wait for your watercolor drawings to dry outside. Or maybe the weather and temperature aren't conducive to lingering outdoors. You can create the basic atmosphere of your pictures, like a colored background, at home before you even decide what to sketch.

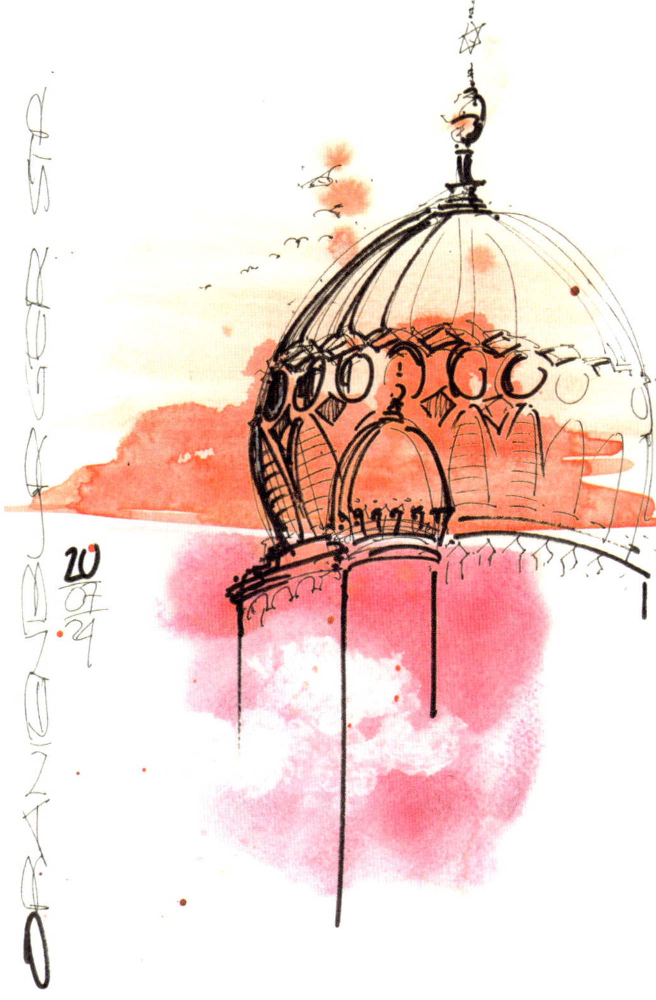

Wet-on-Wet Exercise

1. Moisten watercolor paper with a wide brush and clear water.
2. Apply two or three colors to the wet surface using a wash technique.
3. Control color gradients by adding more pigment or water.
4. Create several variations, allow them to dry, and take them with you for the next sketching session.
5. Add line drawings of your subjects later, on-site.

Switching It Up: Fields of Color First, Then the Lines

When I ask my workshop participants to create color fields without a subject, it's not to save time or because of the weather. I want them to break a common habit. Most people begin a drawing with lines. Outlines help us to grasp things, to get a feel for the proportions of objects and place them on paper. Then they fill in the lines with color. But does it have to be done in this order? Although outlines are not something we can see—neither a tree nor a human being is framed in real life with a black line—we like to create orienting boundaries. It's as if we always want to know exactly where something begins and ends.

Starting out by painting the areas and then adding lines when the subject is in view is a liberating exercise.

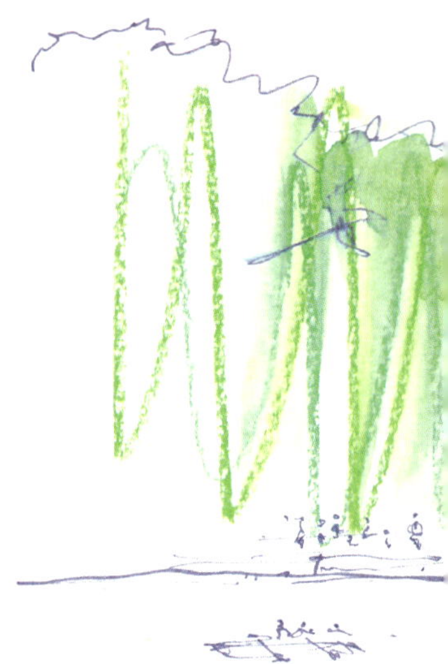

Cemetery in late summer: The colorful background was created a few days earlier. I added this scene with a fineliner pen on-site.

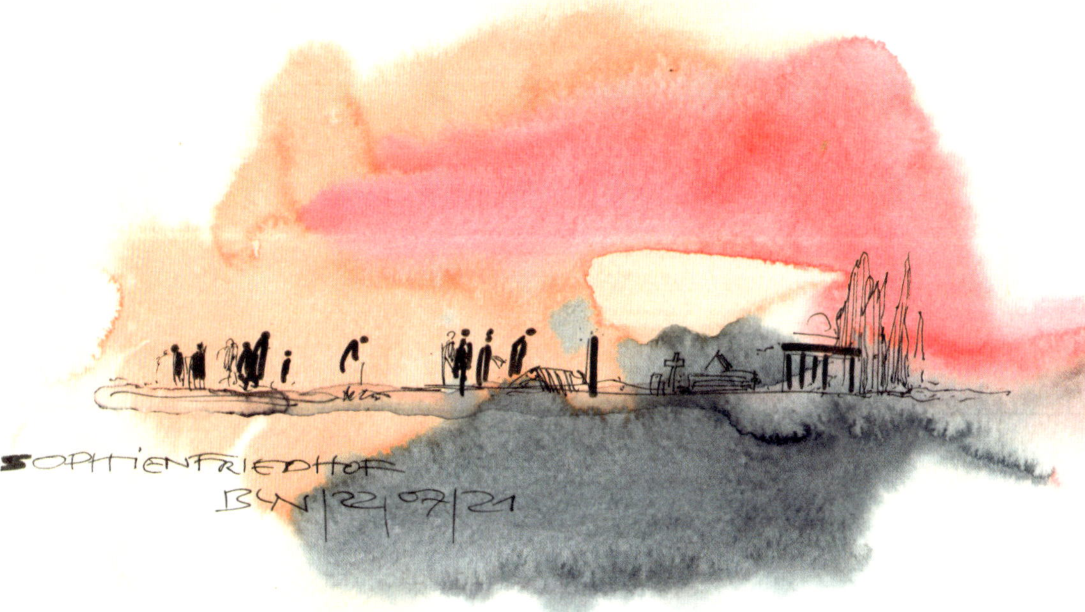

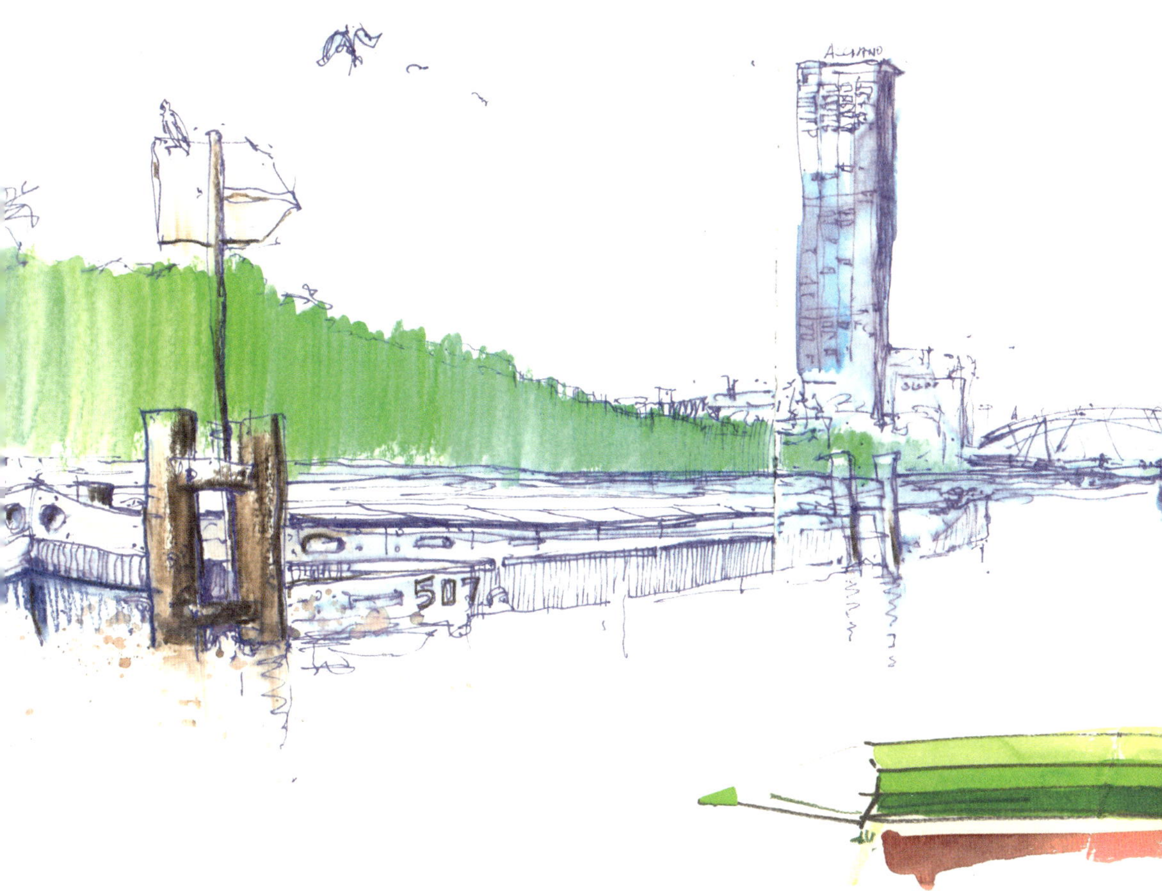

Pens or Paint Sets?

Travel watercolor sets are designed to be compact. The only equipment you need to add are a brush and a water cup. If that's still too much for you, there are even smaller and more compact options.

My smallest mobile painting studio combines watercolor pencils and water brush pens. With watercolor pencils, painting is as easy as drawing with colored pencils. Their "lead" contains special pigments and binders that allow you to blend the colors with water. First, draw lines and areas with watercolor pencils. Then blend the colors with the water brush pen to create wonderful transitions and color gradients without the need for a paint tray and water cup!

Another option that allows you to leave your paint set at home is to use water-soluble brush pens. They combine the precision of a colored marker with the freedom of a watercolor brush.

Detour: Capturing Clouds

Skies and clouds are worthy of their own consideration. Many sketches don't need a sky at all. The closer the horizon is to the top of the picture, the less space there is for sky and clouds. This kind of composition emphasizes elements in the foreground and middle ground—without competition from cloud formations (see page 36).

Yet clouds are popular subjects and a lifelong passion for some painters. The spatial effect and atmosphere of a landscape are ultimately determined by the sky.

Don't Draw Clouds

Before we try to sketch clouds, let's be clear: Clouds are rarely drawn with pens and pencils. Instead, we make the watercolor paint do the work for us. Wet-on-wet is the perfect technique for quickly conjuring clouds on paper.

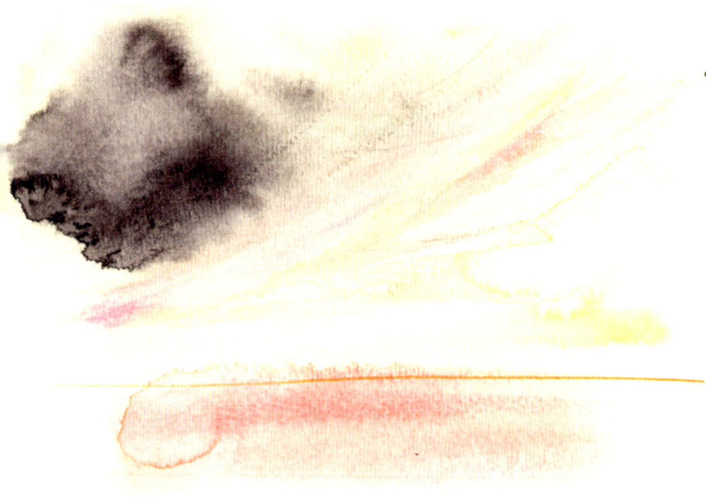

Exercise: Clouds

1. Moisten the watercolor paper with plenty of clean water.
2. Add two to three colors to the wet surface.
3. Leave space for clouds in the white paper or dab them out after with a cloth.
4. Let the paint dry.
5. Suggest a landscape with a few lines.

Perspective Using Clouds

Clouds are collections of tiny water droplets, materially intangible phenomena in the sky. Certain types, like cumulus clouds, though, appear very three-dimensional and physical. They seem to have size, weight, and light and shadowed edges. This three-dimensionality leads us back to the trick with depth. Using clouds, three-dimensionality can be skillfully "built into" the image.

Rules for Three-Dimensionality

1. Arrange your clouds by size: large in front, small behind.
2. Note the light and shadow: light at the top, dark at the bottom.
3. Clouds have a vanishing point: Linear cloud stripes meet on the horizon.
4. Color gradient: dark blue at the top, lighter at the bottom near the horizon.

Experiment with the Sky

Watercolors invite you to experiment. After your first experiences with watercolor cloud structures, you'll feel more confident using the principle of "controlled randomness" in your pictures. Try out wet-on-wet effects at home.

Test different color combinations and weather situations on watercolor paper before you go outside. It's fun to experiment with the drama of the sky. Along the way, you'll develop your own "library" of visual moods that you can access anytime you're outdoors.

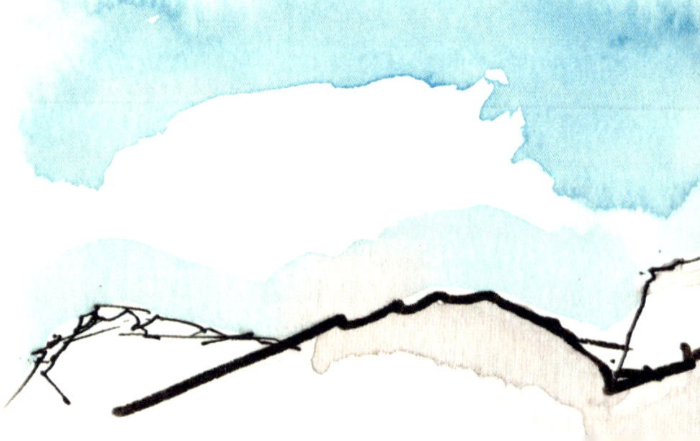

Cloud drama: The dry edges of the watercolor paint create their own shapes. The large cloud in this picture consists entirely of the white of the paper background. Use this method to create natural cloud shapes.

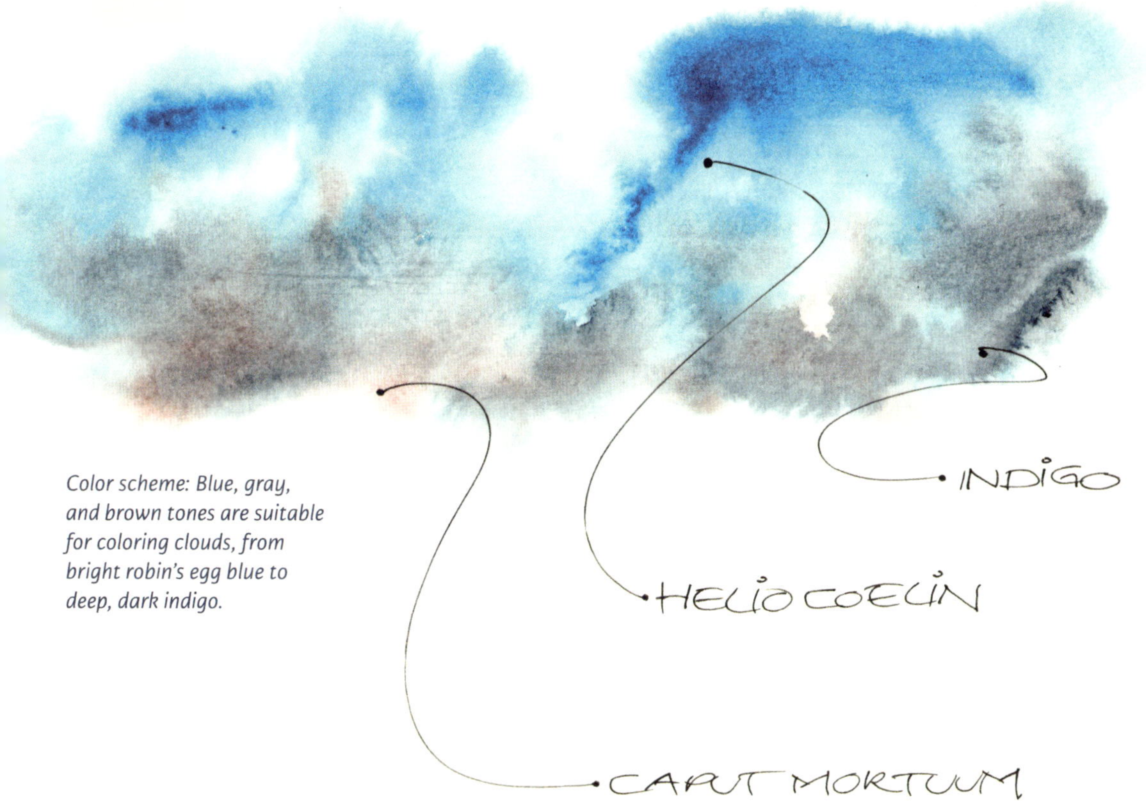

Color scheme: Blue, gray, and brown tones are suitable for coloring clouds, from bright robin's egg blue to deep, dark indigo.

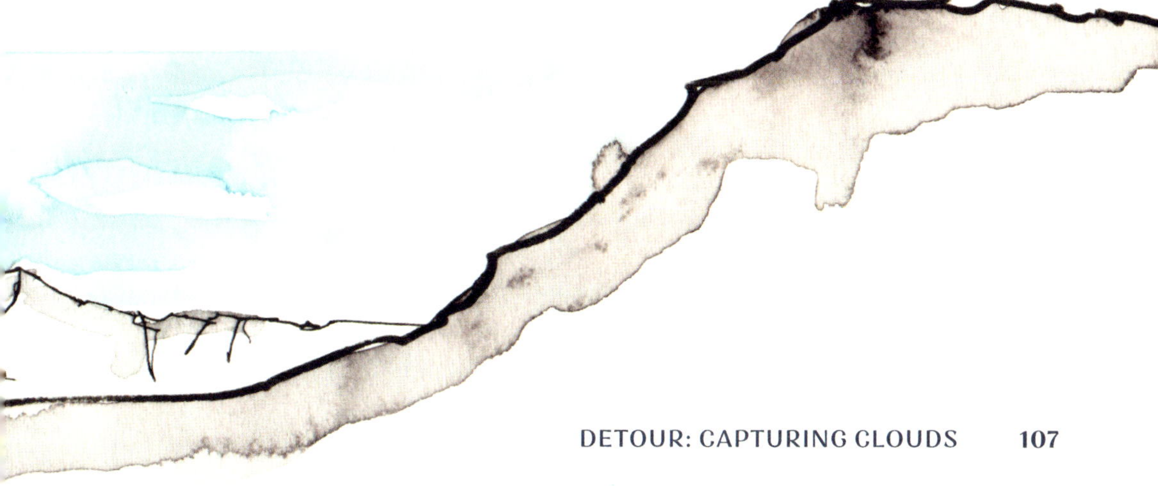

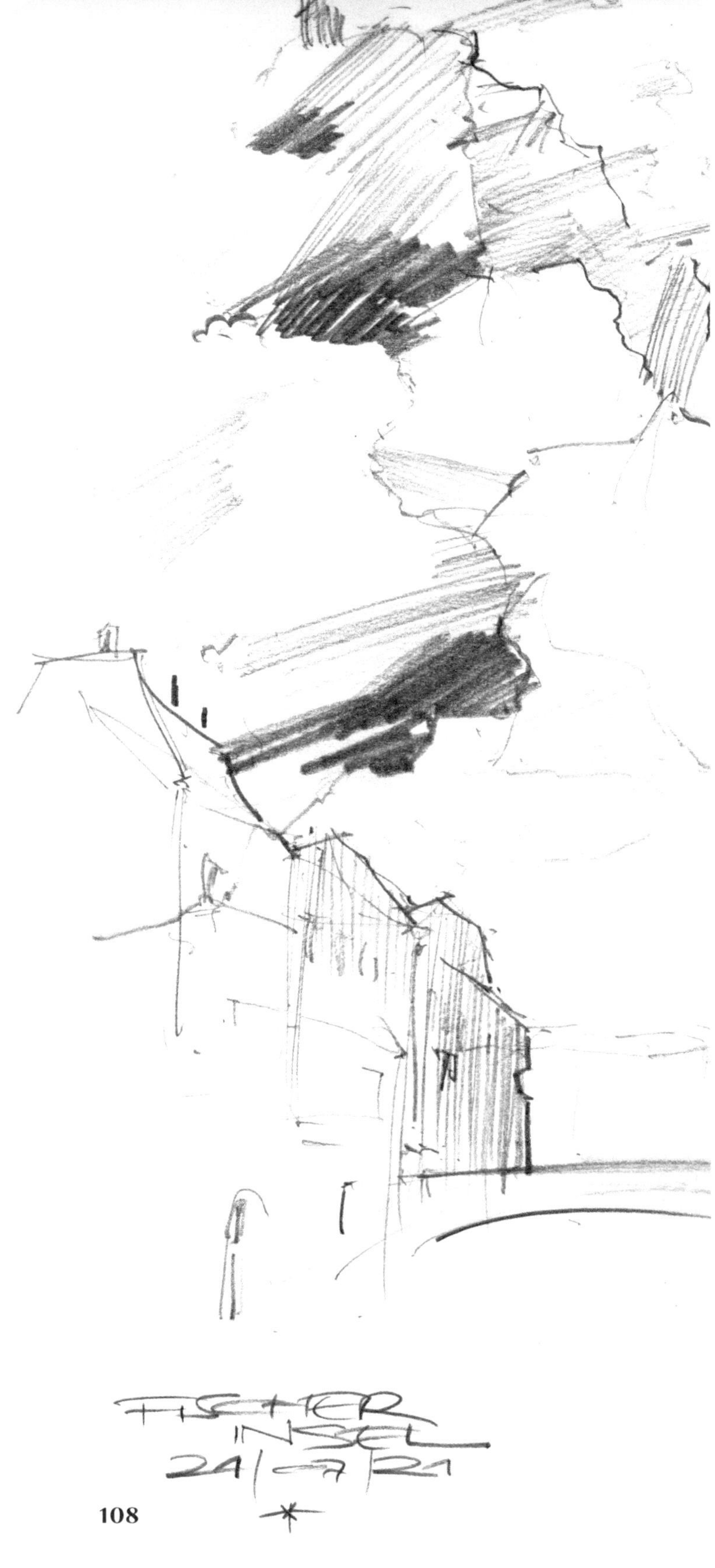

Dry techniques are also used to depict clouds. Skies and clouds can be created effectively with just a few hatching strokes. Don't forget that generous areas of blank white paper provide interest and contrast.

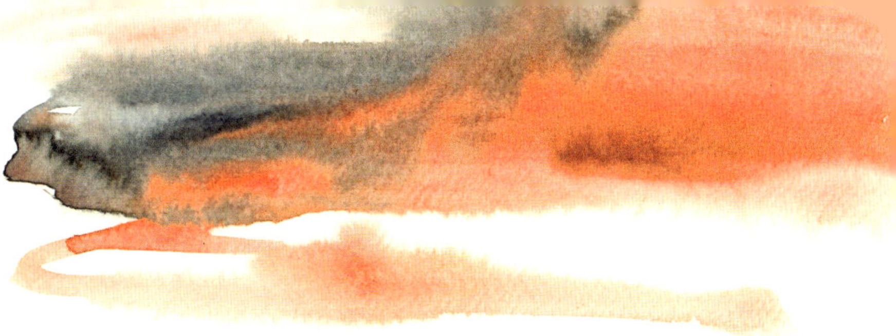

You can also add bright segments to cloudy areas afterward, as I've done here for a snowfall in the mountains. Water-color paint can be erased to a limited extent. Alternatively, a thin film of opaque white can be applied.

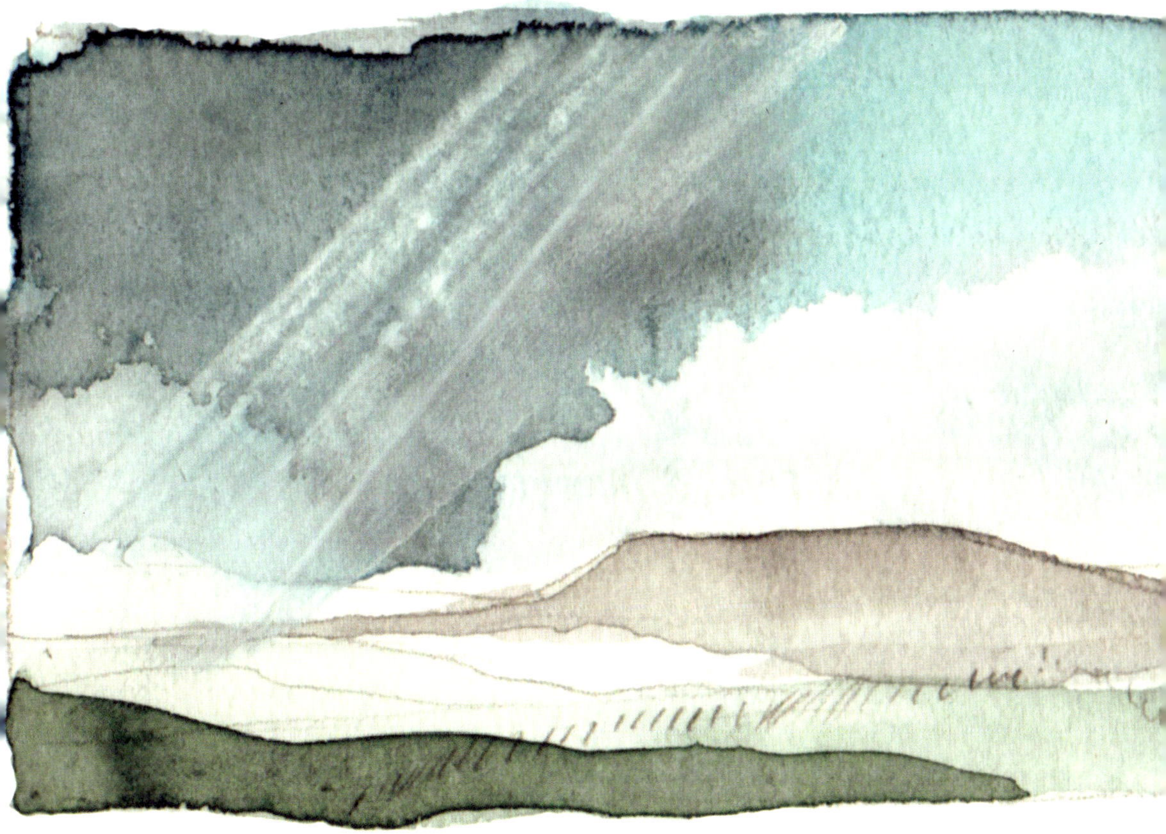

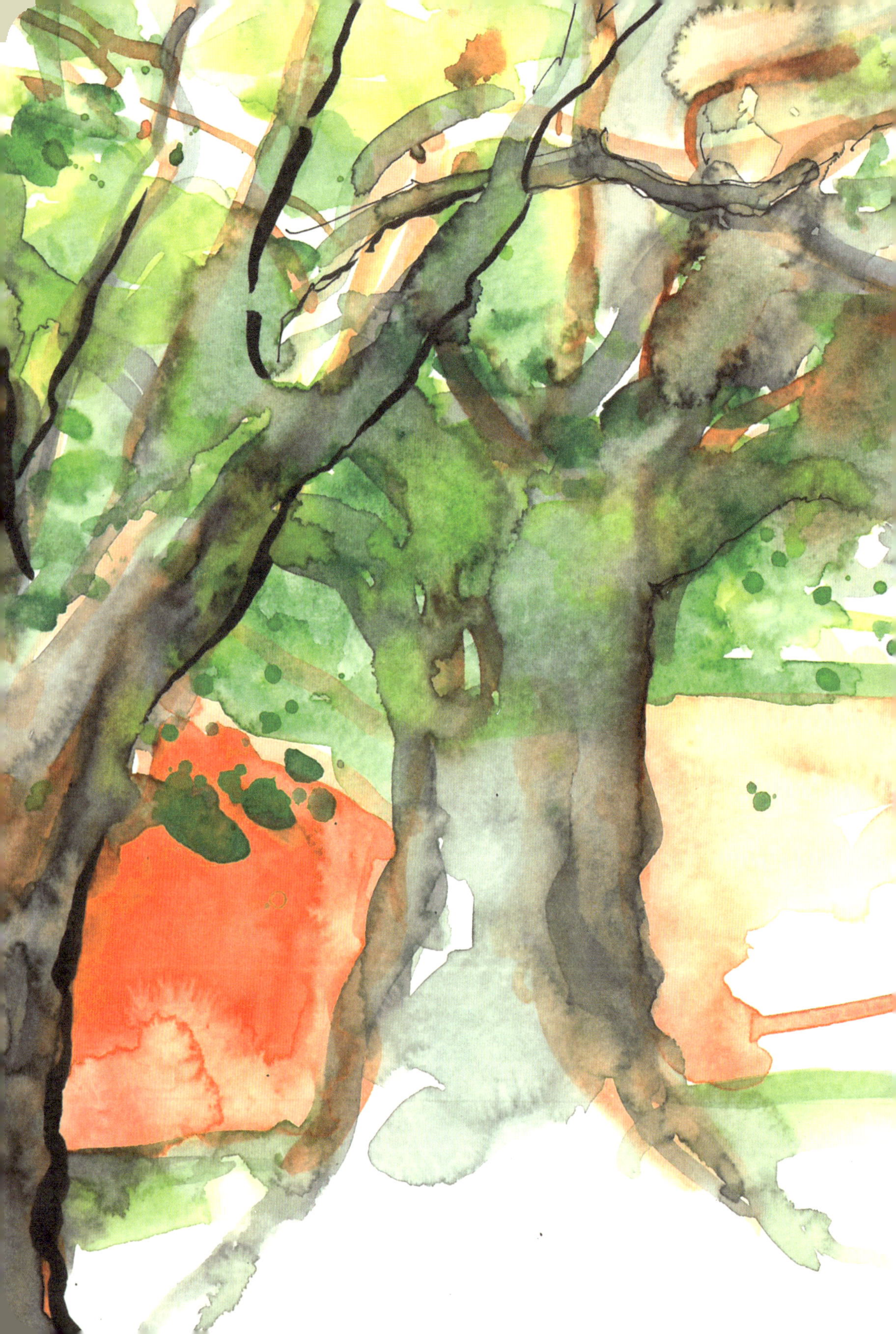

Trees, Forests, and Color

Nature's vibrant shapes and colors offer artists a welcome change from the built environment of cities. Experiences in the great outdoors—in wintry forests, along summery country lanes, in bright valleys, or on spring meadows or hidden paths through the undergrowth—leave lasting impressions both on our minds and in our sketchbooks. A natural ecosystem like the forest thrives on diversity and simplicity in equal measure. In the following chapter, you and I will look over the shoulder of nature as artist. In doing so, we will encounter the artistic challenge of omission as well as the creative freedom of color.

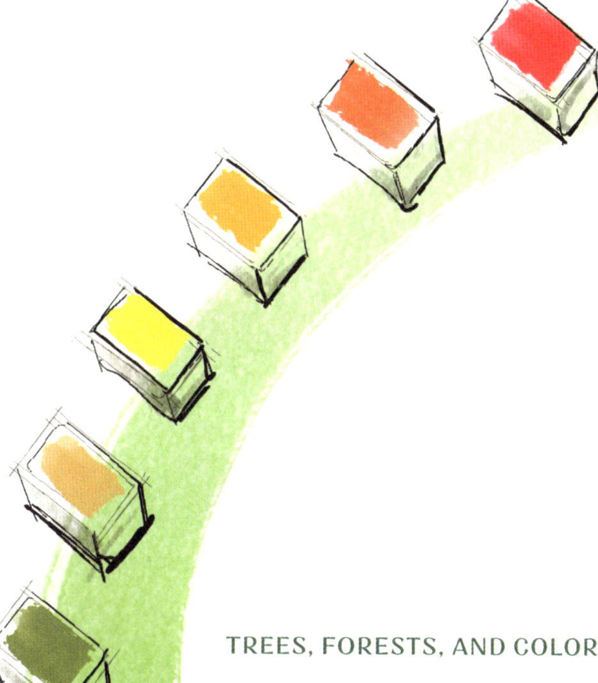

Detour: Drawing Trees

Trees occupy a special place in the following pages. Whether as solitary figures in the landscape or as a group in the background of a picture, trees are an integral part of many natural scenes. Trees are rewarding subjects for drawing practice. Observe them carefully: Their shapes, structures, and surfaces can be studied in passing.

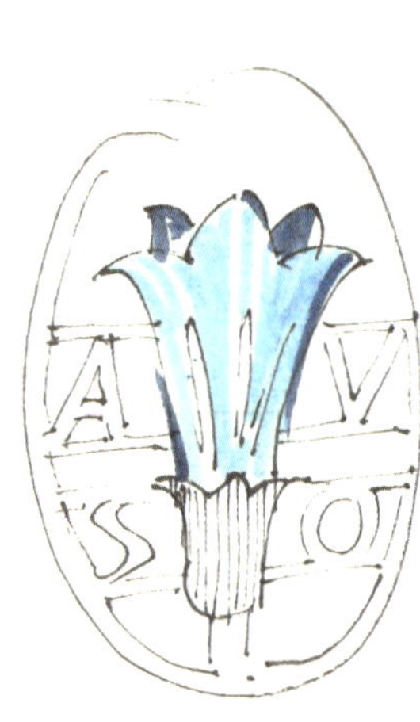

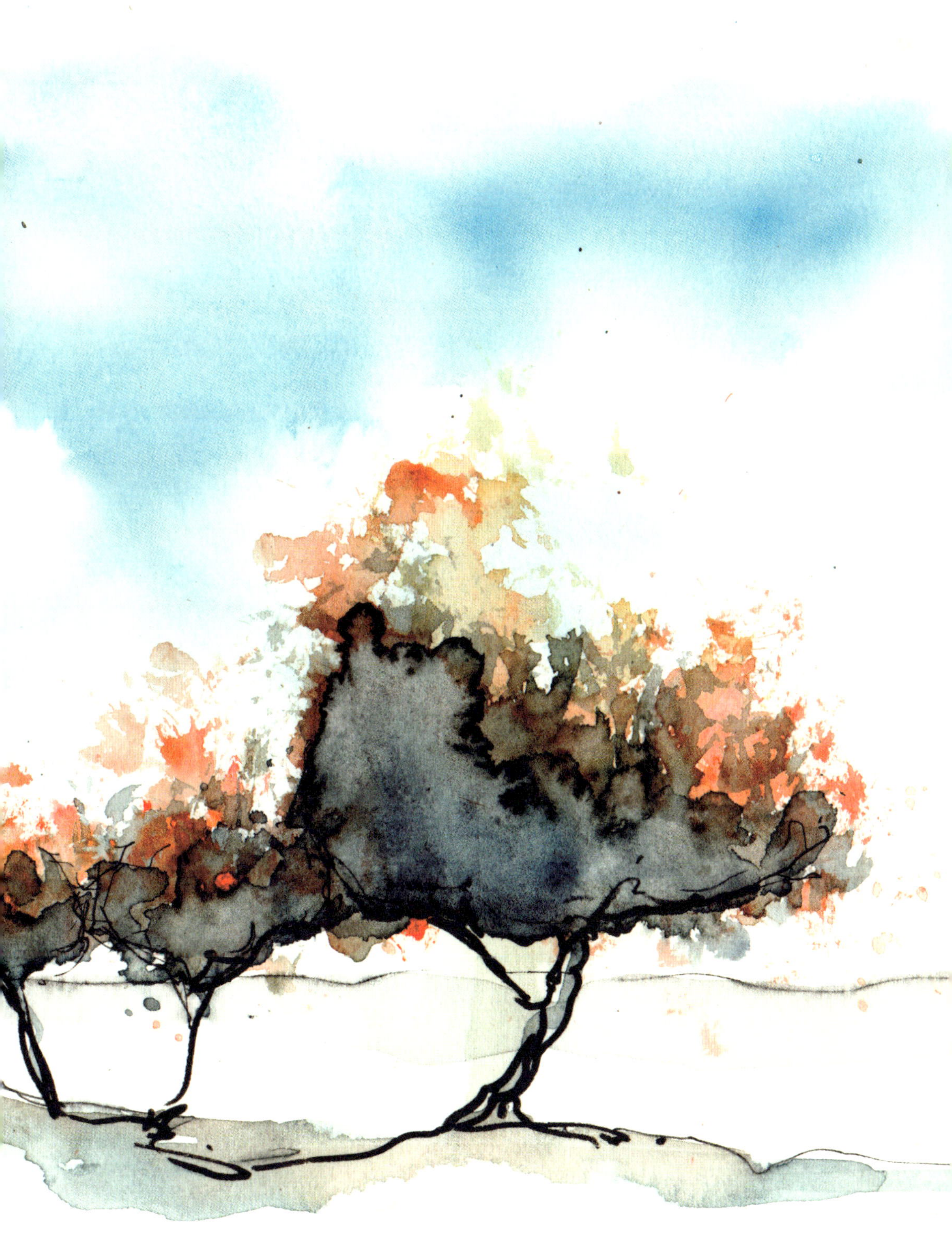

Practice Doodling Trees

Start with a warm-up exercise: Doodle trees. This exercise
demands that you let chance play a major role. The pen glides
across the paper, and shapes emerge almost by themselves
through doodling, lines, and spiral movements. The result isn't
planned—and you won't end up with a "standard" tree. Instead,
you'll gain an appreciation for the shapes found in nature.

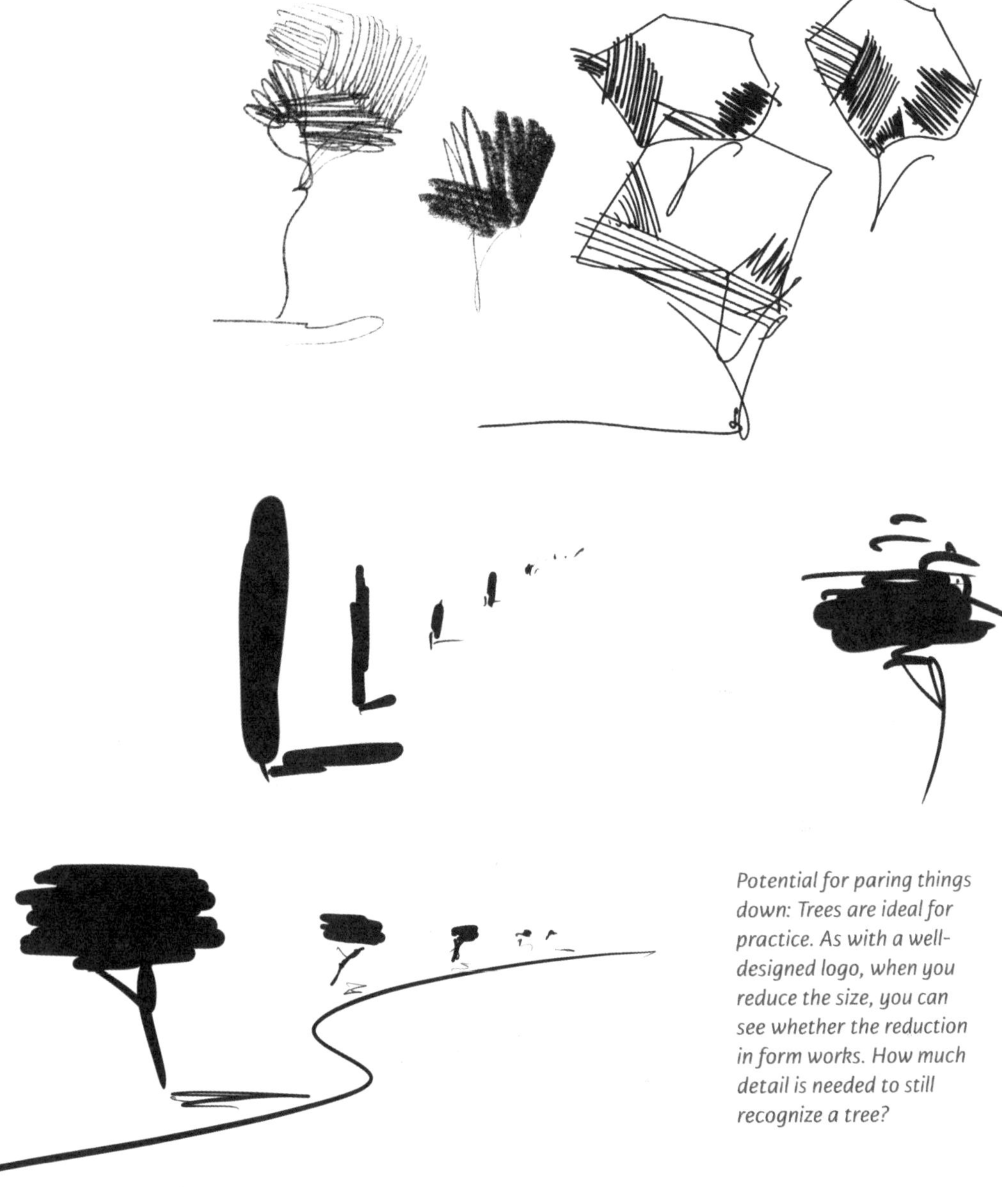

*Potential for paring things
down: Trees are ideal for
practice. As with a well-
designed logo, when you
reduce the size, you can
see whether the reduction
in form works. How much
detail is needed to still
recognize a tree?*

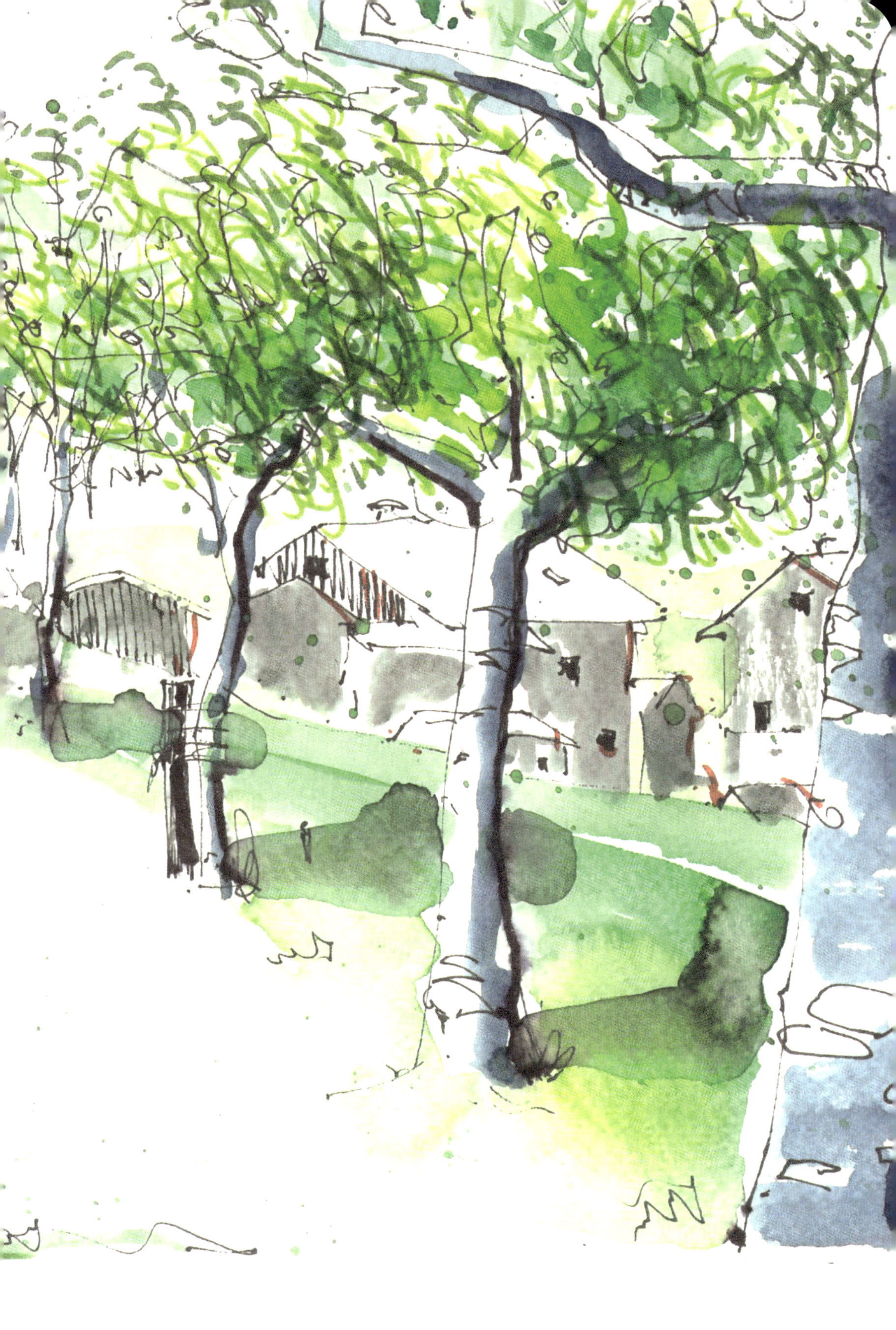

Tree Species

You don't need any prior knowledge of botany to tackle the
diversity of trees in drawing. A little observation is enough
to distinguish the essential characteristics of deciduous and
coniferous trees, as well as exotic species. What is the basic
shape? What is the size ratio between the trunk and the
crown? In which direction do the branches grow?

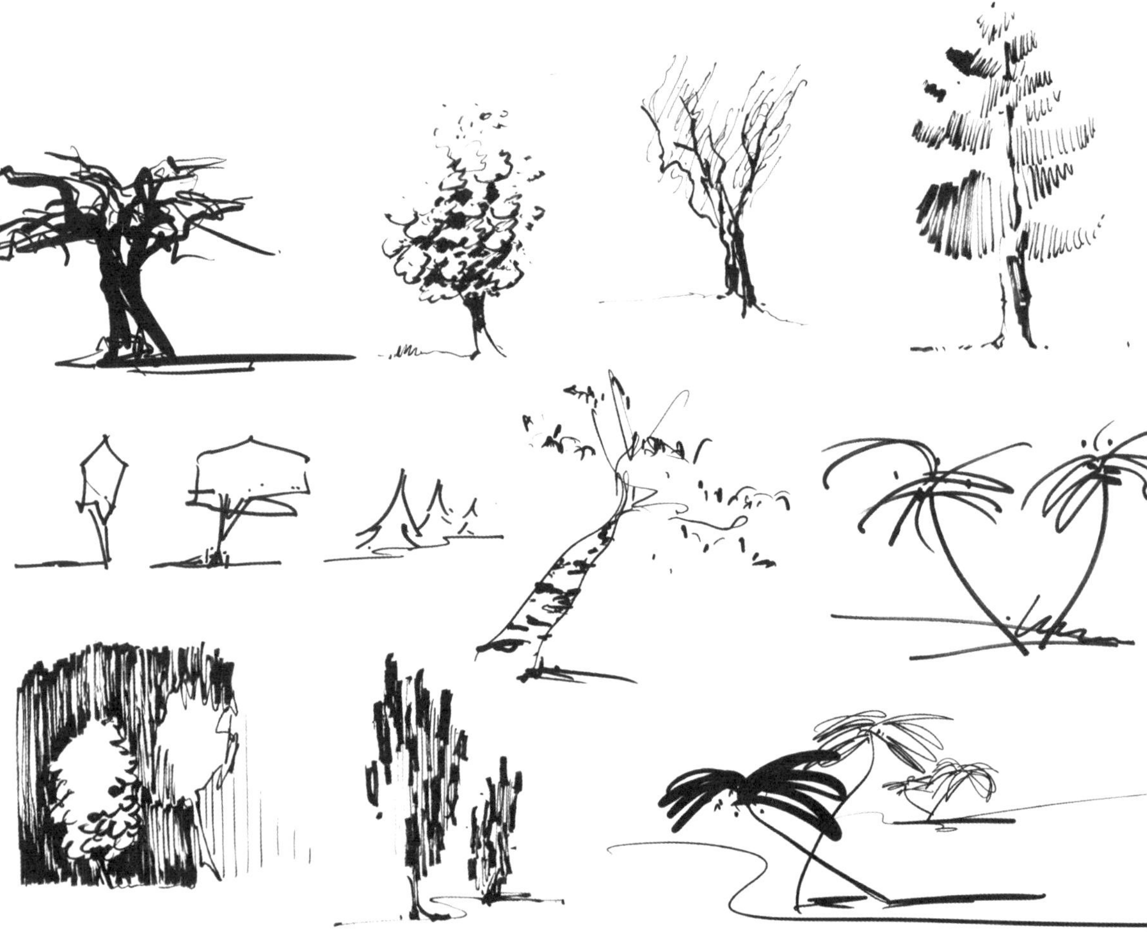

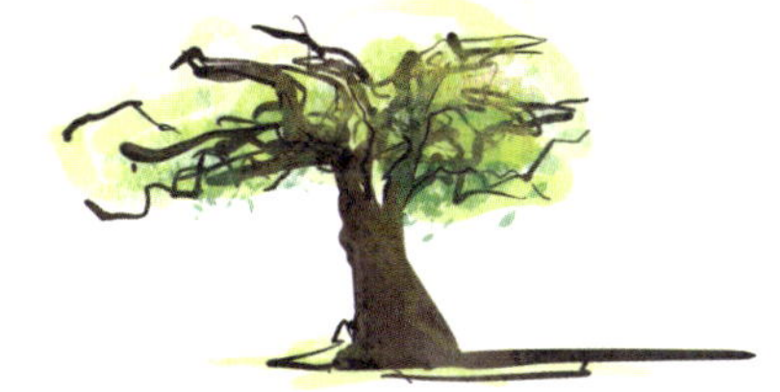

Seasons

The classic exercise: Draw a tree in all four seasons. Whether with pen and brush or on a tablet—try it yourself. Broad-leafed trees like a free-standing oak or beech are most suitable. Observe characteristic changes that go beyond color: from delicate to dense foliage, from a full tree crown to bare branches.

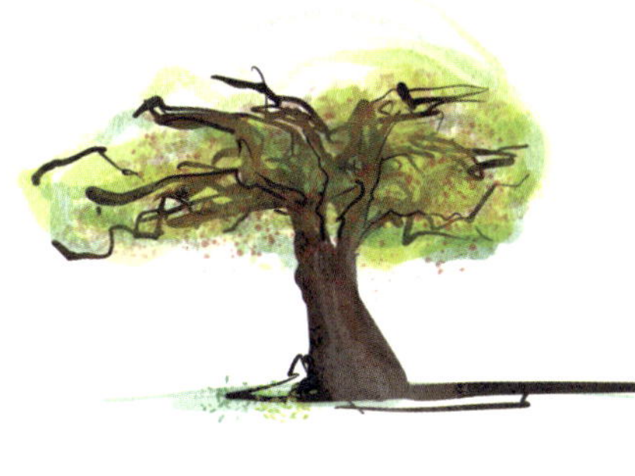

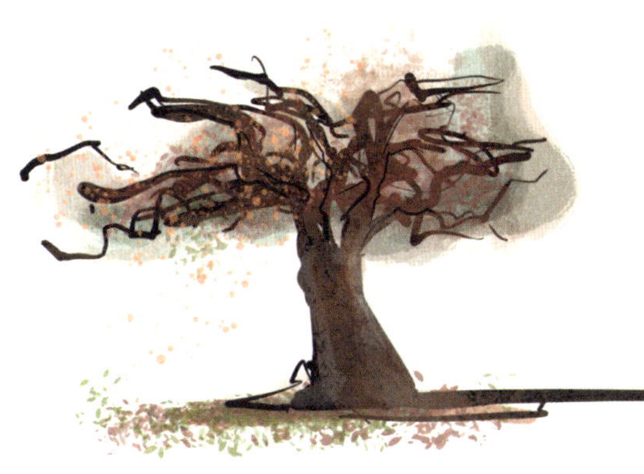

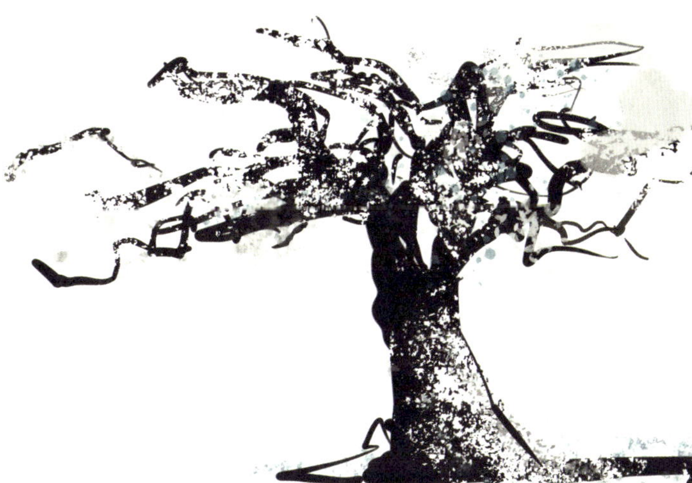

Tip: A tree template can be duplicated any number of times on a tablet. The seasons change in a playful experiment with different levels.

Your Own Portable Library

To quickly incorporate trees, people, vehicles, or animals into my drawings, I collect templates in a sketchbook that I can refer to while traveling. For example, I can consult them when I need to remember the shape of apple trees, how I sketched a hiking group a few days prior, or what it was that I needed to remember about cars. Separate from your sketchbook, create a collection of recurring "prototypes," and add new variations to it over time.

Your library of template sketches will continue to grow as you travel and do the exercises in this book. Starting on page 204, you'll add people, birds, and cars!

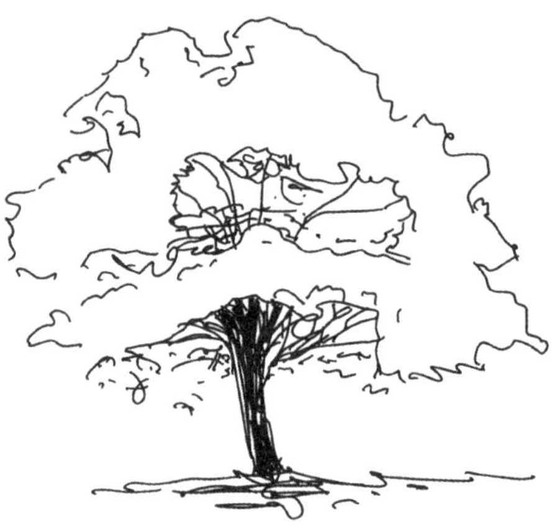

Checklist for Sketching Trees

1. Analyze the shape of the crown, branches, and trunk.
2. Simplify and minimize details.
3. Use quick pen strokes and brushstrokes.
4. Distribute light: bright at the top, dark at the bottom.
5. The tree crown shades the trunk.
6. Avoid trunks that are too straight.
7. Embed the tree in the landscape (see the following double-page spread).

Tip: Instructions for crafting a sketchbook without glue or binding. It's a practical solution when you're on the move and need a new sketchbook.

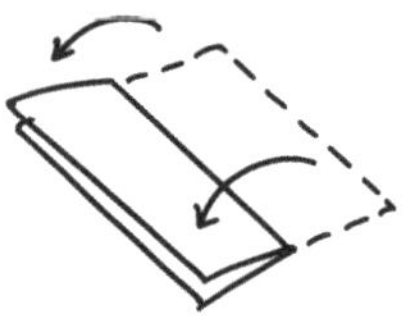
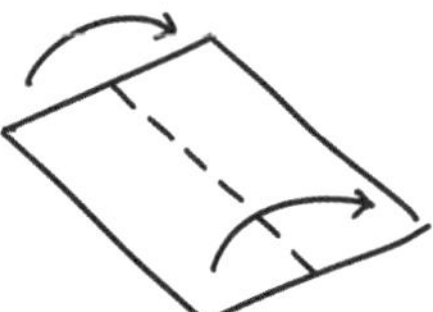
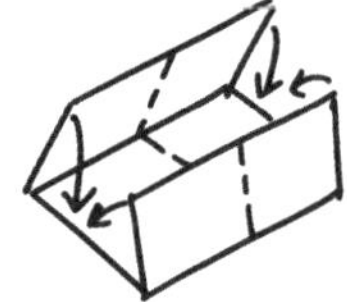
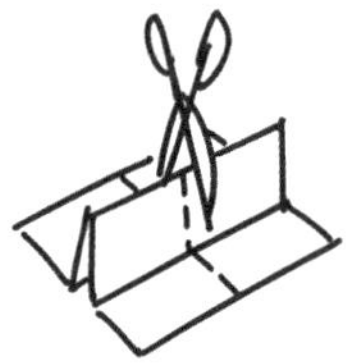

Summer sun: Generous gaps in the tree canopy let light shine through these fruit trees. Don't skimp on the white of the paper for trees, either!

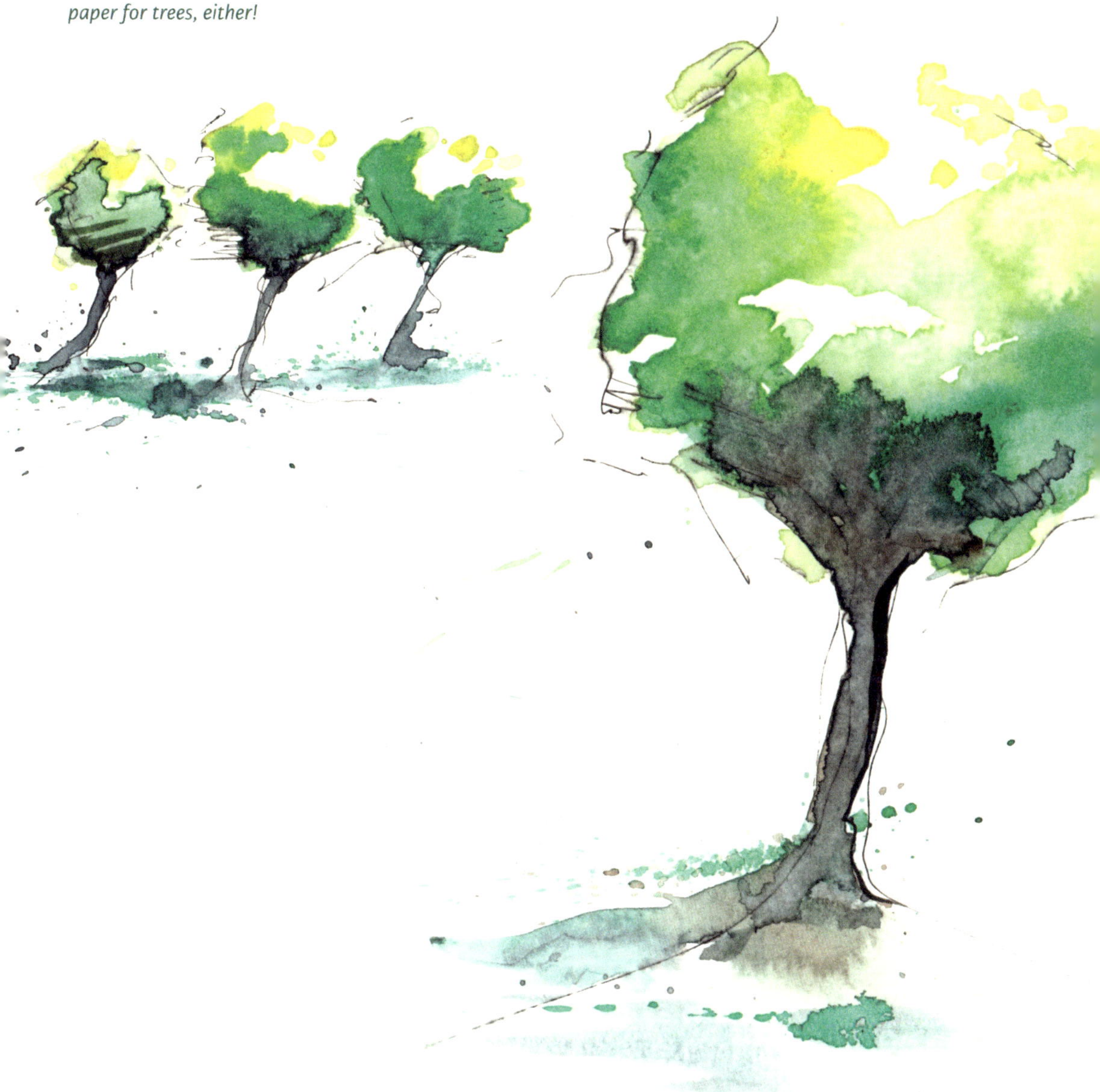

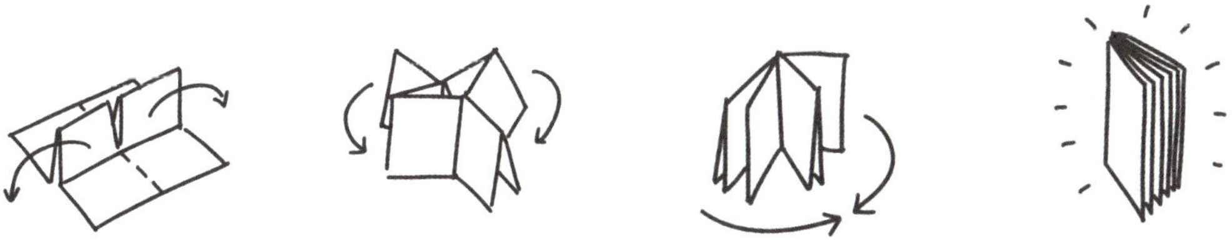

Groves and Forests

While individual trees create strong accents in the foreground of a drawing, groups of trees and forest edges can provide depth in the middle ground and background. Trees merge to form silhouettes and ribbons, and their individual shapes diminish.

When sketching groups of trees, I try to work as efficiently as possible. I use quick strokes to define the upper and lower edges. Hatching of varying densities creates three-dimensionality in the tree crowns. The trunks are only hinted at.

Forest edges in the background can be created just as easily with a brush and watercolor paint. Rounded contours represent deciduous forests, while individual protruding tips represent coniferous forests, depending on the brushwork.

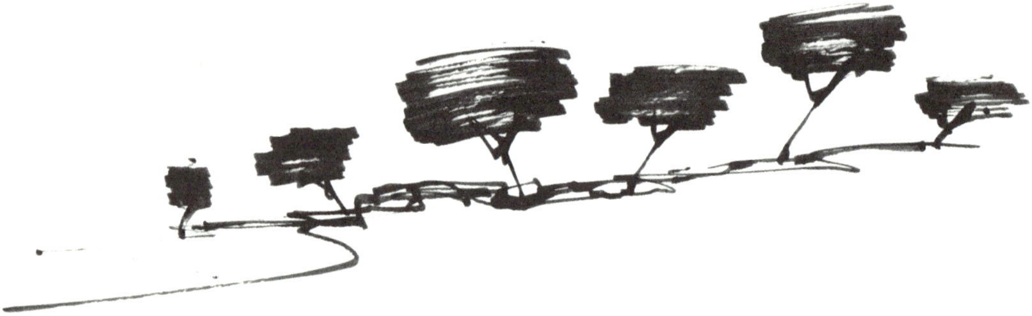

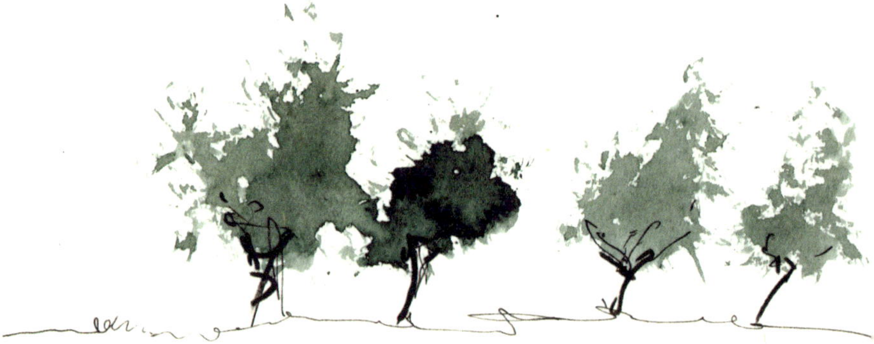

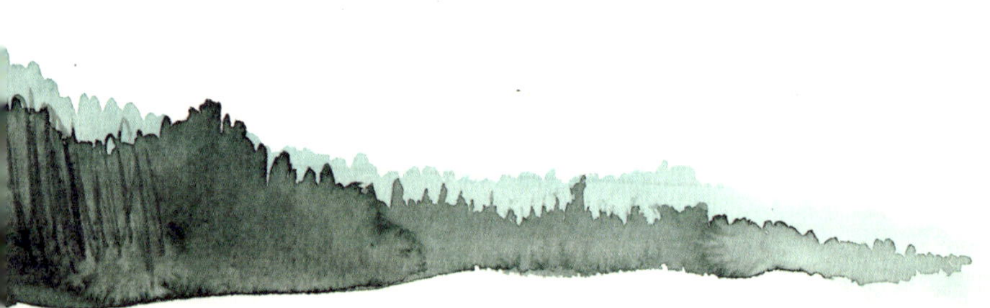

Stippling trees: Using a semidry watercolor brush is less gentle on the brush but much more effective.

Pay attention to the rules of atmospheric and color perspective: The farther away the edge of the forest is, the lighter and cooler the color tone.

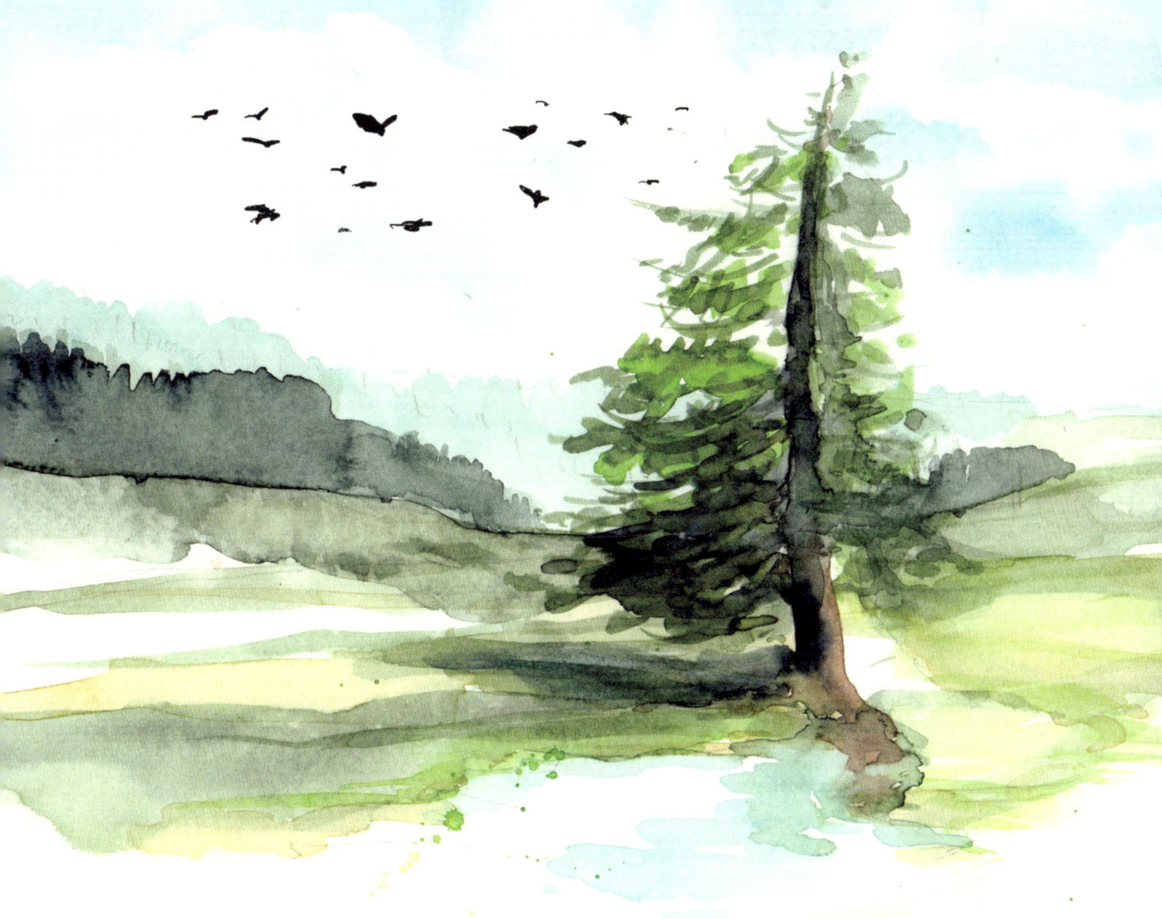

Embedded in the Landscape

Trees grow out of the ground. Pay attention to their organic
transition from the ground to the roots to the trunk. A topographical line is well-suited for integrating trees into the overall
landscape: for example, the bank of a river, the valley floor of
a mountain range, or the edge of a meadow.

Firmly embedded in the landscape, trees stand side by side.
To the viewer, the line suggests natural shadows on the ground.

Mystical Mentors

There are places where I feel especially inspired to draw.
One of them is the Brachtalm in Chiemgau, in the foothills of the Bavarian Alps. At a height of 3,773 feet, it is
surrounded by practically untouched forests and meadows. As you venture deeper into the forest, you enter
an almost mystical wilderness created by the skeletons
of standing and fallen trees. They were giants killed by
storms—now lying in the grass, or stretching bare toward
the sky, overgrown with lichens, mosses, and shrubs.

I captured this mysterious subject in the fading
light of an autumn day using only a pencil and some
indigo blue.

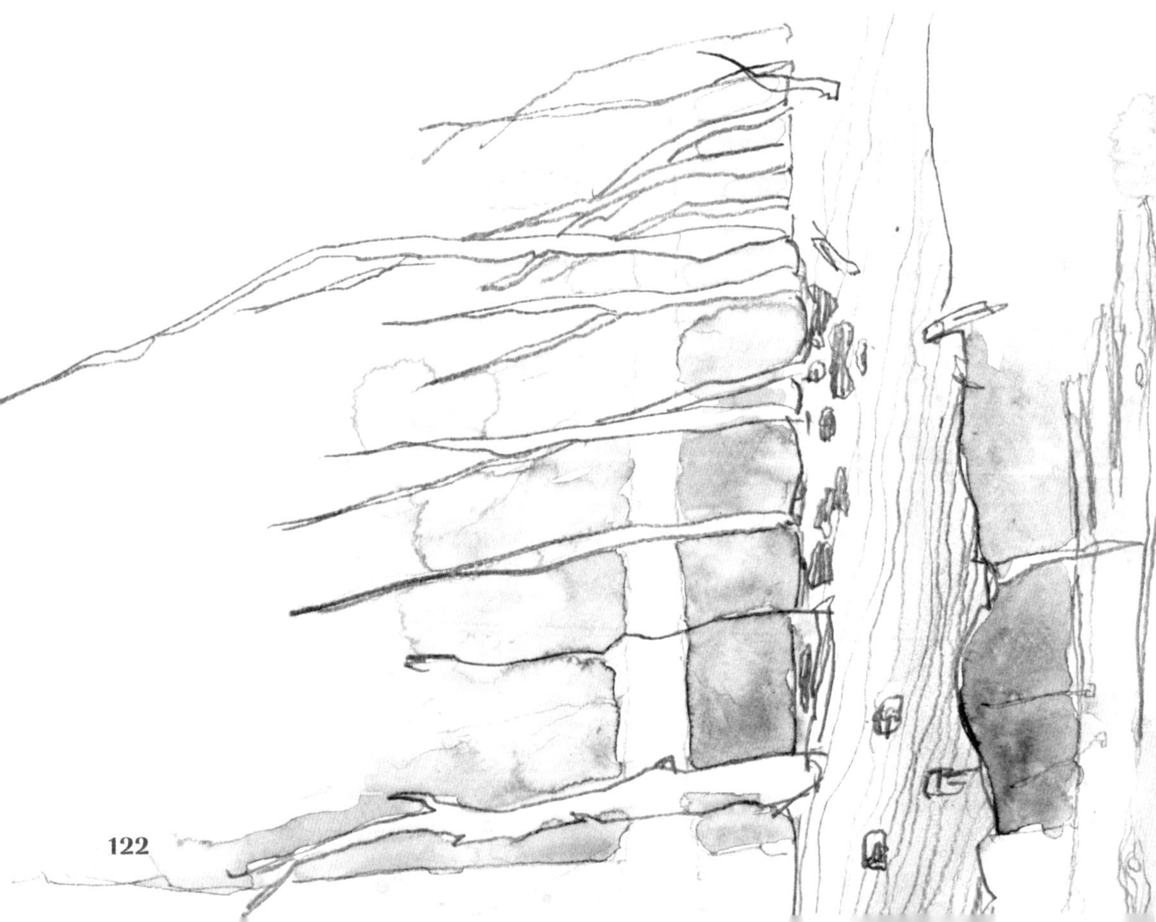

Tip: Glazing and wash techniques
are suitable for coloring trees (see
Watercolor Techniques on page 98).
My choice of colors varies with the
seasons: fresh May green to muted
perylene green in summer, cool
indigo—as seen here—in fall
and winter.

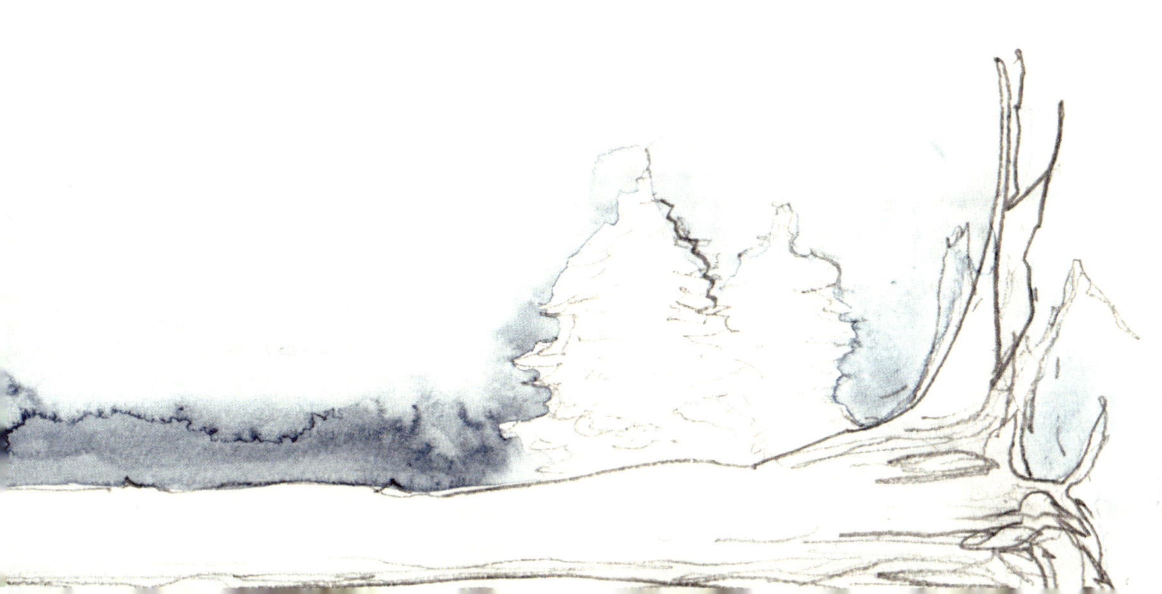

Shrubs, Grasses, and Other Plants

Bushes and shrubs are more elements to add to sketches of nature. Here, reeds, a meadow edge, and grasses along the path divide the image horizontally and calm the composition. Again: Don't adhere too closely to reality.

Your own, readily available style is more useful when sketching outdoors than trying to create a true-to-life image.

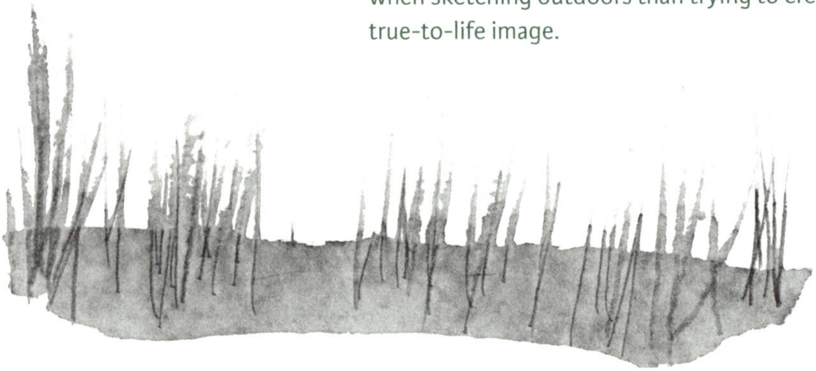

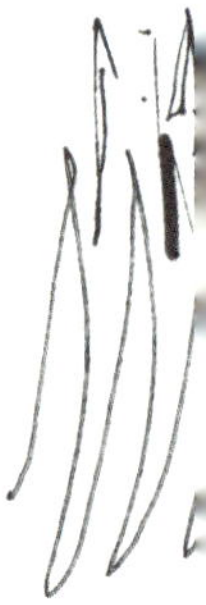

Tip: For depicting fine grasses in watercolor, use a palette knife or the tip of your brush to "pull" individual blades of grass out of the still-wet paint.

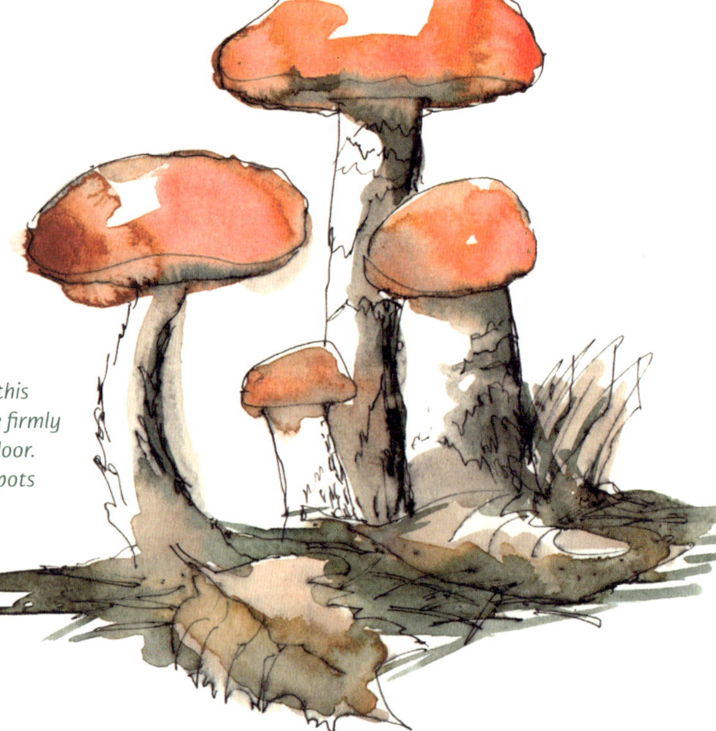

Too good to harvest: In this picture, the red caps are firmly anchored to the forest floor. Overlapping and light spots add depth.

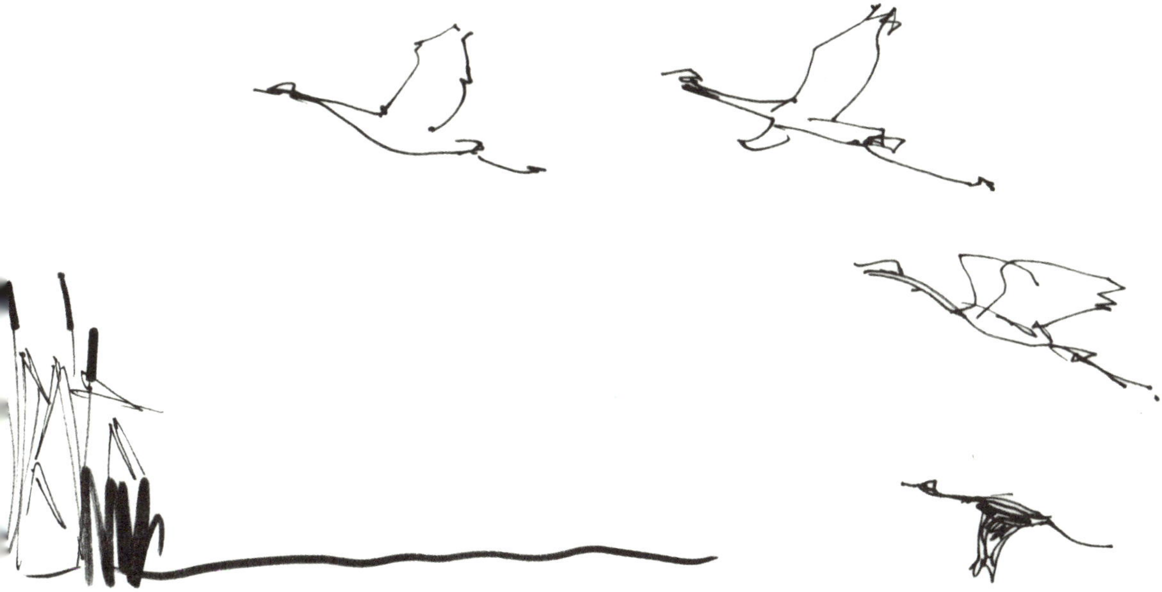

Simply sketch a continuous line on
paper using the one-line technique,
and the meadow edge is complete.

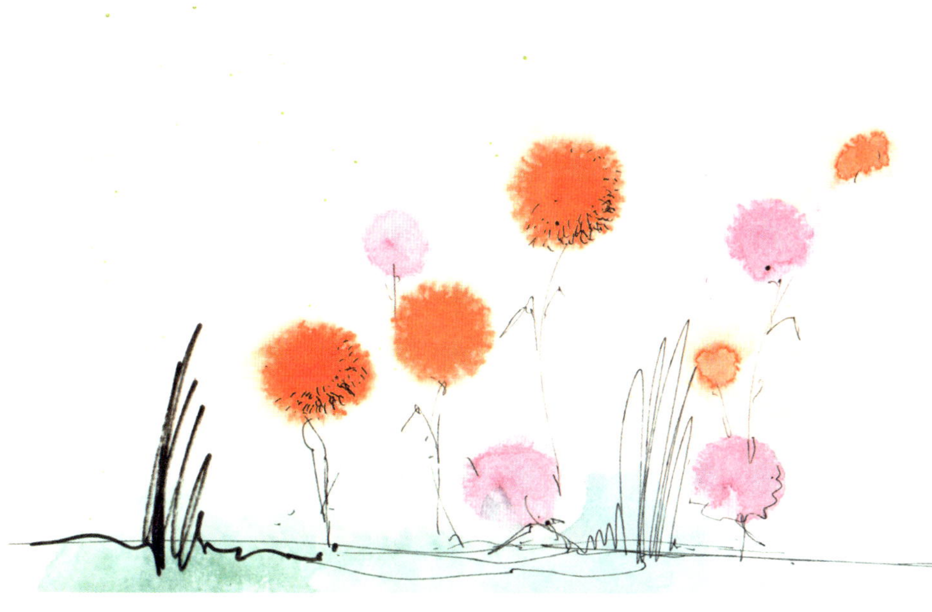

The Art
of Omission

This is a good place to practice leaving things out.
Drawing means reducing and simplifying. Capturing
every branch and every leaf of a tree neither provides
us with more visual information nor is it particularly
enjoyable. This also applies to many other subjects
outside the forest, like roof tiles on buildings or
paving stones on a street. Try it for yourself!

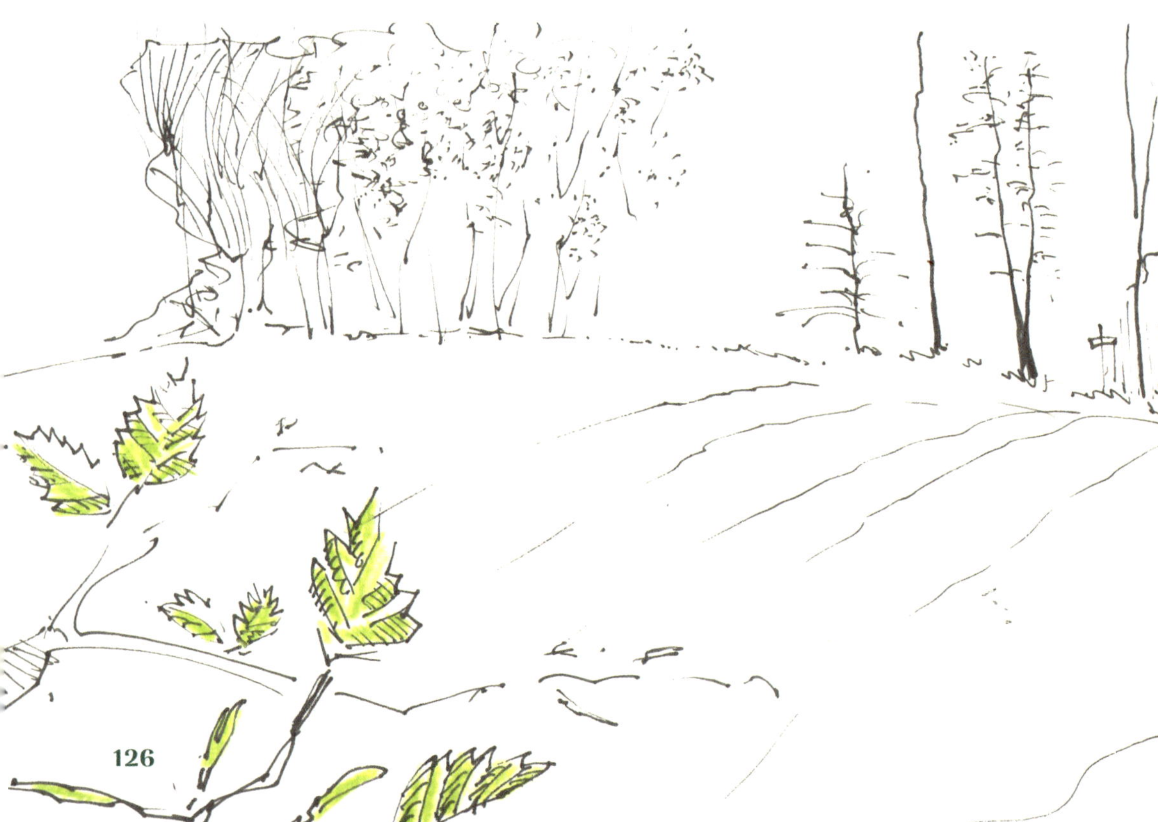

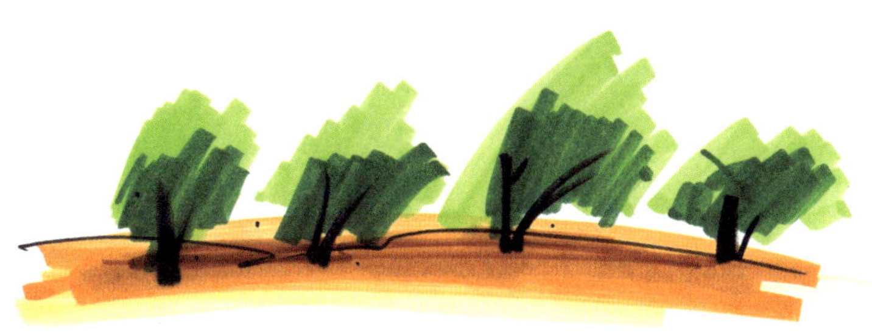

A few powerful strokes in shades of green and brown are all that's needed. This group of trees is very abstract, yet easily recognizable.

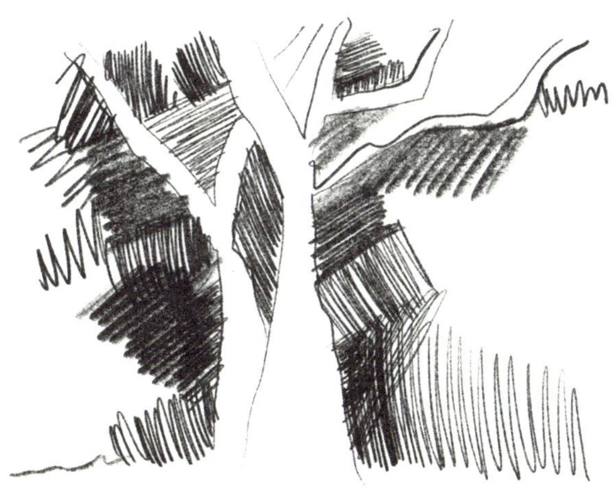

In this sketch, only the shape of the trees is left blank. A few leaves are colored in on the meadow below. Both examples show how our imagination automatically completes images.

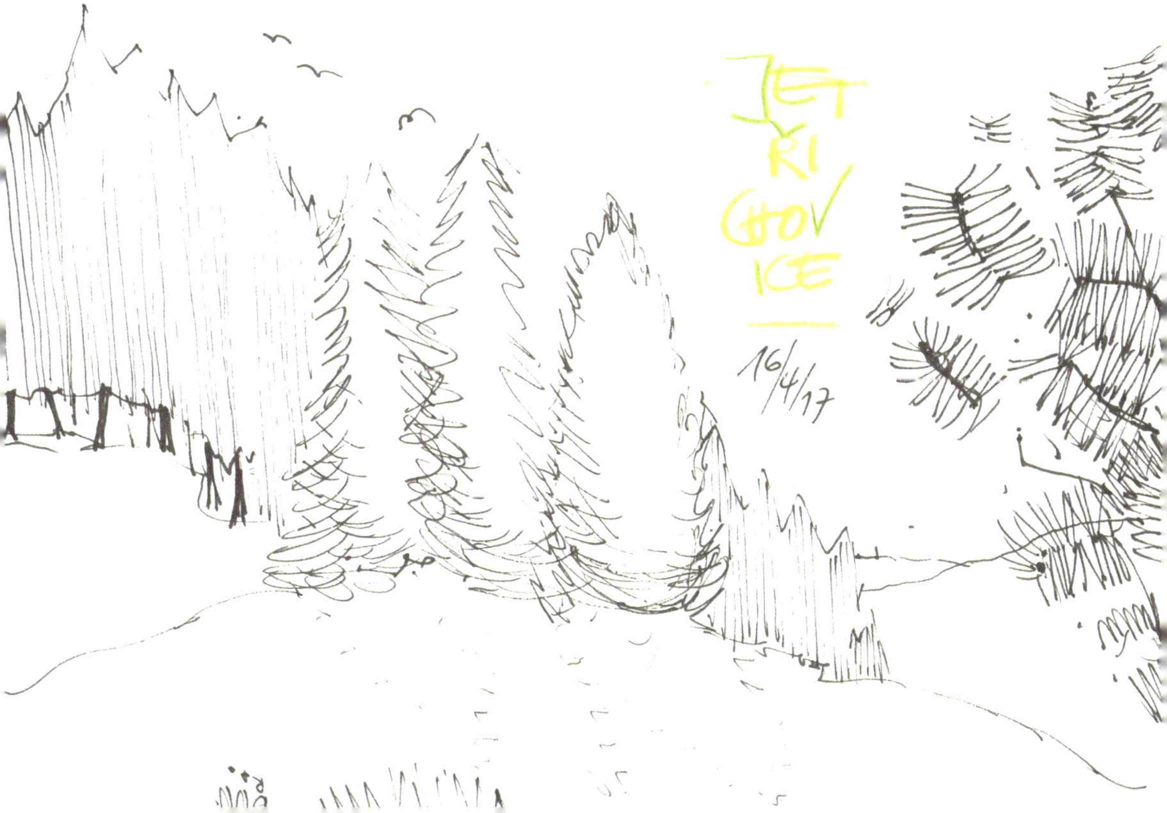

Ways to Practice the Art of Omission

1. Take a straight-on view instead of using perspective: Draw trees, houses, vehicles, and people directly from the front. The two-dimensional depiction provides solidity. Composition, light, and shadow ensure three-dimensionality.

2. Reduce to basic shapes: Almost every tree can be reduced to a basic geometric shape. A cypress to a cylinder, a fir to a triangle, a pine to a rectangle. This reduction is best practiced in black and white.

3. Emphasize silhouettes: Leave out the lower lines of buildings completely. A hard boundary to the ground looks unnatural, while a clear roof contour is even more interesting.

4. Reduce figures: When sketching people, leave out the feet entirely to make the figure appear lighter. The head and upper body are more expressive than the hem of the pants and shoe size.

5. Leave out colors: Fire up the viewer's imagination. The fact that the meadow is green, the sky is blue, and the concrete is gray does not always have to be shown in the picture. Leaving out color or using it sparingly is often more interesting than a lifelike representation.

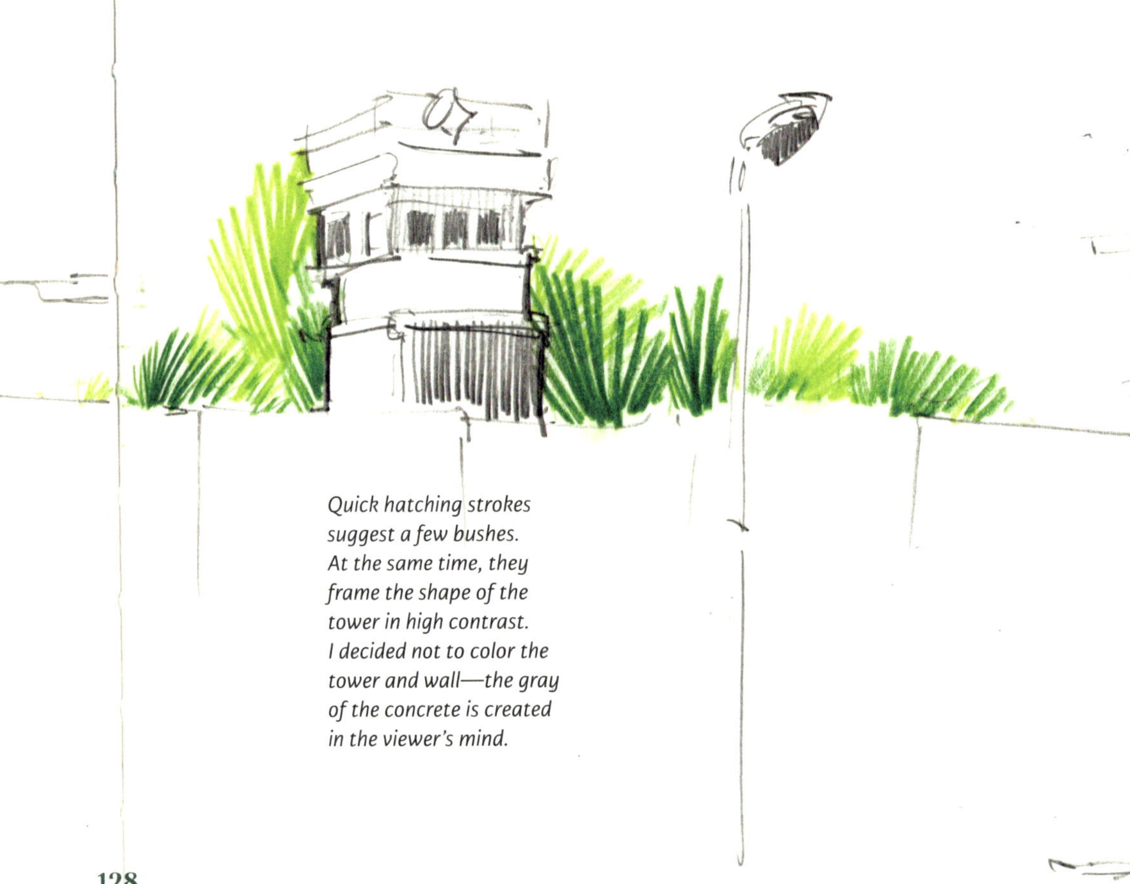

Quick hatching strokes suggest a few bushes. At the same time, they frame the shape of the tower in high contrast. I decided not to color the tower and wall—the gray of the concrete is created in the viewer's mind.

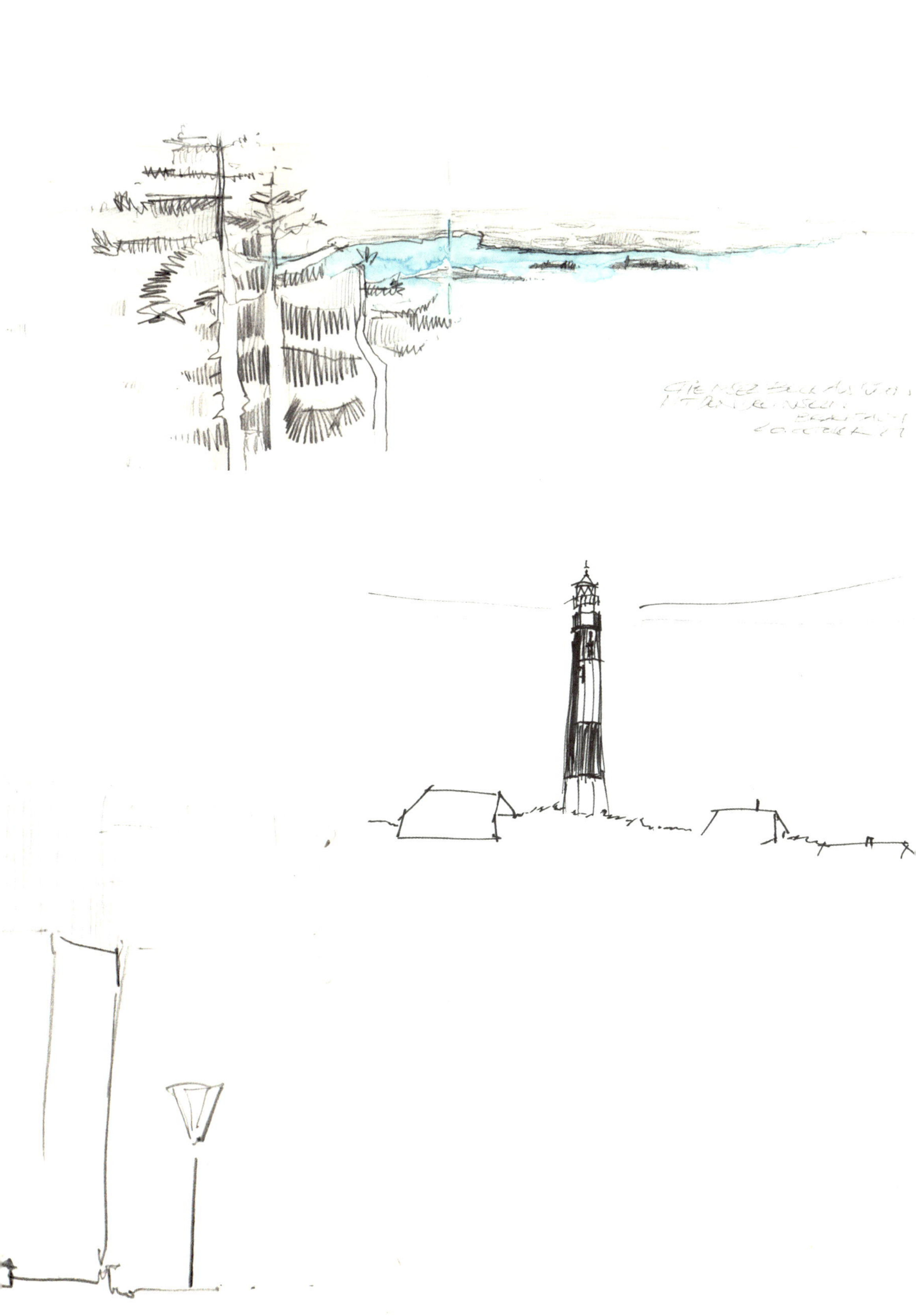

The Freedom of Color

What happens when color is added to a black-and-white sketch? What effect does the line drawing of a landscape or an object have compared to a colored representation of the same?

Without color, a drawing seems "aloof"; it conveys something indeterminate, an unfinished draft (this can also be done intentionally). As soon as color is added, we come closer to reality. This means we have more information about the nature of an object, the character of a scene. But we also have more creative and narrative freedom—a freedom that some beginners struggle with because color can save a picture, but it can also ruin it. Let's delve a little deeper into the world of color on the following pages.

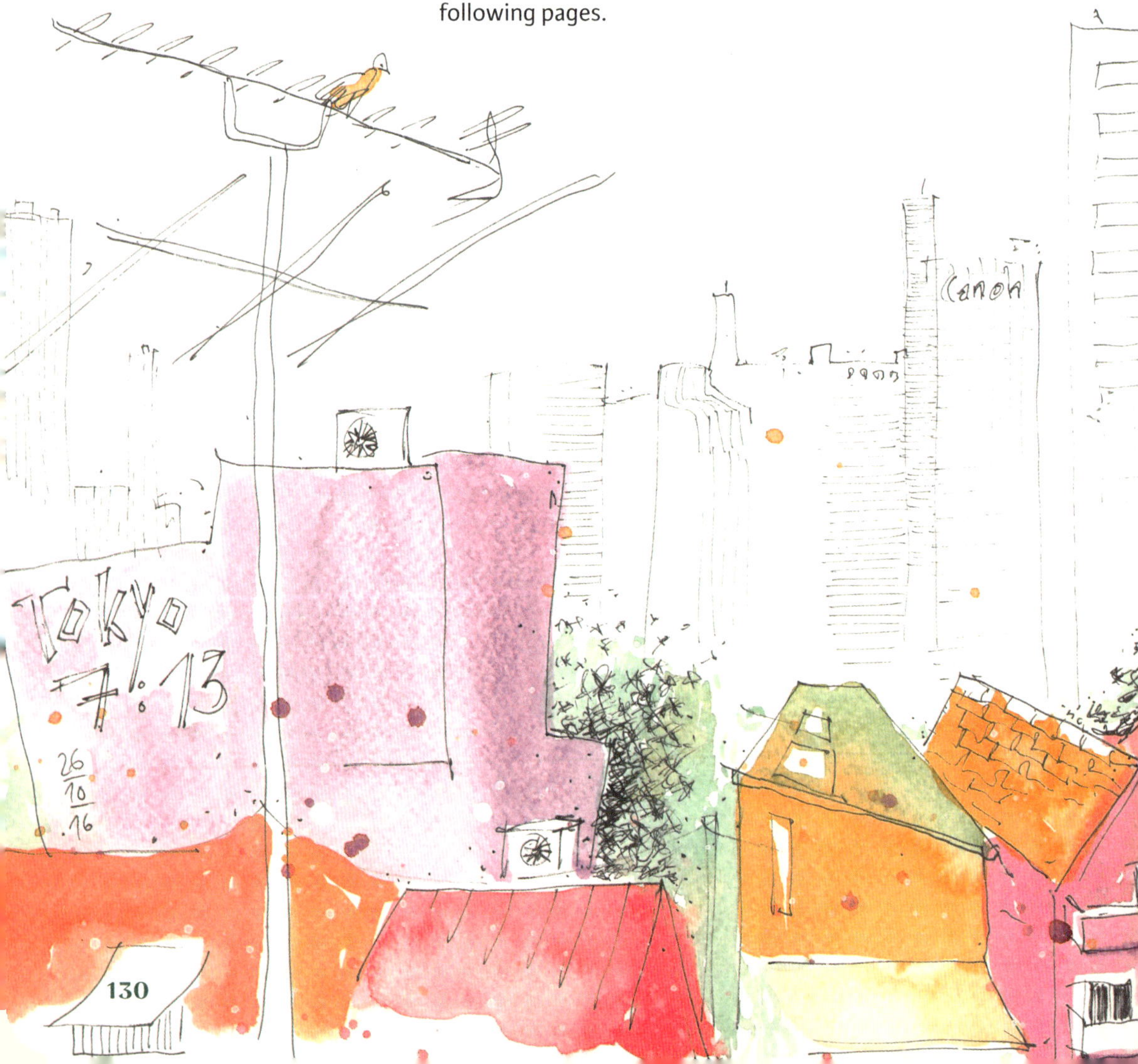

Less Is More

This design adage also applies to the use of color. Apply colors deliberately to highlight important things in the picture. When creating a sketch, decide which parts of the picture are important and highlight them later with color. Too many focal points in the picture cancel each other out. In the same way, a firework of colors won't increase the impact of your drawing.

Real Versus Perceived Colors

Unlike outdoor photography, sketching gives you the advantage of being able to move far away from the "real" colors of your subject. Making your own intuitive color choices that deviate from nature is part of the freedom of art. No one will question your perception of color on that day and in that place. This allows you to intervene in the narrative and achieve certain pictorial effects through color. To stimulate emotions, not to record facts.

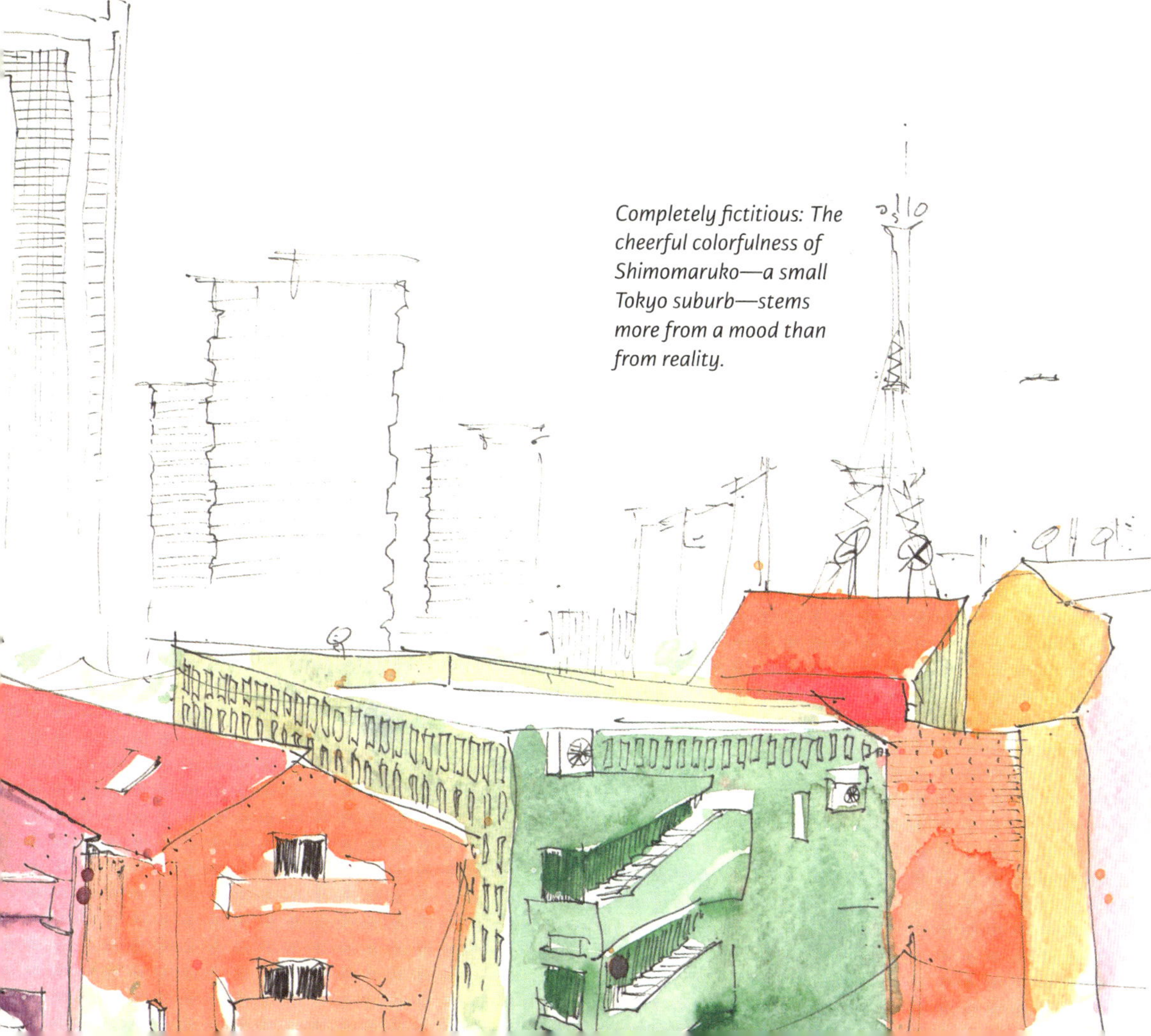

Completely fictitious: The cheerful colorfulness of Shimomaruko—a small Tokyo suburb—stems more from a mood than from reality.

You're moving outdoors with your sketchbook. Quick lines are filling up the page. Now you want to add some color to the picture. Should you open your watercolor set? As we learned in the landscape chapter, colors influence a picture's composition and effect. So, we need to use colors deliberately and systematically. Models like Johannes Itten's twelve-part color wheel help us understand the effect of color contrasts and harmonies and use them in our sketches.

Itten's Color Wheel

With his color wheel, Bauhaus teacher Johannes Itten, also a proponent of outdoor lessons, gave us a reliable tool. Three primary colors (yellow, red, blue) mix in pairs to form secondary colors (orange, violet, green). The mixture of adjacent primary and secondary colors (e.g., yellow and orange to yellowish orange) results in six more colors, the tertiary colors.

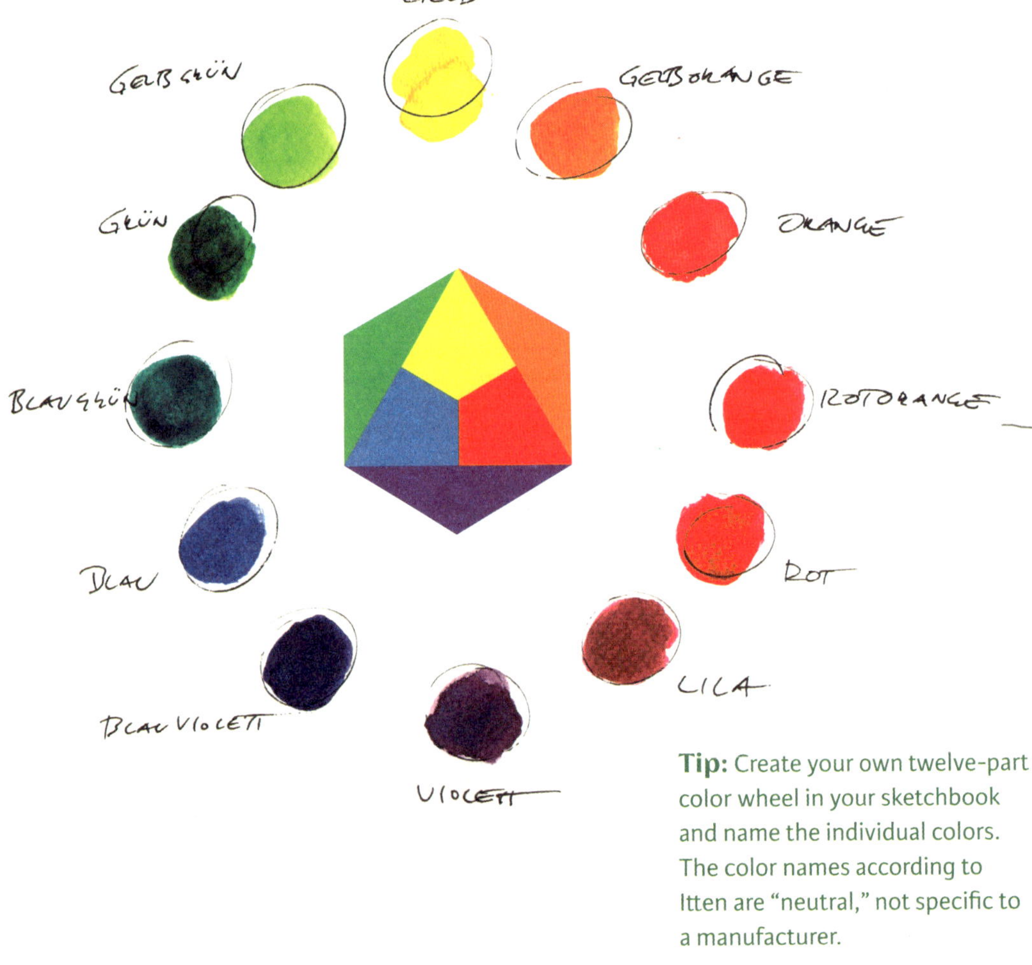

Tip: Create your own twelve-part color wheel in your sketchbook and name the individual colors. The color names according to Itten are "neutral," not specific to a manufacturer.

Pure and Mixed Colors

All colors on the color wheel are pure colors, not lightened, darkened, or further mixed. But how do we assign mixed colors like ochre and brown to this model? To transfer the color theory to the world of travel, think of a globe as a three-dimensional color model: Pure colors would be located at the equator, white at the North Pole, black at the South Pole. All the millions of possible mixtures would be located in between.

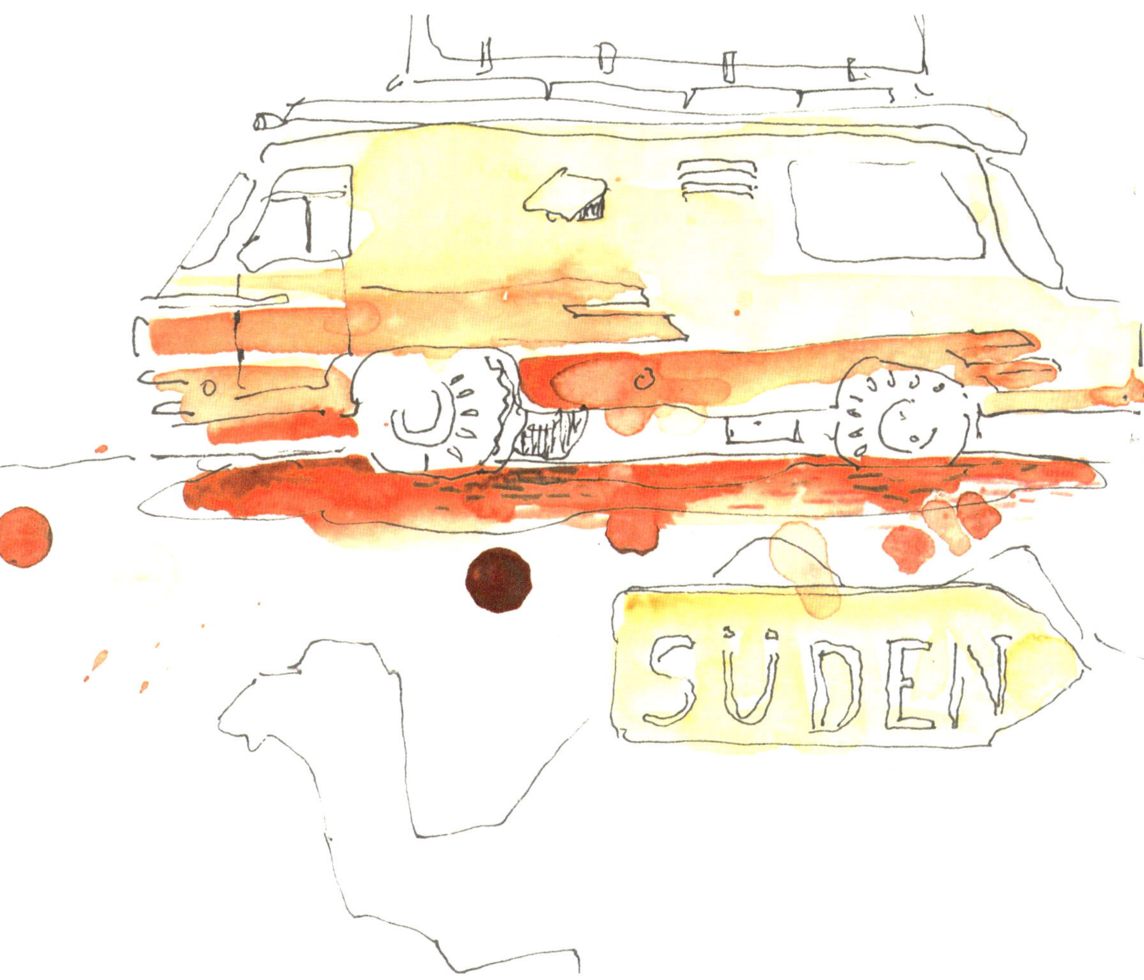

Color Contrasts and Harmony

Contrast and harmony—How do they go together? Should contrasting things harmonize? It's all about the right combination and quantity. How do we arrange colors so that they look good together?

Monochrome Color Harmony

Let's approach it carefully. You can't go far wrong with just one color. A dark watercolor, indigo or caput mortuum, finely modified by adding water, produces a variety of nuances. The mood of the drawing is carried by a single color and radiates a certain calm. Instead of watercolor, I like to use sepia ink for historical buildings—another monochrome technique (see the next chapter).

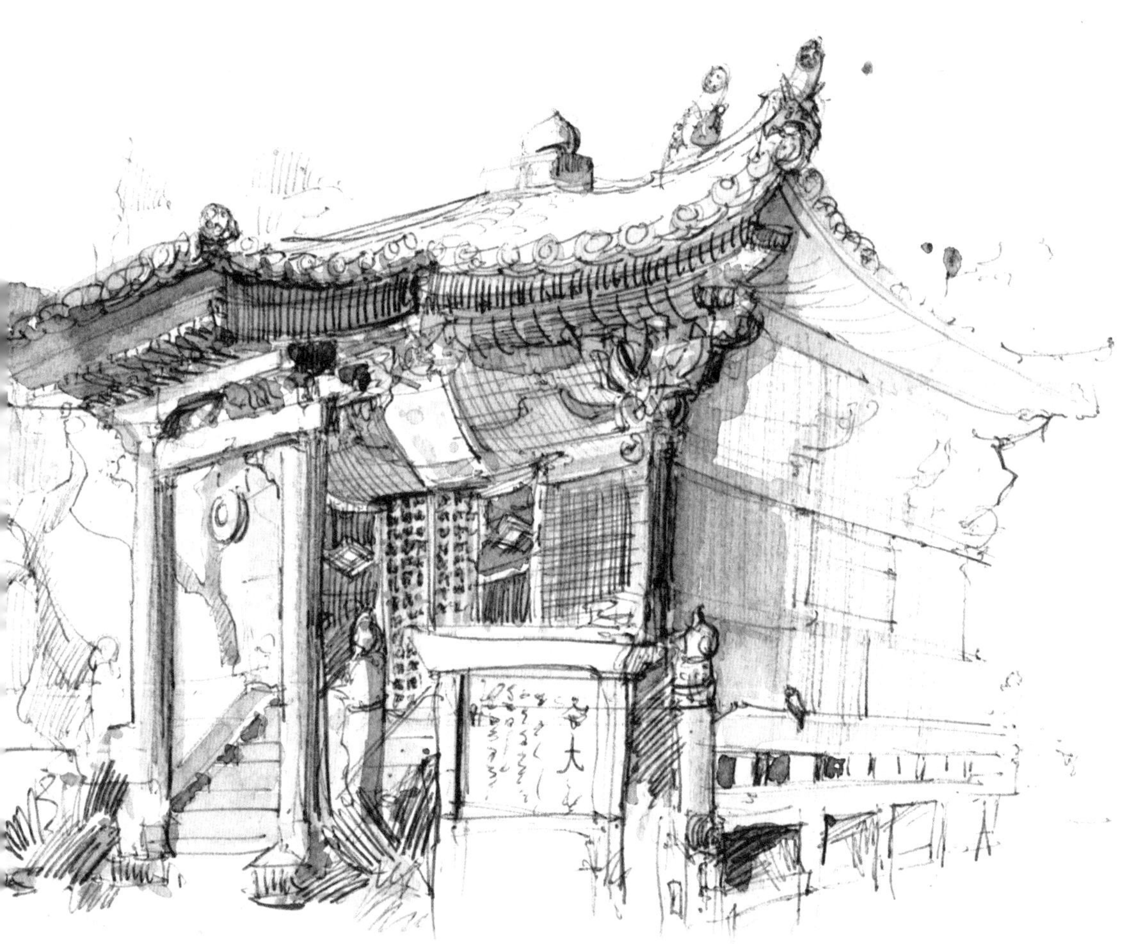

If you add a few direct neighbors from the color wheel to the chosen base color of your picture, things will still be harmonious. Yellow, orange, and red line up easily, as do shades of blue and green.

Tip: Depending on which segment of the color wheel you use, the "basic temperature" of the picture can be determined from the outset, even if the sun is not shining while you're drawing.

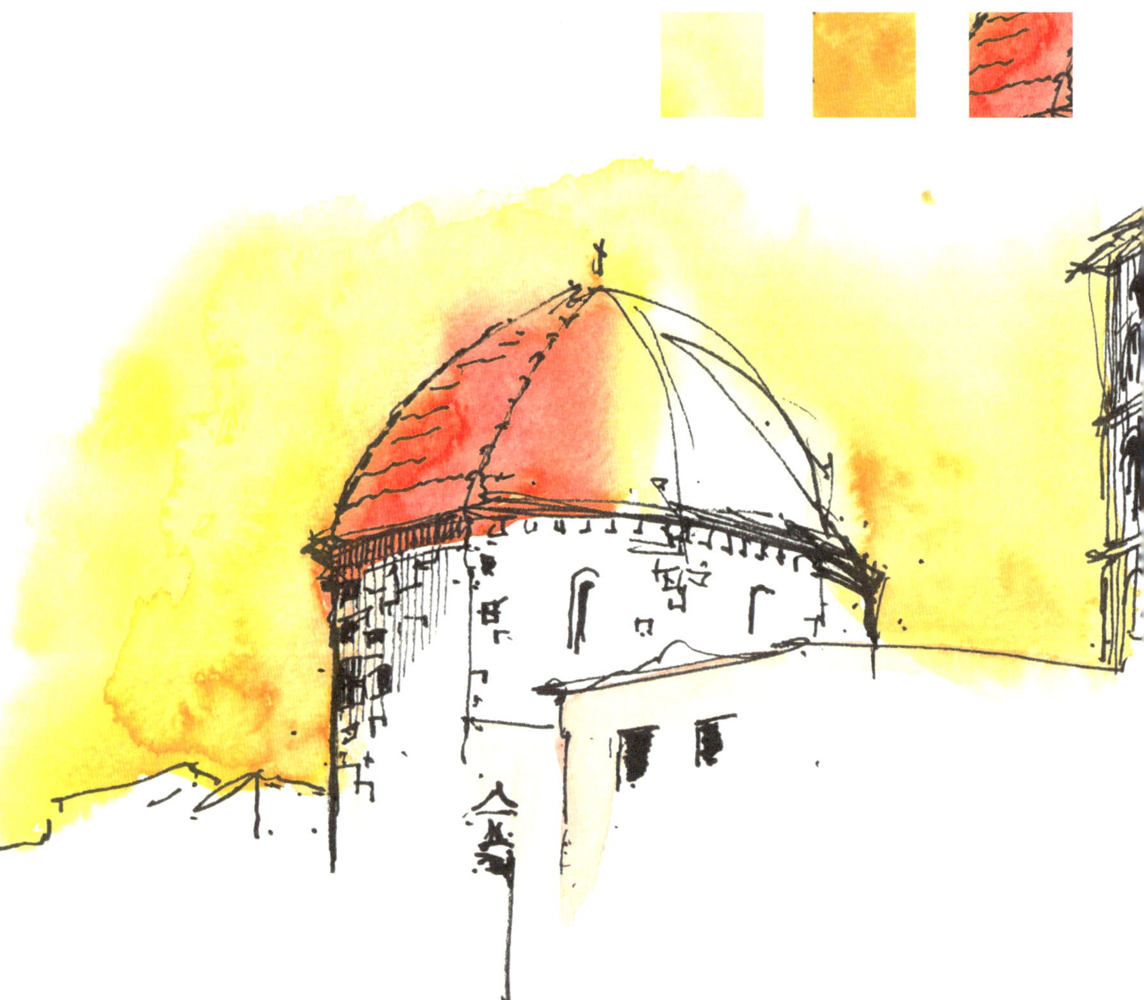

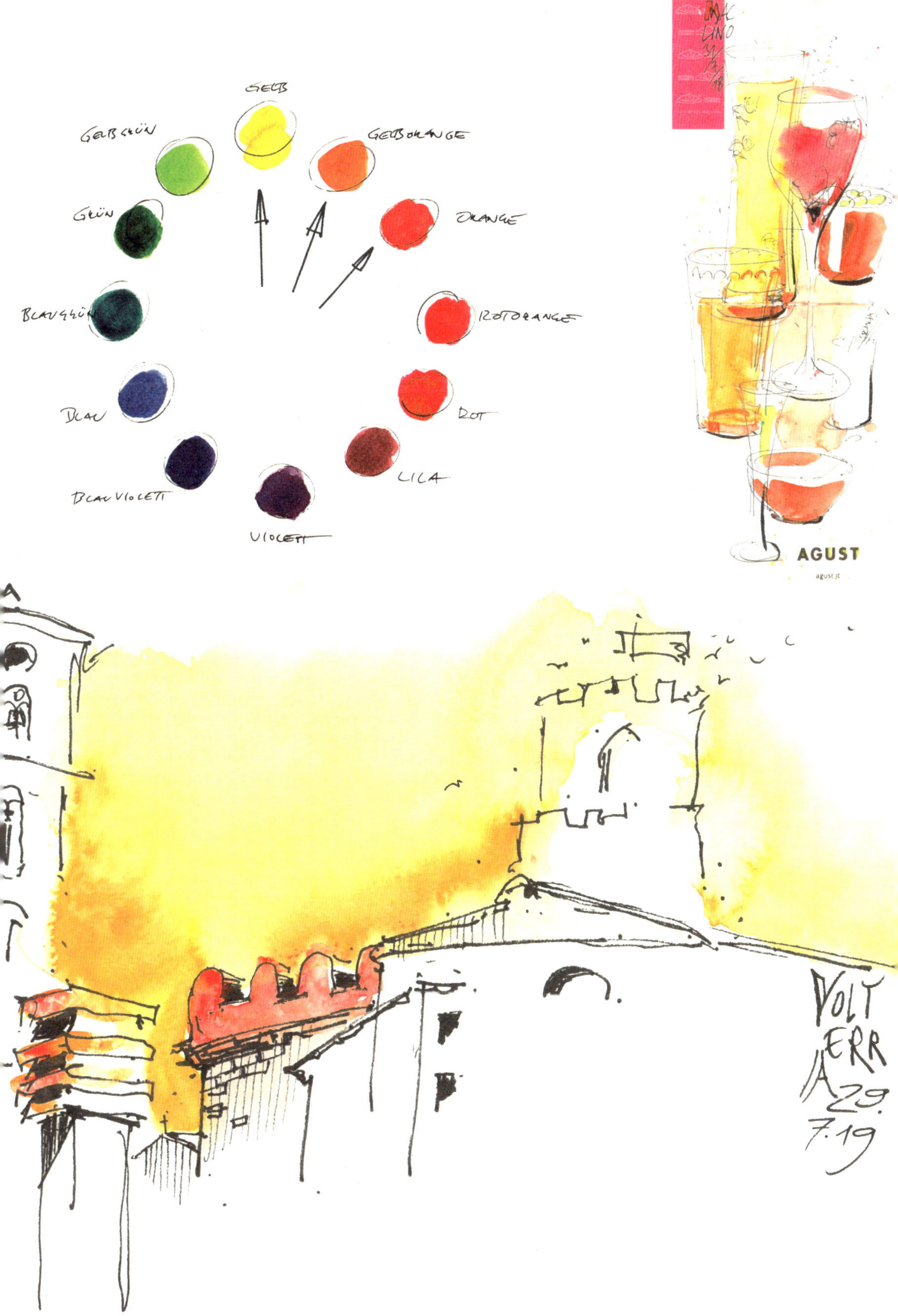
GELBGRÜN
GELB
GELBORANGE
GRÜN
ORANGE
BLAUGRÜN
ROTORANGE
BLAU
ROT
BLAUVIOLETT
LILA
VIOLETT
AGUST
agust.it
VOLTERRA
29.7.19

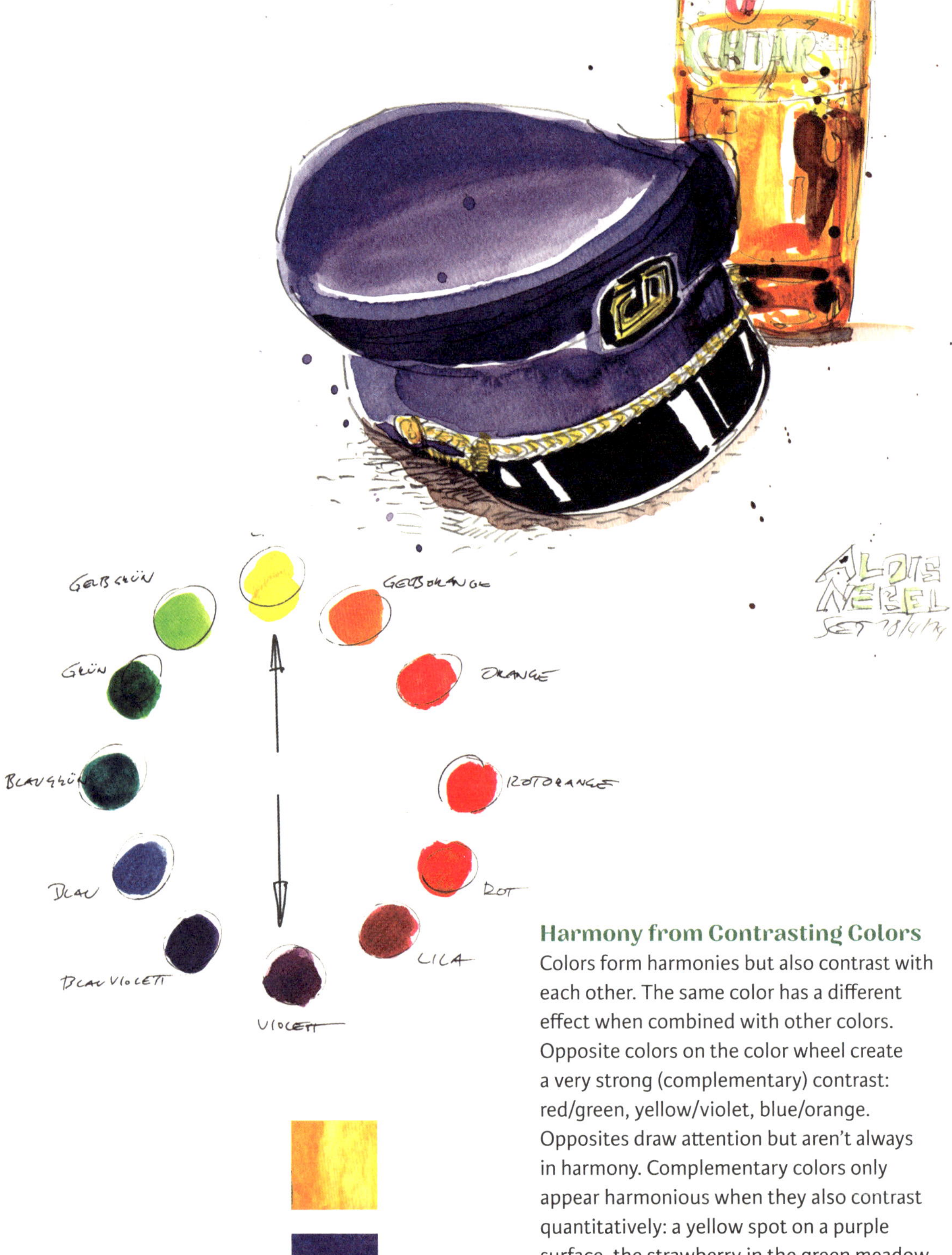

Harmony from Contrasting Colors

Colors form harmonies but also contrast with each other. The same color has a different effect when combined with other colors. Opposite colors on the color wheel create a very strong (complementary) contrast: red/green, yellow/violet, blue/orange. Opposites draw attention but aren't always in harmony. Complementary colors only appear harmonious when they also contrast quantitatively: a yellow spot on a purple surface, the strawberry in the green meadow.

Tip: To prevent complementary color areas from "outshining" each other, I place dark separating areas in between or leave some white paper.

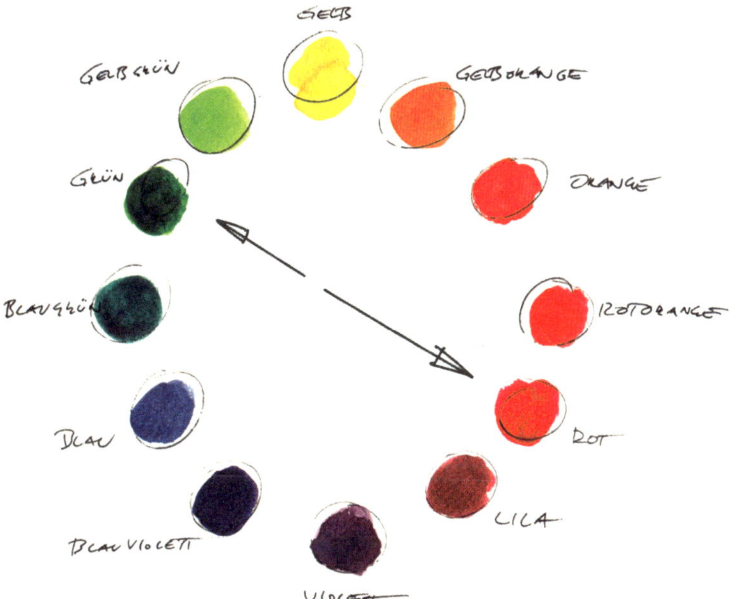

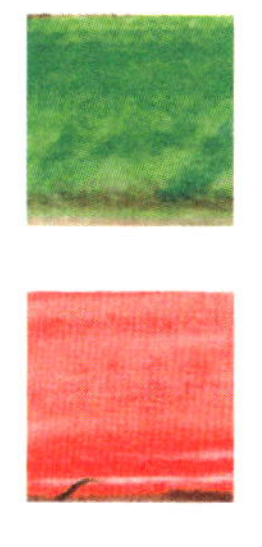

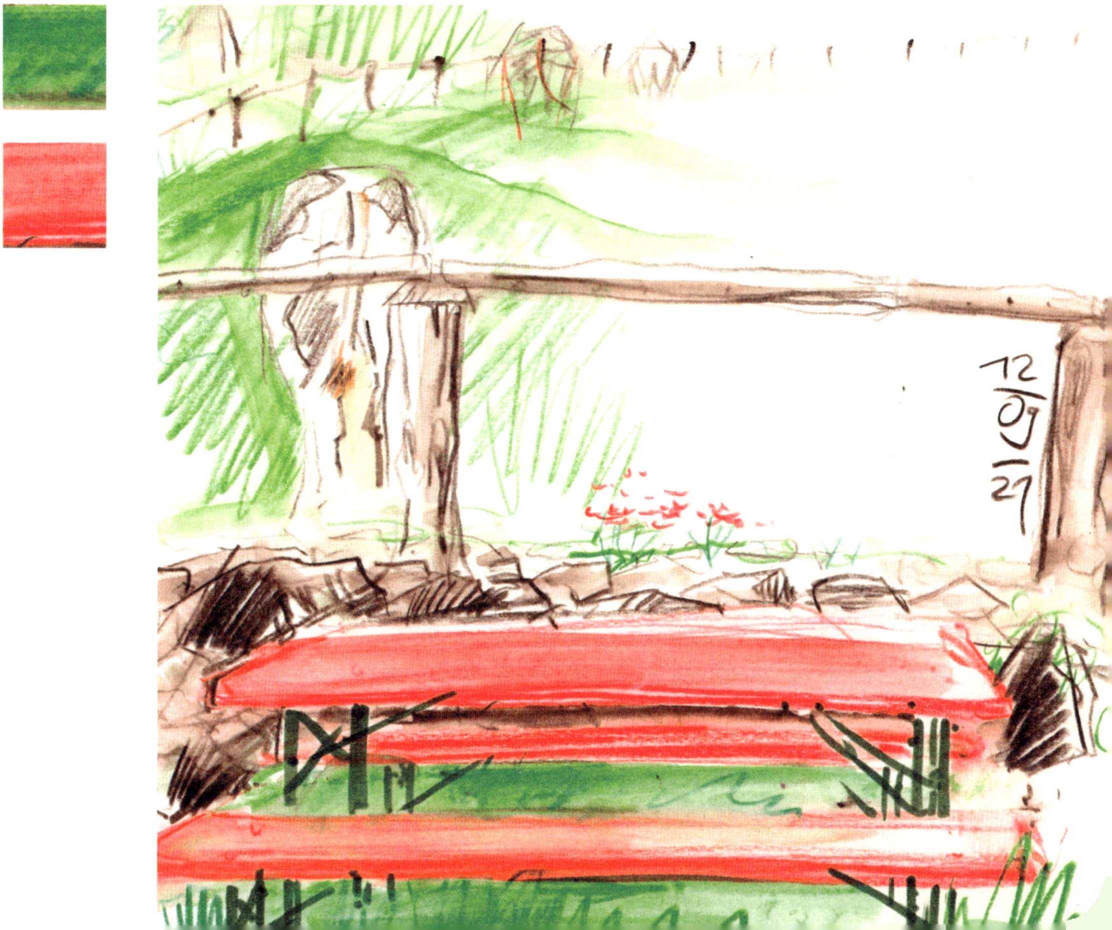

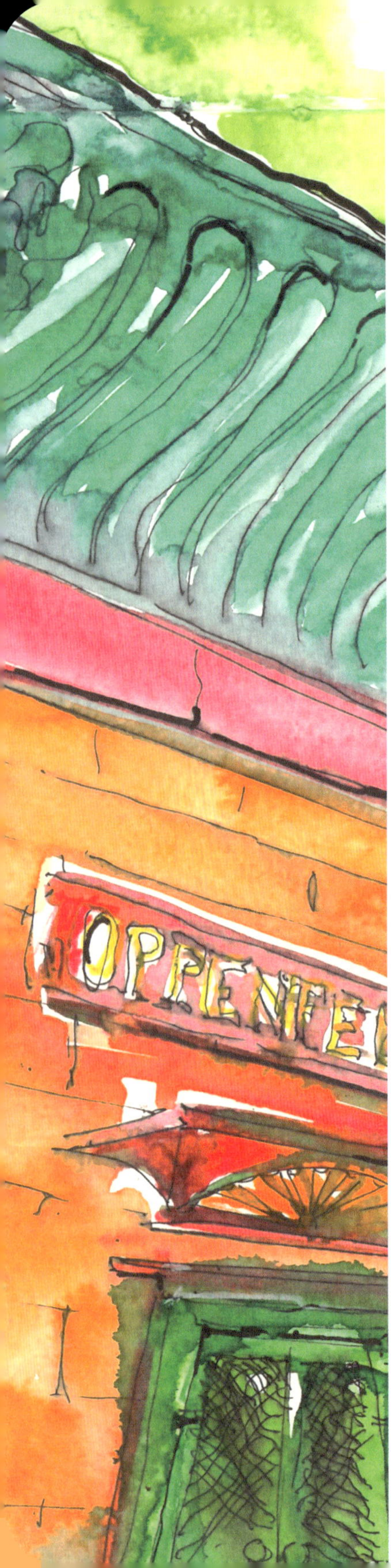

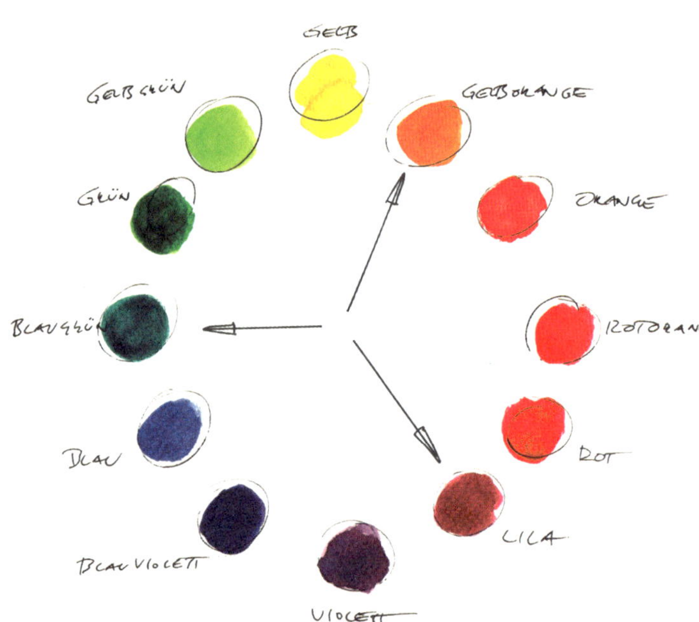

Harmony of Three or More Colors

Now we're really mixing things up. Using triadic and tetradic color harmonies is a good way to continue working freely—but not haphazardly—with color. Colors that are evenly spaced within the color wheel produce harmonious color tones, while irregular spacing tends to lead to disharmony in the combination of colors.

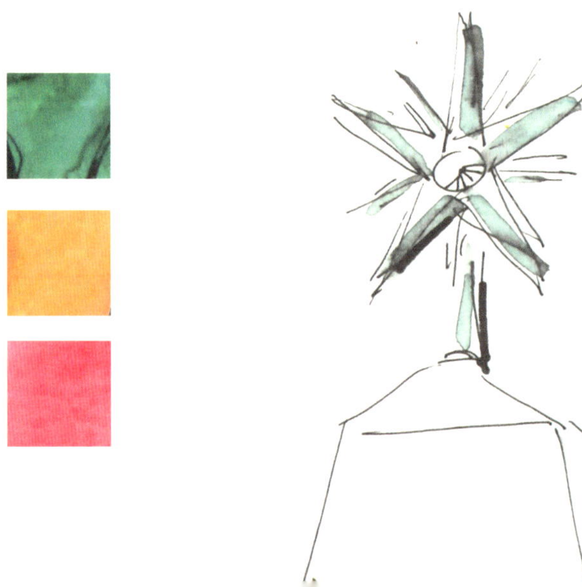

Triadic Harmonies

If I choose three colors spaced equally apart on the color wheel, this is called a triadic harmony. The colors are arranged in a triangular shape within the color wheel. Two triadic harmonies are already formed by the primary and secondary colors.

Tetradic Harmonies

If I choose four colors spaced equally apart on the color wheel, this is called a tetradic harmony. The colors are arranged in a square within the color wheel.

You'll often find two or three colors from a triadic or tetradic order already in your subject. Don't be afraid to exchange or add real colors to complete a color harmony you need for your picture.

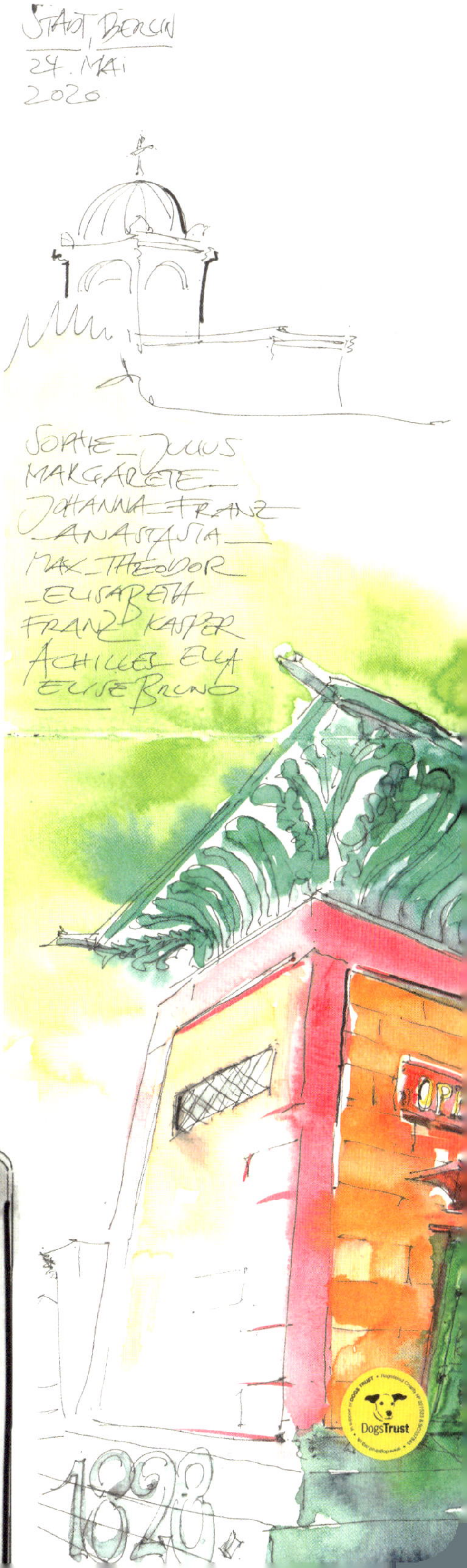

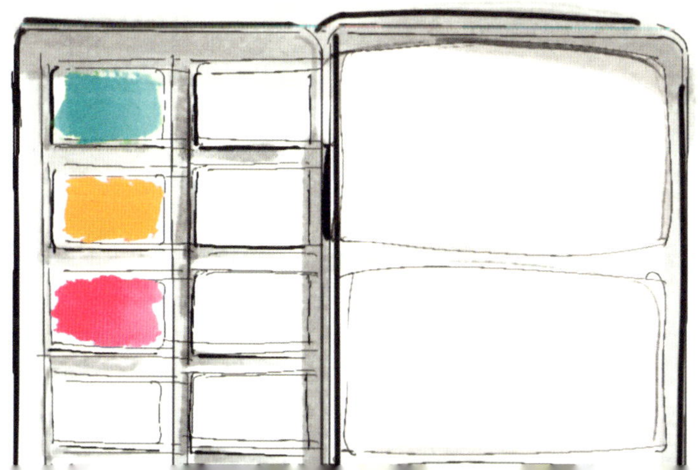

Harmony of Saturated and Unsaturated Colors (Quality Contrast)

Too much pure, saturated color is usually not good for a picture. It looks loud and arbitrary. Pure colors are more effective when combined with muted, unsaturated colors like gray, brown, or beige. Single pure colors stand out best in neutral surroundings; otherwise, they drown each other out.

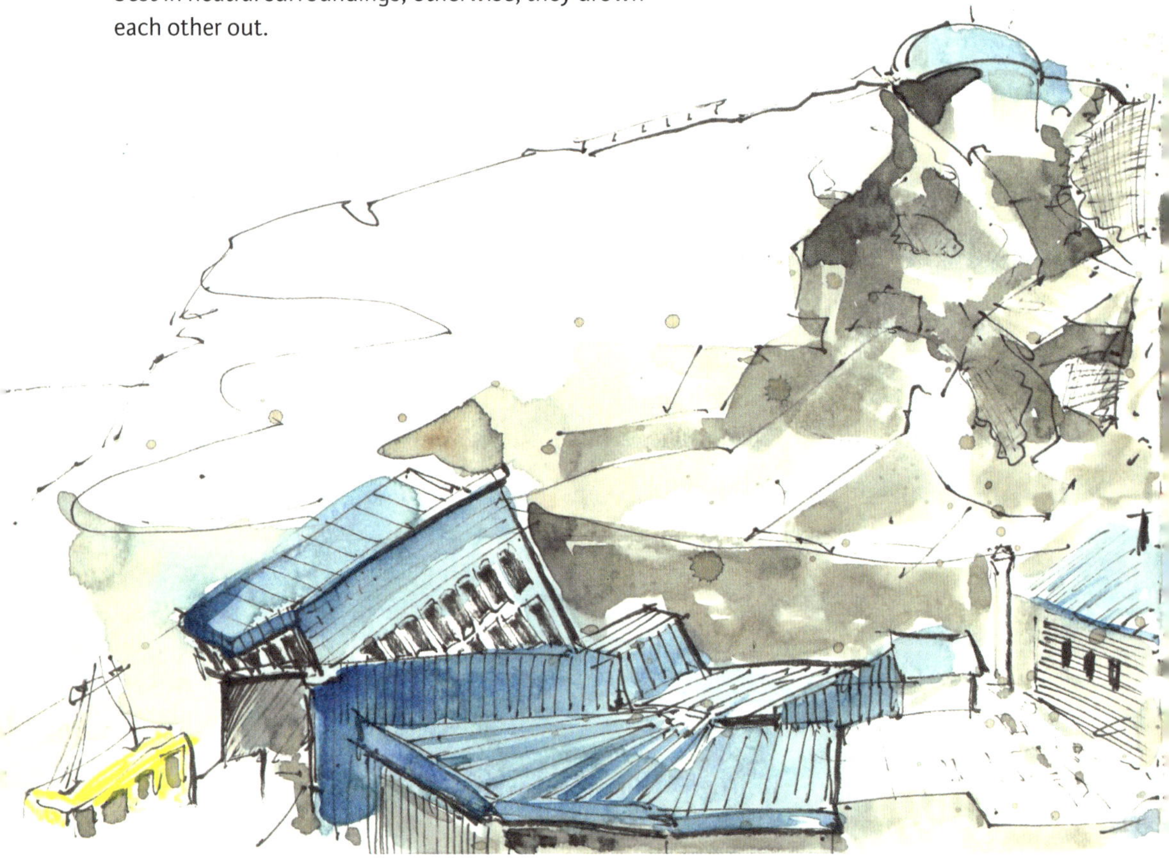

When pure colors meet: A clear, quantitative contrast calms the image—only a little yellow against a lot of blue in the roof surfaces.

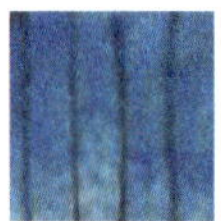

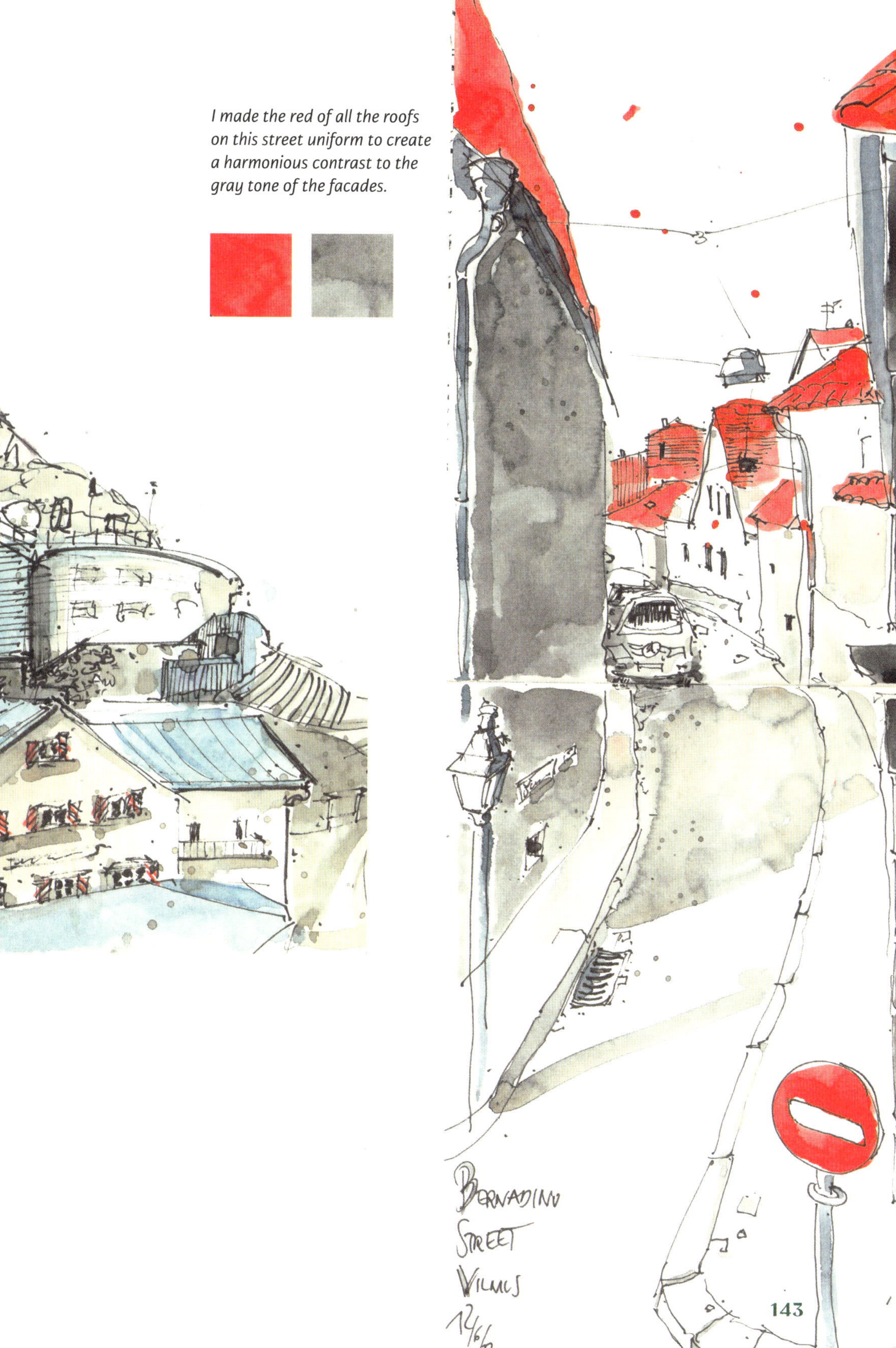

I made the red of all the roofs on this street uniform to create a harmonious contrast to the gray tone of the facades.

143

Harmony of Warm and Cool Colors
(Warm-Cool Contrast)

The combination of warm and cool colors creates appealing effects. While warm colors suggest closeness, picture elements in cool colors move into the distance (see Atmospheric and Color Perspective on page 76).

Warm colors have a heightened impact next to cool colors, and vice versa. The "temperature" that a color conveys to us only emerges in the juxtaposition. You can find an example of this to the right.

Warm yellow against indigo blue: Subconsciously, we also perceive the material and assign "cool" to the cast iron of the lantern.

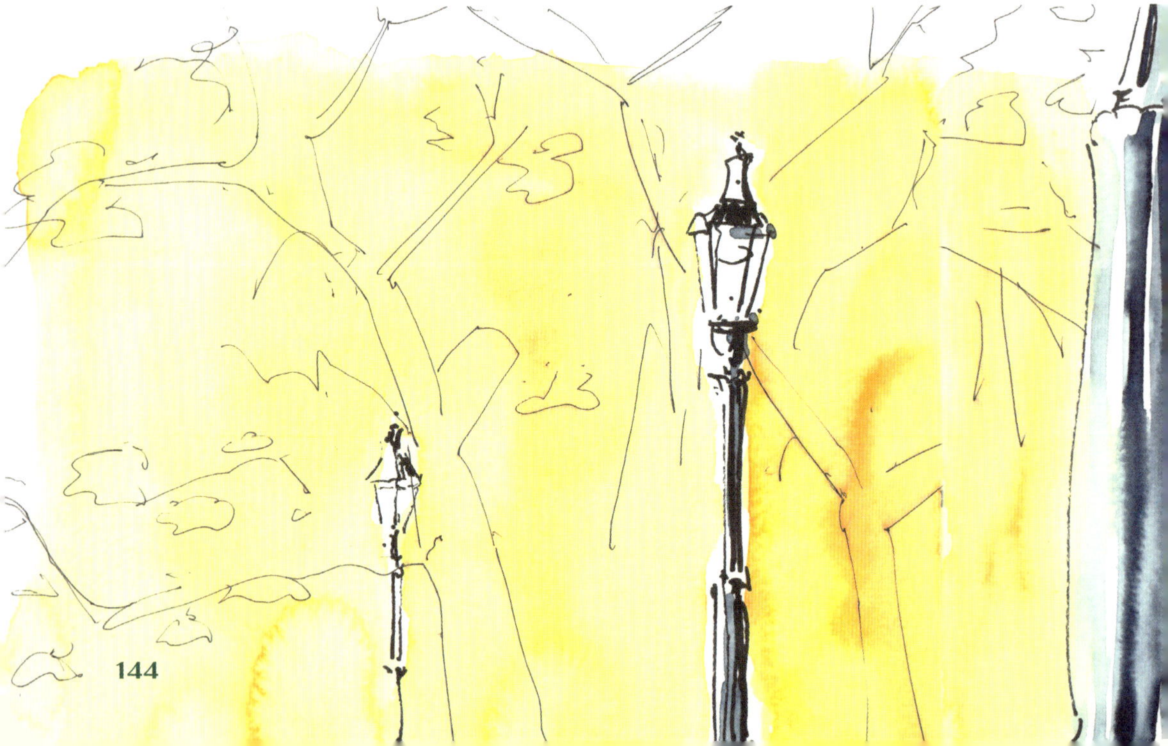

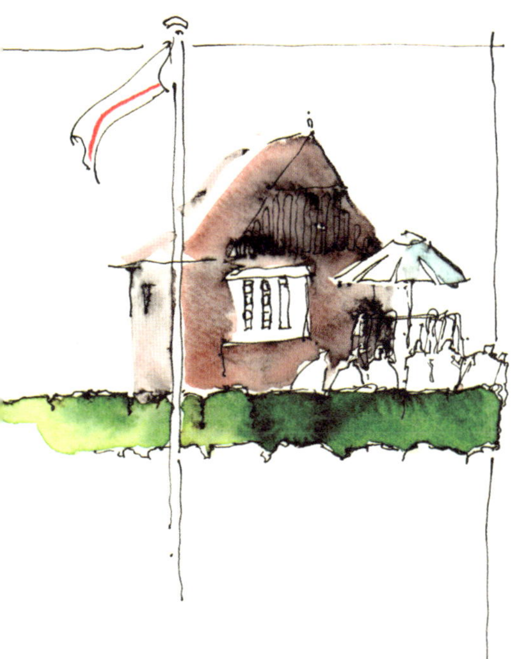

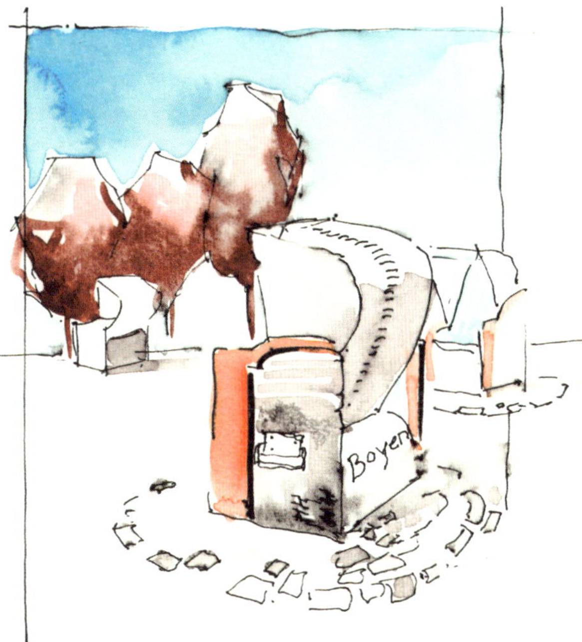

The purple of the house appears as a cooler color compared to the yellow-green of the hedge.

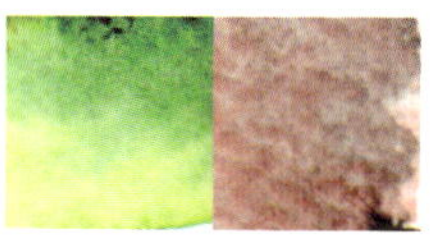

The same purple (here trees) is perceived as a warmer color compared to the blue (sky).

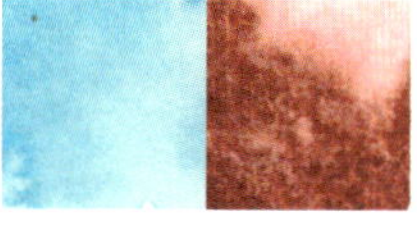

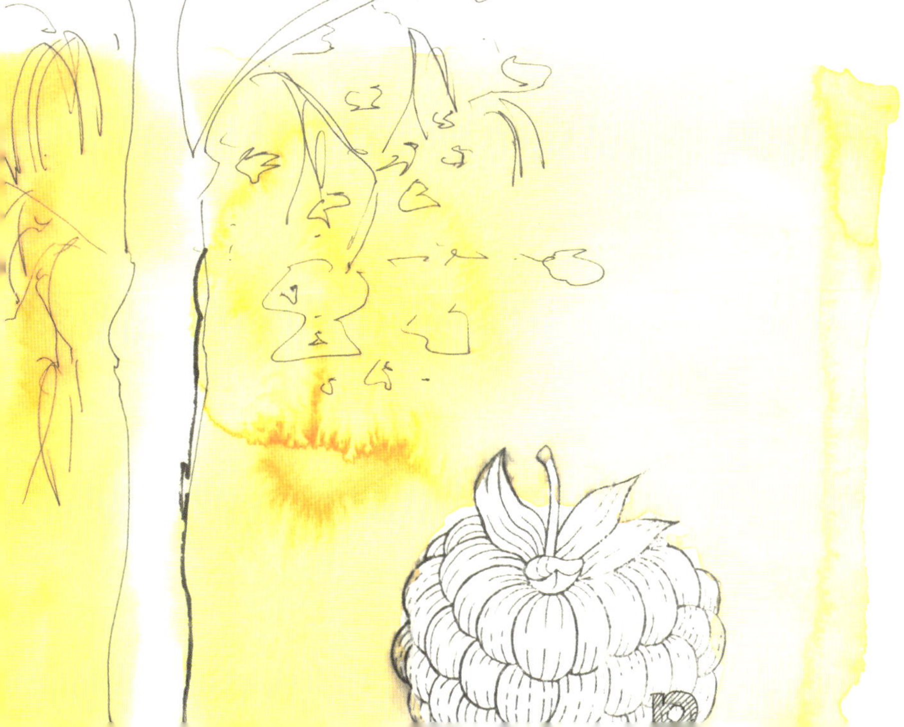

Colors Define Our Style

All theory aside, the effect of colors varies from person to person. Color perception remains a subjective matter for which only limited universal rules can be established; we are too influenced by culture, upbringing, and personal experience.

Favorite Colors

Just as you're drawn to your favorite places, just as one landscape type is dearer to you than others, you will always fall back on a palette of favorite colors. That's understandable. Some artists always use the same color palette and make it their trademark.

Maybe it's time to leave the comfort zone of your favorite colors with your next purchase of drawing materials, your new sketchbook, or your upcoming sketching tour.

Whether you're inspired by a fresh new watercolor set or undiscovered places, it's always a good idea to embark on experiments with color.

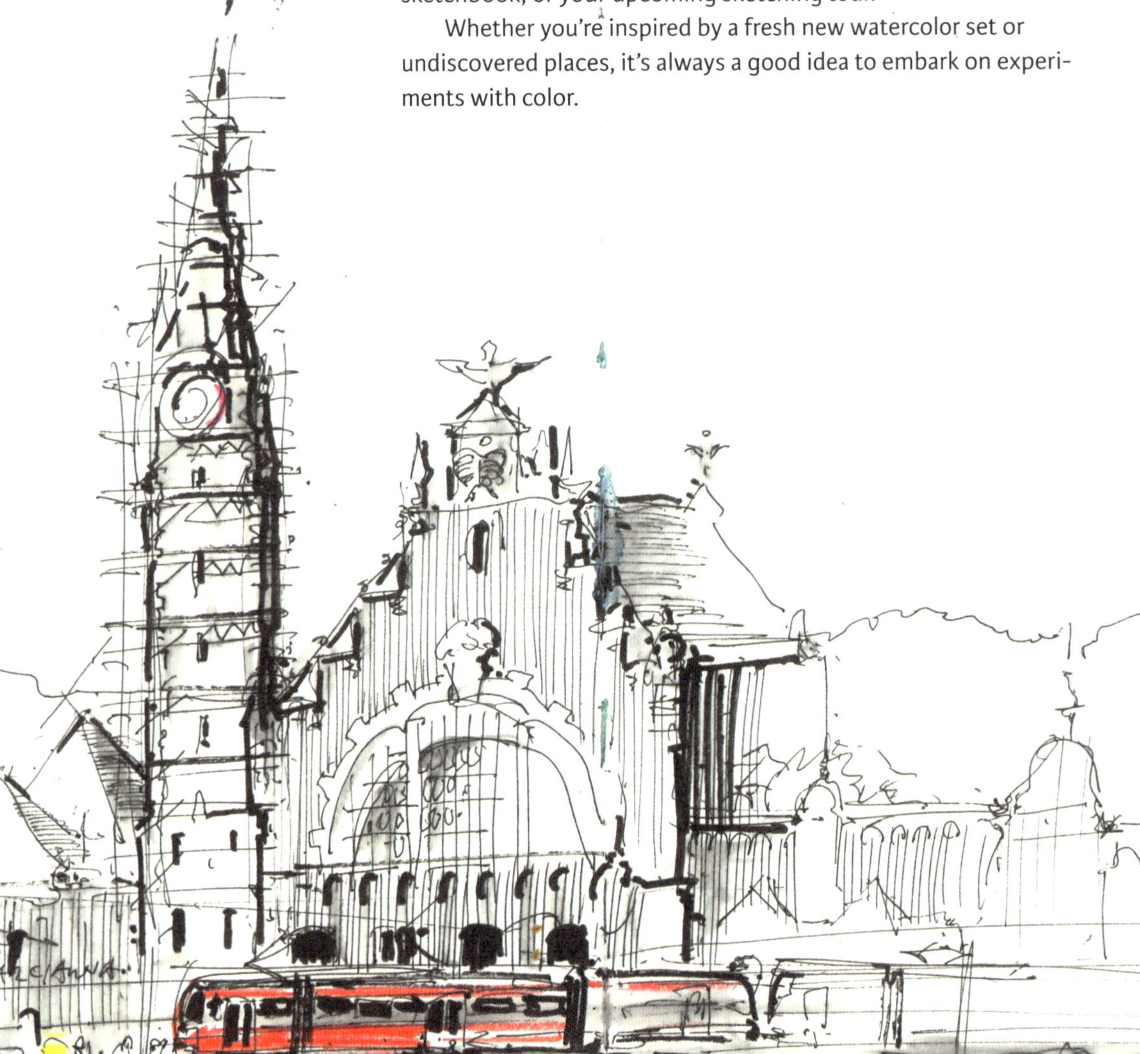

Color Cards: Putting It to the Test

I made my own color cards with the manufacturer's color codes to use while traveling. There are three good reasons to always have your own color cards with you:

1. The color is easier to assess on paper than on your watercolor palette; the colors in the little pots can be deceptive.
2. Harmonious color combinations can be mixed and matched by placing the cards next to each other.
3. If you buy additional colors, you don't have to search long for the color code.

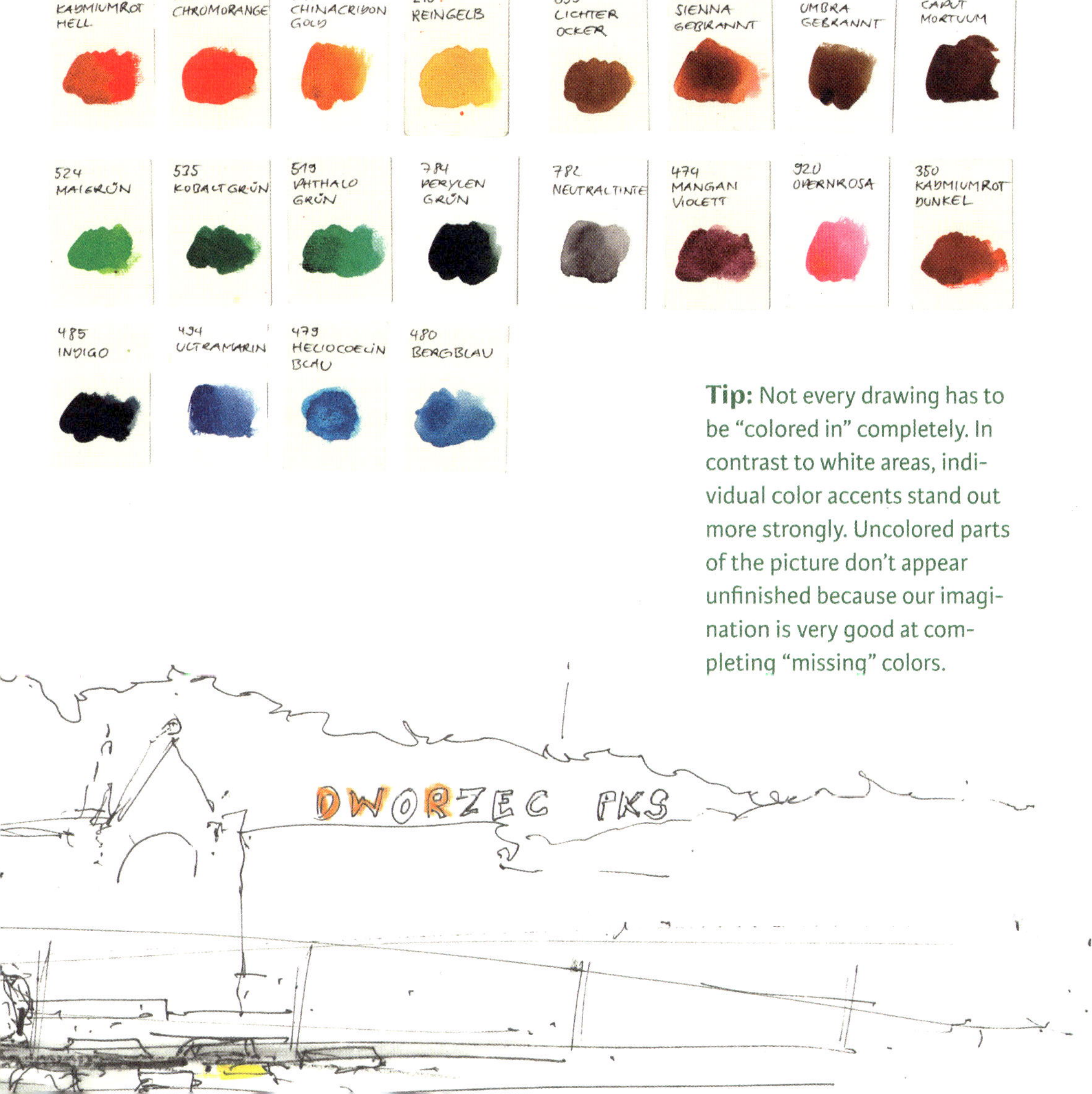

Tip: Not every drawing has to be "colored in" completely. In contrast to white areas, individual color accents stand out more strongly. Uncolored parts of the picture don't appear unfinished because our imagination is very good at completing "missing" colors.

Towns and Locales 6

Let's stay outdoors, but leave the wilderness behind for more civilized locations. In the previous chapters, we looked at ways to capture a landscape in a sketchbook while keeping our feet dry and examining natural forms and colors along the way.

In urban areas, other visual stimuli attract our attention: big-city architecture, traffic arteries, crowds of people. Or on a smaller scale: tranquil street scenes in small towns, historic squares, the slow pace of life.

All of this belongs in your sketchbook.

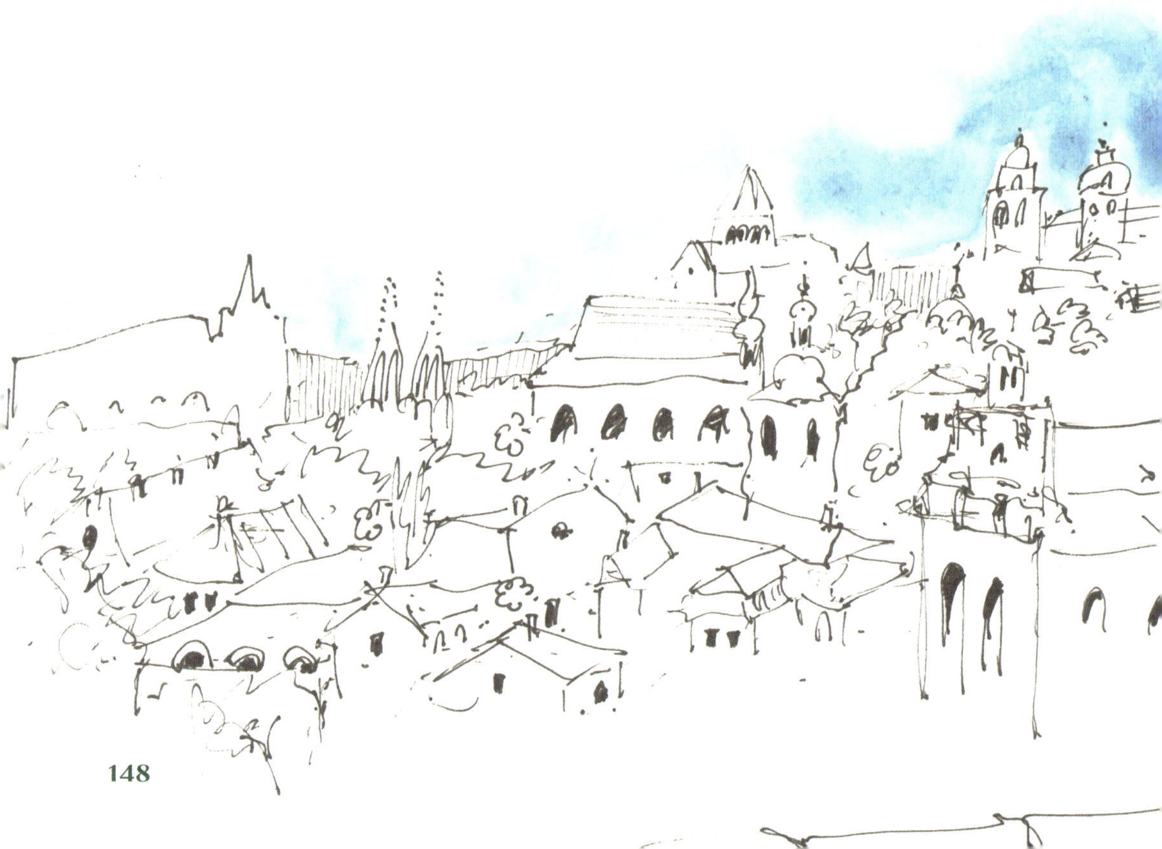

Drawing should be fun. It can enhance a trip, take you
out of your everyday routine, and provide a creative
spark. Don't spend too much time searching for the
ideal place to draw. Pay attention to where you are right
now. When you arrive at a new place, your perceptions
are intense: a certain light, an architectural style, the
clothes people are wearing. Try to capture that first
moment in your sketchbook.

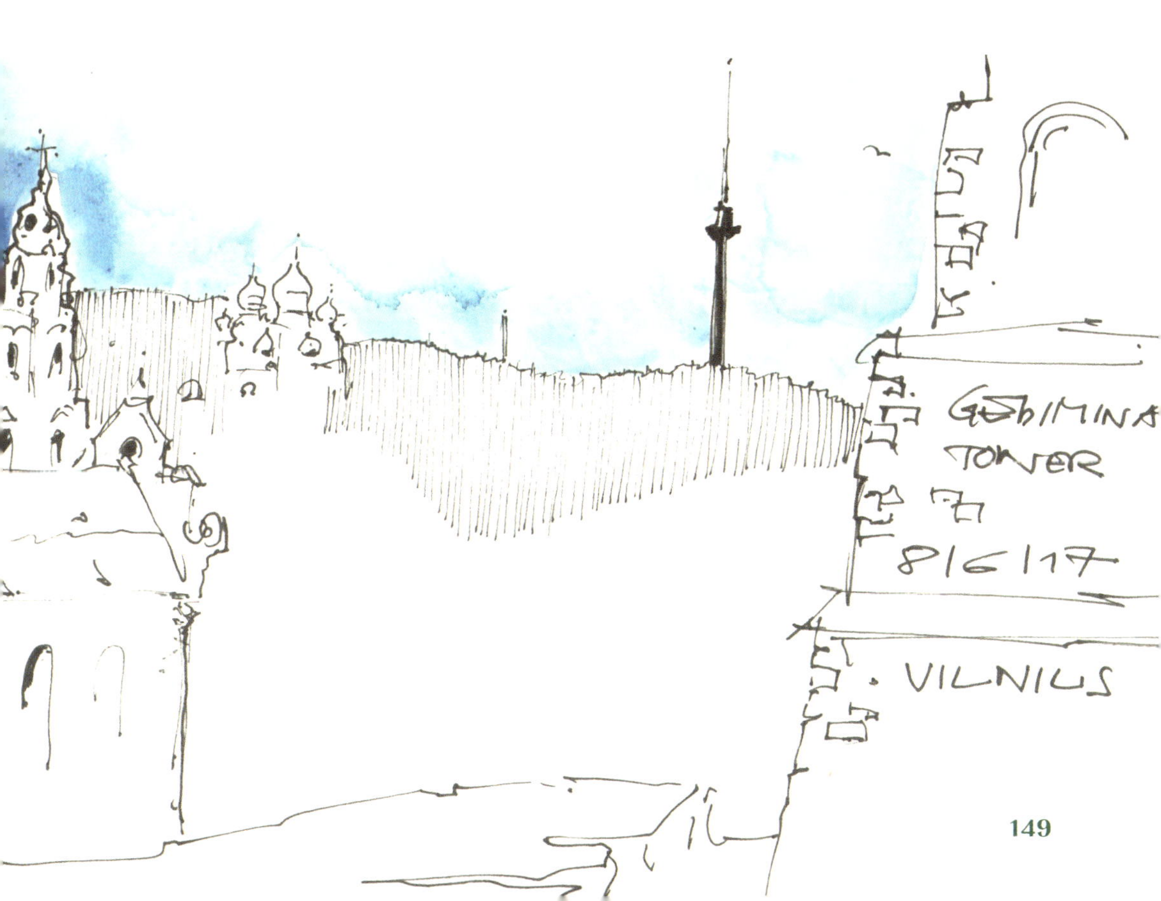

Detour: Seaside Towns

Some travel sketchers love the cosmopolitan character of large port cities; others prefer the picturesque charm of a remote coastal village. Both are appealing subjects, especially when you discover what lies behind the picture-postcard backdrop. Wander with a trained eye through steep, curving streets and winding alleys, past weathered houses and squares with their blend of beauty and decay. Draw what fascinates you about seaside towns from your own perspective.

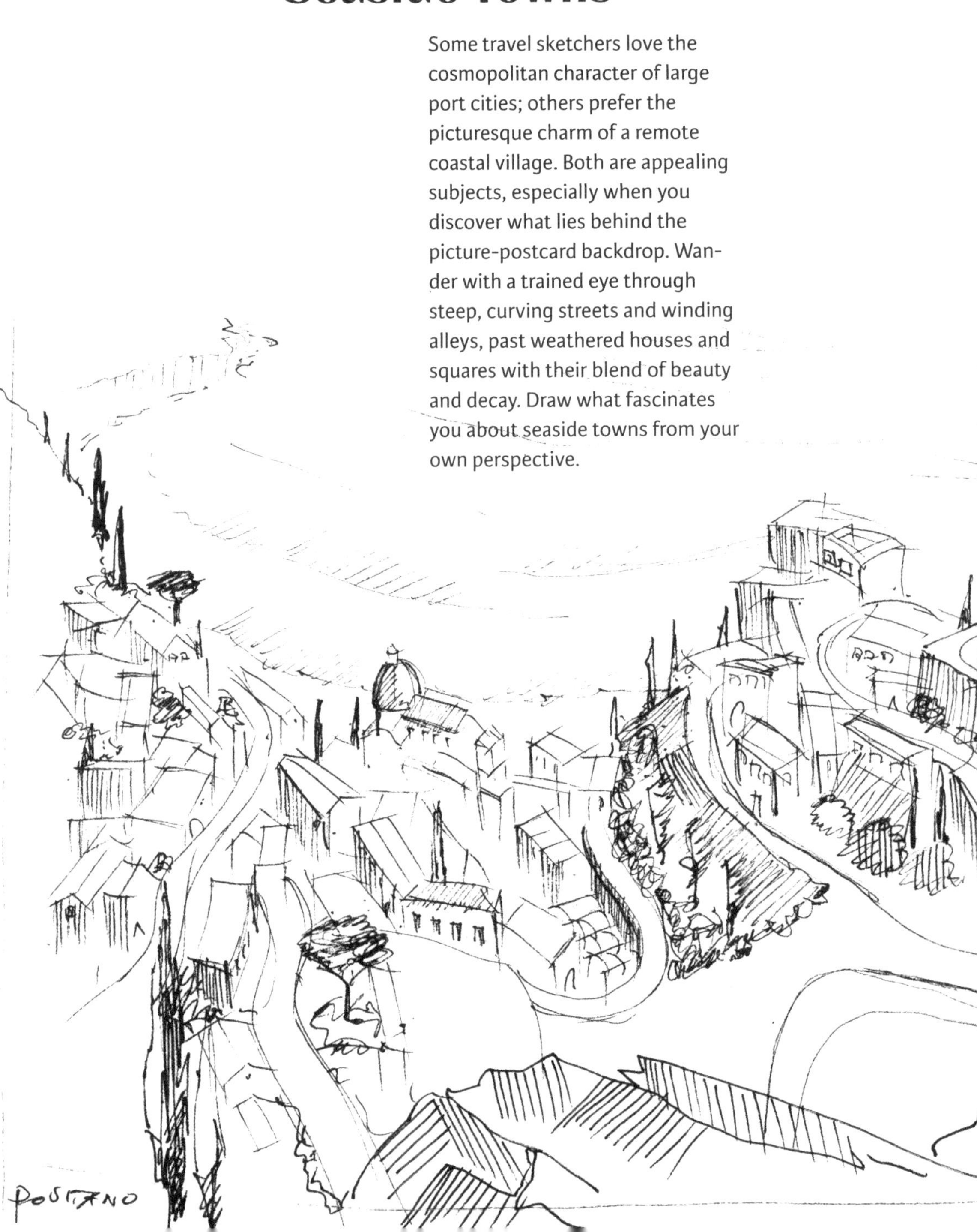

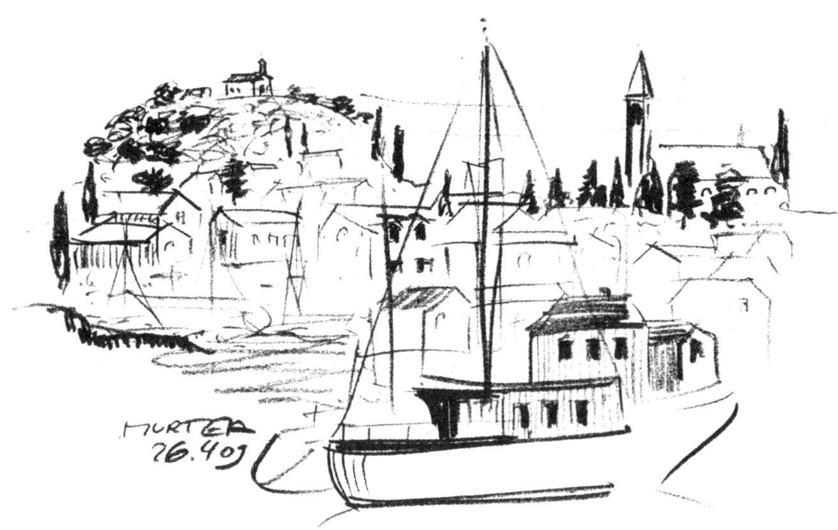

Drop anchor and draw: The ship is still moving and I have yet to set foot on land, but I like to use the moment of arrival to make a quick sketch. A few strokes and a couple of minutes of my time are all it takes.

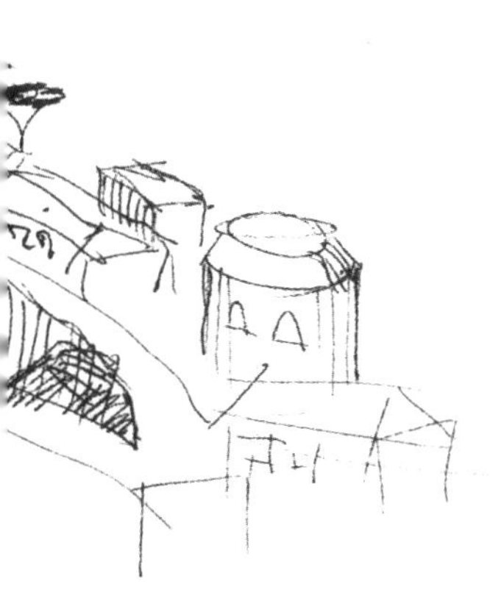

Tip: Up and down the Amalfi Coast: To better capture the picturesque streetscape of Positano, I chose a location high above the town— far from the crowds of tourists.

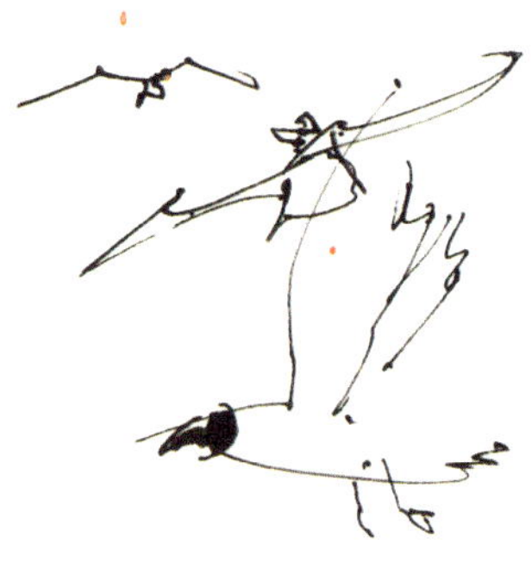

Your Perspective Matters

Instead of staying at the harbor and gazing out to sea like everyone else, I recommend venturing farther inland into the seaside towns, into local life, to the subjects in the second row.

That's what I did for my watercolor sketch in the village on the Ligurian coast on the right. I left the hustle and bustle of the harbor behind me and took up position in the shade of an entranceway. From there, my gaze wandered through the alley in front of me. The buildings seemed to be moving toward each other, so close and narrow that only a three-wheeler could fit through.

Via Roma: The curved retaining walls between the houses create an extraordinary effect of depth. I used fineliners and warm watercolors to modulate the tunnellike composition. The only spectators were the seagulls.

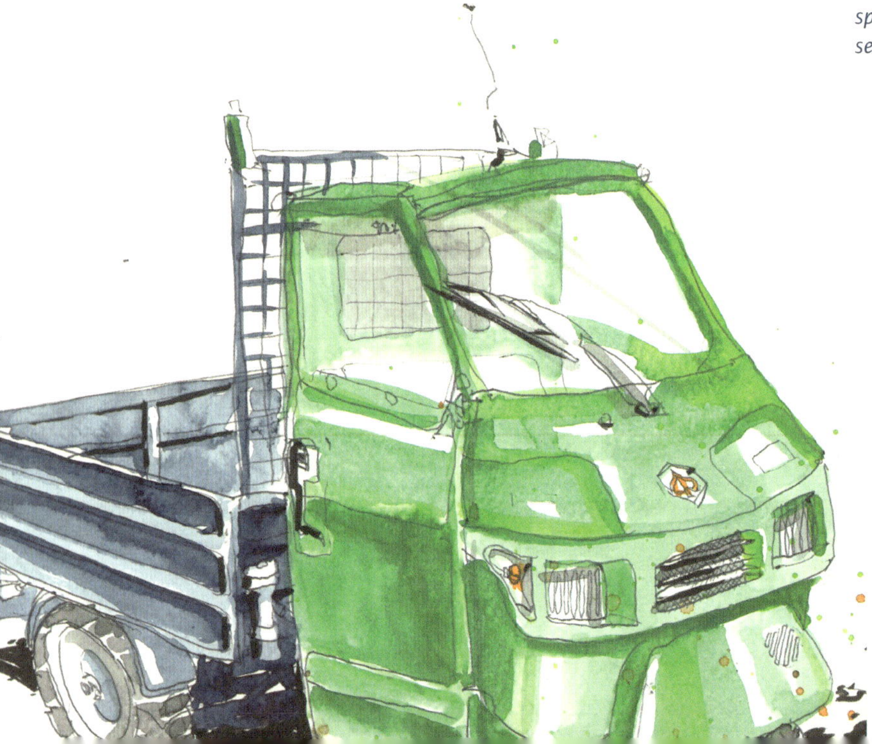

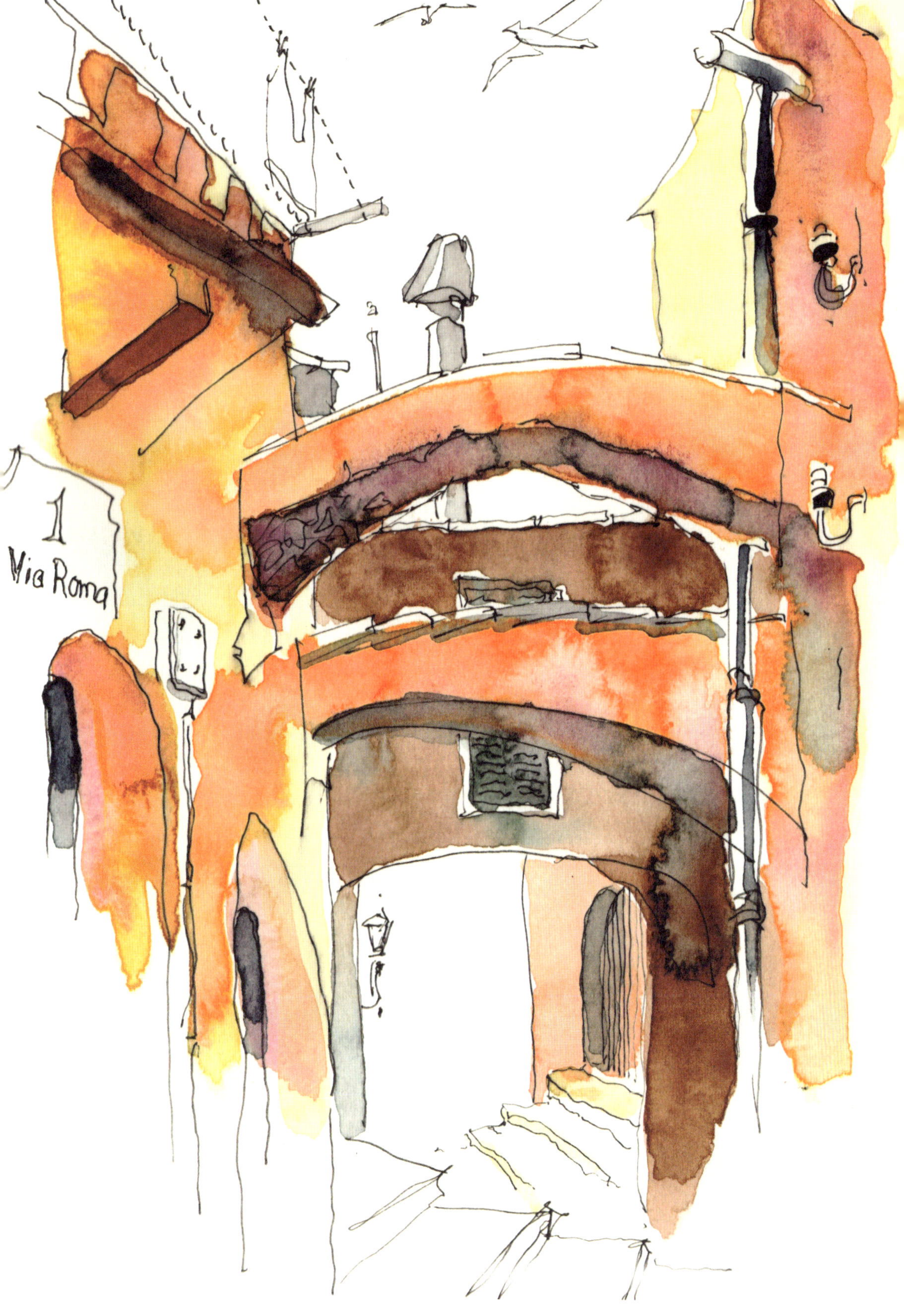

1
Via Roma

Experiment with Color and Light

Not only the geography, but also the colors and light characterize
a seaside setting: Southerly sunlight casts harsh shadows and
intensifies the hues of lush green vegetation, bright blue skies,
and garishly colorful architecture.

My Tips for Successful Color and Light Effects

1. Assign clear light and shadow sides to a building. Facades facing
   the sun appear brighter. Areas in shadow, like building edges,
   balconies, and window cornices, appear dark and stand out
   in contrast.
2. Trees and plants appear three-dimensional and natural when you
   combine two shades of green. In the case of the palm tree below,
   I used May and cobalt green.
3. Emphasize the southern ambiance with strong color contrasts.
   In my drawing, I used the complementary contrast between the
   palm trees and the casino facade.
4. With watercolors, light and dark gradations of a color are best
   achieved using the glazing technique (see page 99).

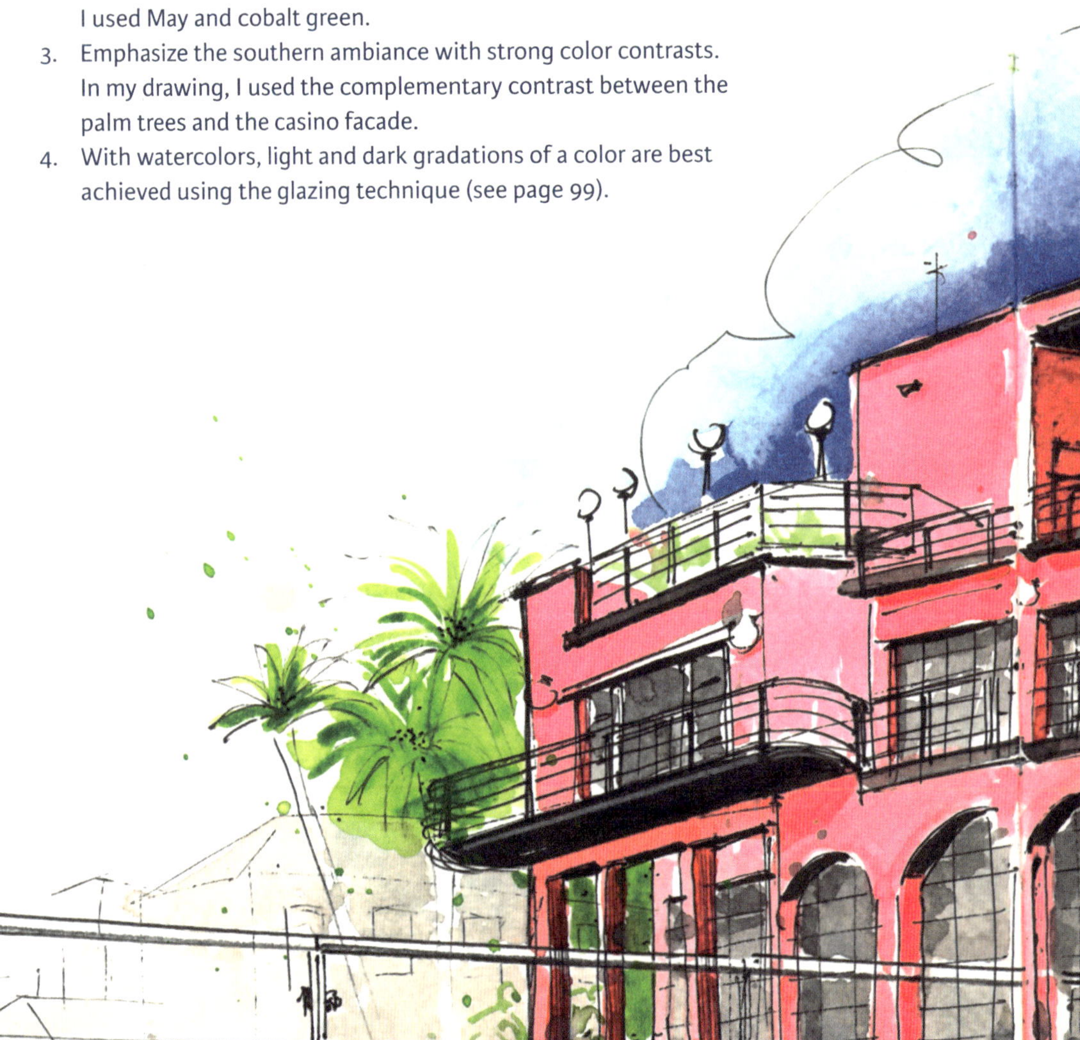

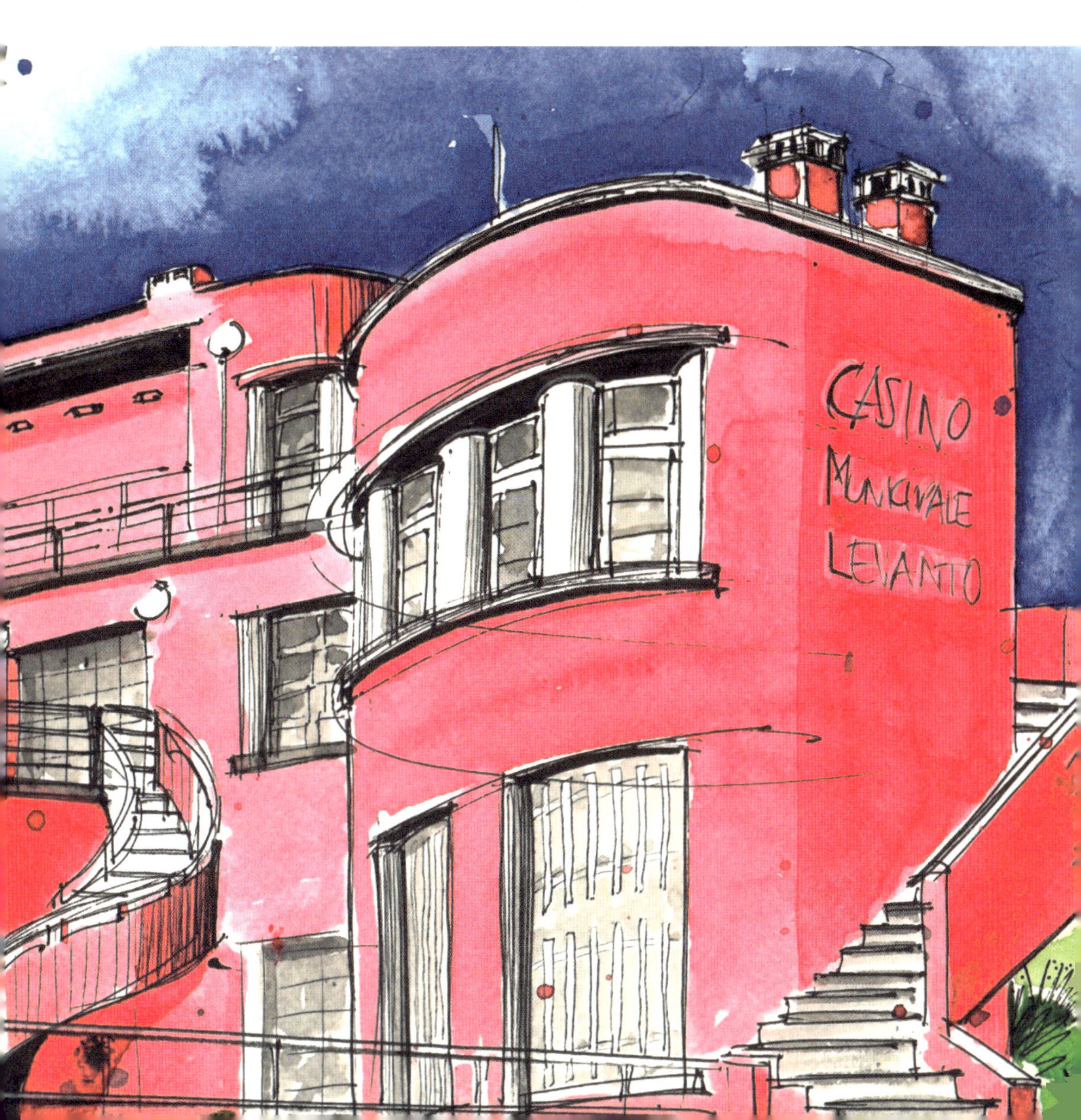

CASINO
MUNICIPALE
LEVANTO

Patina Everywhere

Abandoned places, vacant locations, decaying industrial wastelands, and harbor areas are wonderful places to linger with a sketchbook. Boat wrecks, rusted tools, and crooked sheds are sources of inspiration for drawing. I use sepia ink to make the patina visible. I emphasize decay by exaggerating cracks, rust, and leaks in my sketches.

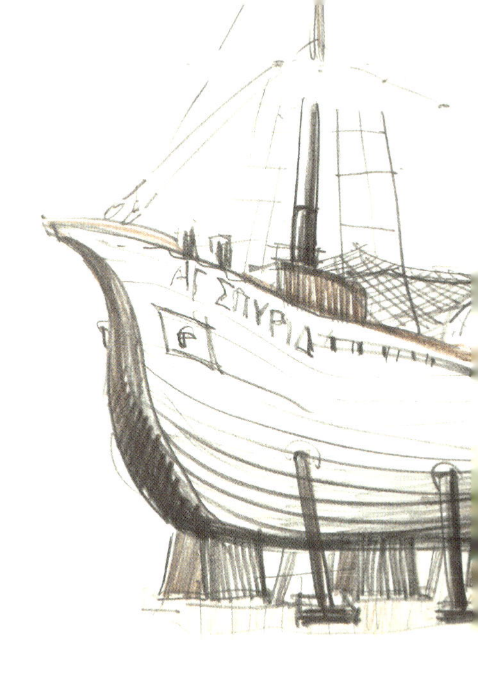

Drawing Time

A mixed line drawing using pencil, ink pen, and a few brushstrokes documents the stages of decay. Hatching and torn lettering accentuate the surface of the boat hull.

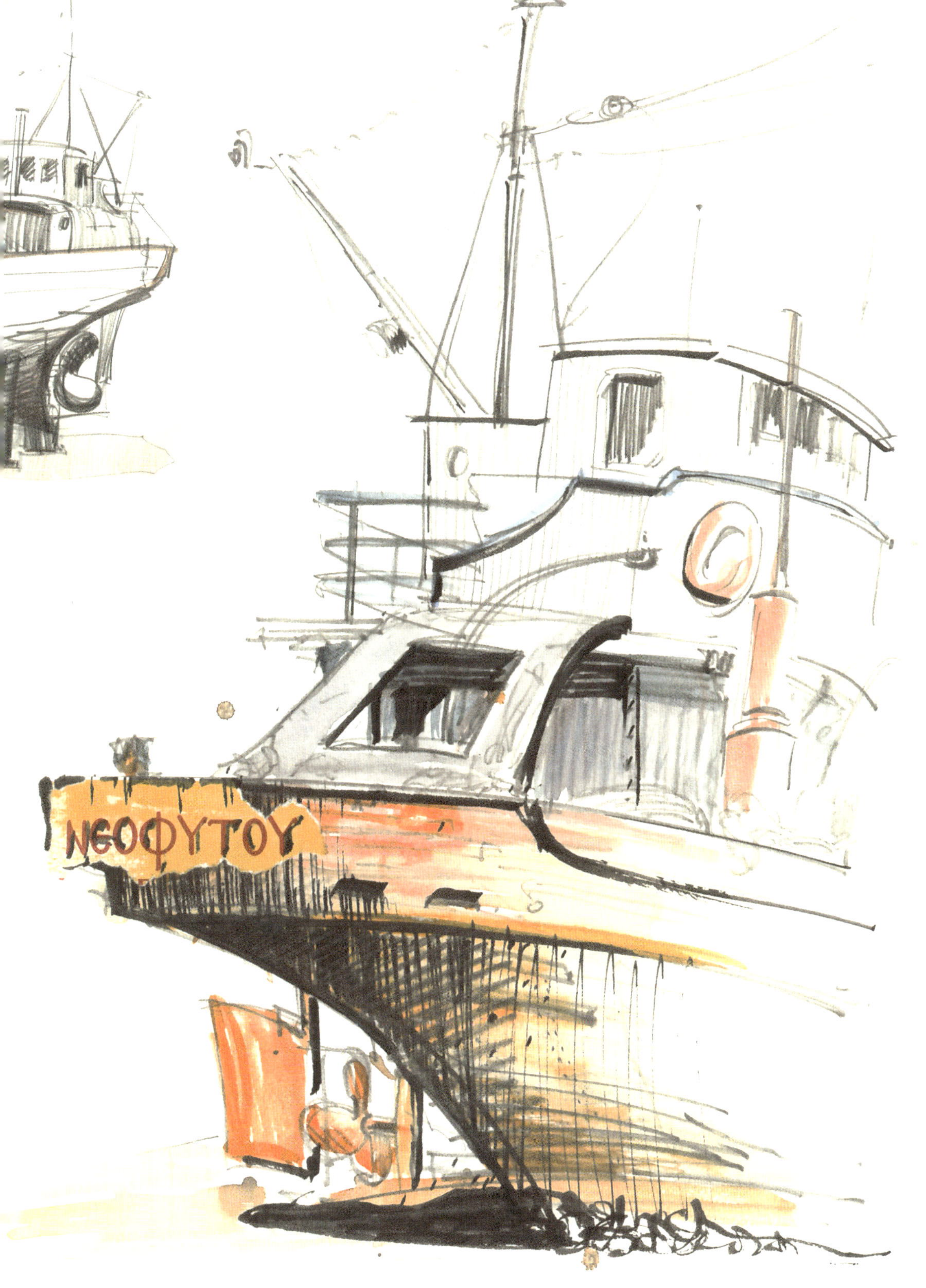

ΝΕΟΦΥΤΟΥ

A Simple Maneuver

When you leave the harbor or approach a city from the sea, the place spreads out to present itself for a brief glimpse that you should capture in your sketch-book. Even though a lot of visual information floods in at this moment (rows of houses, a church, city walls), the objects appear flat and two-dimensional.

The greater the distance, the less spatial the buildings on land appear. The perspective changes to a panorama view, and this simple effect makes sketching much easier. Facades and roofs form basic rectangular, trapezoidal, and triangular shapes. So, to simplify the drawing, increase your distance from the subject.

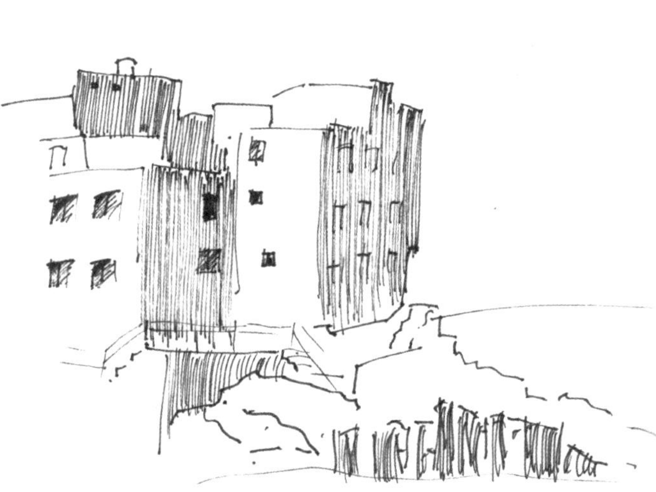

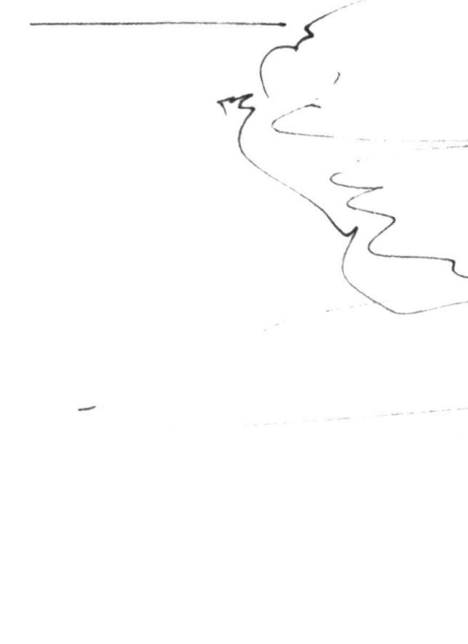

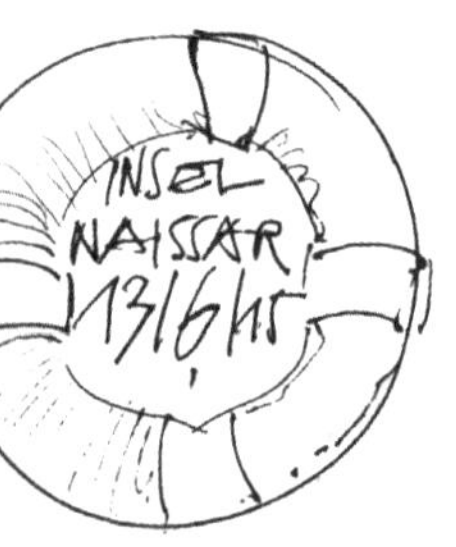

Tip: Rent a rowboat and paddle out a little way. You'll see that putting some distance between you and your subject will make drawing it easier.

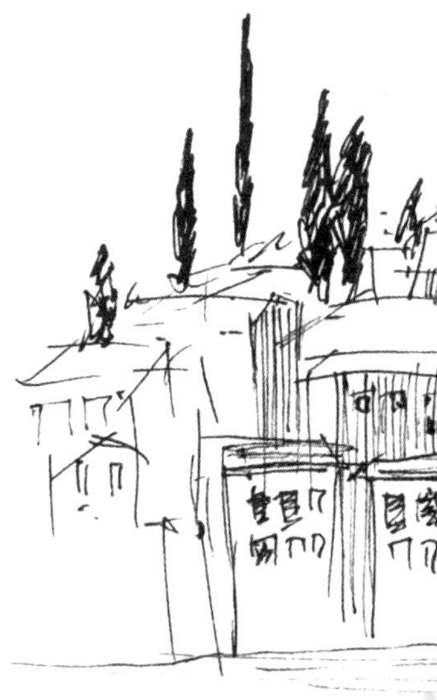

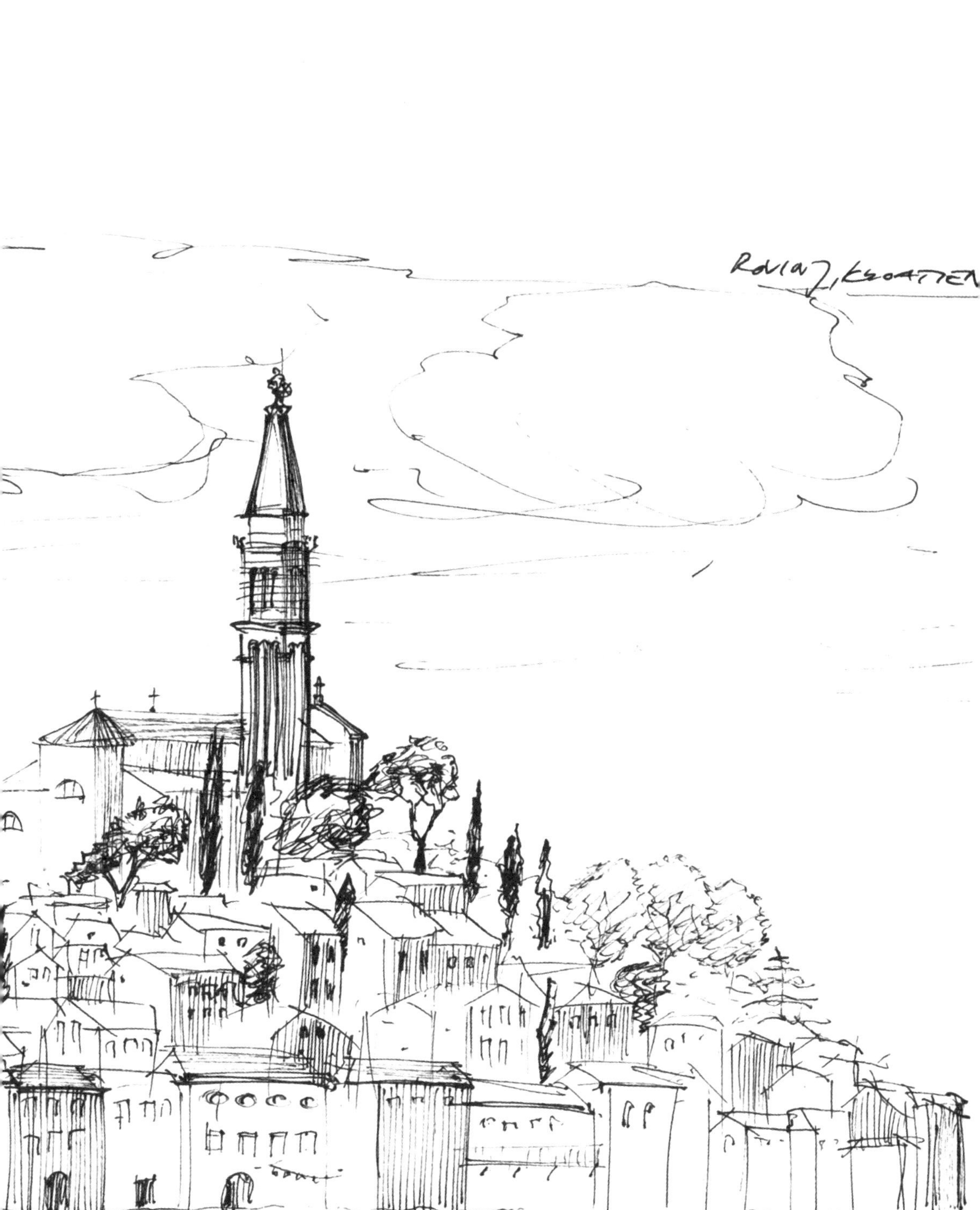

Rovinj, Kroatien

Where and When I Sketch

To get started, lower your expectations and don't hold your work to high artistic standards. In my experience, the place and time don't always have to be perfectly in sync. Even popular destinations like Tuscany don't always automatically spark an inspirational flame in me. Instead, I relax and open myself to everything around me. I watch, I doodle, I fantasize, I digress. I let myself drift into drawing. Sometimes in the morning. Sometimes in the evening. On a boat on a lake, during a break from hiking in the mountains. Guided by the light, the mood, the space around me.

Even as a professional artist, I enjoy the freedom of not having to create a "presentable" sketch, picture, or illustration. When you're not working for a client, no one will be judging you. Draw for your own pleasure, not for the critical eyes of others.

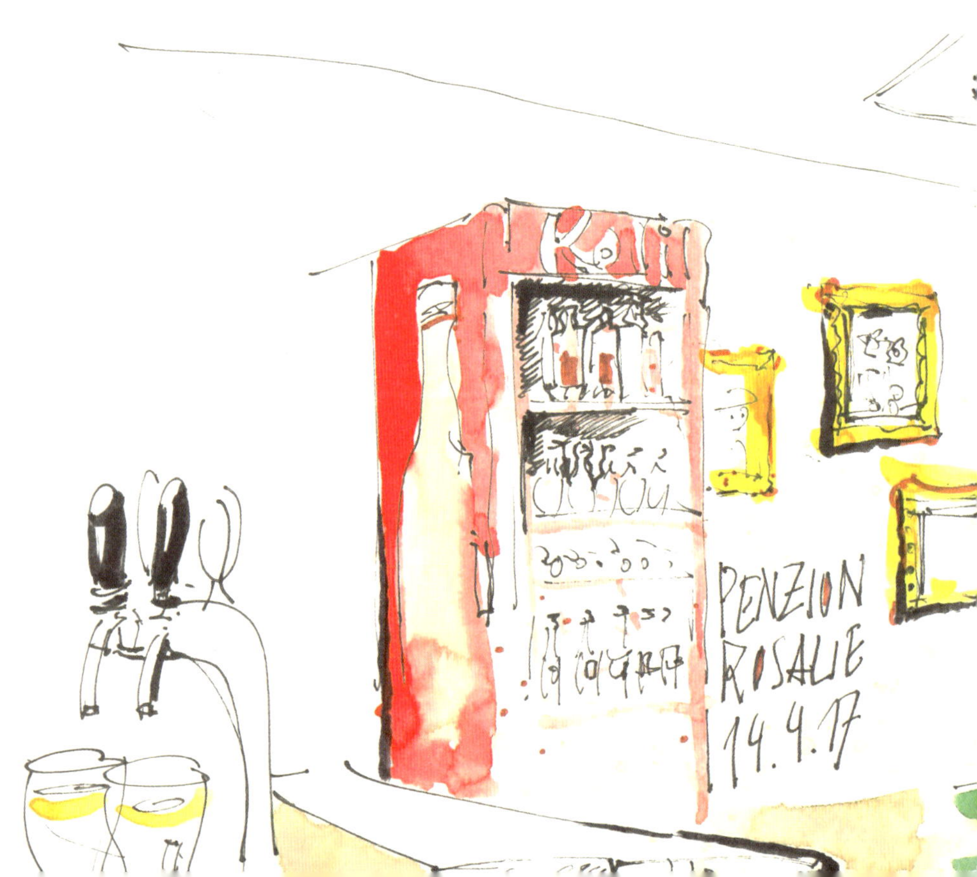

Tip: A protected spot makes it easier to draw without being disturbed. The corner table in the pub, the shady spot under a tree, or the wall of a house behind you keep prying eyes and the weather at bay.

Your drawing place doesn't have to be as cozy as your own sofa, but you should still feel comfortable enough to spend a few minutes quietly observing.

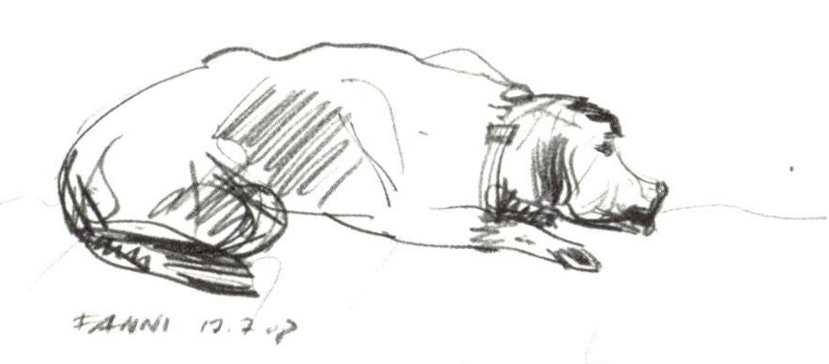

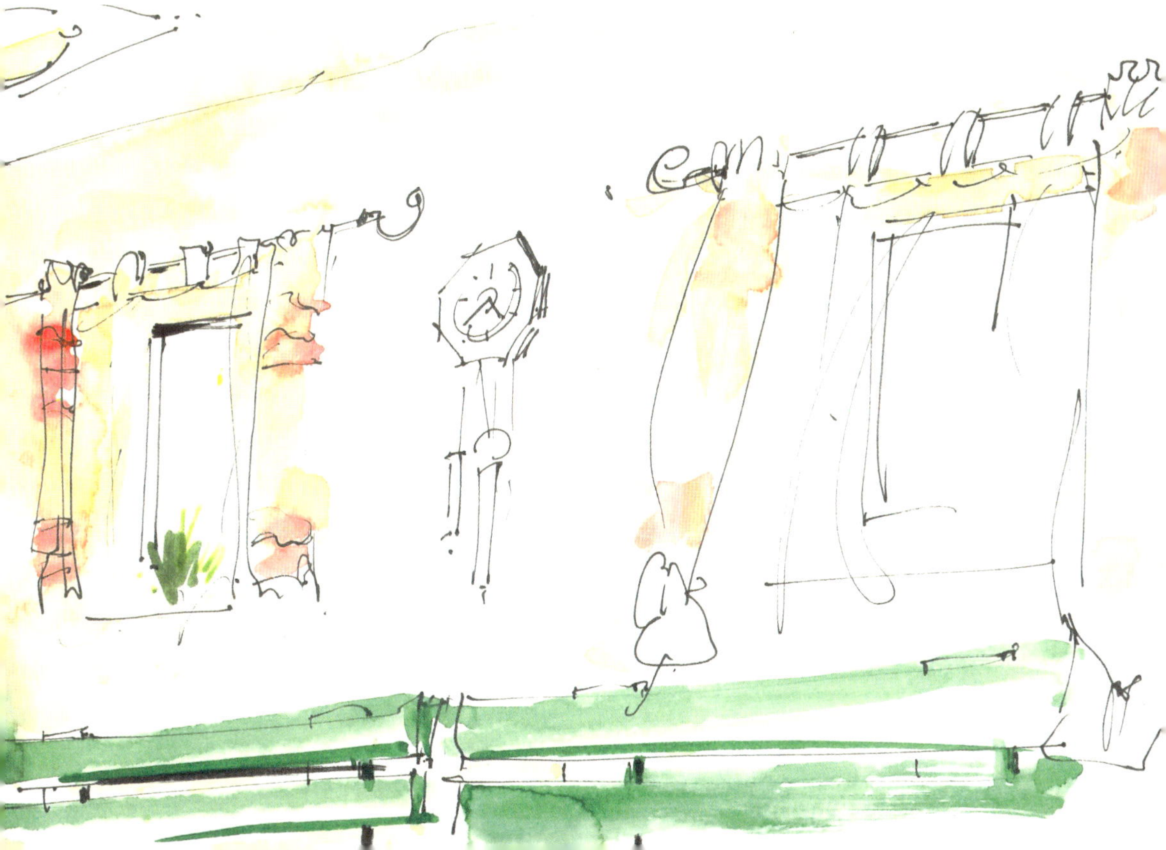

Use Downtime to Sketch

How much time do you spend waiting every day? The bus is late. The train is stopped on the tracks. Your friend is late for your planned lunch. The meeting can't start without a missing participant. Whenever external circumstances force you to do nothing, the brief lull in activity can lead to an interesting observation or a great sketch. How often is your patience tested when traveling—at the airline counter, waiting for a ferry, stuck in traffic in a long tunnel? These are all involuntary breaks that are ideal for drawing. A little finger exercise for in between, a snapshot on paper.

A Quick Sketch

Time is a crucial factor when sketching on the go. Calm, reflective moments and situations where you need to work quickly are both valuable drawing opportunities. Always carry a pen and sketchbook with you, just like you do your wallet or cell phone. Short scenes on the street (traffic lights turning red; a dog running through the frame) are good practice. Quick strokes and the appeal of the unfinished make them all the livelier. Leave out the details; color can be added later.

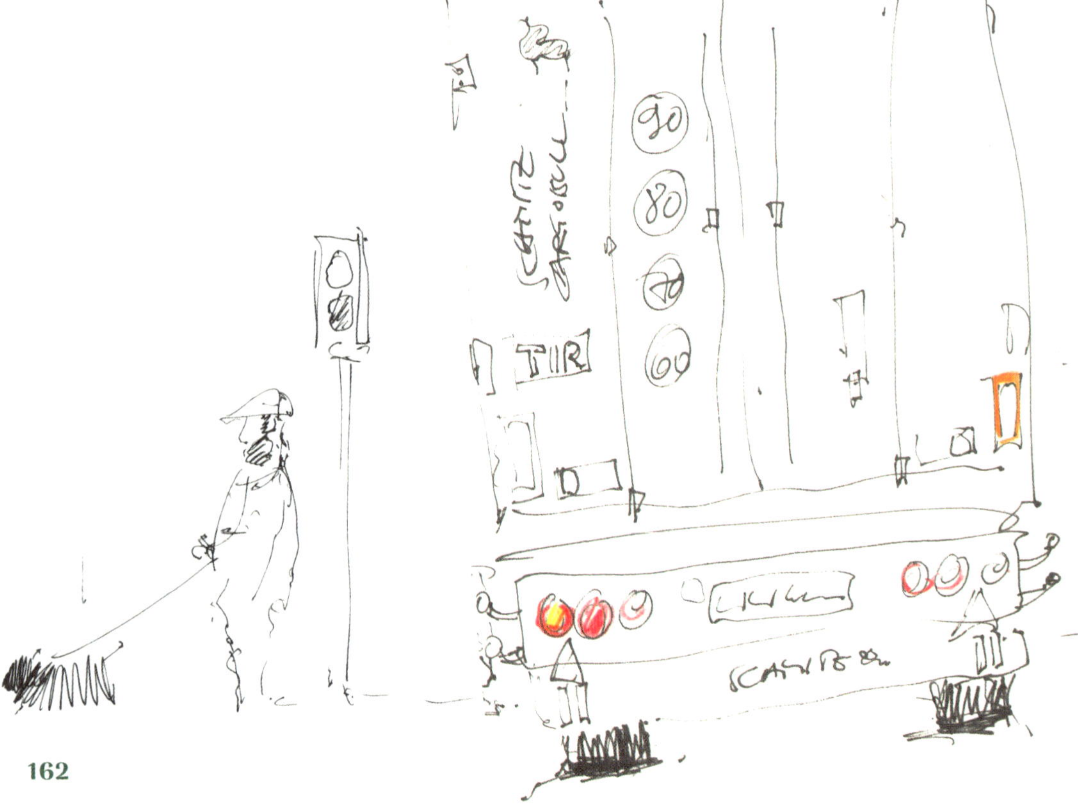

From my travel diary: traffic jam in the Caucasus. They're blue. They're red. They're white. Plain. Patterned. Lettered. Polished to a high shine. Completely covered in dust. Repaired multiple times. Half empty or overloaded—with 40, 5, or 10 tons. Bumpers touching for miles, trucks are lined up as far as the eye can see, to the horizon and beyond. They're from Hungary, Georgia, Ukraine. The drivers—lying down, sitting, their eyes fixed on the distance or closed in semisleep—wait to be cleared at the Russian border. Stoic, it seems to us as we drive past them in the opposite direction. Pausing only briefly for my sketch. With quick strokes, I captured what touched my travel companion and me: the patience that hung in the air and filled us with a deep sense of calm.

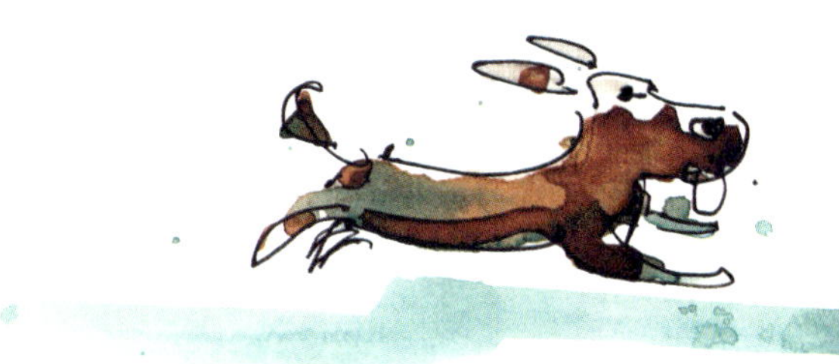

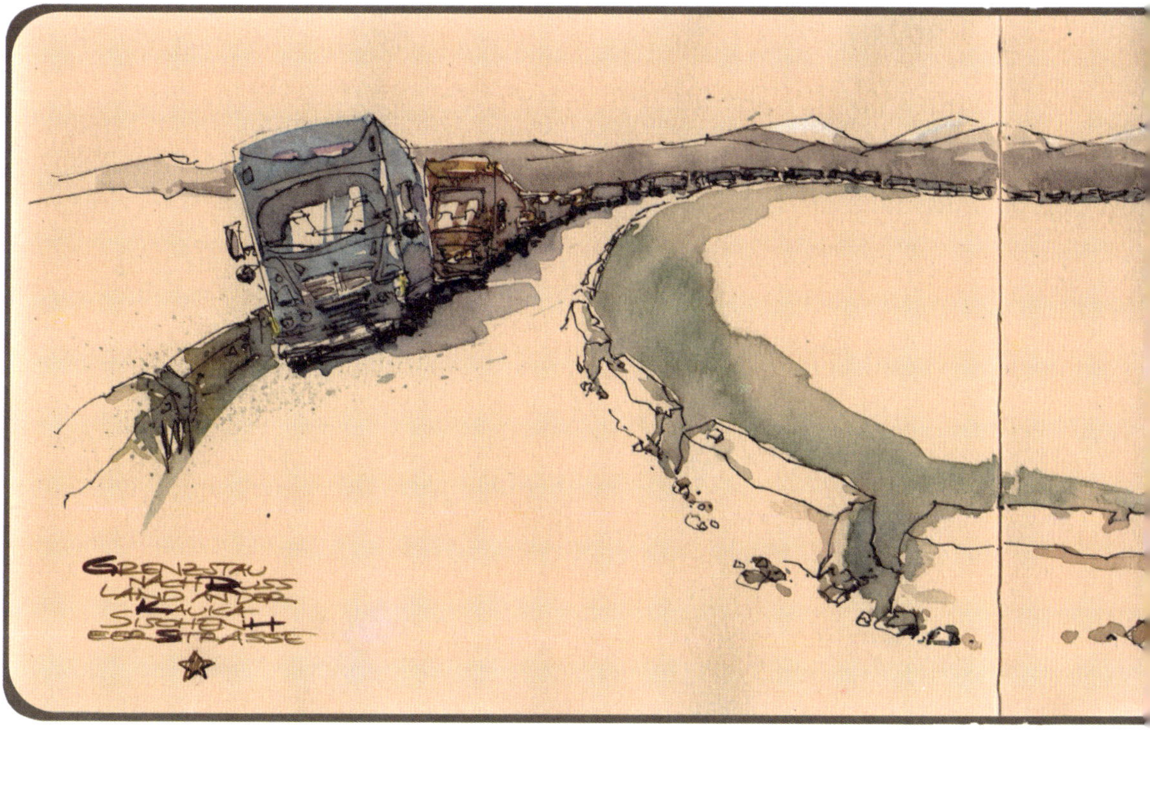

Travel Companions and Surprises

When I'm sketching on the go, I'm usually distracted.
I constantly stop to capture a moment on paper, which
sometimes means longer waits. A friend of mine (not
an artist) has been accompanying me on trips across
Europe for years now. The time we spend together is very
important to me, but most of it is taken up by drawing.
Not exactly the best conditions for a carefree traveling duo.
And yet we always return with a sketchbook full of impressions that we shared.

Why? I only travel with people who share my curiosity
about foreign places and my interest in slow observation.
Everyone collects impressions in their own way: by drawing,
writing, taking photographs, or simply letting the place
work its magic on them. When you travel solo as an
illustrator, you have surprising encounters along the way.
Passersby are often happy to comment on your work
and strike up a conversation. Setting aside a few difficult
encounters, I've met many interesting people this way.
If you draw while traveling, you won't be alone for long.

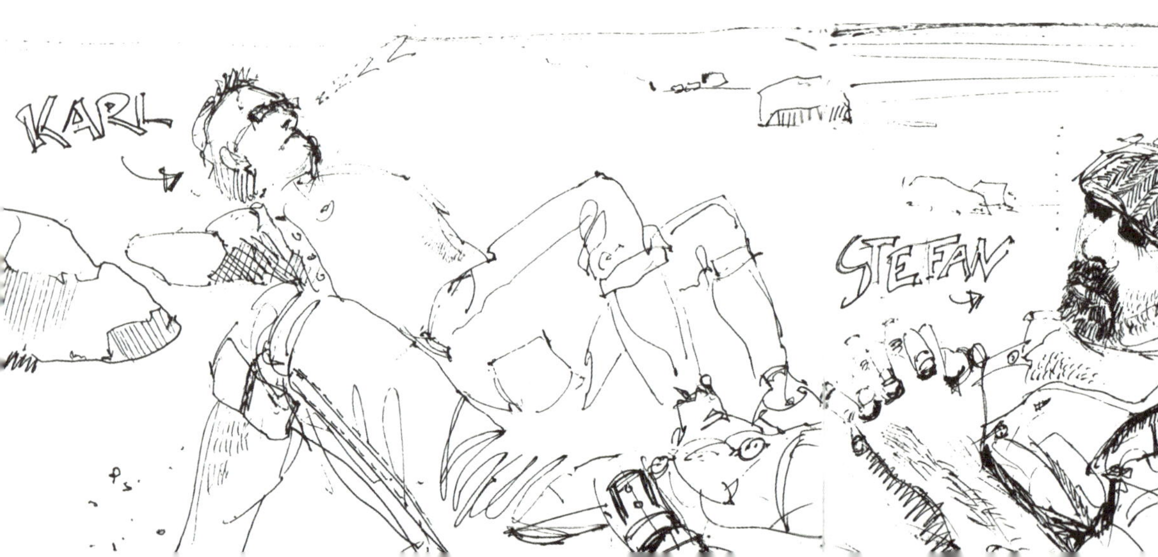

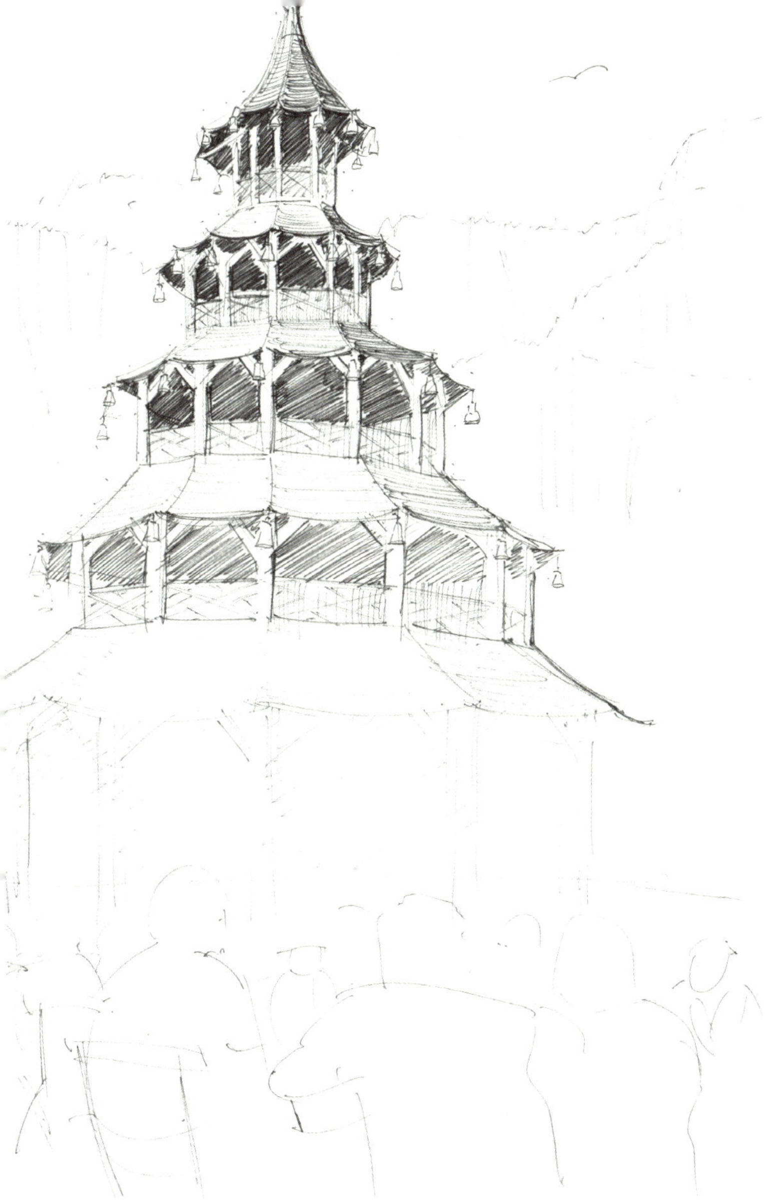

Tip: Children can brighten up a drawing tour. They're good observers and capture subjects in their own unique way—like my daughter did in her sketch from the outskirts of a town.

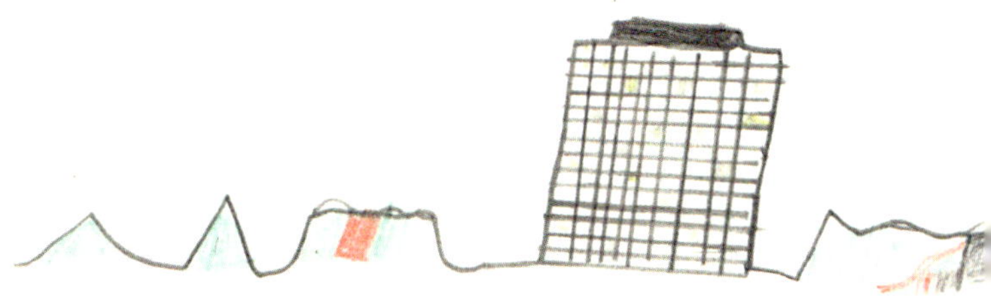

Time Series

Sometimes it's hard to find something that captures your imagination. You're outdoors, but there's nothing to draw in sight. A few sparse impressions come into view (everyday objects, endless landscapes, faceless architecture), but it doesn't seem worth the effort to get out your paper and pen.

In this case, try changing your approach. You can get a lot out of unremarkable subjects by using time sequences, sketched "tracking shots," or object series.

Observe your subject over time. Moments string together like imaginary film shots, as you pass by, from different angles, a few seconds apart, or over the course of a day.

Create a series of sketches and add the location and time of the event. In retrospect, your drawings will gain meaning and tell a little story through attentive observation.

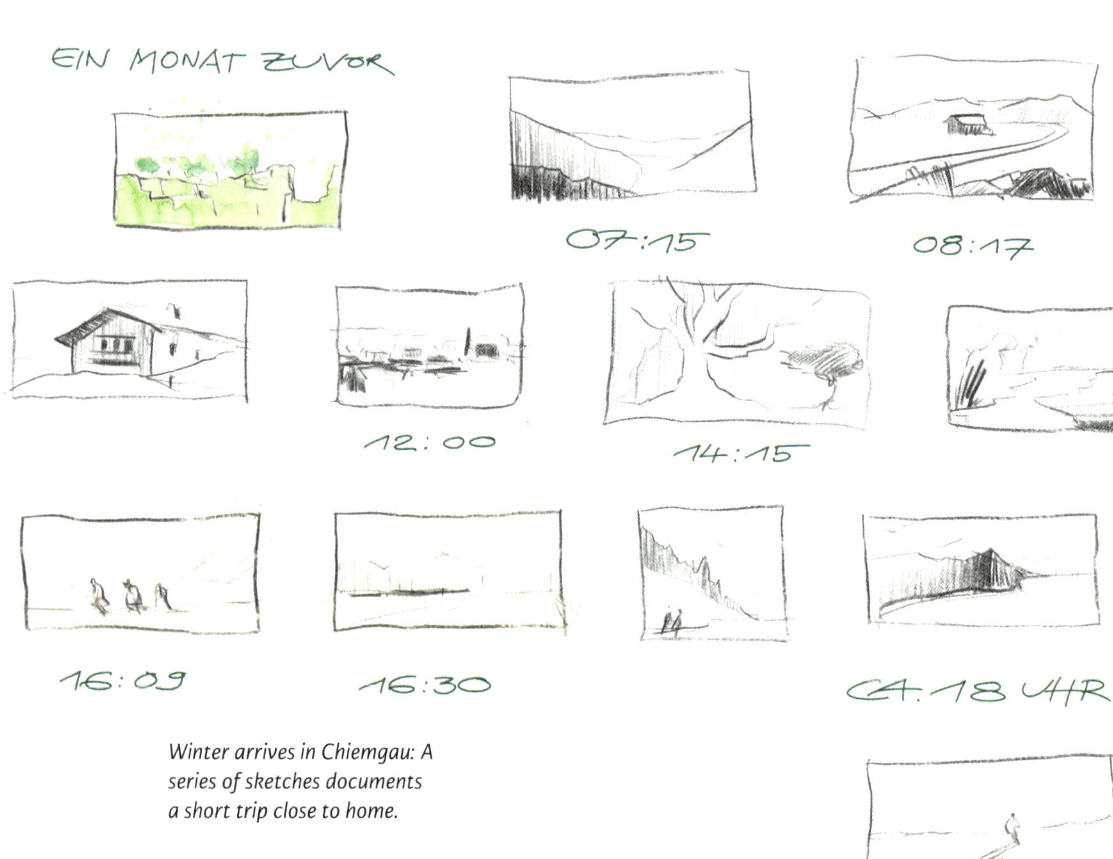

Winter arrives in Chiemgau: A series of sketches documents a short trip close to home.

A talking windmill: Windmills are a rather mundane subject on the German coast, even though they vary in shape and construction from place to place. But on the island of Amrum, my interest was piqued: The mill in the main town of Nebel "speaks" with its sails at different times of the day.

Depending on the position of the blades and the occasion, visual messages are sent to the islanders every day. To capture the variety of shapes of the windmill in a sketch, I took a virtual tracking shot around the object. I explain this method on the following pages.

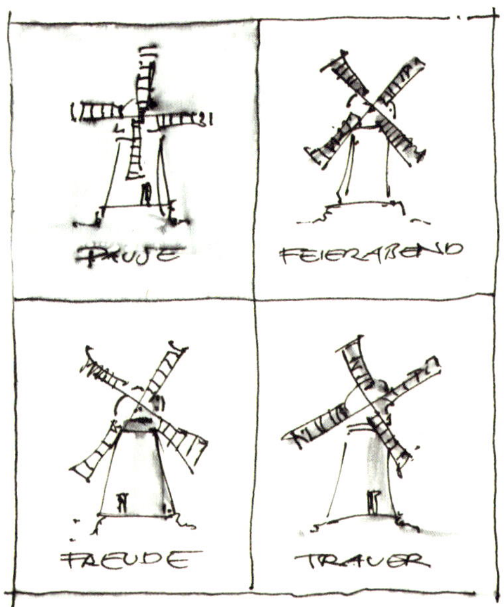

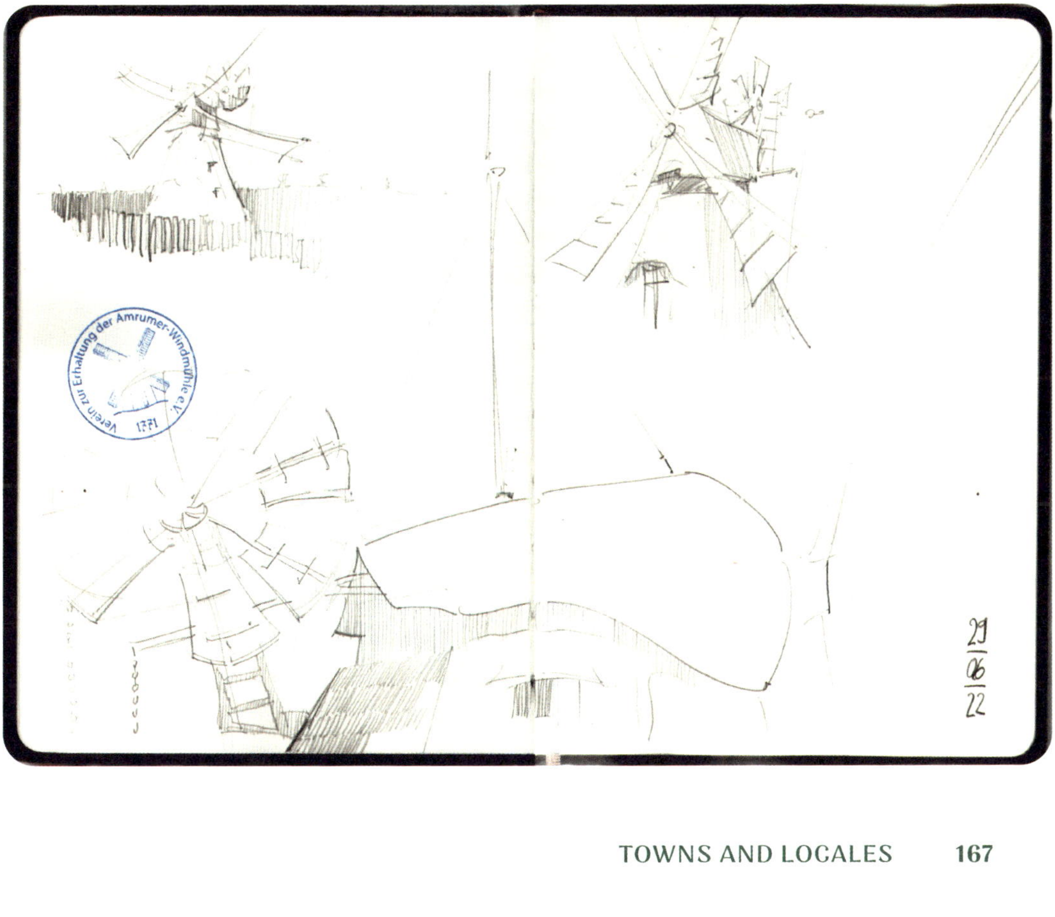

Tracking Shot with a Pencil

Everyday objects that accompany you on your travels or equipment that reliably fulfills a function are used hundreds of times and yet rarely given a second glance. All these objects can tell interesting stories when viewed through the right lens. Look at one of your favorite items through the virtual lens of a film camera. Sequences are good alternatives to intricate single drawings. Instead of details, variations in form and presentation catch the viewer's attention. Don't commit yourself to one version, but find a subject and create a series with as many variations as possible. The more, the better. It's a bit like designing in retrospect: What could a different design look like? What effect would small changes have?

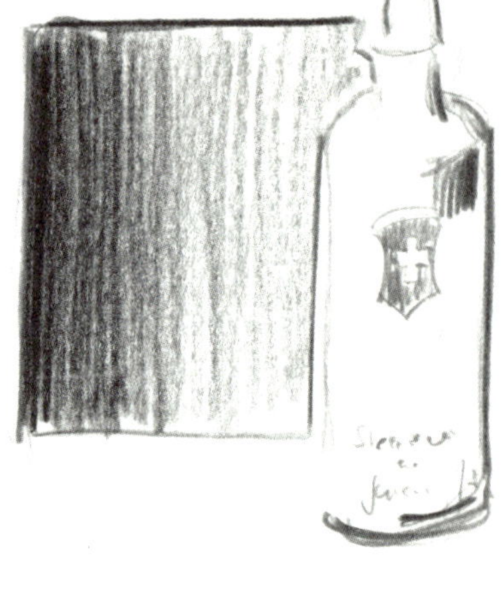

Exercise: An Object Tells a Story

1. Pick an object you've brought along outdoors.
2. Look at it very closely from all angles.
3. Record your observations in mini sketches using a pencil or felt-tip pen.
4. Zoom in on important details and pan the "camera" for interesting angles and unusual perspectives.
5. Combine the sketches into an interesting sequence of individual shots, right in your sketchbook. Alternatively, draw each sketch on separate pieces of paper, cut them out, arrange them, paste them in— and you're done.

Variations on a hat: One felt hat—a hundred ways to wear it. This series of sketches shows the wide range of possibilities.

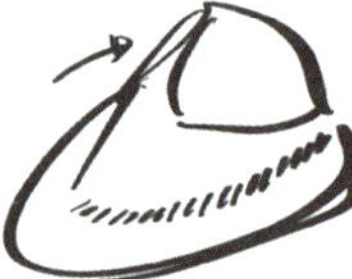
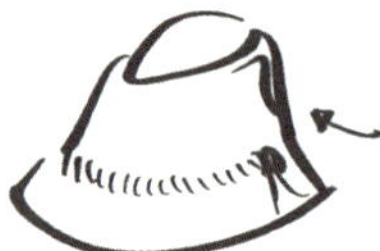
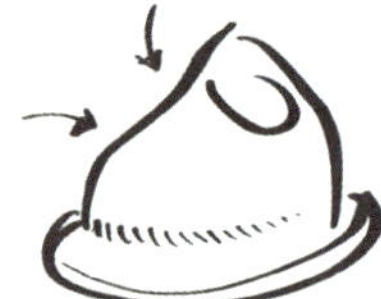
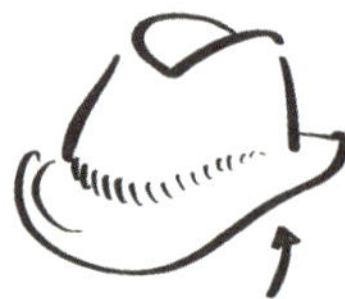

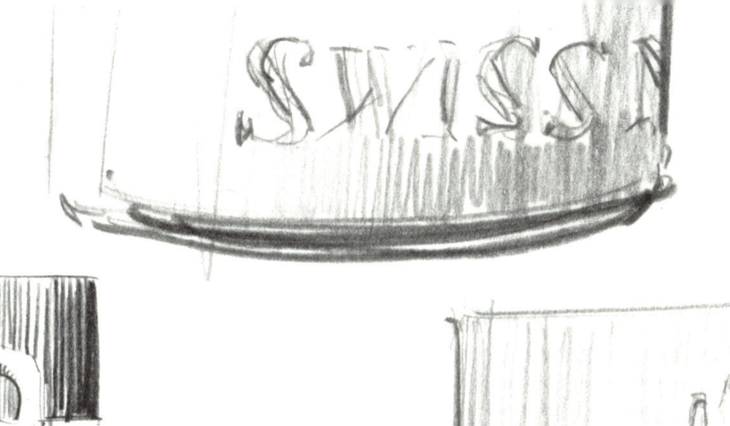

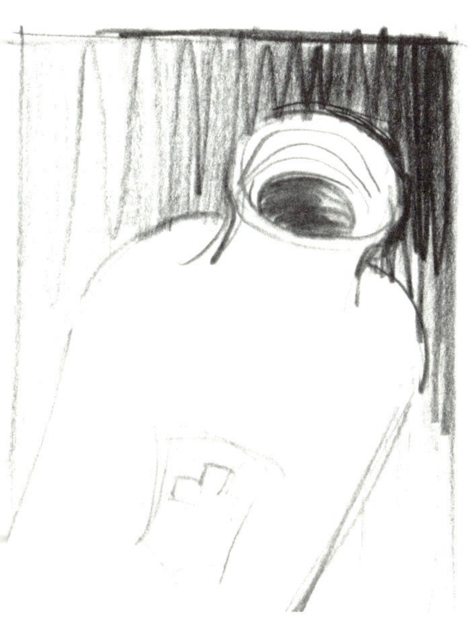

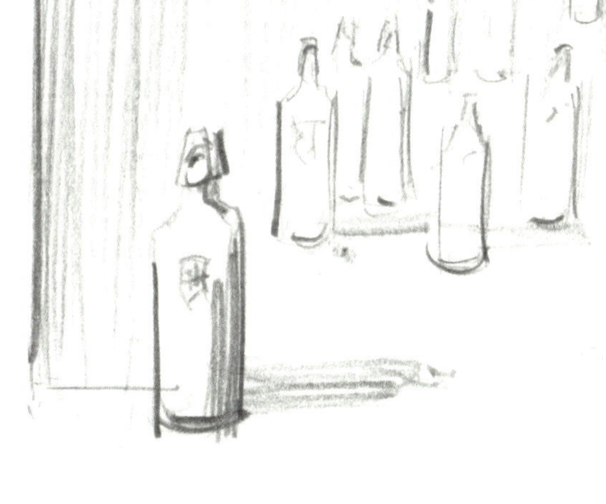

A tribute to the water bottle: Keeps drinks cold and hot, and it's unbreakable. The main character is the object itself.

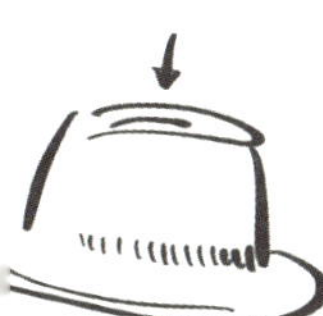

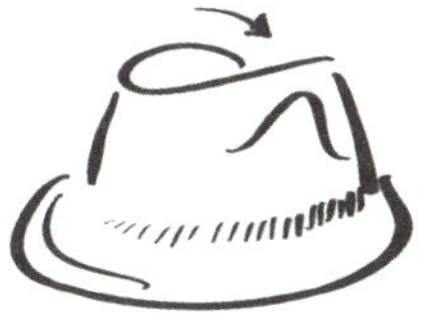

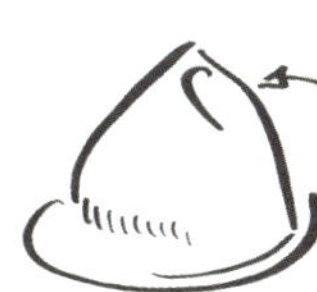

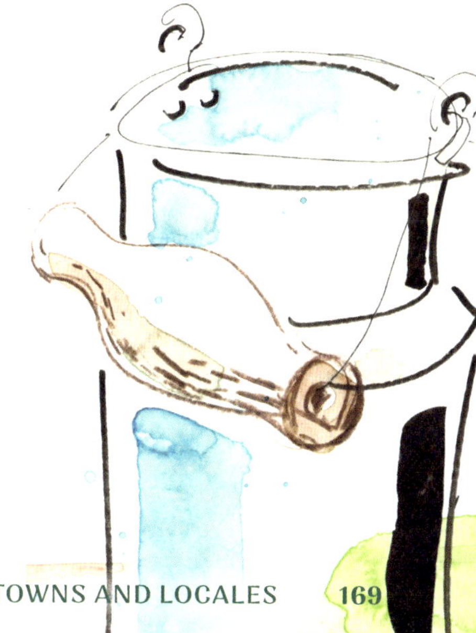

Collecting Things

Here's another technique for when you're on the
go, especially when you're lacking inspiration or
during breaks: Draw a collection of objects. You
won't have to move from the spot or look for the
perfect place to draw.

When I don't find a subject that really interests
me, I turn my attention to minor details. Signs,
streetlights, house numbers, sewer hole covers,
trash cans. There's always something to discover,
and sometimes it takes a second glance to notice
something typical of a place. Later, after the trip,
when comparing different "snapshots" in your
sketchbook, you'll see that collected sketches
can often capture the character of a place
very accurately.

All kinds of travel accessories are also suitable
for collecting: pocket knives, sunglasses, caps,
backpacks. Add the location and date, and these
sketches are guaranteed to bring back memories.

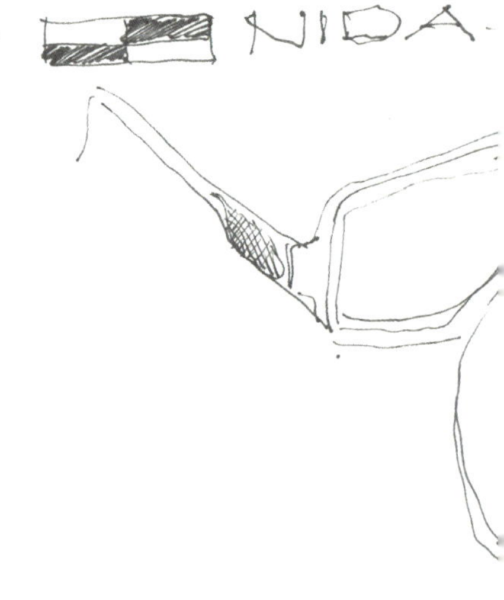

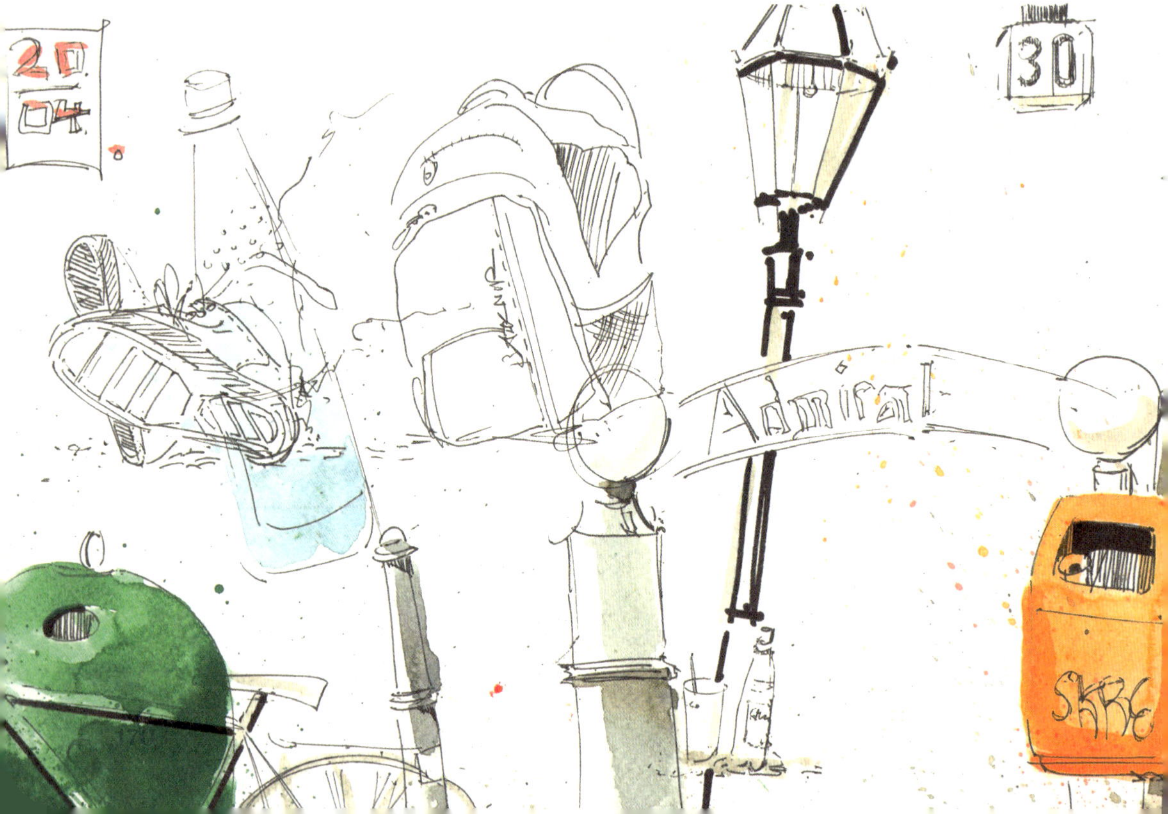

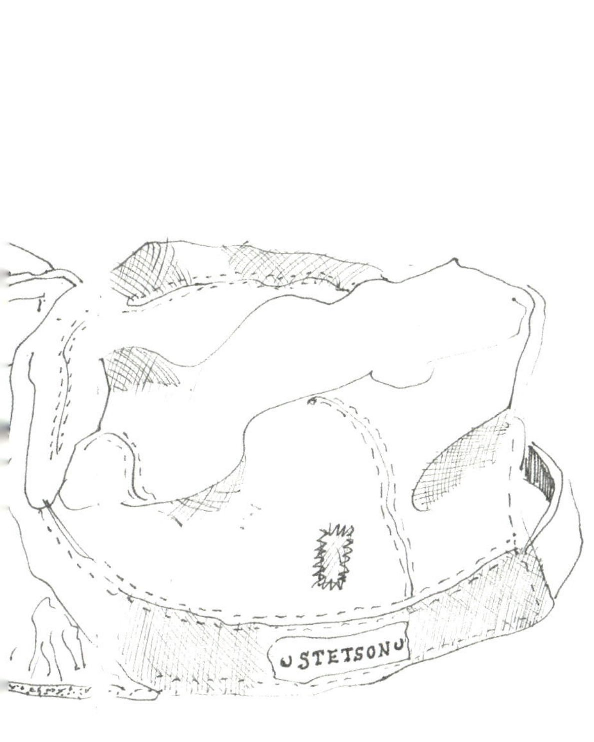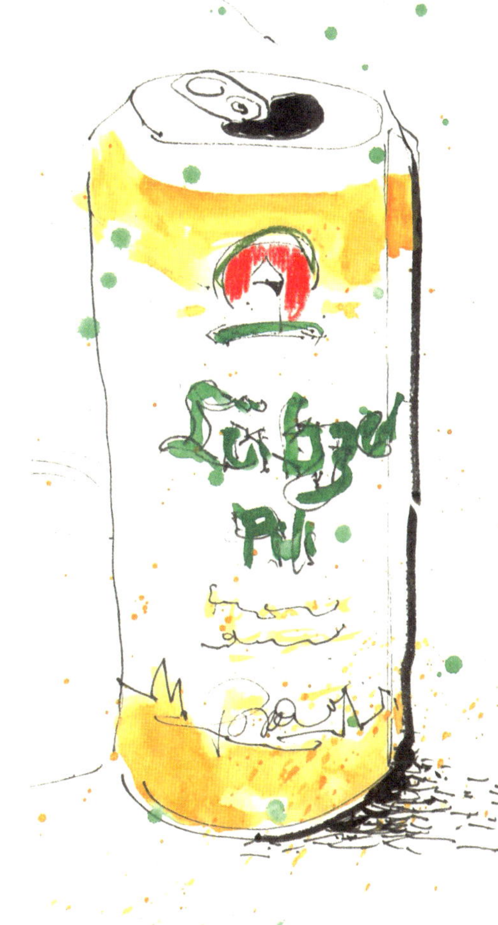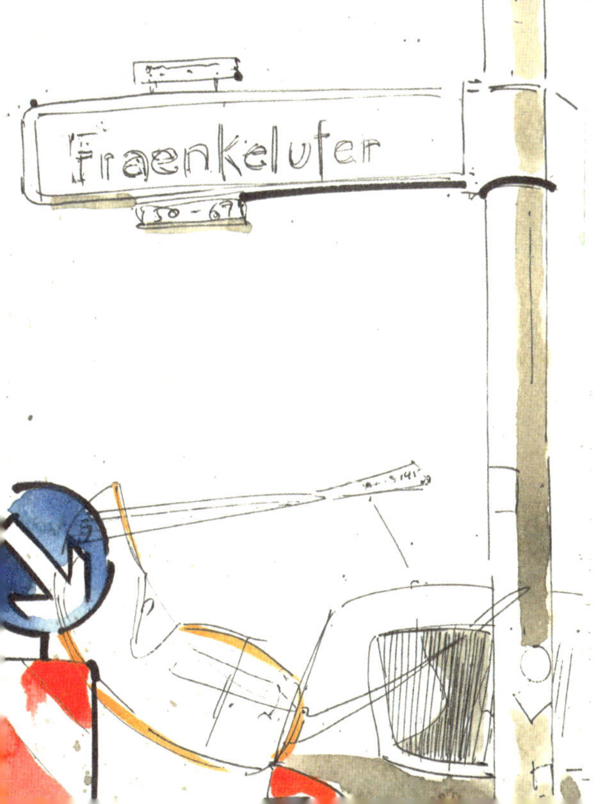

The face of Berlin:
Garbage can—
orange. Practical
detail—house
numbers are listed
right below the
street name.

Detour: Rural Villages

Generations of plein air painters were inspired by the natural wilderness as well as by the rural idyll of meadows and fields, village squares, and farmsteads. Anyone traveling from the city to the countryside can still understand this fascination today. Here, the world still seems to be in order, everything has its place, and the rural scenery offers reliable subjects to sketch. It's easy to find favorite places to draw. But remember that we're living in the twenty-first century. Pictures of peaceful country life and watercolor paintings with no rough edges can quickly drift into kitsch. If you want to avoid that, swap the idyllic farmyard for an abandoned barn, the shiny tractor for a rusty plow. Even if the clocks tick more slowly when sketching on a green meadow, keep your strokes quick and your eye critical.

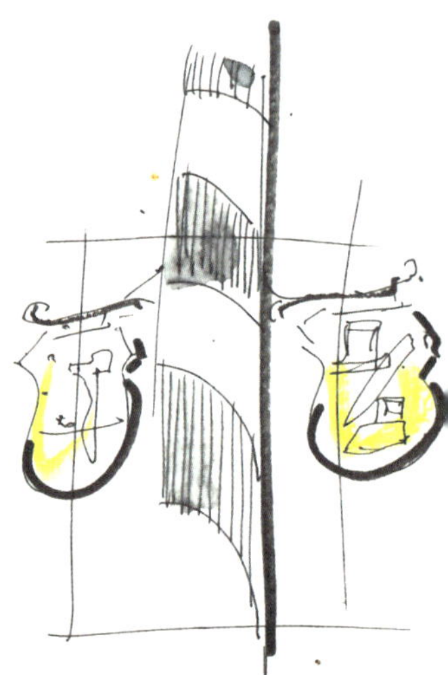

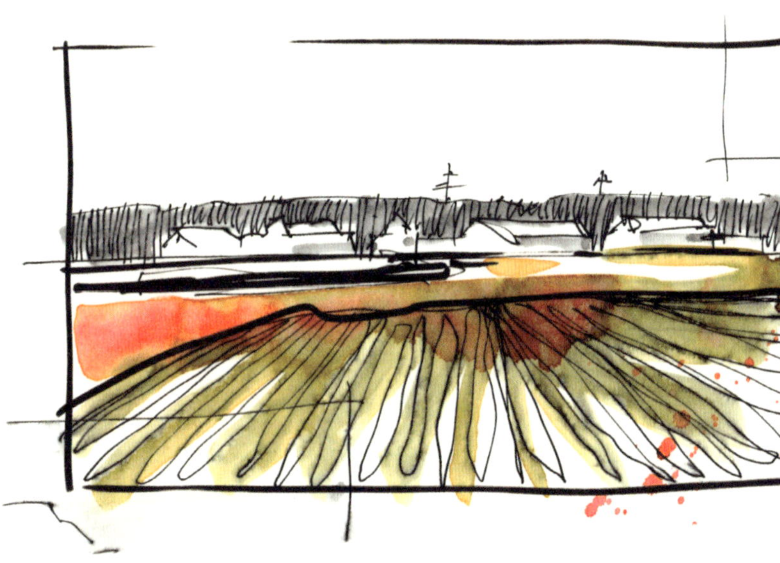

Not just country life: Power lines and traffic signs are part of modern life and belong in your sketchbook.

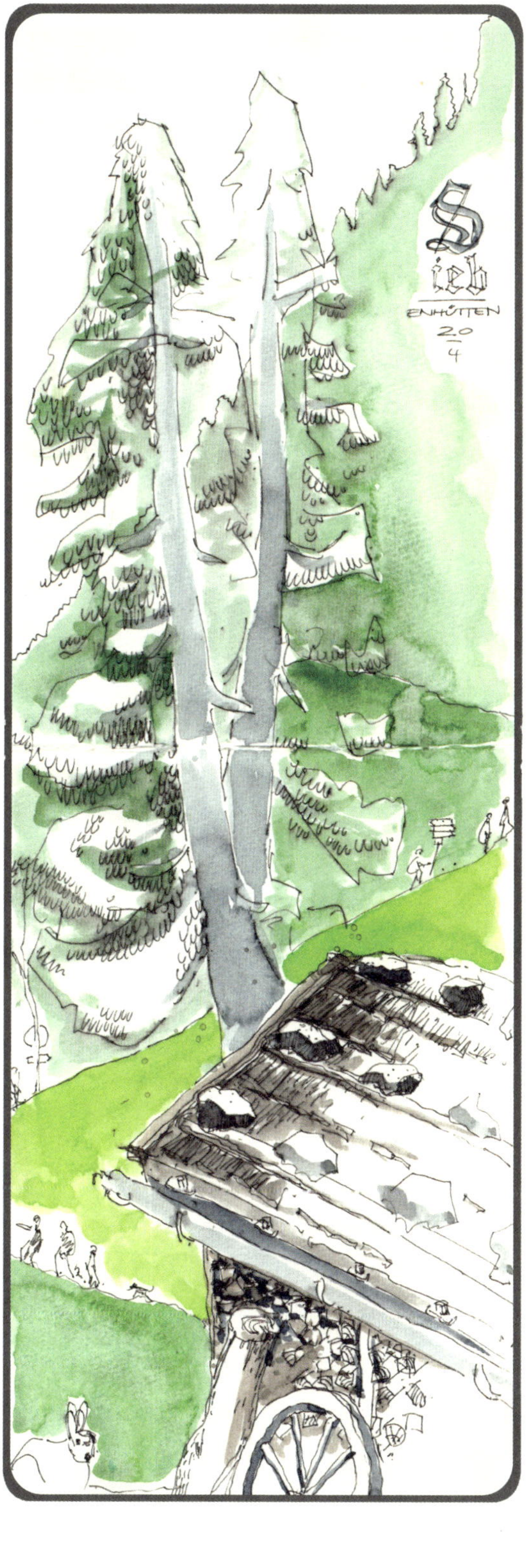

Tip: To prevent a subject from breaking up into individual elements, I join areas of color and lines as seamlessly as possible.

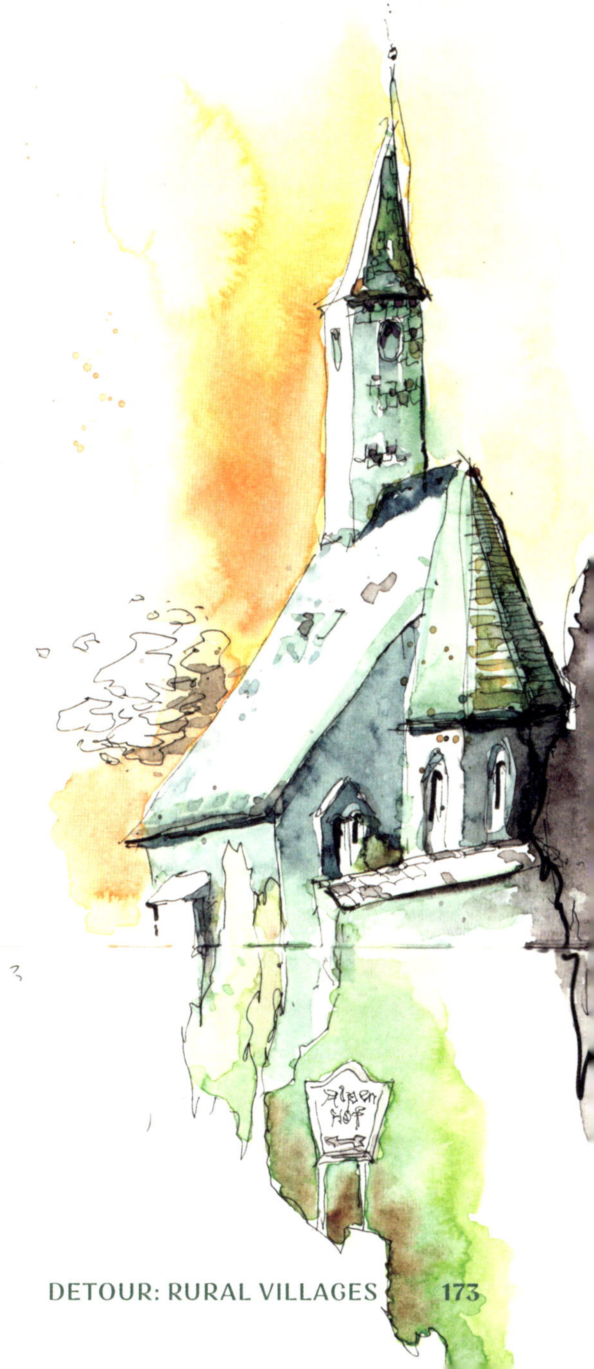

Time Standing Still

Some features of rural towns have changed little or not at all to this day. Farms, livestock breeding, and agriculture have been part of village life for centuries, even if some industries have been replaced by manufacturing and tourism. Traditional holidays and festivities really reveal what makes a functioning village community (ideally you can observe this with a pen and paper at hand). The music, food, and drink are all part of the program. And, of course, everyone's on a first-name basis, even the visiting artist with a sketchbook.

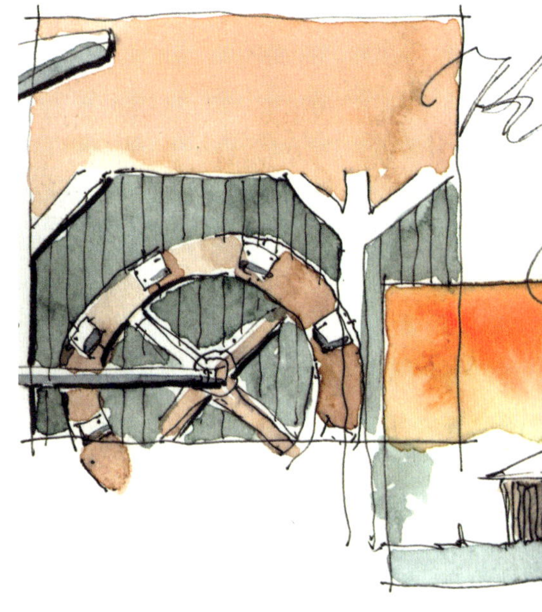

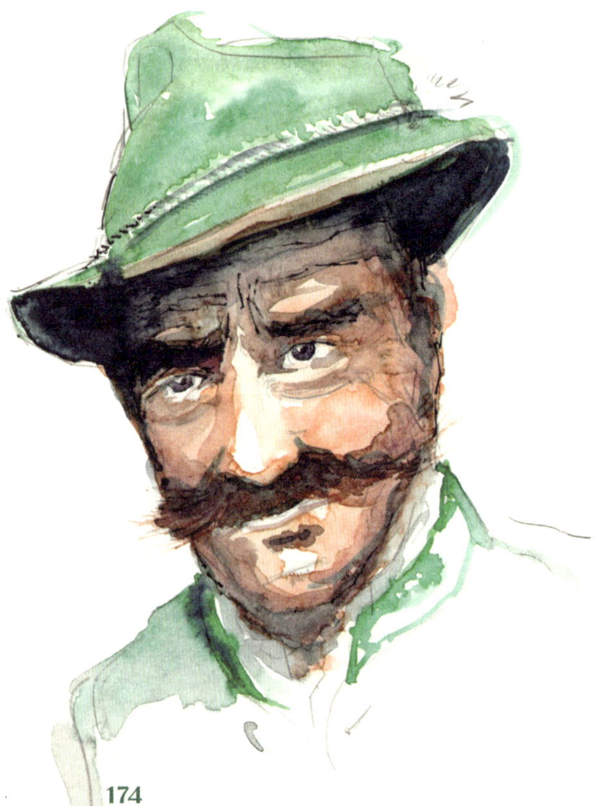

Tip: Don't forget the white space. When coloring roofs, facades, and surfaces, always leave some white of the paper empty. Light and dark areas should be clearly separated from each other and provide light in the drawing.

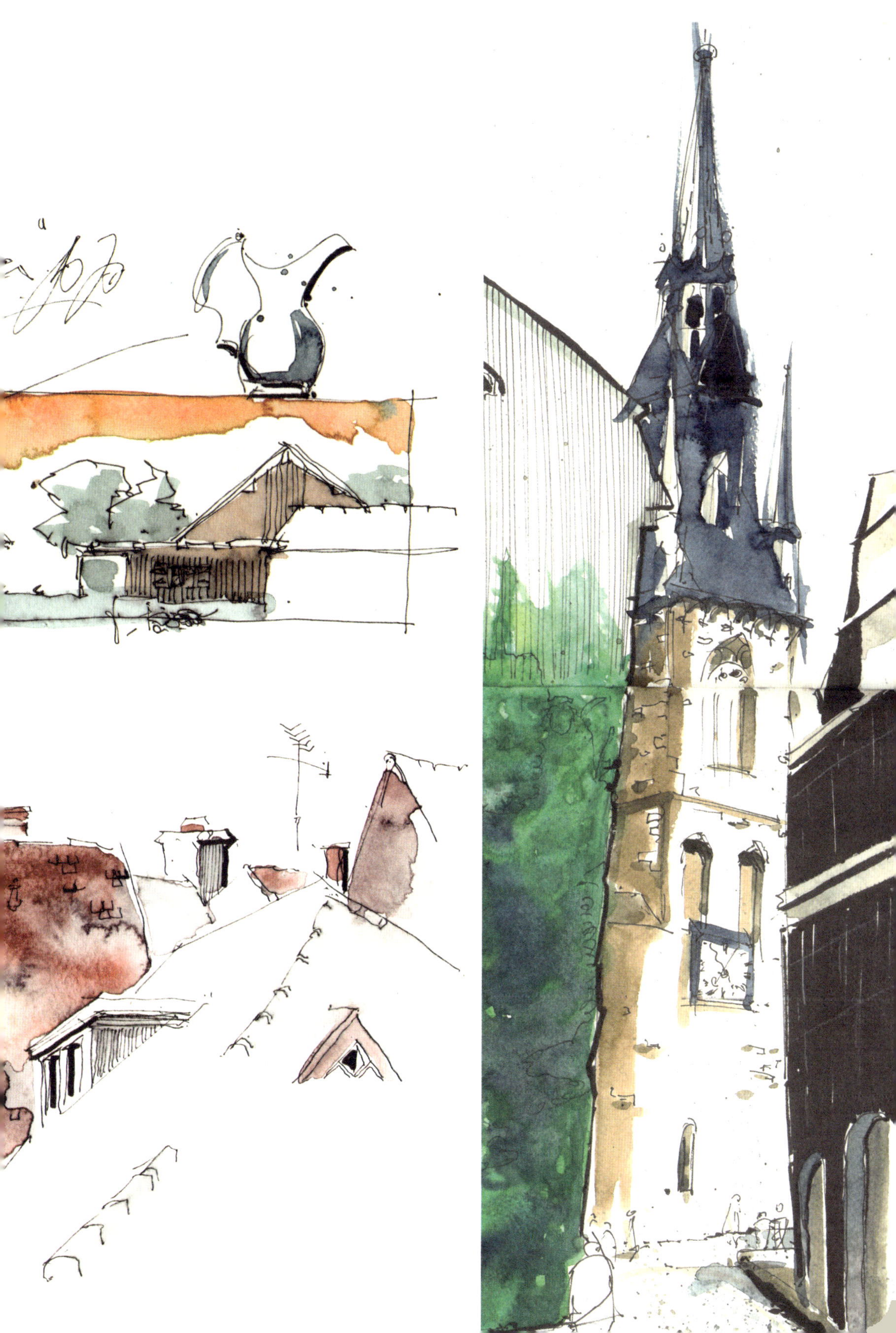

In the Tavern

If you want to find out about the people in the country,
their culture and way of life, go to the village inn. It can
be found in the center of town, usually not far from
the church.

Put your backpack in the corner. Sit down, listen, and
join in. Enjoy a refreshing beverage and a local meal. Stay
on the lookout. Whenever I'm on the road, stopping off at
a tavern is both an opportunity for contact and a source
of inspiration. I even draw what's on my plate, like how
guests photograph and post the dishes served to them
before they reach for their cutlery. Smartphone or
sketchbook: Which appetite lasts longer?

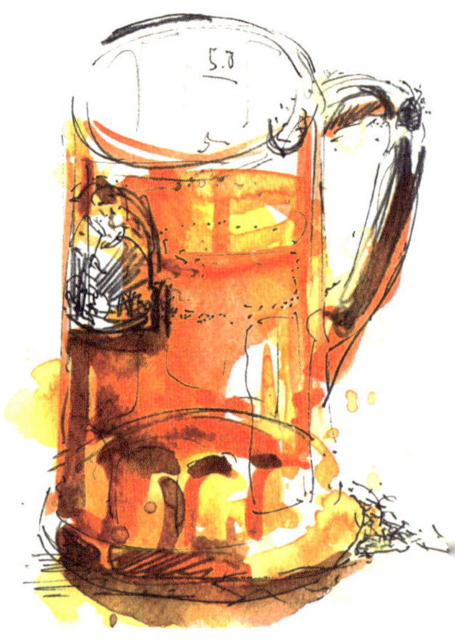

Tip: Glasses and drinks are
best depicted by applying
watercolor washes and glazes
(see the exercise on
page 100).

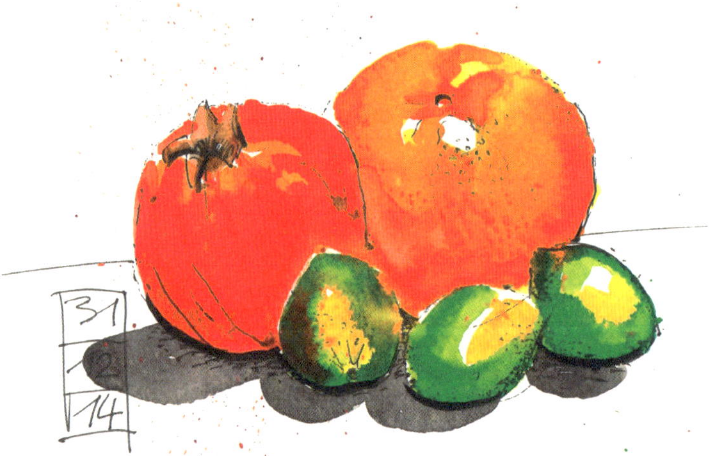

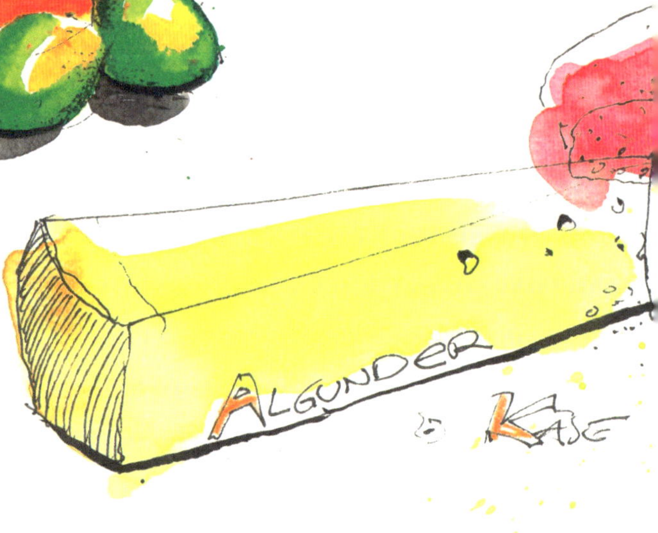

Noted in My Sketchbook:
One Man's Philosophy

A Bavarian village pub: In the early evening, I sit down at a table with a corner bench, alone. I order a beer, unpack my sketchbook and some pens. My eyes scan the interior and the guests. Linger briefly on one or the other. Wander back to the paper. I'm engrossed in my first strokes when a deep baritone sounds next to me. "Are you a painter?" I peer into a bearded face reddened by alcohol. "I'm an illustrator," I reply. "Can you make a living with that?" my counterpart asks. "It's enough," I reply. "That's all you need, then. And as long as there's a beer in it, it's all good, right?" the bearded man grumbles contentedly and raises his glass to us artists.

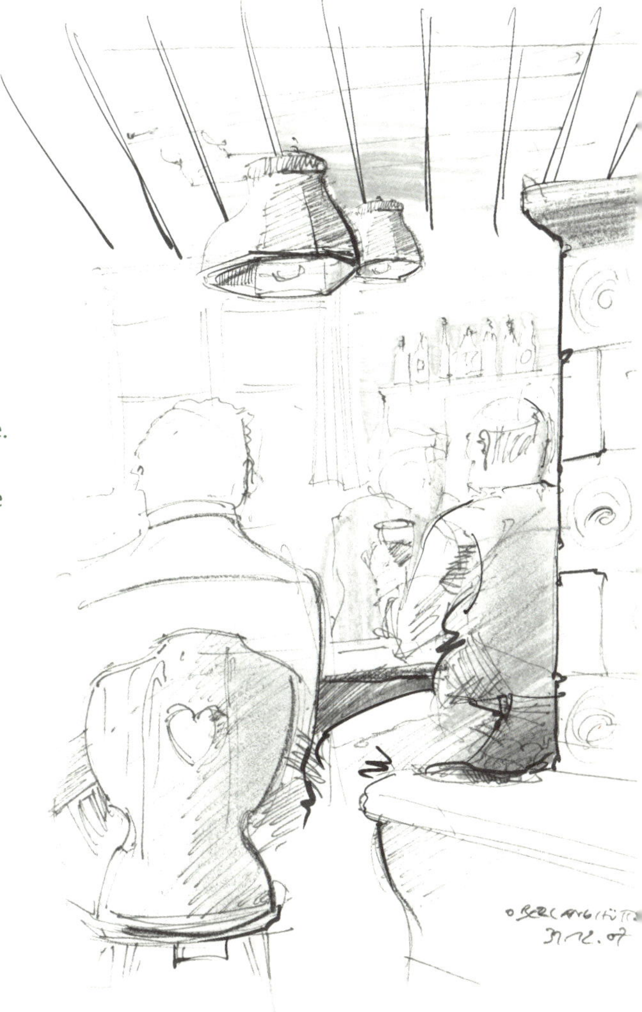

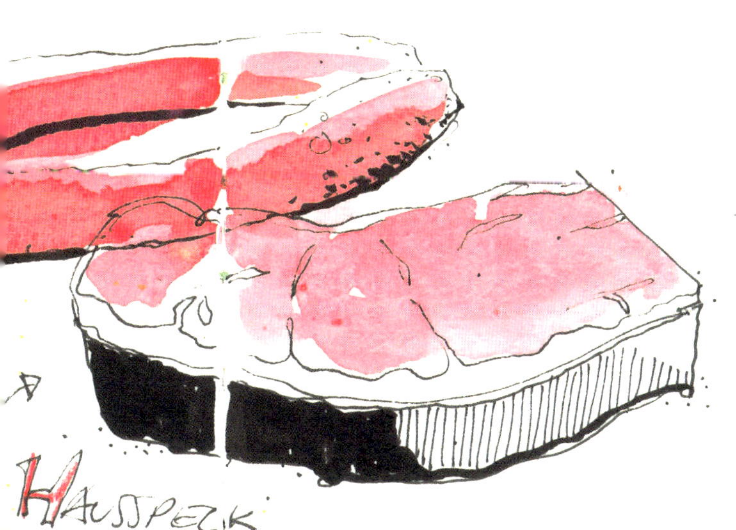

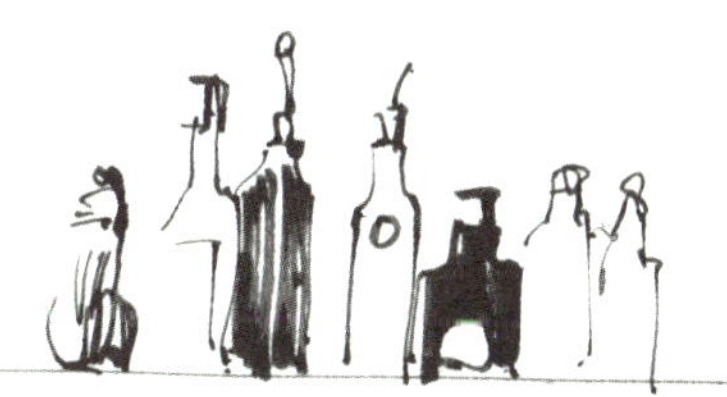

The School of Seeing

A Change of Perspective

Digital images are in such abundance that many subjects degenerate into clichés—places that have been visited thousands of times. It's hard to find anything new to draw. Everything's already been seen, photographed, shared, liked. Pictures have a short half-life. The choice of subjects is a challenge for every artist, in every familiar or unfamiliar place, in every situation anew. When you find yourself depicting the same subjects over and over again, repeating yourself in your choices, it's time for a change of perspective. And it's simple to change it in no time.

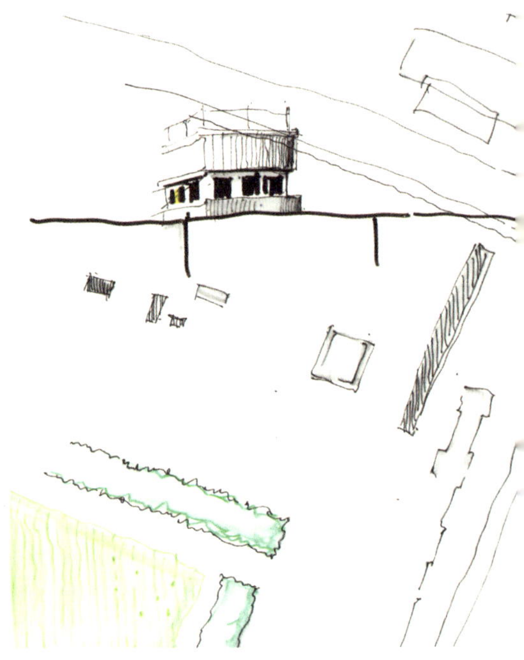

Suggestion no. 1: Change your viewing angle. For example, look at the scene from above (you can do it without a drone), or shift your eye level drastically downward (frog's-eye view).

Suggestion no. 2: Hardly anyone gets from A to B today without the help of GPS and digital maps. Transfer the view on your route planner to your sketchbook. Terrain lines, symbols, routes, and altitudes entered by hand leave an authentic impression.

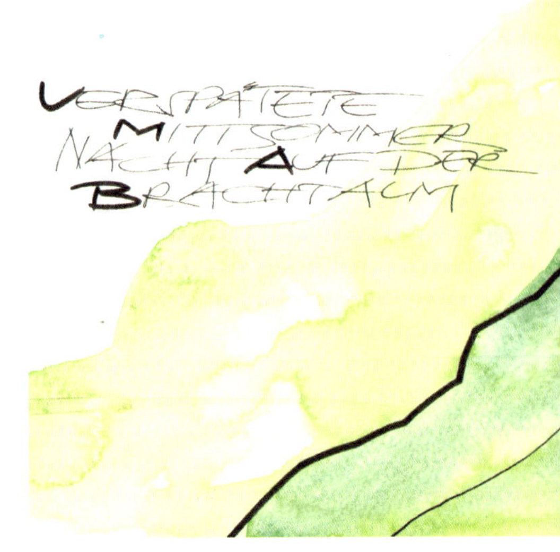

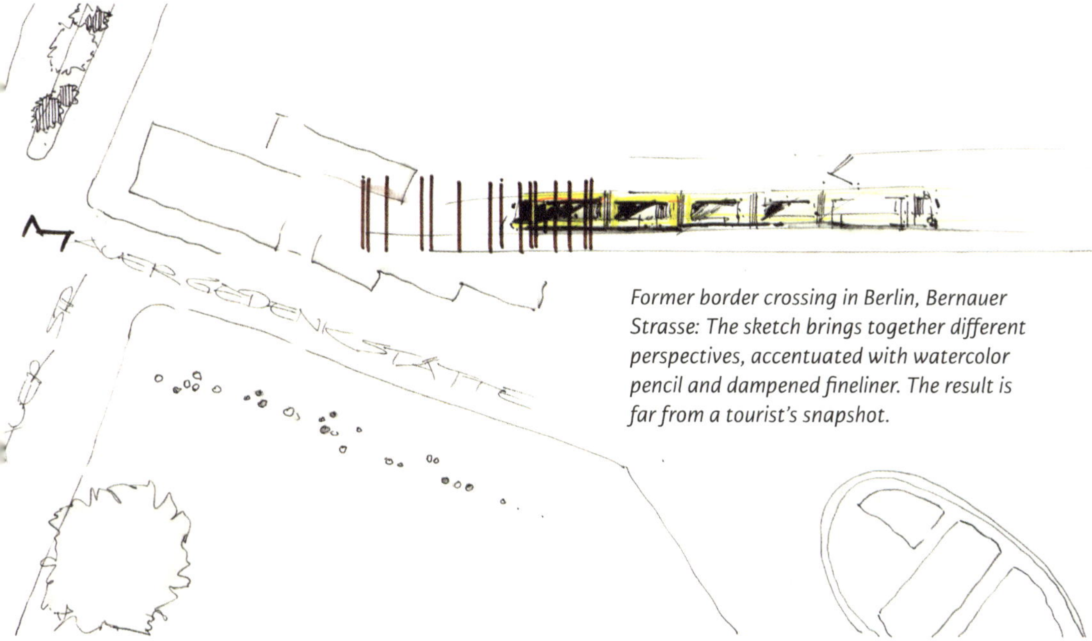

Former border crossing in Berlin, Bernauer Strasse: The sketch brings together different perspectives, accentuated with watercolor pencil and dampened fineliner. The result is far from a tourist's snapshot.

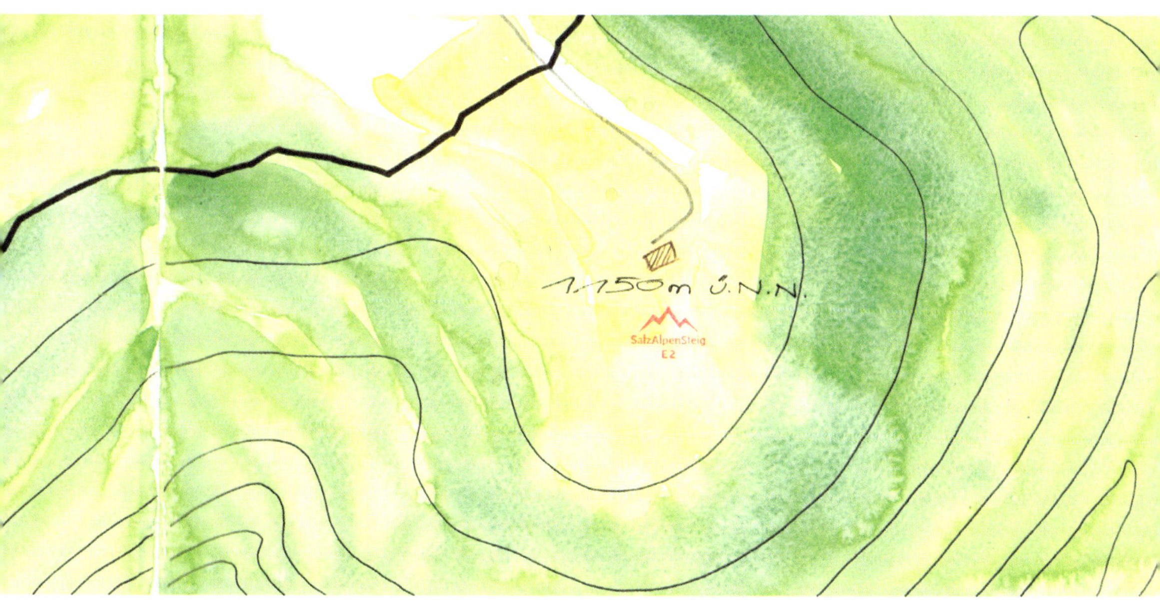

Orientation Aids

When I prepare for a sketching
workshop, I first get an overview
of the location. Places are explored,
a map of worthwhile drawing spots
is created in my head and on paper.
You can approach a new city by
sketching a preview from a bird's-
eye view. Free city maps are available
at any tourist information office to
inspire you.

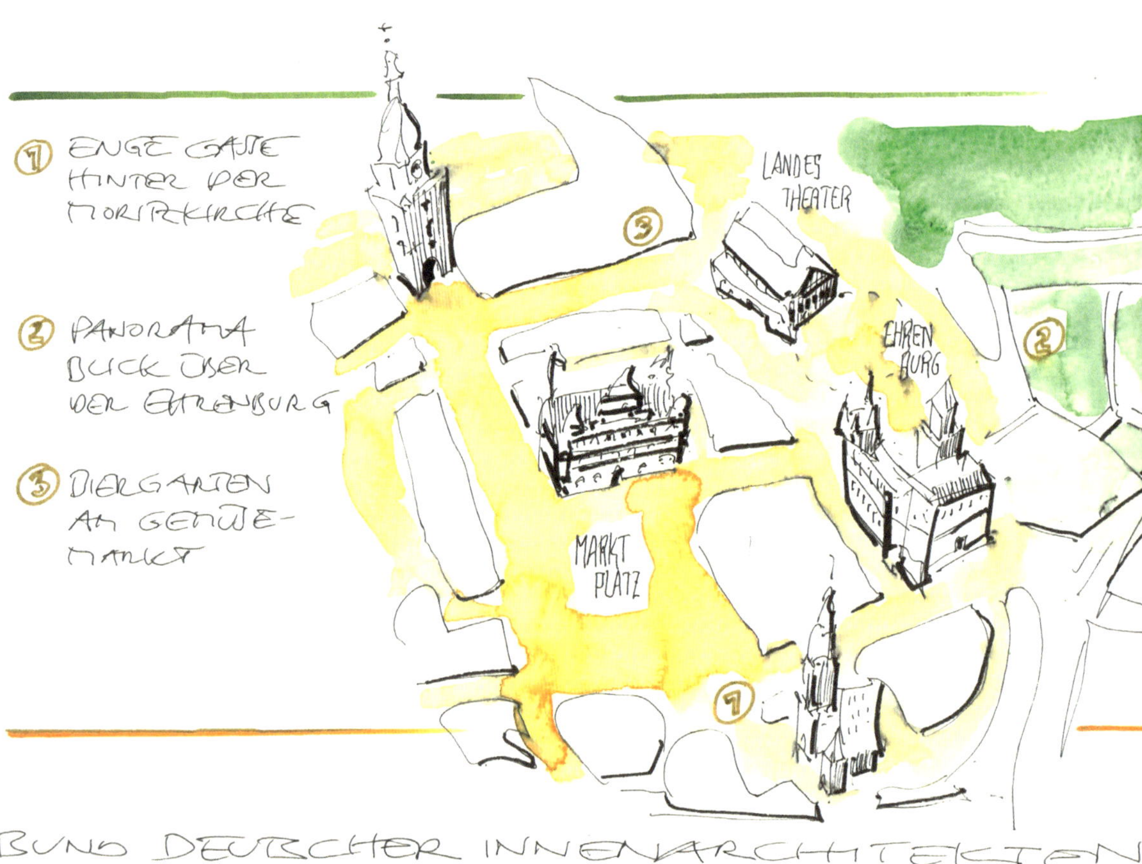

Bird's-eye view: Drawing spots
in Coburg, Germany. I only
indicated the location of alleys
and squares in simplified form,
sketched important buildings
from above, then highlighted
them in watercolor.

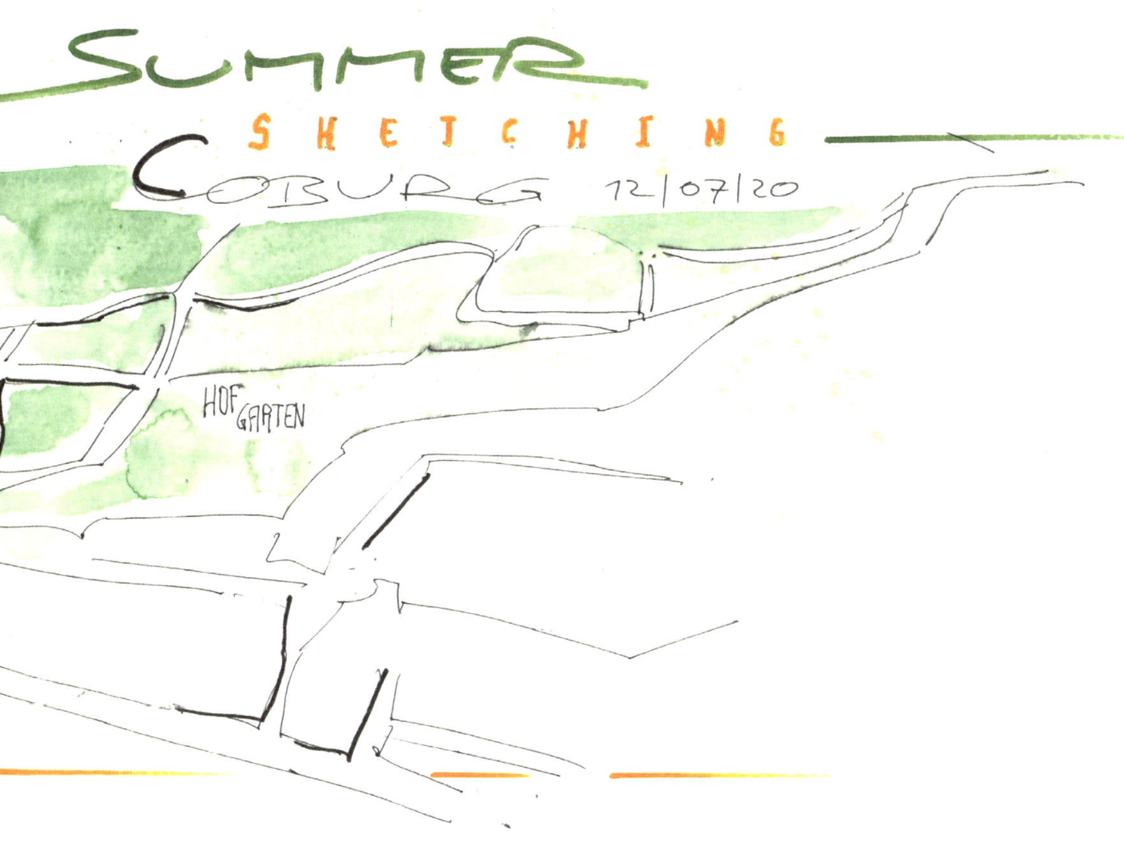

SUMMER
SKETCHING
COBURG   12/07/20
HOFGARTEN

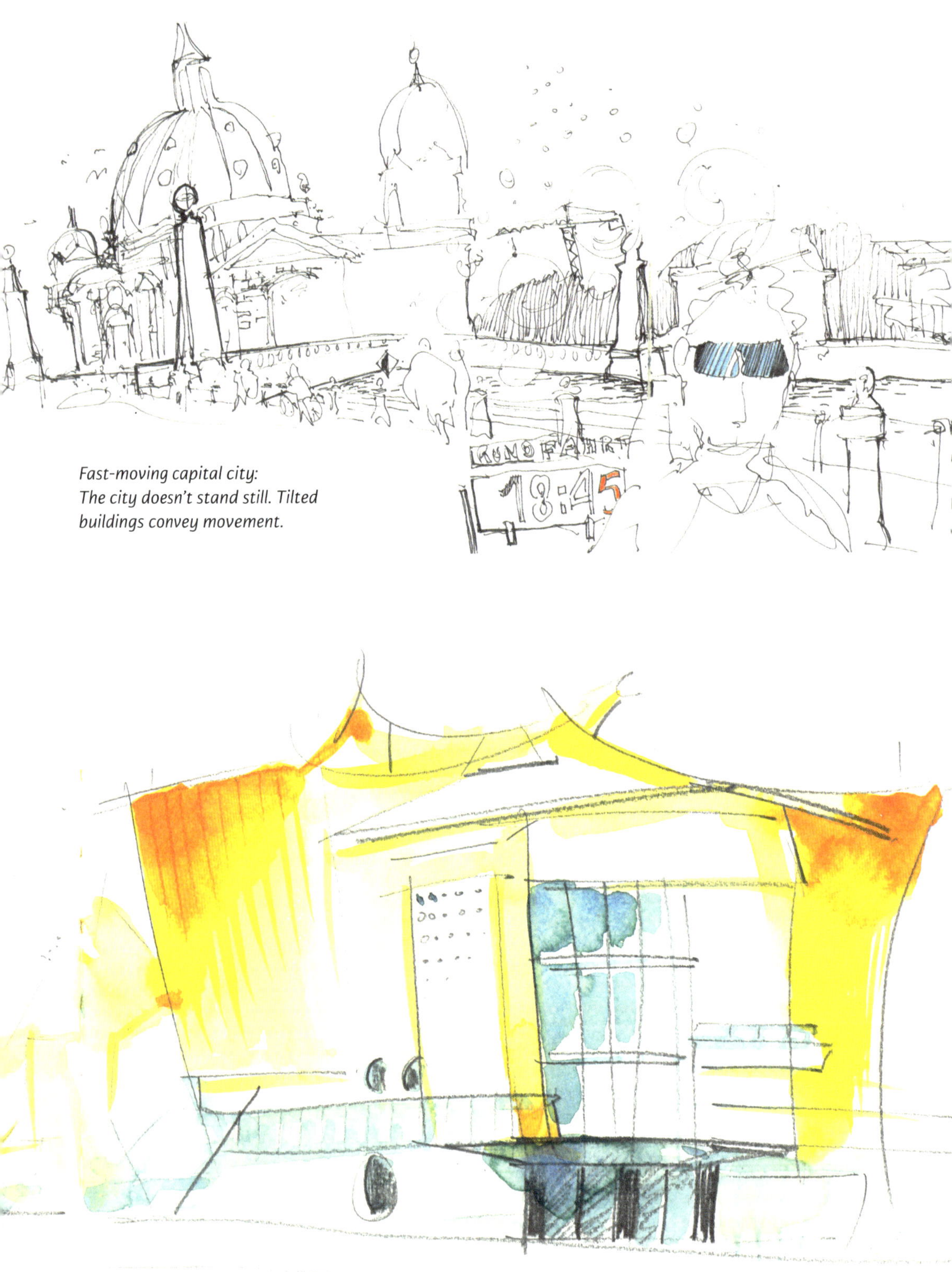

Fast-moving capital city:
The city doesn't stand still. Tilted
buildings convey movement.

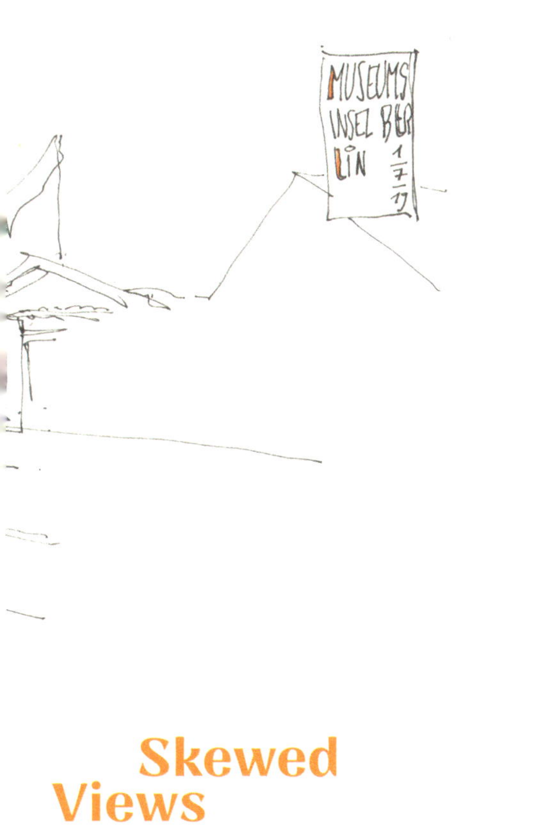

Skewed Views

Forget for a moment what you've learned about perspective: horizon, vanishing points, and foreshortening. Of course, they all help you to create drawings with correct perspective, but it's not how your picture is "constructed" that matters to a viewer, but the impact of the picture, its message. Houses seem ready to topple over. A Gothic tower stretches into infinity. Buildings emerge, expanding at the roof and contracting at the base. To create tension and dynamism, your pictures can be a little "skewed." An unusual perspective is more narratively effective than reality.

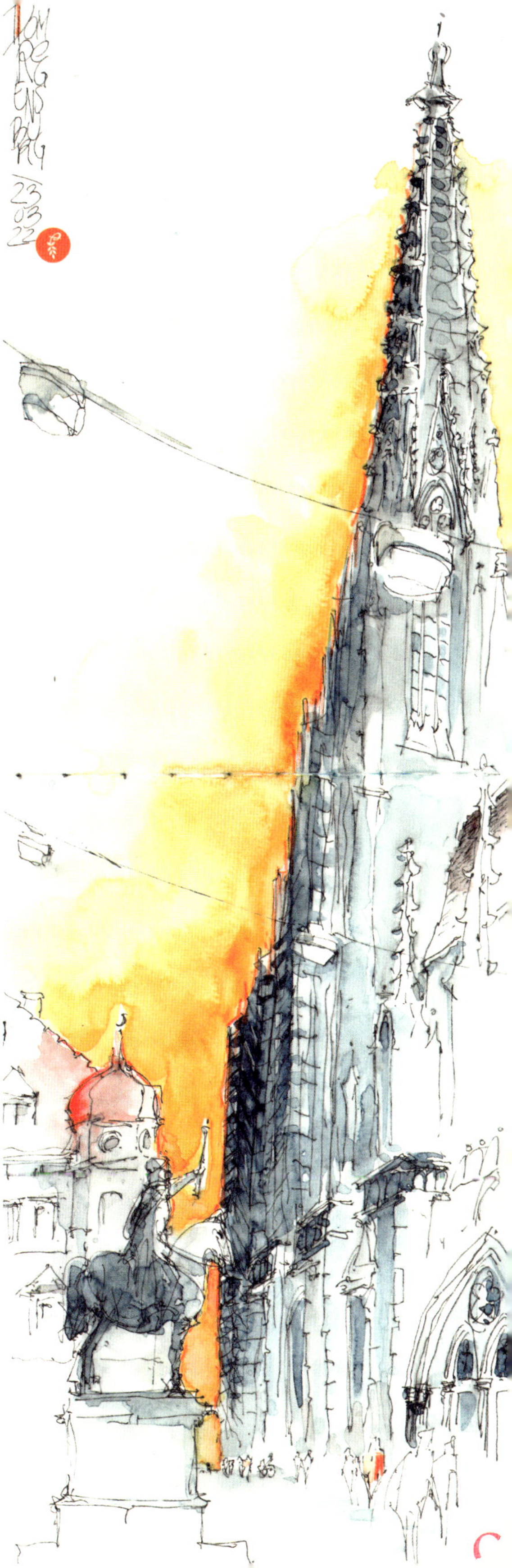

Upending Expectations

The little cup, the big table. The blue sky, the green meadow. The mighty oak, the tiny beetle. I prefer to break with viewing habits and upend expectations. Create suspense in your travel sketches by replacing the true-to-life with narrative pictorial statements. Make mountains out of molehills. Enlarge small things, swap top and bottom, color the tree blue. Once again, the advantage of drawing over photography becomes obvious: You decide for yourself what the components of your picture look like. The story behind the subject takes precedence over logical construction.

Beware of fire beetles: While sketching in Georgia, curious beetles joined me on the paper. When greatly enlarged, they draw attention to the foreground of the picture. Their striking red color is a warning signal to potential predators.

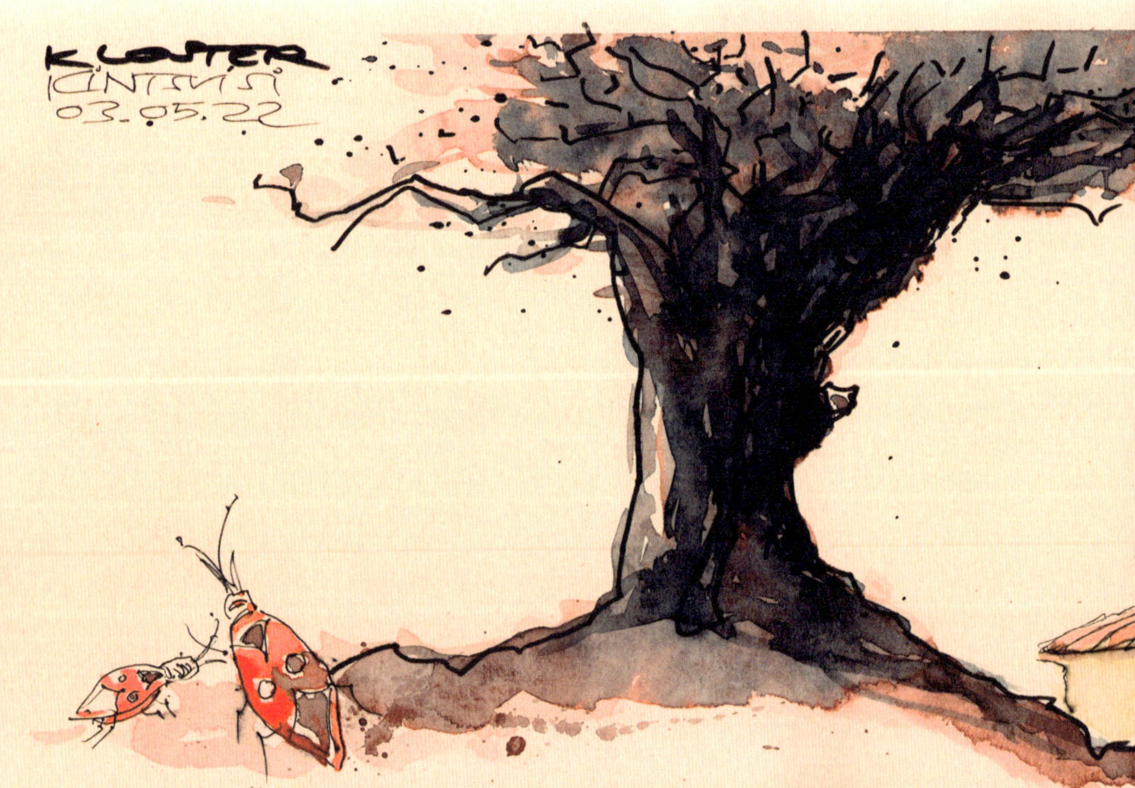

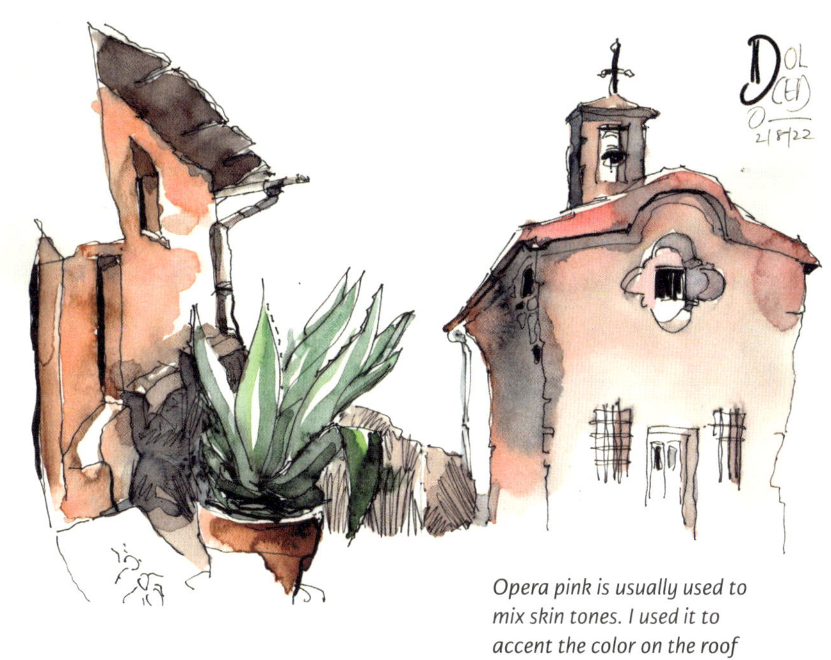

Opera pink is usually used to mix skin tones. I used it to accent the color on the roof of a Ligurian village church.

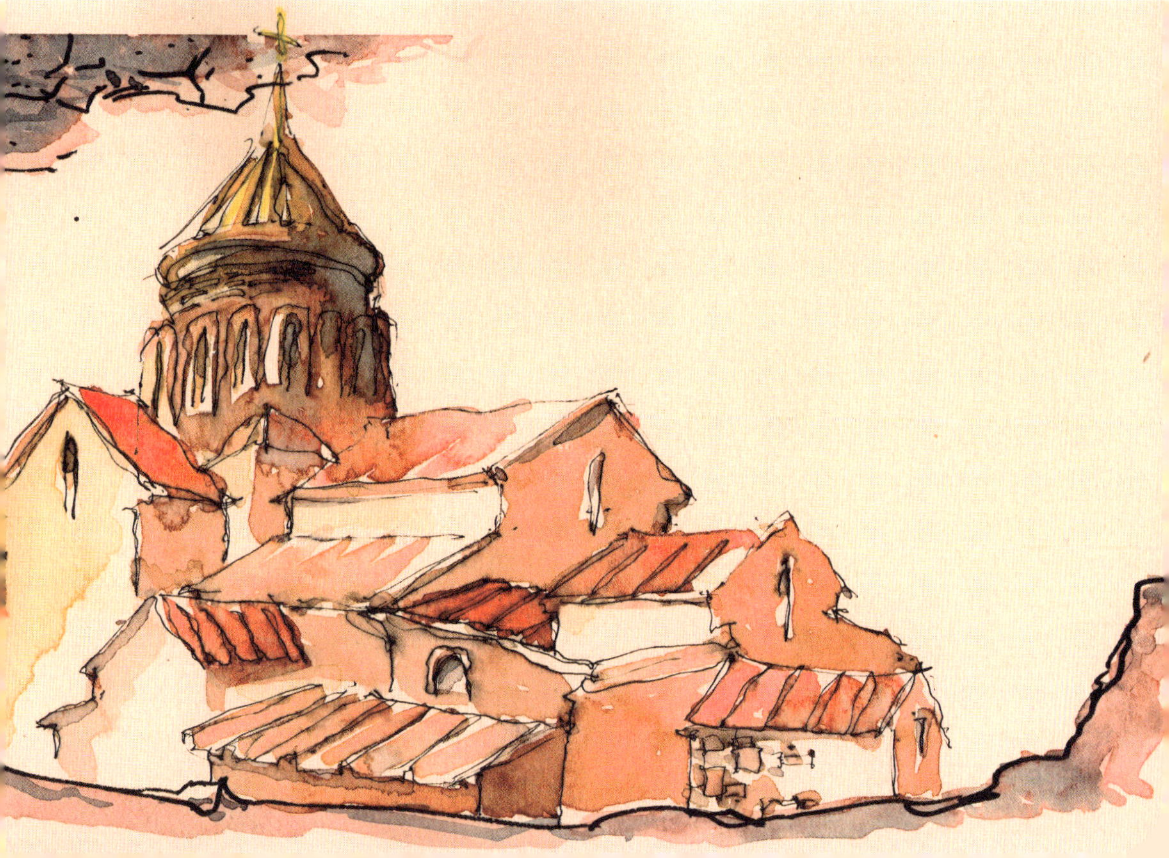

Challenging Places

There are places where you'll find it difficult to draw. You won't see a trace of beauty, romance, or comfort, but instead sadness, ugliness, alienation. So, what can you do with an empty sketchbook far from the charms of Italy?

For my workshops, I sometimes choose places that don't lend themselves to drawing at first glance. It's a good exercise in the school of seeing, of visual mindfulness, to face the challenge of difficult-to-draw places. Here's some advice on how you can elicit drawings from "challenging" places.

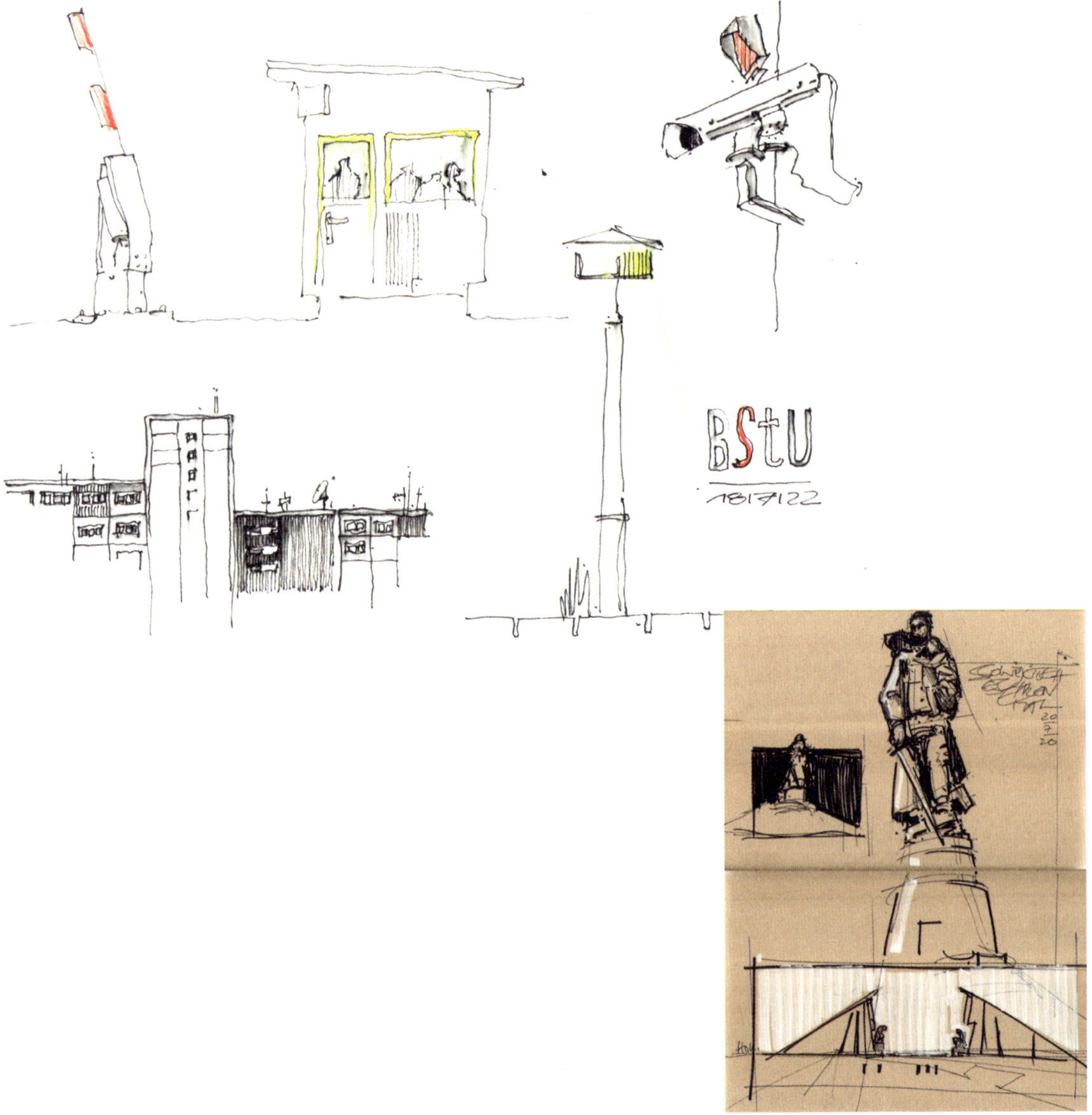

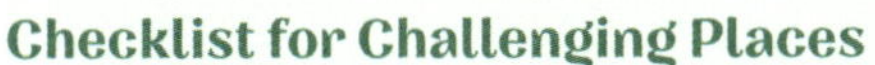

Checklist for Challenging Places

1. Don't steer clear of places like memorials, monuments, or buildings with a political past.
2. Take your time in the place; observe closely.
3. Look for remnants of the past in conspicuous and inconspicuous objects, building details, and signs: old-fashioned, dilapidated, historical.
4. Collect your finds on a page of your sketchbook. Together they tell a story.
5. Use color, light, and shadow to emphasize the atmosphere of the place.
6. In noisy, cramped, drafty, unpleasant places, choose a position where you can work well.

Tip: I like to depict historical buildings like the Palace of Culture and Science in Warsaw— a "gift" from Stalin to Poland—in sepia ink.

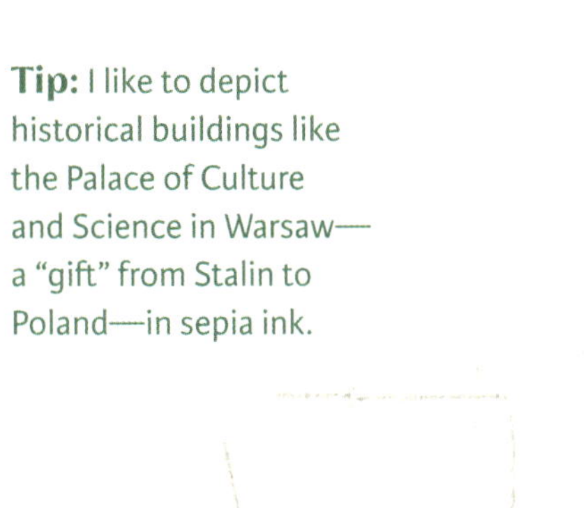

Stillness

In every village, every small town, and every big city, you can find retreats that keep the noise and hustle and bustle of civilization at bay for a while. They're great places to linger and draw—indoors (museums, churches, coffeehouses) or outdoors (parks, gardens, side streets, backyards).

Cemeteries are ideal for travel sketchers because they can be found all over the world. They're quiet places where you can unpack your sketchbook and drawing utensils undisturbed. Many cemeteries are surprisingly lively, and they are always worth sketching. Take a closer look at the stories that statues, stones, and epitaphs have to tell.

German cemetery in the Czech Republic: Portraits in porcelain, two languages in stone. A sketch in black and white with a fiber-tip pen is all you need for this panoramic view.

Whaling stories at night: On the island of Amrum, elaborate gravestones tell sailors' life stories. Plenty of indigo blue and stamps emphasize the mystery of the place. You can find tips on painting night scenes in watercolors on page 228.

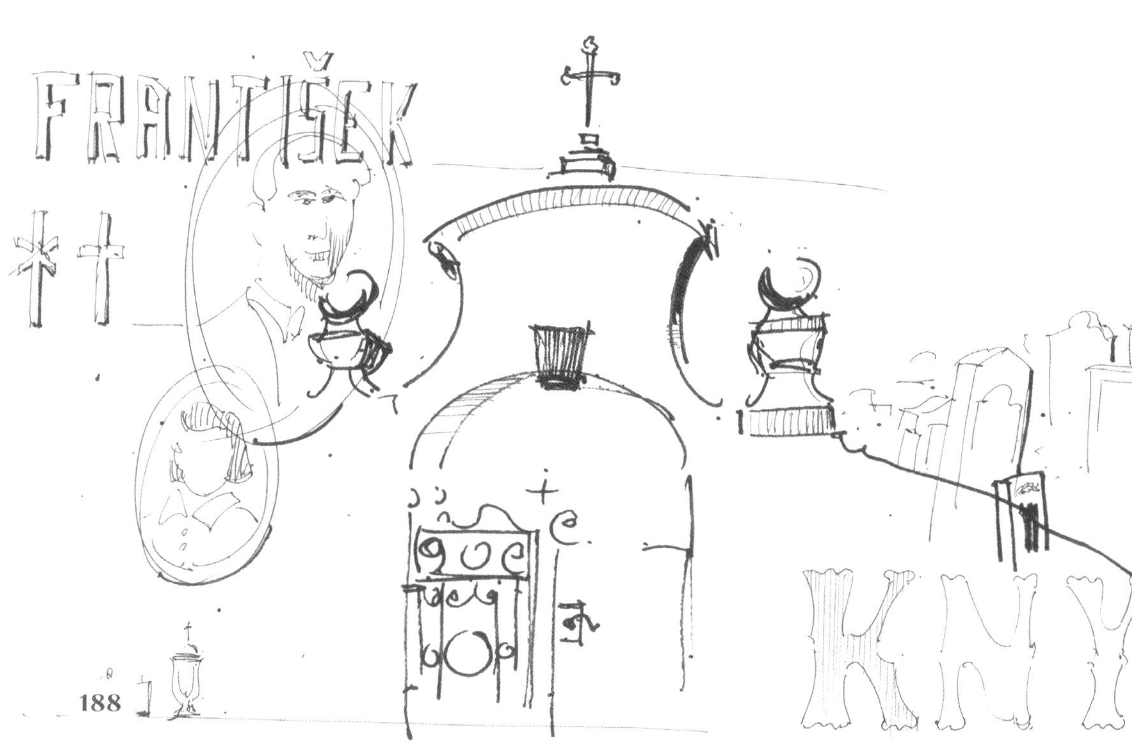

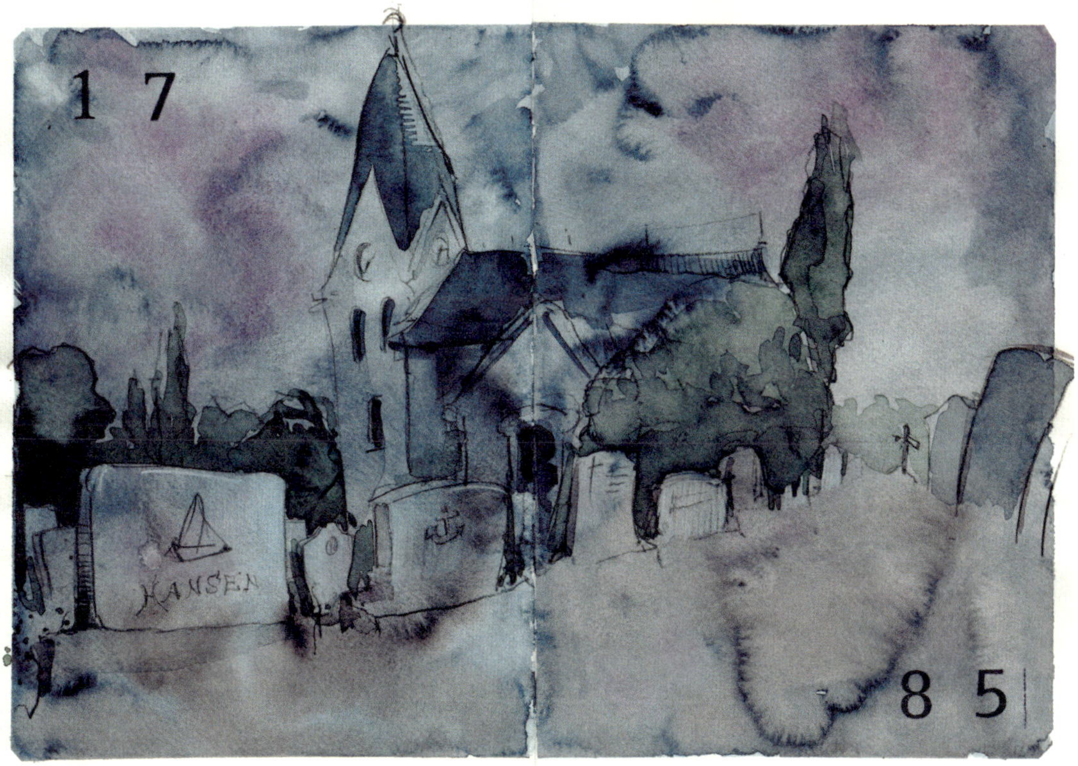

1 7
HANSEN
8 5

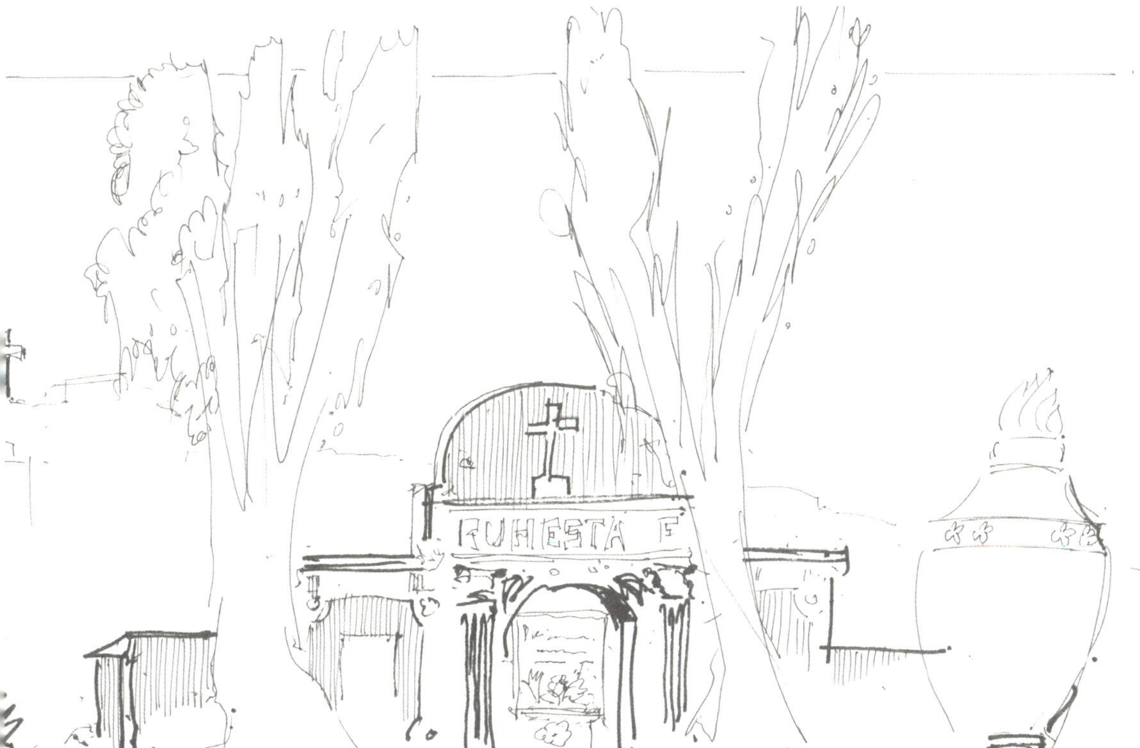

RUHESTÄ F

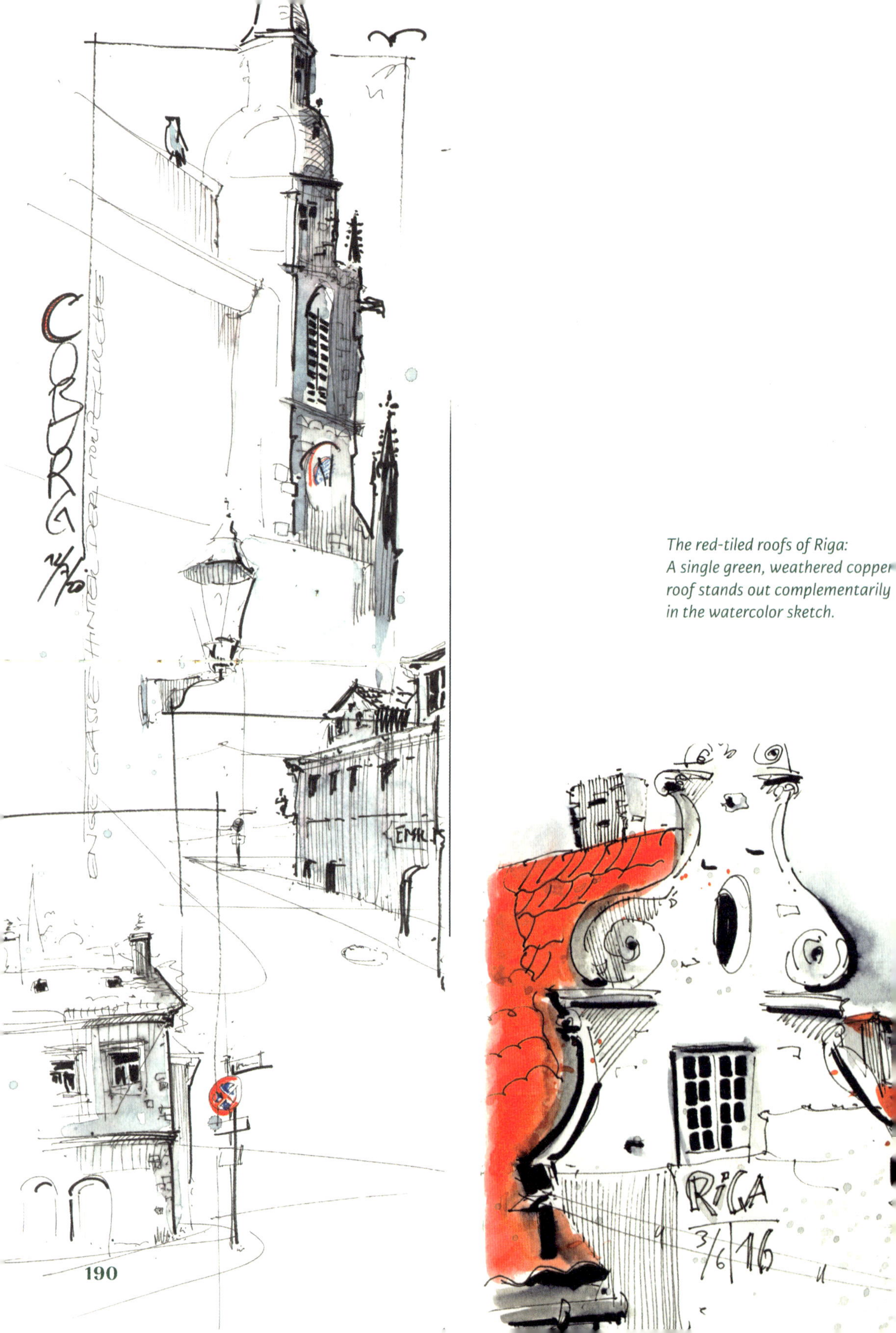

The red-tiled roofs of Riga:
A single green, weathered copper
roof stands out complementarily
in the watercolor sketch.

190

Detour: Historic Towns

Which is worth a sketchbook entry: a romantic old town center or the urban backdrop surrounding it? The stone-carved witnesses to the city's history or the spectacular new buildings?

What's visually interesting—and therefore authentic—is whatever attracts you to a place. Unfamiliar scenes, the view from the hotel window, chance encounters on the street. The smells, noises, voices, colors, and sounds of the city. If you fall back on traditional subjects, like fountains on the market square, you're on safe ground, but also stuck on the well-trodden paths of hundreds of travel artists before you.

The search for what to sketch is subjective. Whether it's a change of scenery in your own country or a trip to a faraway place, what goes into your sketchbook is entirely up to your personal interests, both in a small town or a big city.

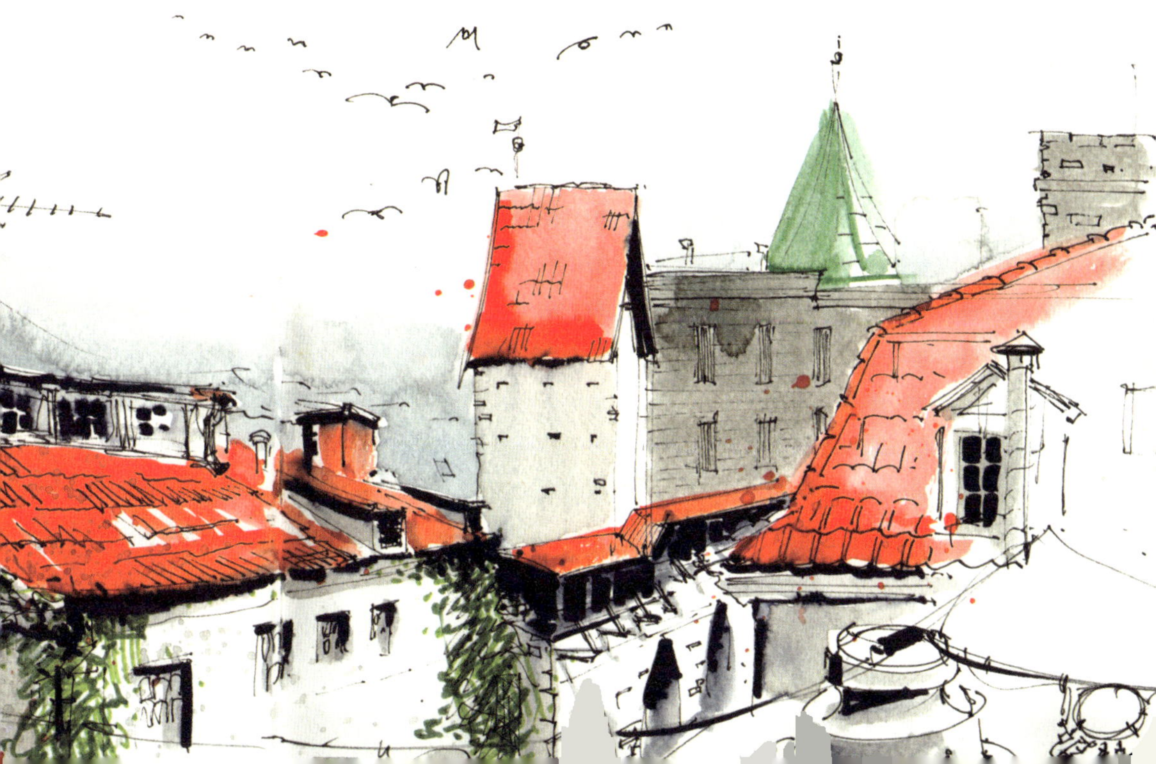

Old or New?

One day, a friend who is an architecture aficionado from Japan visited me in Munich. The Oktoberfest had just been set up, and he was amazed at the structures on the Theresienwiese (the site of the annual festival) in the middle of the city. He wondered which buildings were historical and which were temporary. He was certain his first impressions were correct: The colossal monument of Bavaria must be a temporary backdrop, while the Ferris wheel was certainly a permanent fixture. But he was wrong; I had to smile. How we see a built environment is very personal. Make your own observations, and be open to historical, modern, and foreign places, with fresh city views in your sketchbook. Whether they're centuries old or were built yesterday.

Tip: Simplify roof surfaces. Individual roof tiles are only hinted at; colored surfaces dissolve into a lot of the white of the paper.

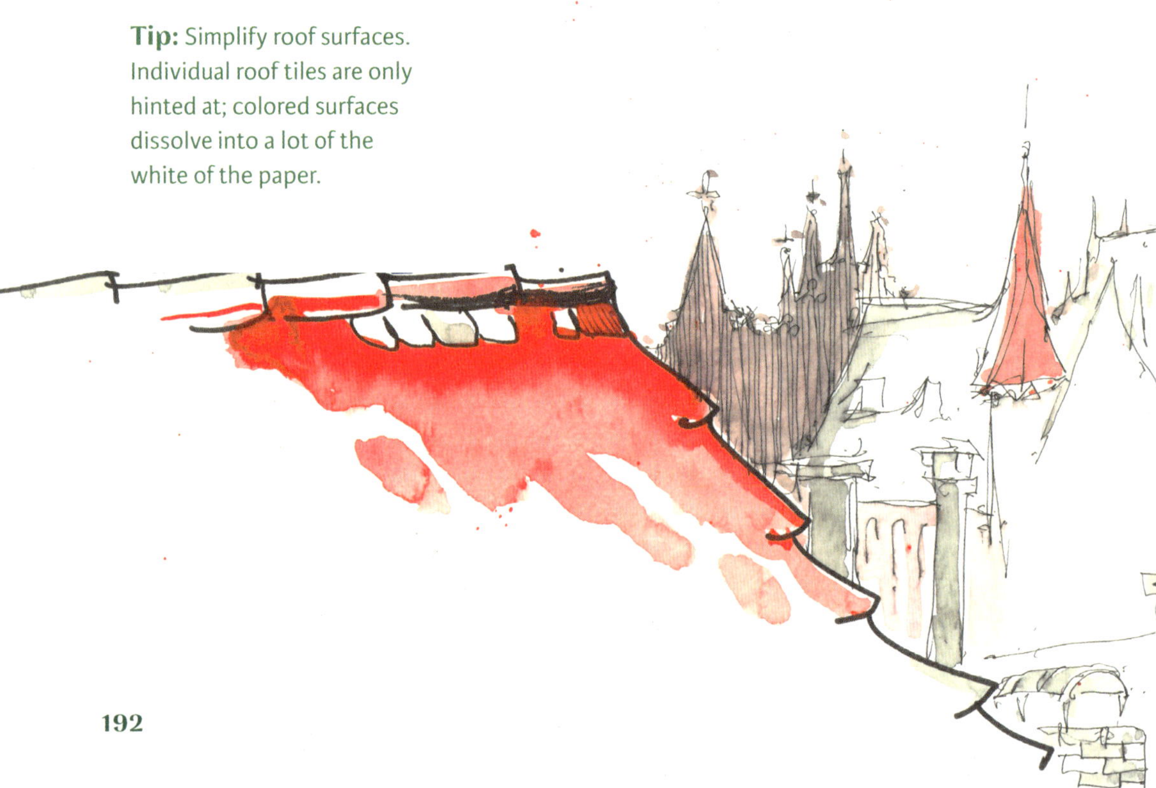

Towers

Towers are reliable landmarks that are
visible from afar. Back in the Middle
Ages, church steeples, city fortifica-
tions, castles, and palaces enticed
onlookers—if only because of the
contrast between their vertical form
and the usual horizontal line of the
landscape. You don't have to be an
architectural historian to realize this.
Then as now, towers in all their
forms are visual focal points that
magically attract travelers and artists.

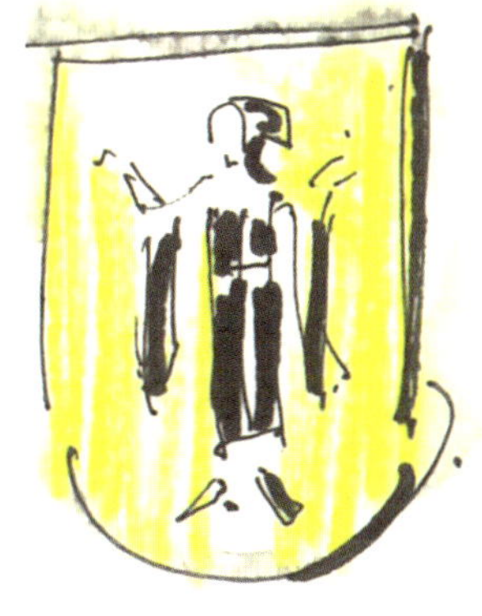

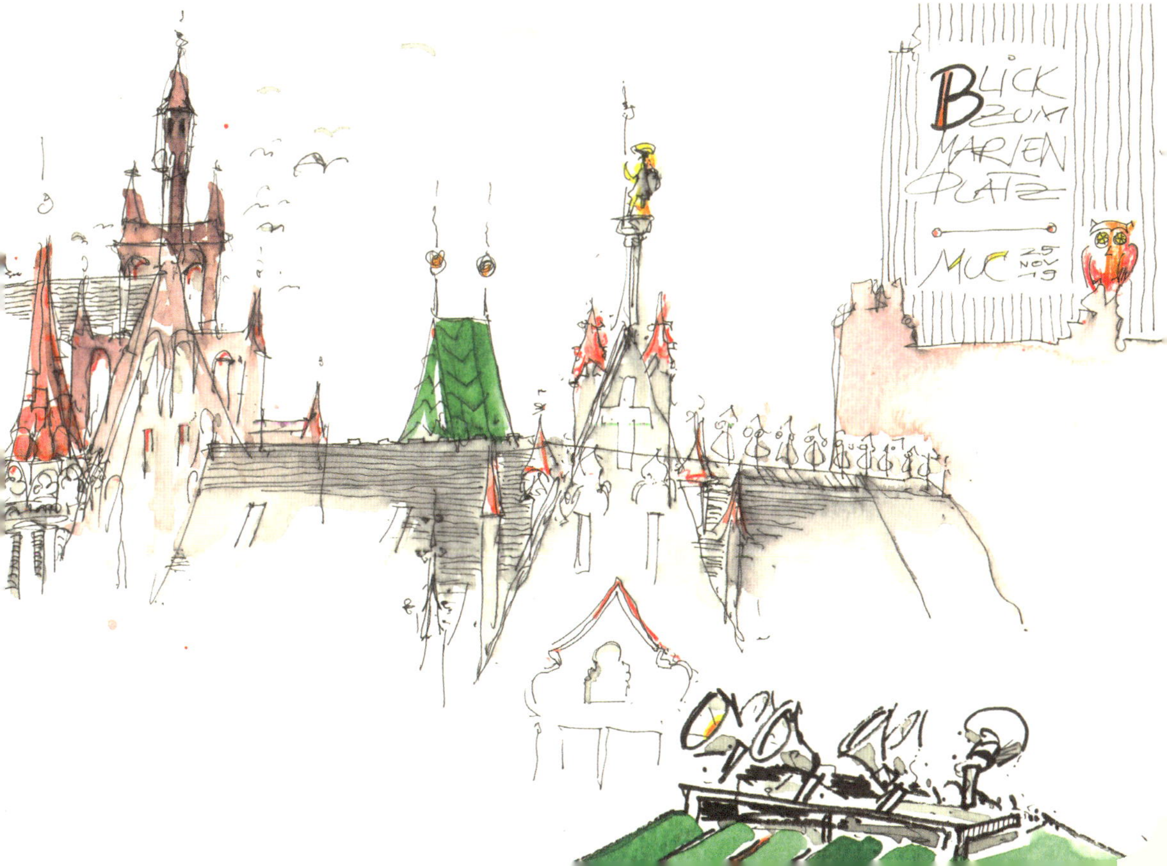

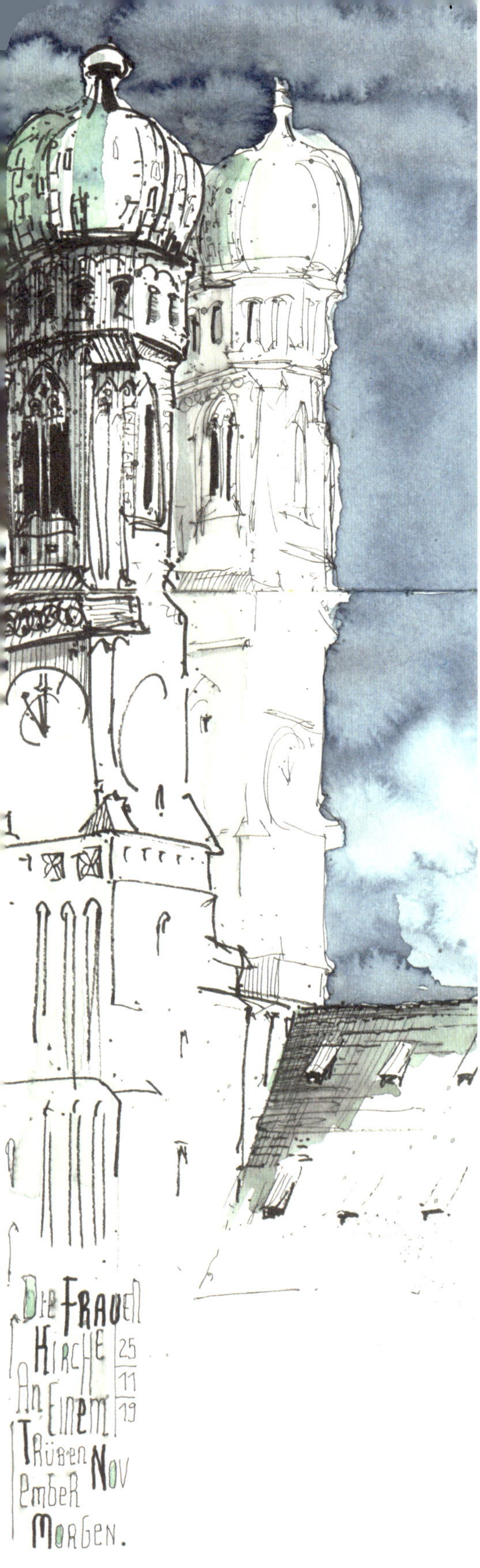

Collecting Shapes

My sketchbooks don't just contain domes and cupolas. As an attentive artist, you may feel the same way: Once your attention is awakened, you'll quickly find more objects to observe. The "collecting" begins. Pagodas that attract the benevolence of the gods. Lighthouses that mark harbor entrances. Wooden churches that borrow their form from nature.

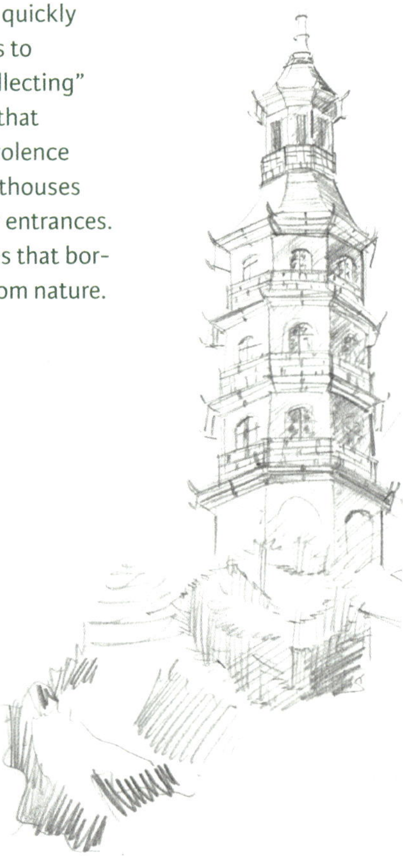

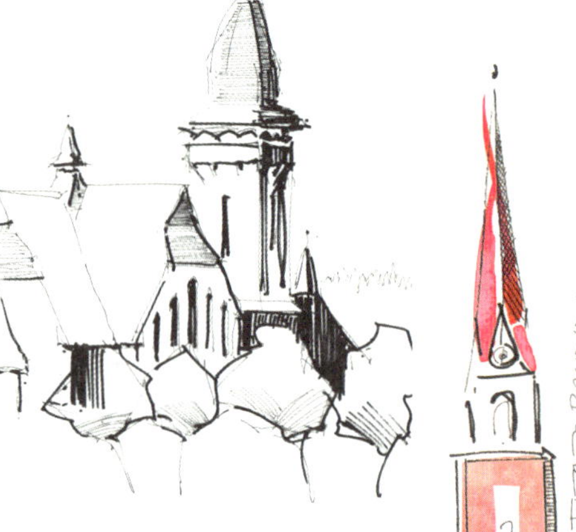

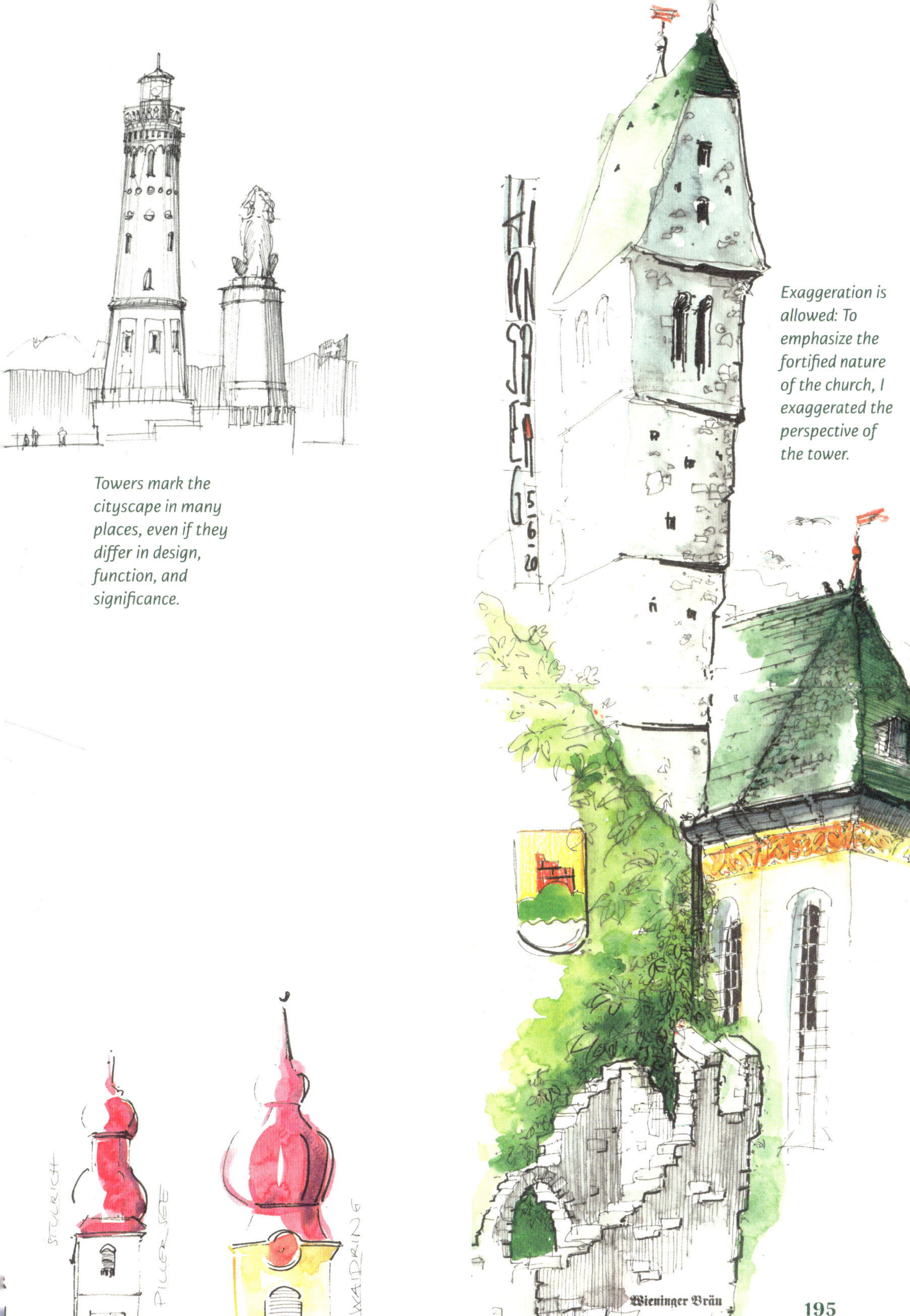

Towers mark the
cityscape in many
places, even if they
differ in design,
function, and
significance.

Exaggeration is
allowed: To
emphasize the
fortified nature
of the church, I
exaggerated the
perspective of
the tower.

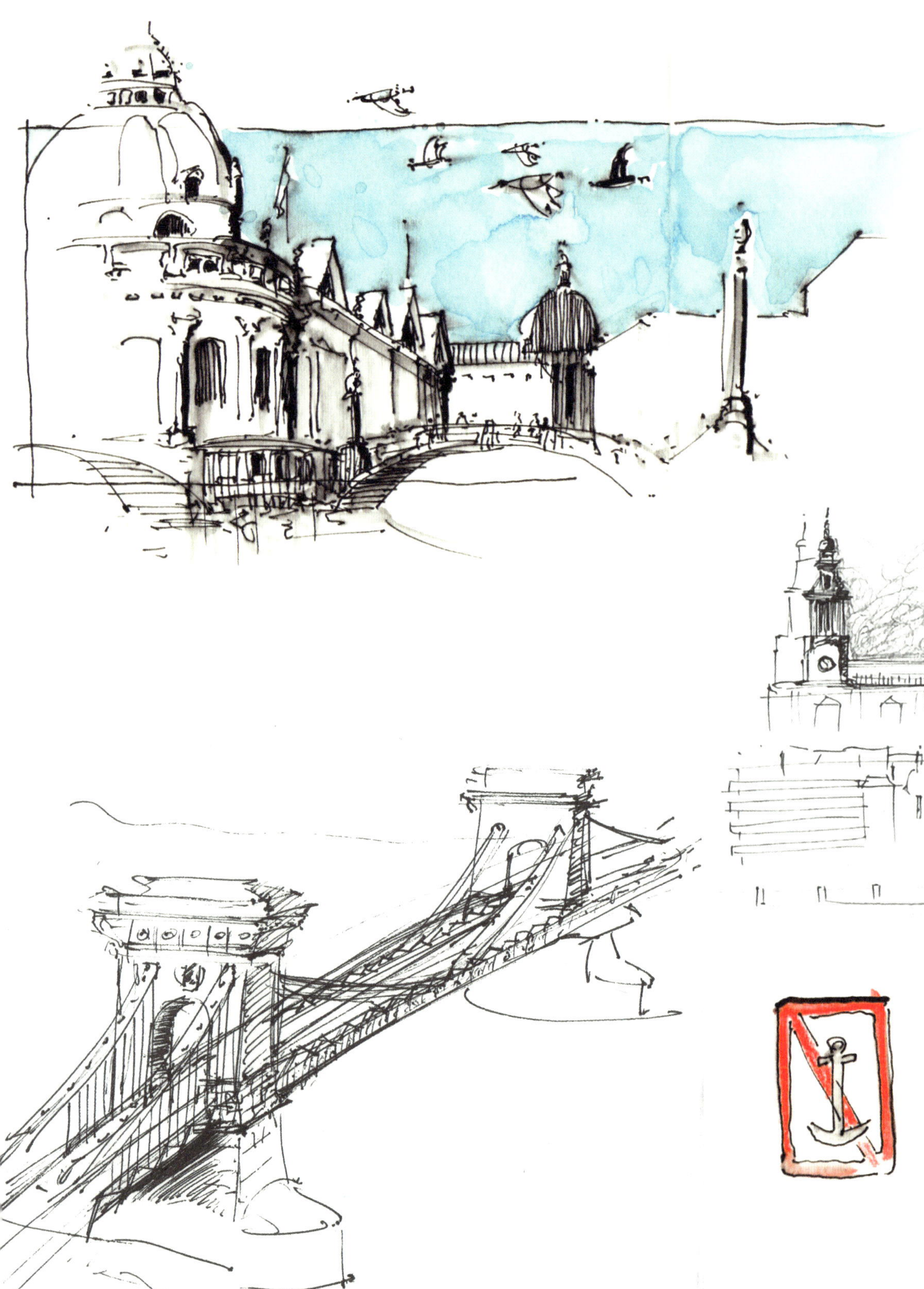

Bridges

Bridges are part of our artistic rendezvous with a city. Many of us might think of the bridges of Venice and Paris when it comes to romantic backdrops. Statistically speaking, Berlin has far more bridges than Venice. Hamburg holds the record in Europe with 2,500, followed by Vienna and Amsterdam. Bridges aren't just urban links. They provide lasting impressions of the city: as photography or drawing subjects, meeting places, historical sites, technological wonders, or movie backdrops.

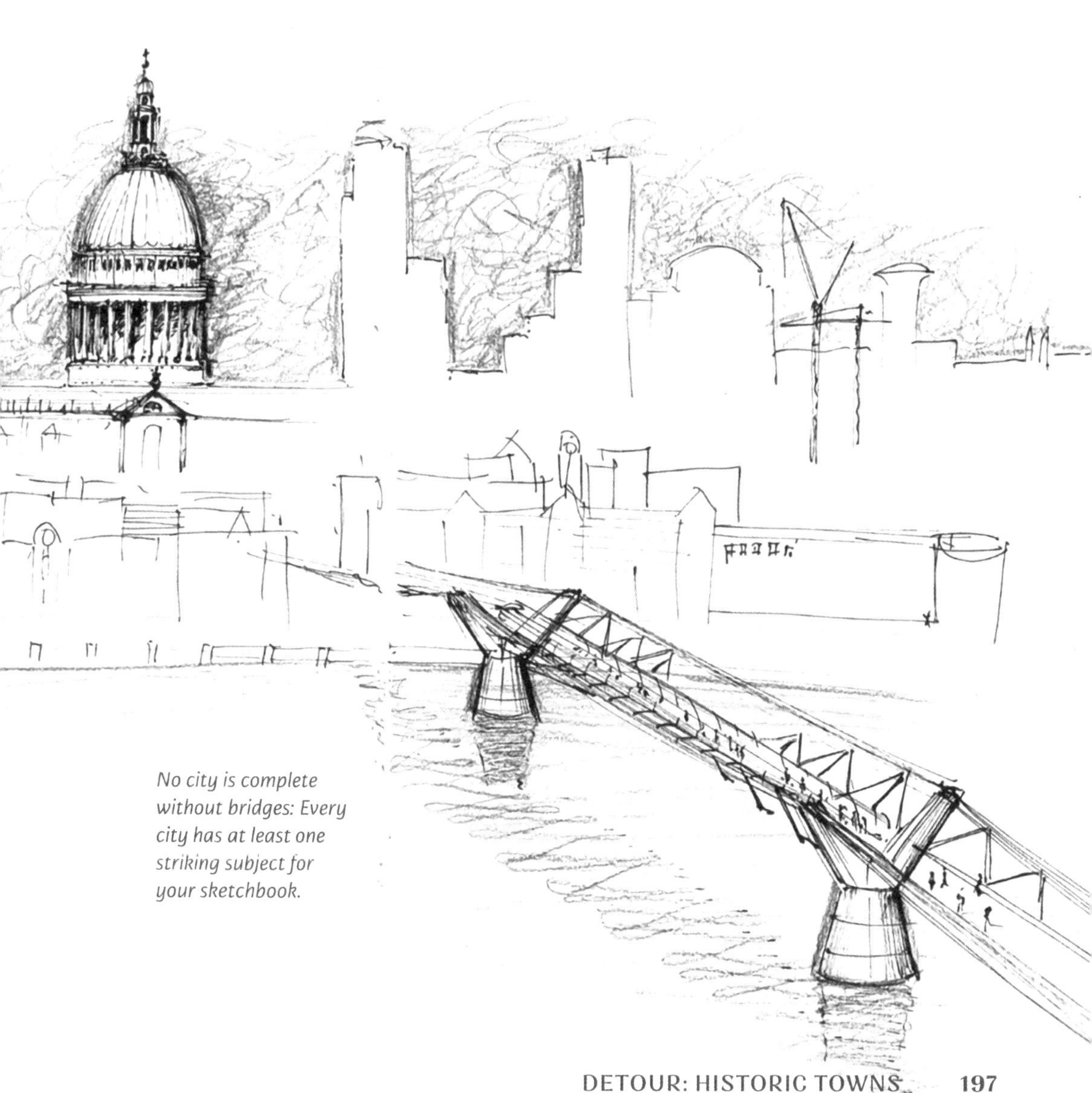

No city is complete without bridges: Every city has at least one striking subject for your sketchbook.

Squares

Where narrow streets and winding alleyways meet, where the urban space unexpectedly widens into a square or marketplace, another enticing world opens to us: shops, businesses, bars, cafés, and restaurants. We've all seen pictures of a sunny piazza in Genoa or Florence (the groan of the espresso machine, the smell of pizza, the rattling of scooters, car horns). How about sketching boulevards and avenues in Paris or New York instead?

The key is to carefully observe what of the place's atmosphere can be captured on paper. There are a few tips on the next double-page spread.

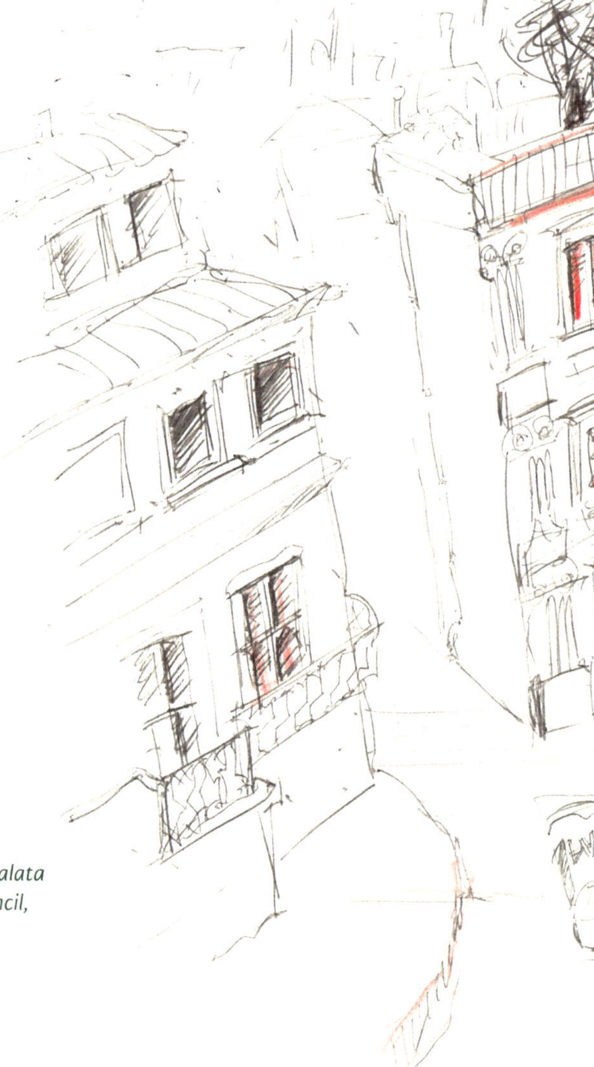

Istanbul from above: view from the Galata Tower café. Ballpoint pen, colored pencil, lots of sugar in my tea.

Tip: Windowpanes are always dark during the day. Left white, they look like empty eyes. So, fill the areas with hatching or dark color, although not every window needs to be meticulously filled in. I show depictions at night on page 228.

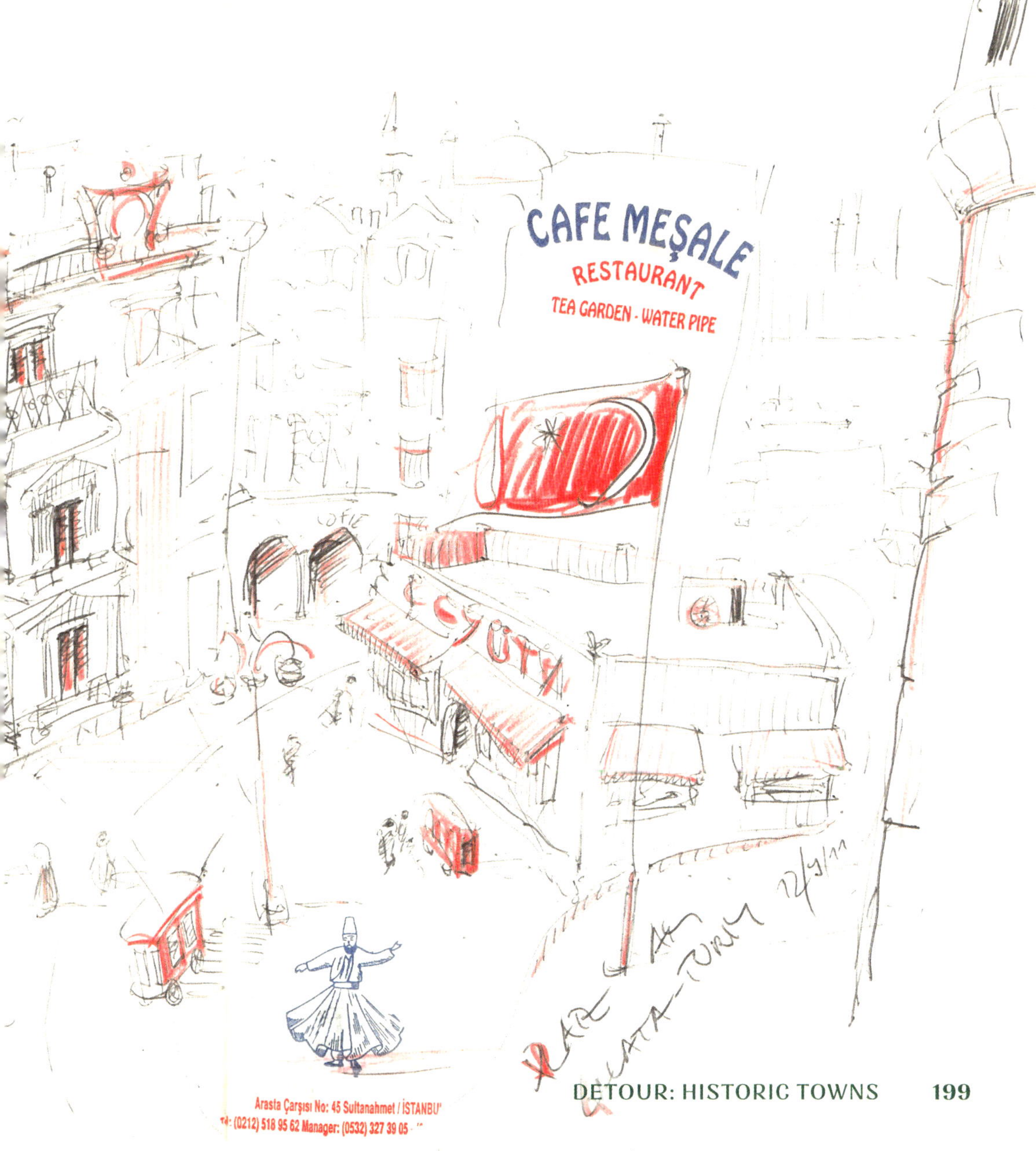

CAFE MEŞALE
RESTAURANT
TEA GARDEN - WATER PIPE
Arasta Çarşısı No: 45 Sultanahmet / İSTANBU'
Tel: (0212) 518 95 62 Manager: (0532) 327 39 05

Drawing Tips for Town Squares, Big or Small:

1. Find a comfortable place to sketch, where you feel relaxed and unobserved.
2. Determine where the center of the square is: your focal point. It can be a building, a monument, a lantern, or similar. But arrange it off-center for a more interesting composition.
3. Limit your subject at the sides: Cropped objects emphasize the space in between.
4. Mix views (buildings straight on from the front) with interesting perspectives (pay attention to vanishing points, see page 38).
5. Increase the depth of the image by using people and objects arranged in perspective.
6. Historical squares are organic structures—falling lines, crooked houses, dilapidated curbs are allowed in the picture.
7. Pay attention to the focal point when coloring. Contrast colored areas with the white of the paper.

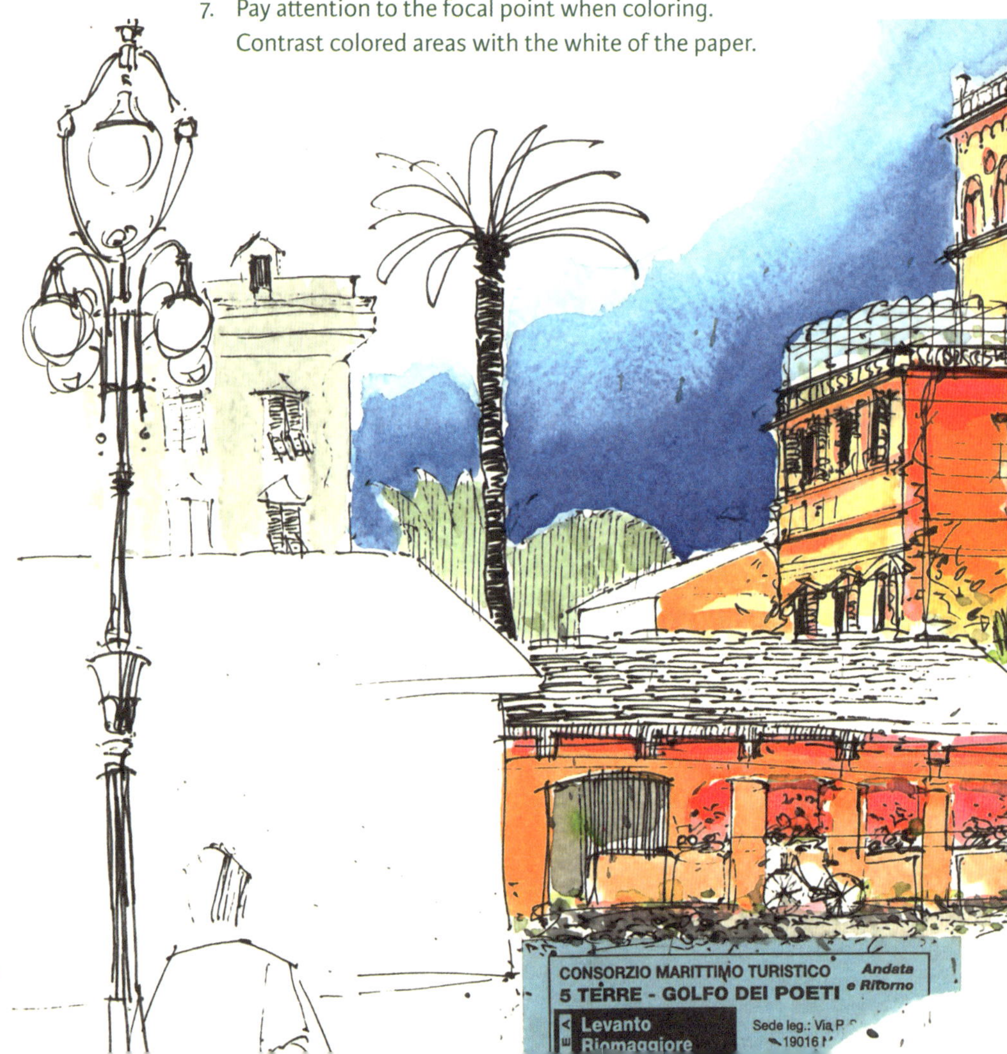

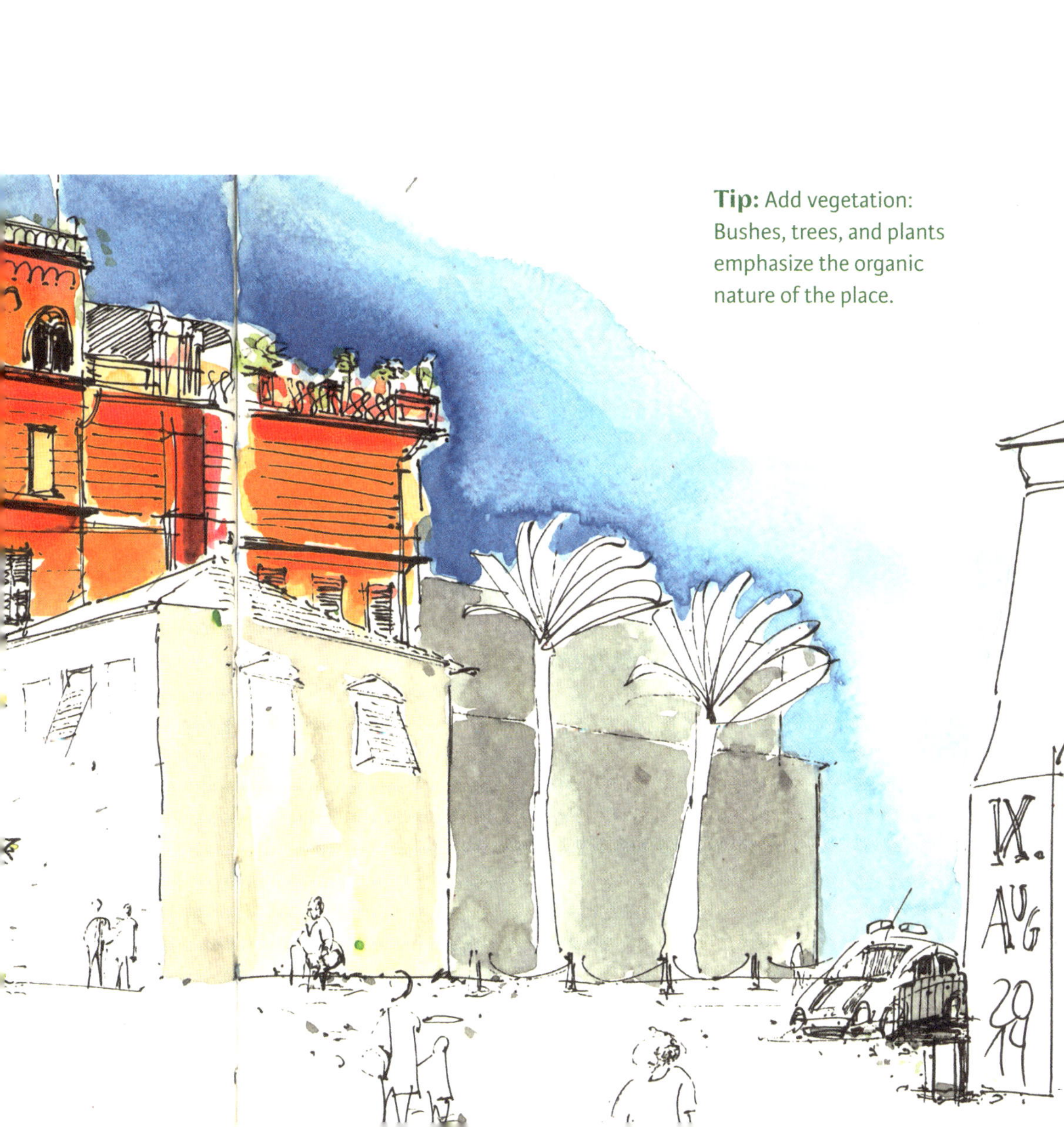

Tip: Add vegetation: Bushes, trees, and plants emphasize the organic nature of the place.

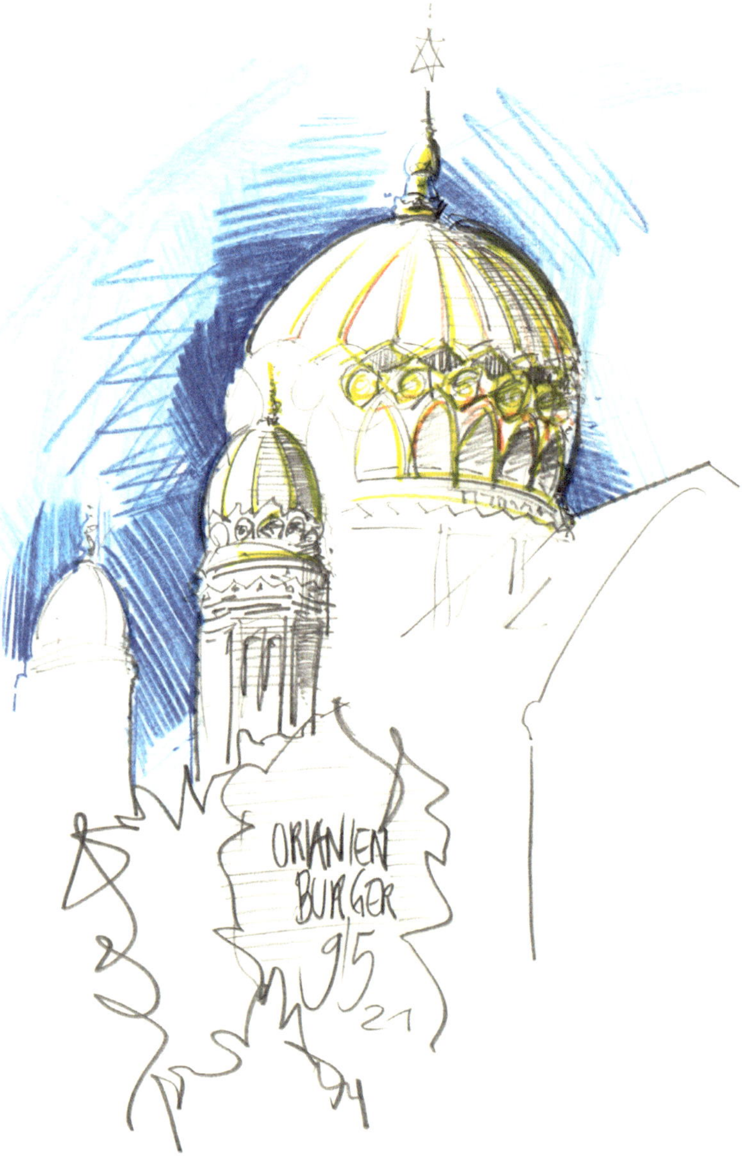

Hatching

Synagogue in Berlin: The richness of detail in
a building can be emphasized with hatching.
The precise line hatching frames the dome
and suggests more building details than are
present in the sketch.

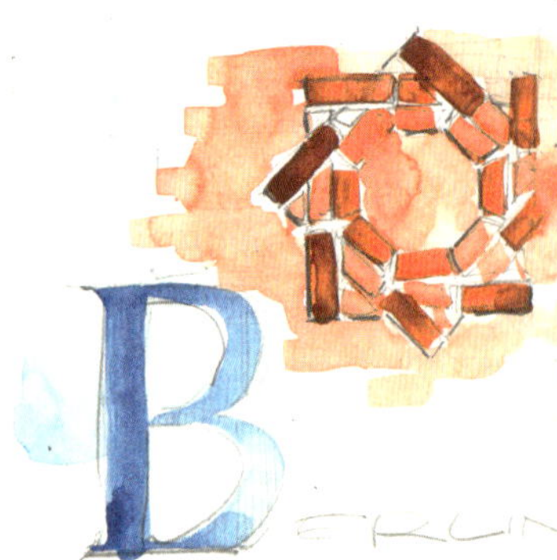

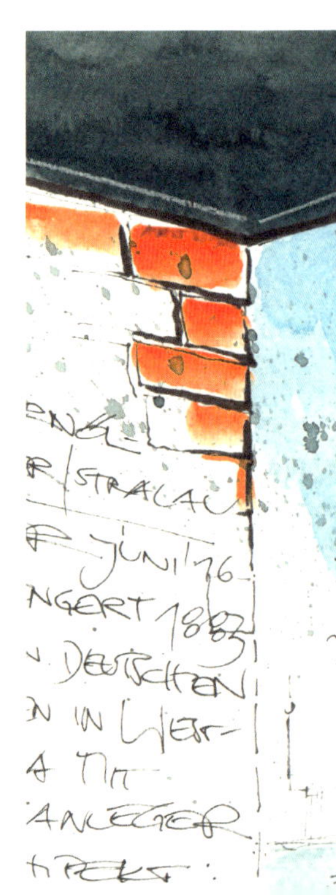

Facades

Facades regularly drive my course participants to despair, even the architects among them. Windows, windows, and more windows. Doors, gates, eaves. Columns, cornices, and stucco. Even before sketching begins, their desire to draw is at an end. It's understandable, considering all the details that the viewer of your drawing can't take in completely, either. Simplify it! Draw parts of the building; omit window struts, downpipes, bricks, or entire facade sections in favor of a dynamic sketch.

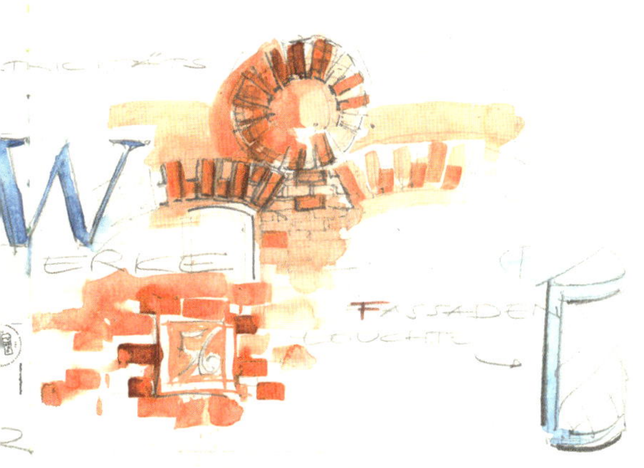

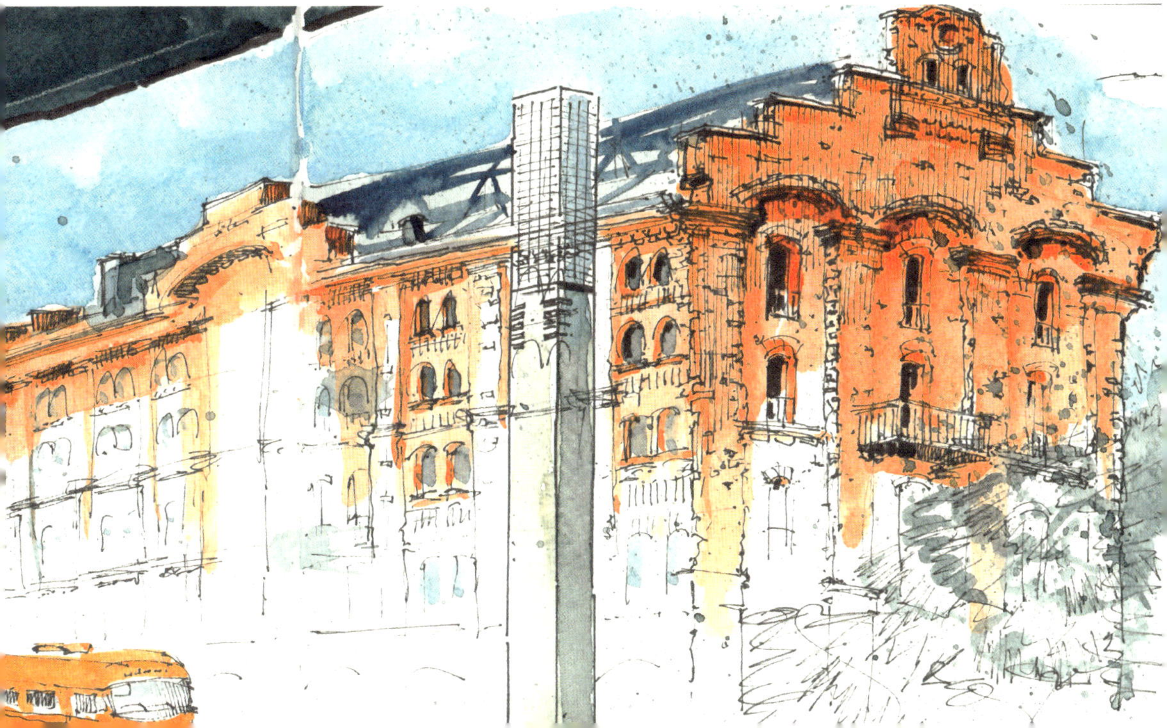

Added Ingredients: People, Birds, Vehicles, Handwriting

Other ingredients should be added to the recipe for lively outdoor scenes. Everything that makes the place look lived-in and natural: people walking their dogs, cars driving past, signs and billboards. Passersby, cyclists, sparrows, and pigeons not only breathe life into your drawings, they may be what prompts a sketch. Miniature stories take place every day in public places, at traffic lights, bus stops, and ticket offices. Fill your sketchbook with actors.

Reminder: Put Templates in a Sketchbook

Expand your sketchbook with additional templates for people, animals, and vehicles. You can use them the next time you sketch, just like you did with the trees. You can find the instructions for folding a pocket sketchbook on page 118.

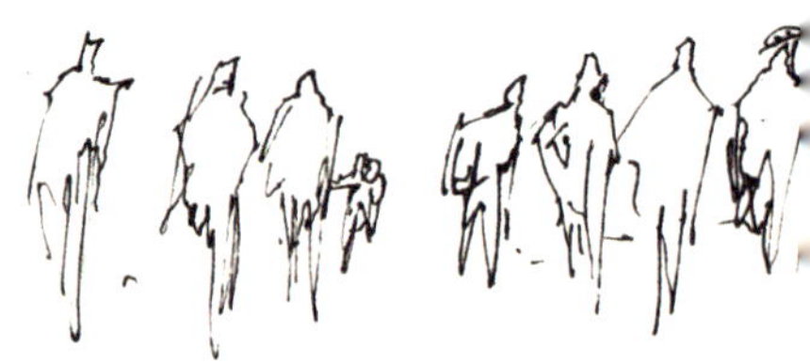

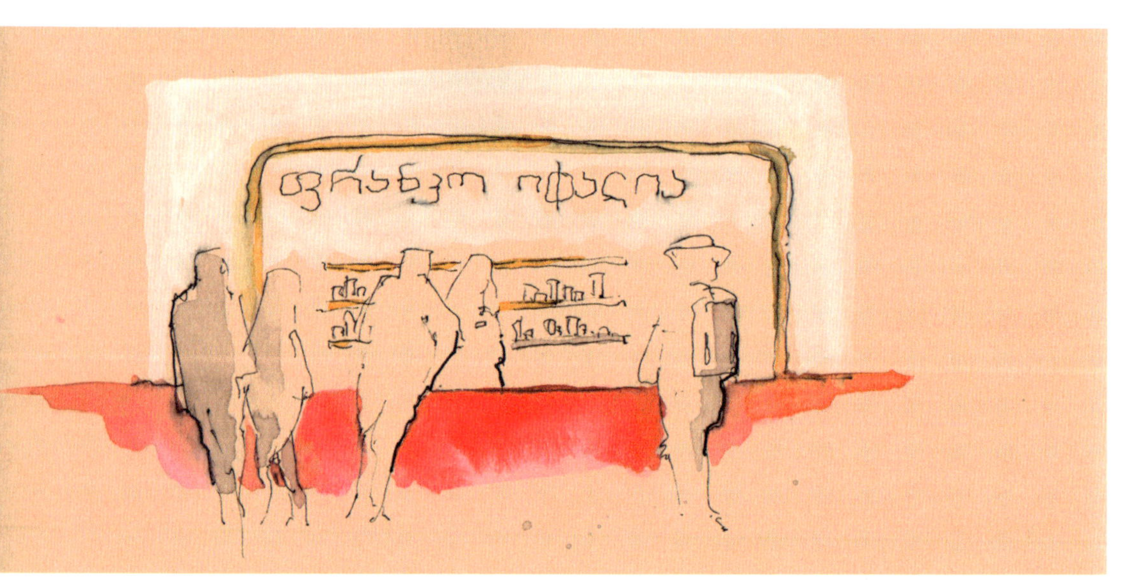

Waiting, Georgian-style: I documented the queue at the phone shop with quick strokes and a little watercolor paint.

People

You rarely see deserted streets and squares in real life. There's a reason why architectural designs and real estate catalogs are filled with people: They paint a positive picture. The same applies to sketchbooks: Pages filled with drawings containing no people seem strange and distant.

There are numerous methods for adding people to your sketches. I'll introduce some of them below. If you're interested in the human figure with all its rules of proportion and representation, you'll need to delve deeper into the subject another time.

Figures as Lines

Simplify and imply: Quick outlines with a fineliner, simple lines, and no details make for lively figures. Don't make the heads too large. Leave out the feet and let the contours fade away at the bottom.

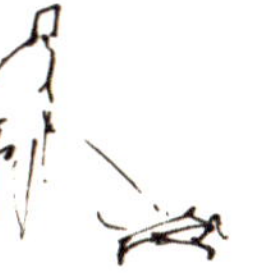

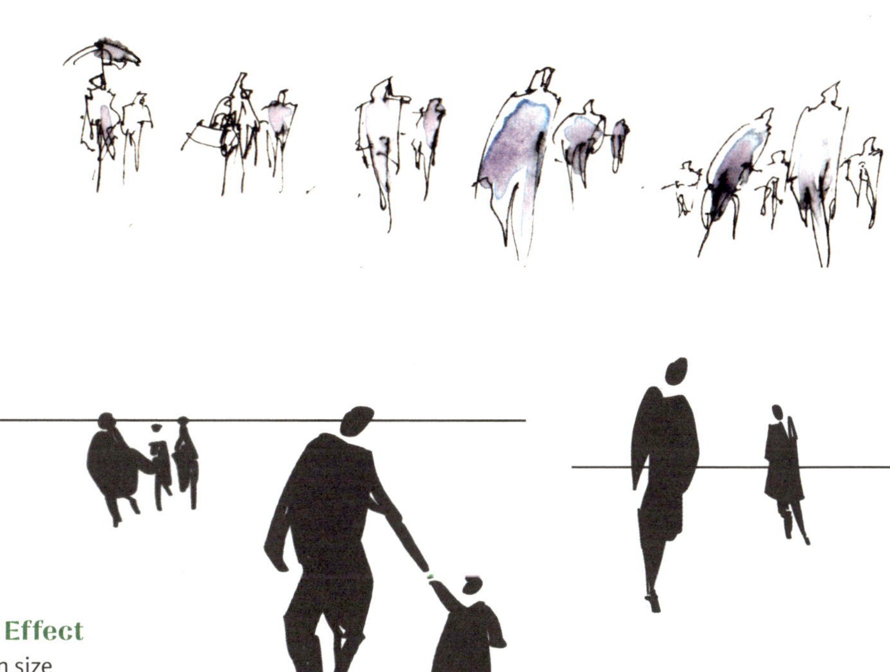

Perspective Effect

The gradation in size creates depth. Left: artist standing—horizon at head height. Right: artist sitting—horizon at midriff height.

Figures as Shapes

Once you've created a few figures with quick lines, experiment with ink pens and brushes. A dot for the head, a broad stroke for the upper body, legs tapering to a point. Model a whole series of figures, varying their posture, gait, and direction of movement.

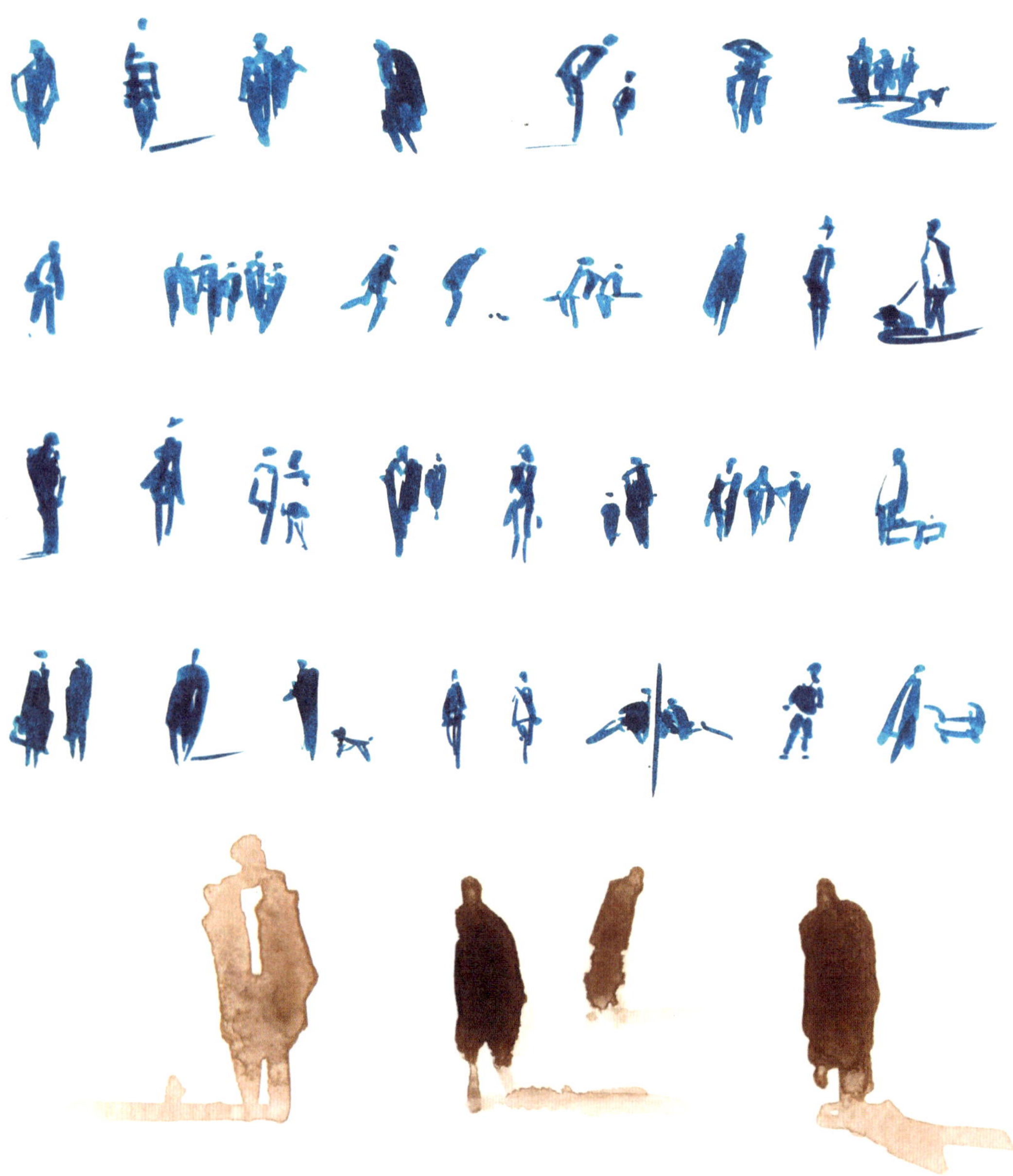

Checklist: Figures and Groups of People

1. Draw quickly rather than beautifully. Warm up with blind drawing or one-line exercises (page 24).
2. Draw heads too small rather than too large.
3. Draw figures more angular than their models.
4. Leave out feet and shoes.
5. Sketch figures directly from the front or from the side.
6. Imply clothing: Add pockets, backpacks, caps, hats, umbrellas.
7. Show people in action and movement.
8. Set figures into pairs and groups; move them around and overlap them.
9. Use figures to create depth (observe rules of perspective).
10. Use color sparingly.

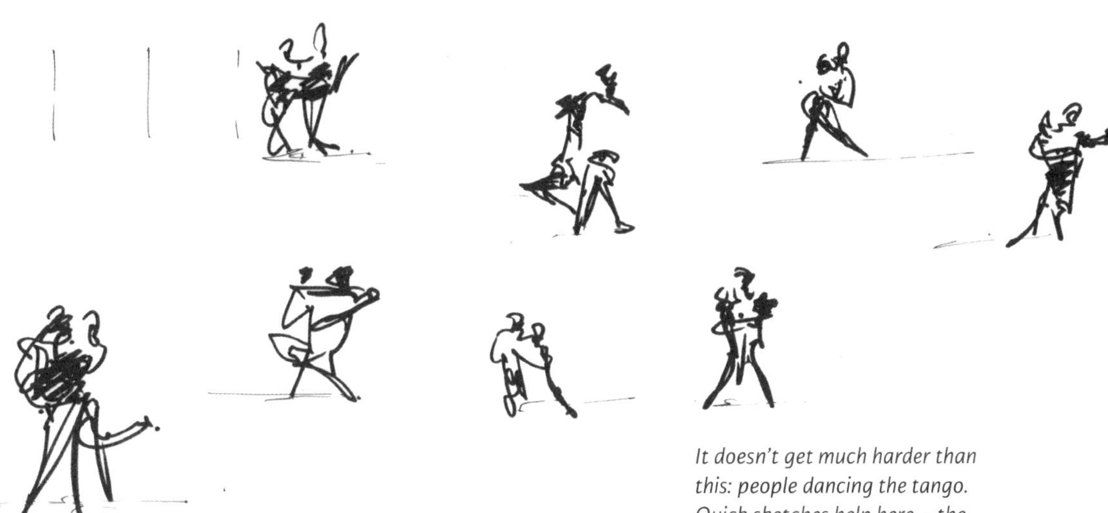

It doesn't get much harder than this: people dancing the tango. Quick sketches help here—the faster, the better.

Tip: Move the brushstroke on the head sideways, bend the upper body, and extend one leg. And just like that, the figure appears to be stepping out of the picture. Shadows provide grounding and dramatic effects.

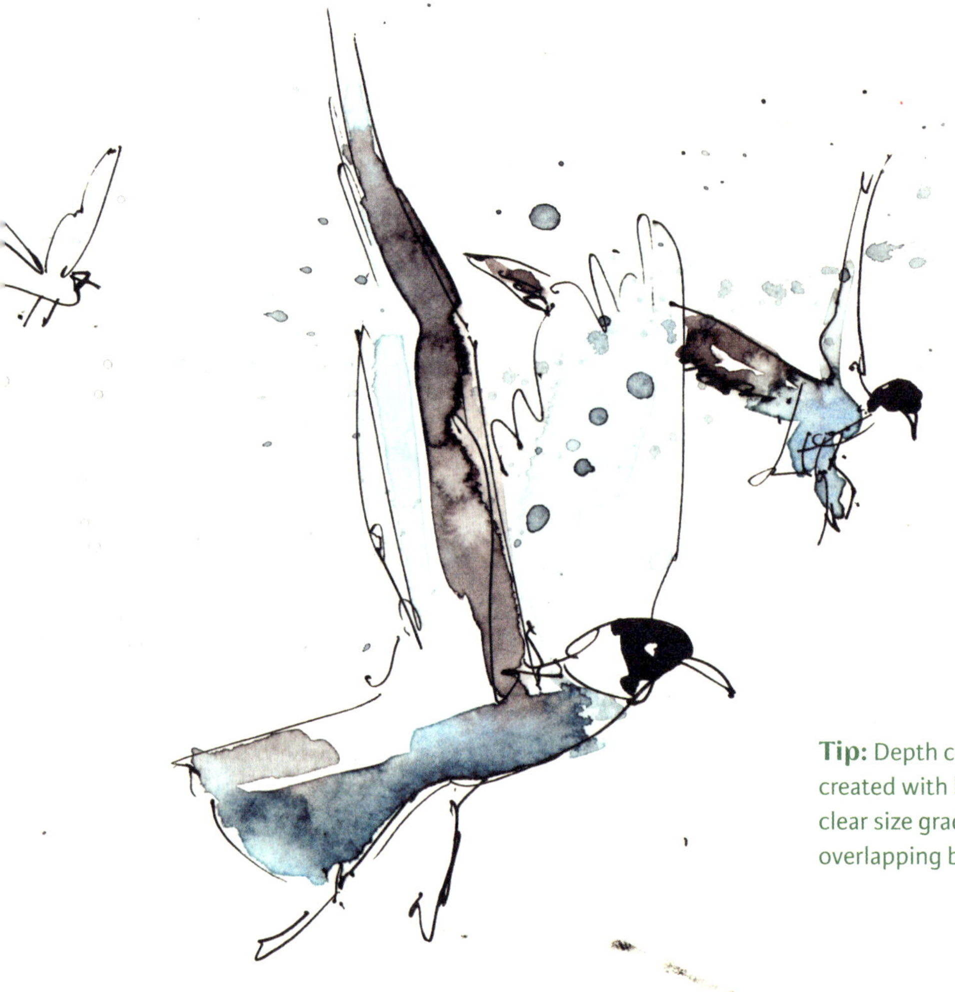

Tip: Depth can also be created with birds through clear size gradation and overlapping bodies.

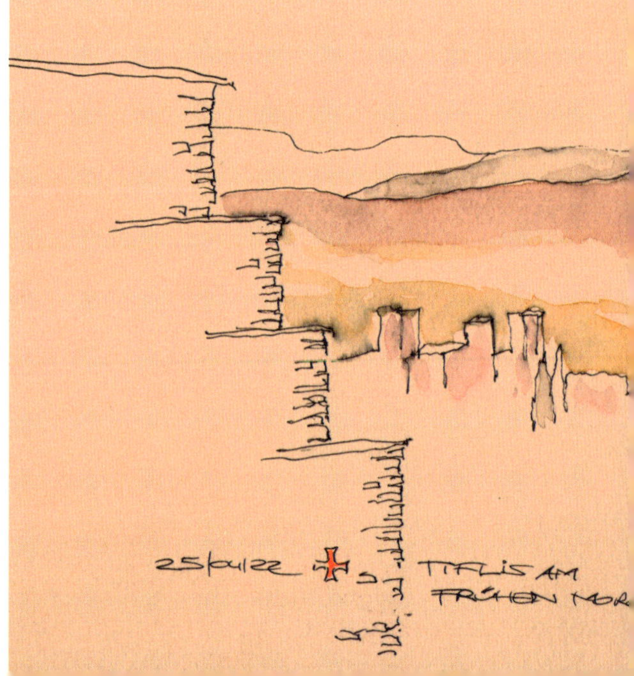
TIFLIS AM
FRÜHEN MOR

Birds

Birds are another "natural" ingredient for pictures. They add scope to landscape drawings and life to city sketches. Simplification also works well when sketching birds. Whether it's a bold sparrow stealing crumbs from a plate or an eagle soaring high above, the differences among raptors, songbirds, and shorebirds seem big at first but can be captured with your pen using just a few distinctive features. Over time, you'll develop a repertoire of templates that you can refer to at any time when you're outdoors. I show examples of body proportions and flight patterns on the following double-page spread.

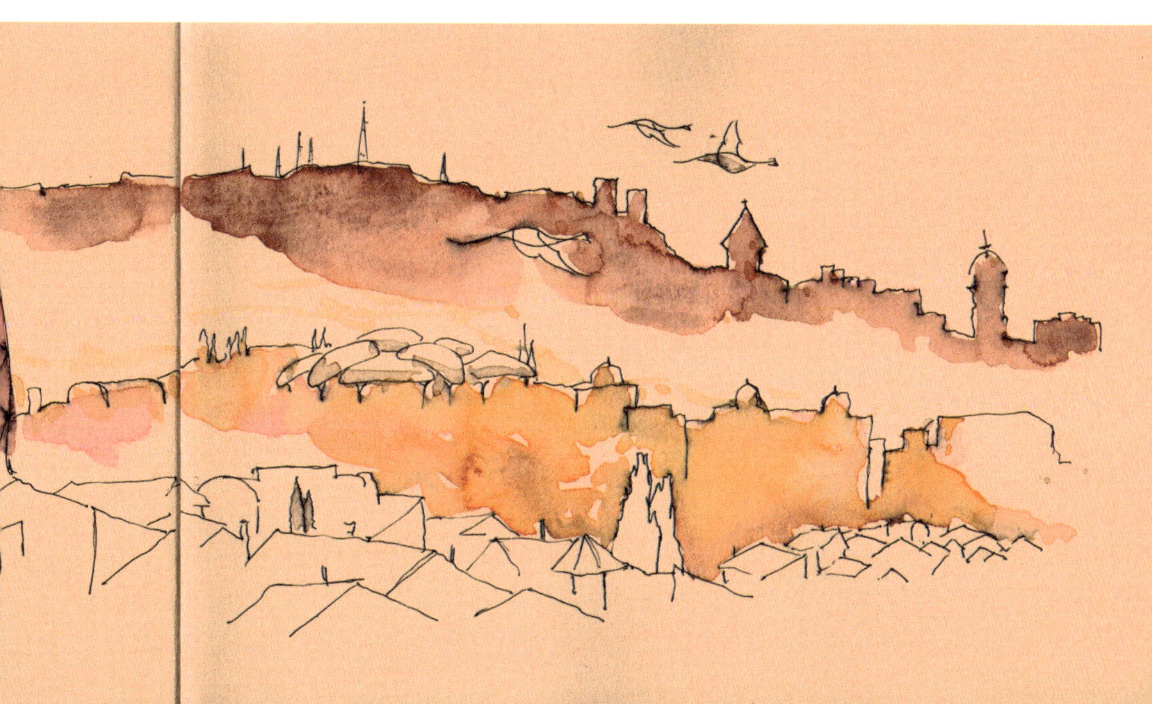

Cranes over Tbilisi: disappearing act. I later added these rulers of the skies from memory with just a few strokes. Birds are wonderful for complementing the view of a landscape or city.

Experiment with Basic Shapes and Proportions

If you observe closely, you'll soon recognize basic shapes and proportions: The open wing of a goose or duck is about as long as its body. The torso, head, and wings can therefore fit into a square. For cranes, herons, and storks, the ratio is 1:2. In birds of prey, it is even greater.

So, when drawing (not just birds), examine what basic shapes there are, how they are composed, and how they relate to each other in terms of size. With a little attention, you can discover basic patterns everywhere that make it easier to draw natural forms. As with trees (page 112), this also applies to birds.

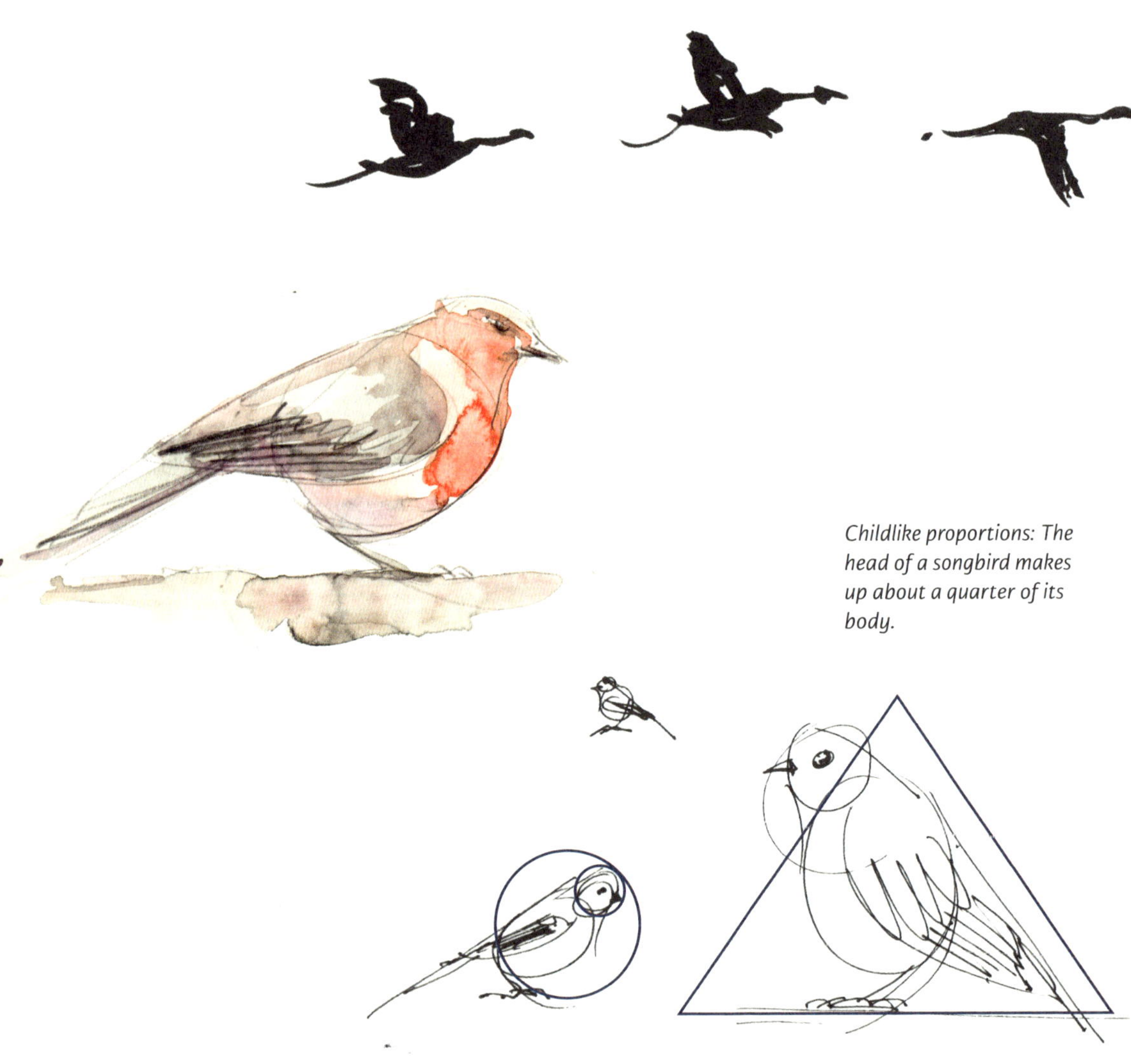

Childlike proportions: The head of a songbird makes up about a quarter of its body.

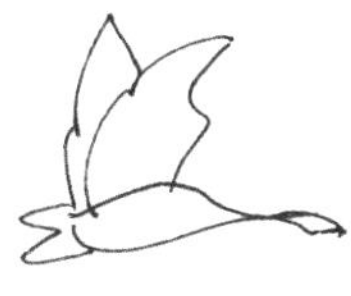
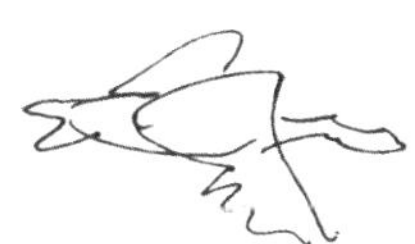
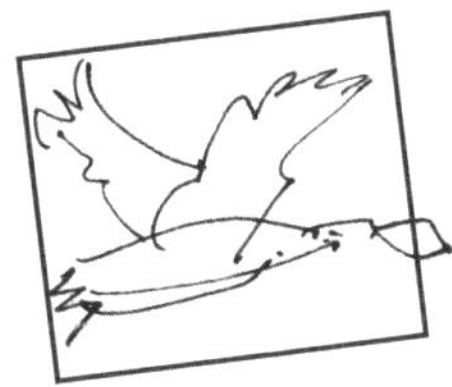
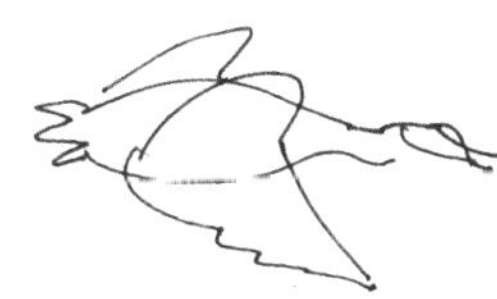

Comparison of birds in flight: large bird of prey, small bird of prey, duck.

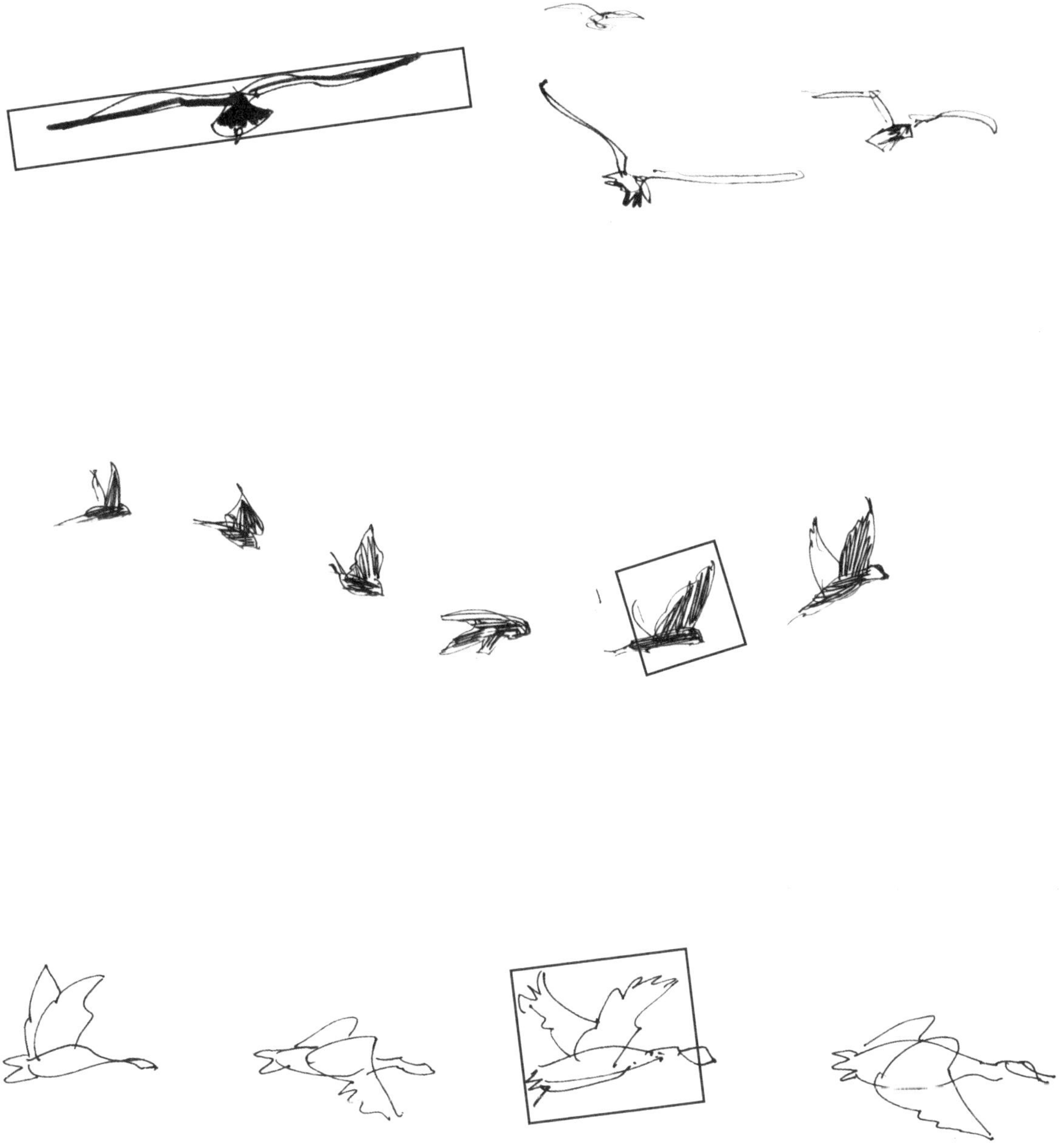

Vehicles

Put cars in the picture! Since vehicles, power lines, satellite dishes, and trash cans don't exactly contribute to the beauty of a city, they're often omitted from drawings. Yet there are few places in the world where you won't find these "ugly" signs of civilization.

Should you draw only beautiful things in your sketchbook? Behind the aesthetic debate lies an opportunity for every artist because everyday products describe the present in which you live. Drawings of things and places capture the era. As street scenes and entire neighborhoods change, in just a few years your sketchbook will become a time machine. Phone booths already look nostalgic in drawings today. Will mailboxes be next?

Don't be afraid to exaggerate: The highways between Azerbaijan and Georgia certainly don't have seven lanes. This sketch on tinted watercolor paper represents adventure on the road.

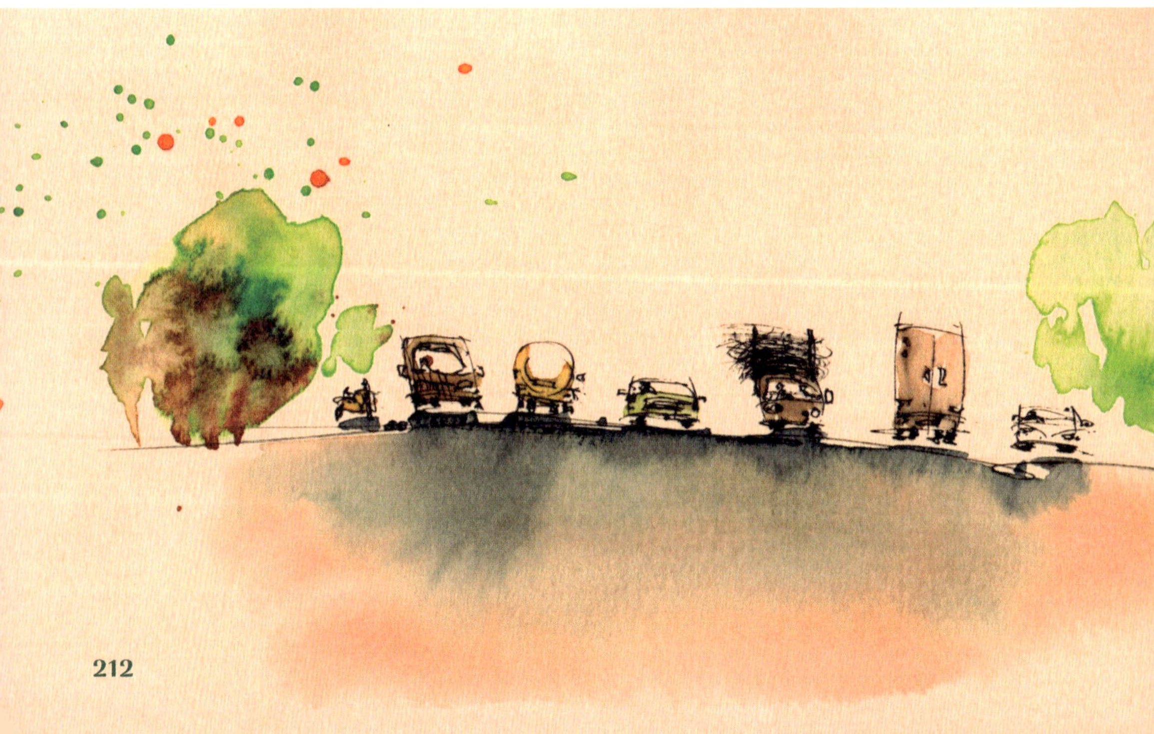

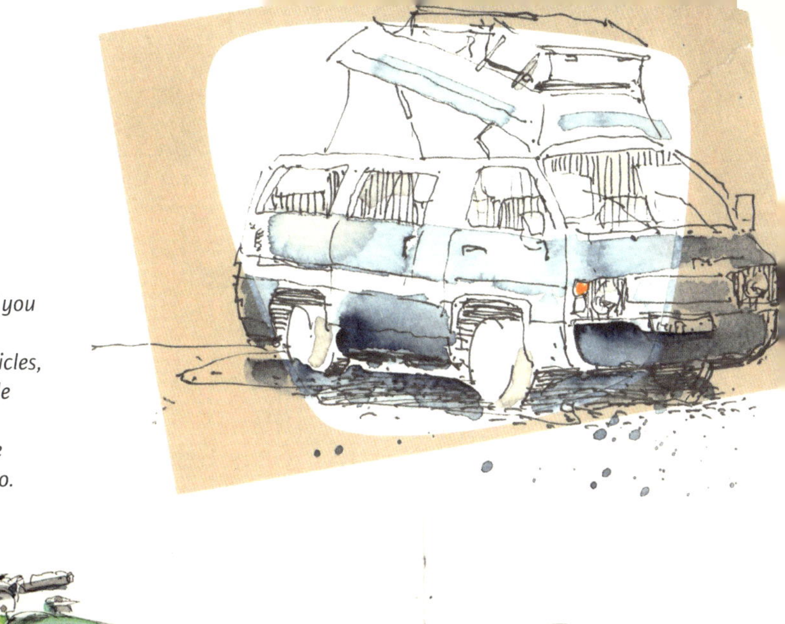

Well parked: If you
want to draw
stationary vehicles,
museums, trade
fairs, and car
dealerships are
the places to go.

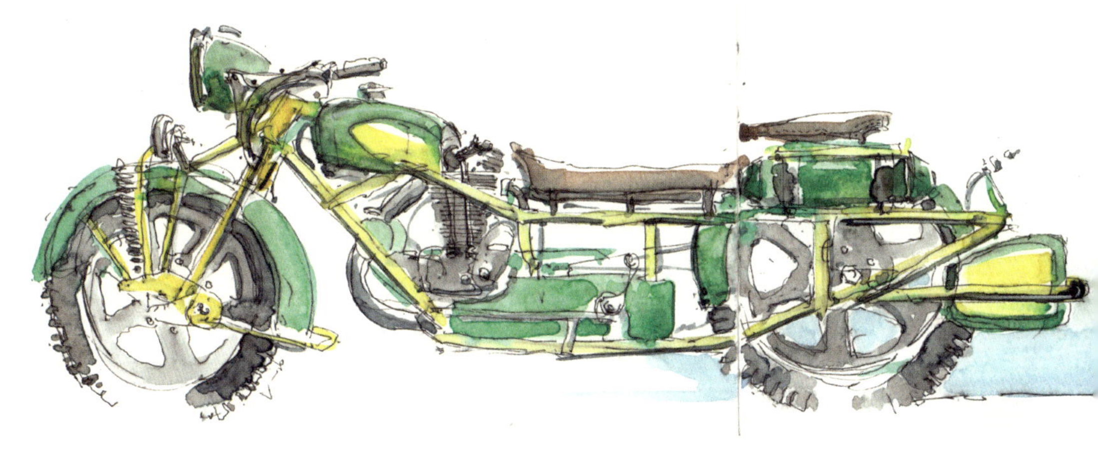

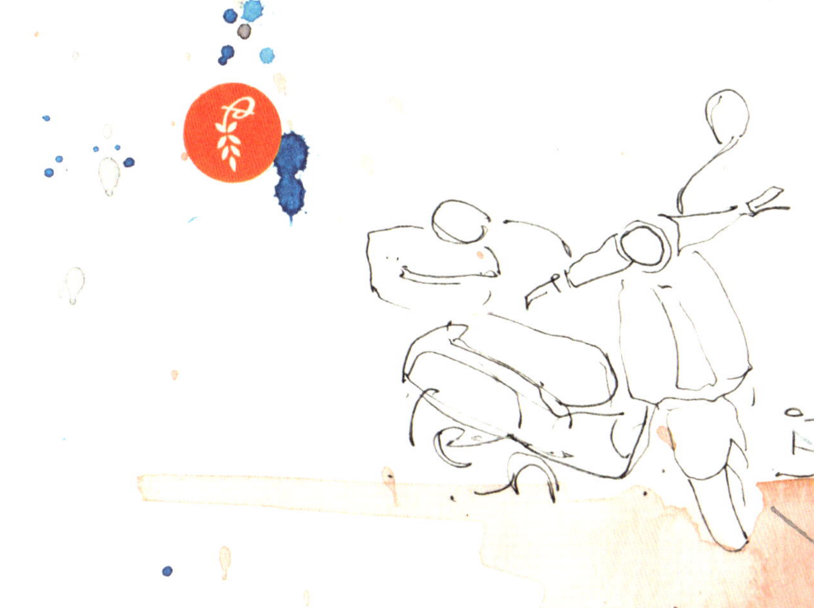

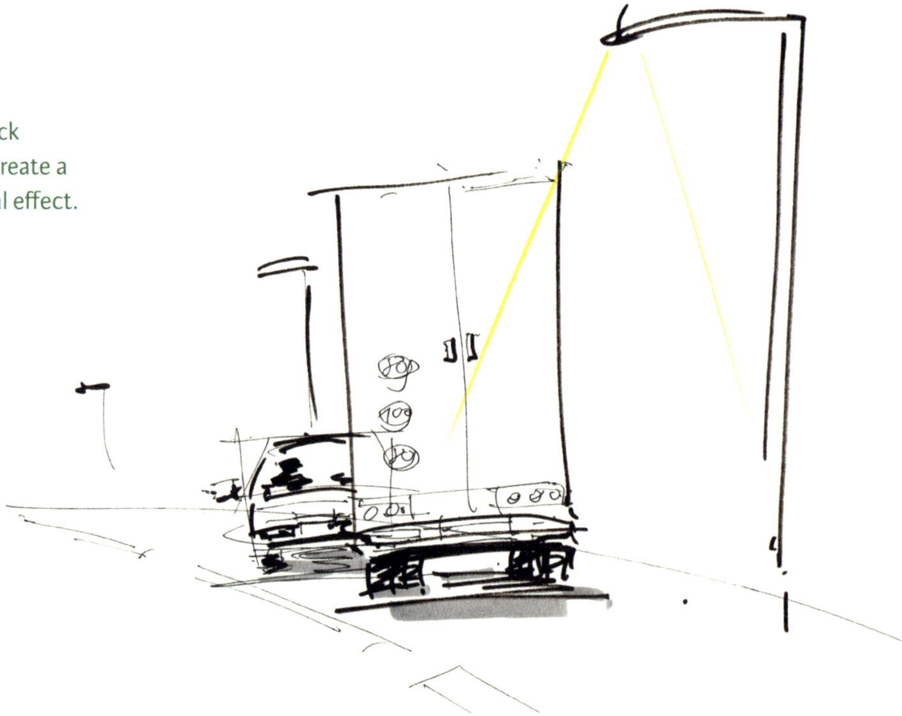

Contemporaries

Vehicles are a reliable indicator of contemporary tastes: Yesterday's elegantly shaped sports cars are today's electric scooters, hybrid cars, and angular SUVs. To make drawing easier, forget the design dictates of the automotive industry and develop your own repertoire of quickly sketched vehicles.

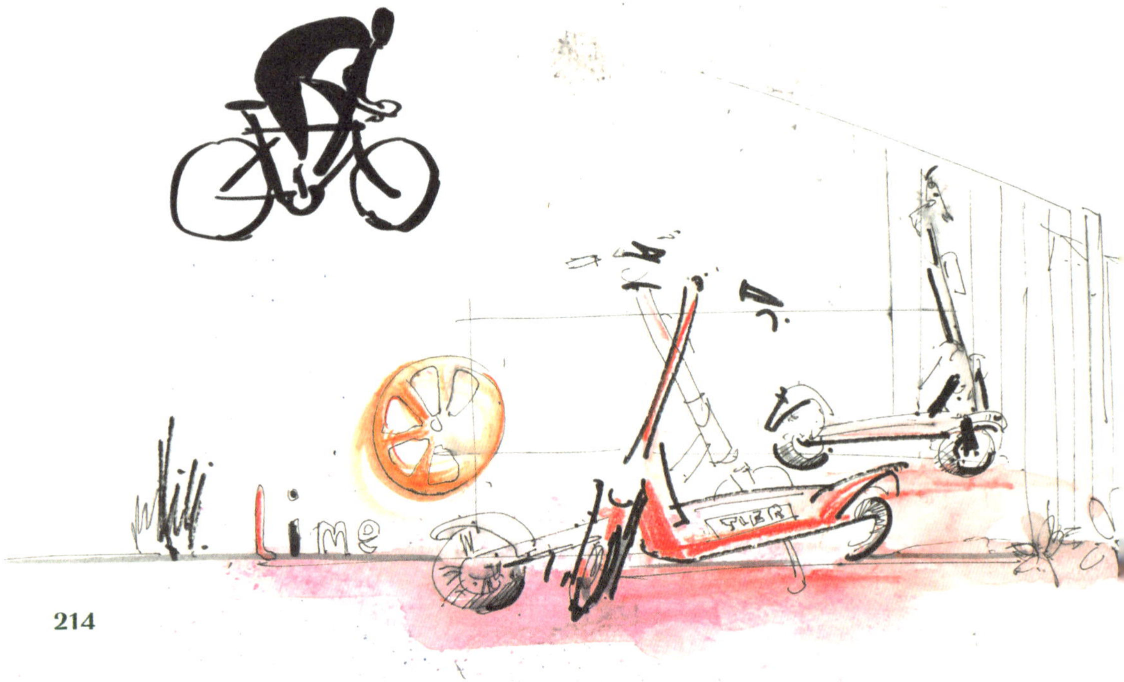

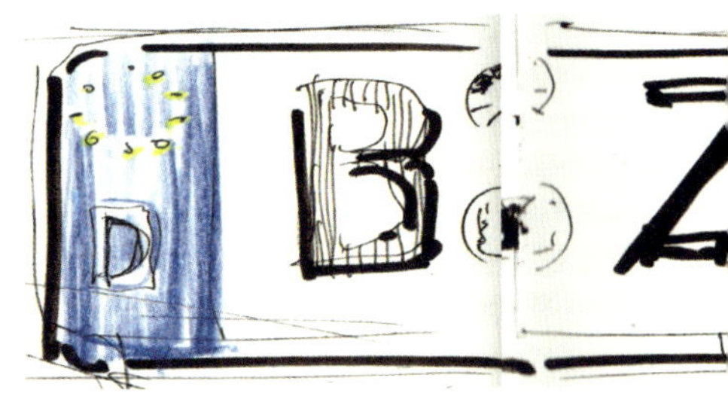

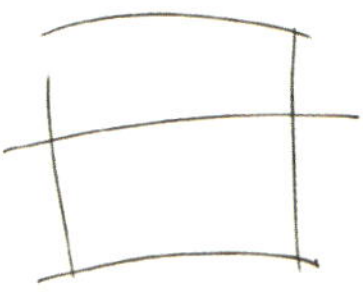

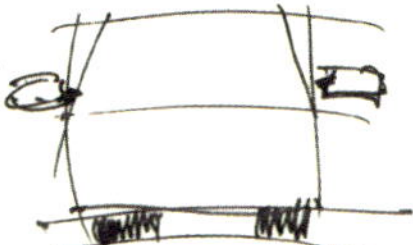

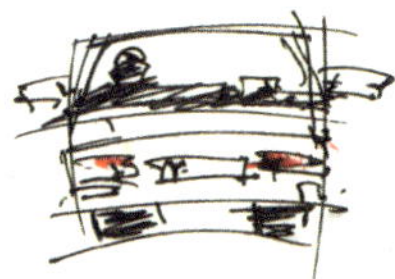

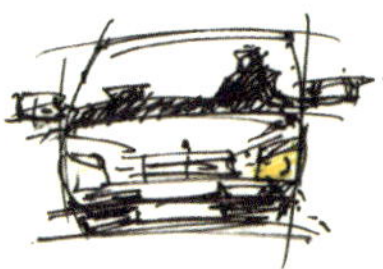

Checklist for Cars: See Them as Boxes!

1. Limit your drawing to front, rear, and side views. Start with a square on a baseline. Draw the window edge about halfway up.

2. From this height, draw two lines sloping inward to indicate the side windows. Add the vehicle floor, wheels, and exterior mirrors.

3. Define the front and rear: Draw the driver's silhouette on the left or right, and highlight the brake lights and headlights in color.

4. Intensify the shadows on the edges of the vehicle and the ground.

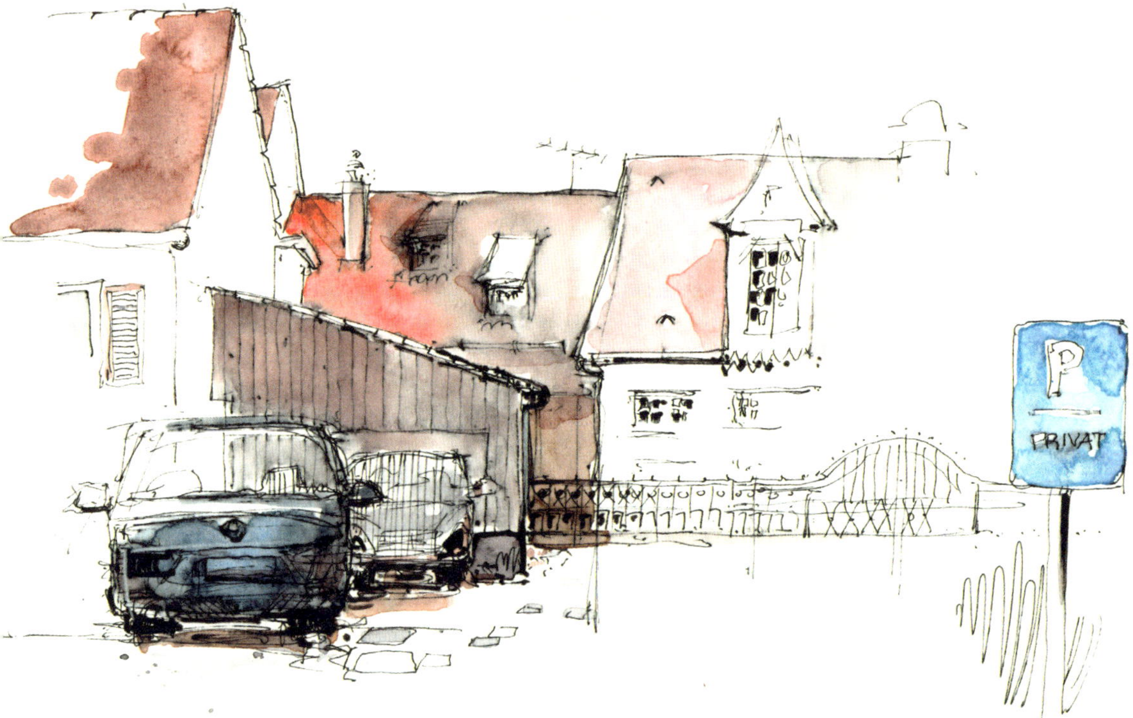

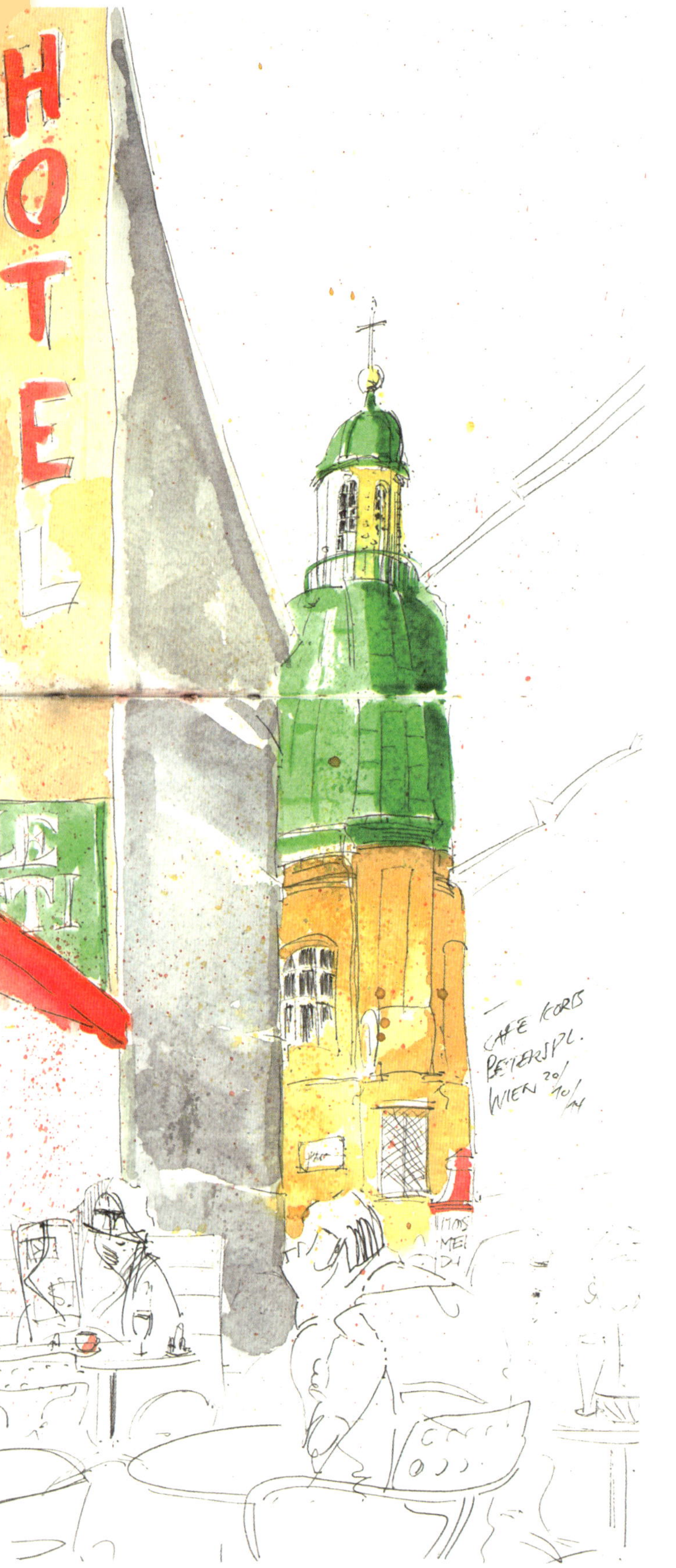
HOTEL
CAFE KORB
PETERSPL.
WIEN 20/10/14

Tip: Text blocks should match the shape of existing elements and the format of the sketchbook page. Writing in narrow columns emphasizes vertical shapes, while text in long lines emphasizes panoramas and landscape formats.

Handwriting

Handwriting is a recurring element in my sketchbooks. It's not just to note the place and date in the margin. Handwriting has both an artistic and narrative influence on your drawings.

Writing Is Part of the Composition

Just like all other parts of an image, text elements also contribute to the overall composition. A block of text or eye-catching individual letters carry "weight." Use handwriting deliberately to draw the eye to a specific point in the image or to balance a lopsided layout. Only add the location and date at the end.

Writing Tells a Story

I use writing for comments and notes to capture the atmosphere at the place where I'm drawing: weather conditions, original sound bites from loudspeaker announcements, or snippets of conversation from the neighboring table. This is how marginal notes become little stories. And the sketches become a graphic novel.

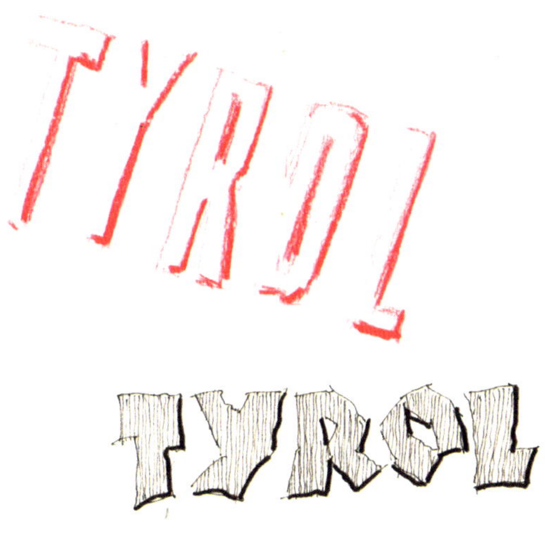

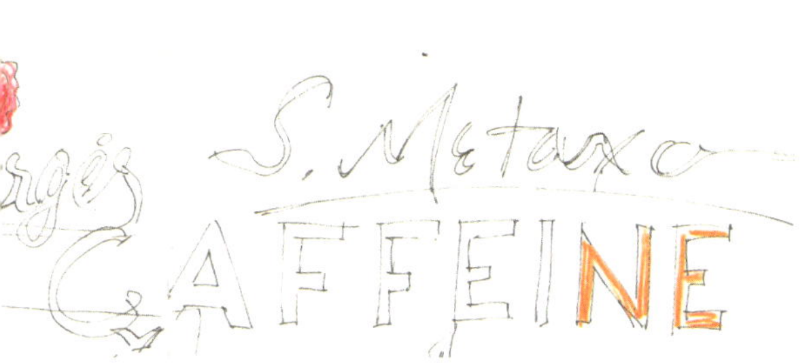

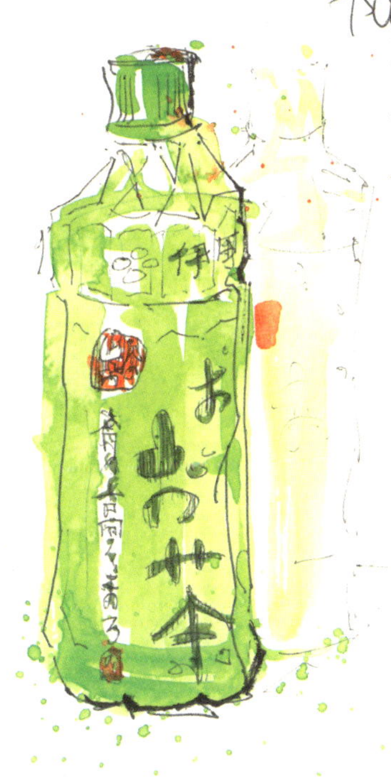

My Writing Set for Traveling
This is my normal sketching handwriting.
As a designer, I like to use capital letters:

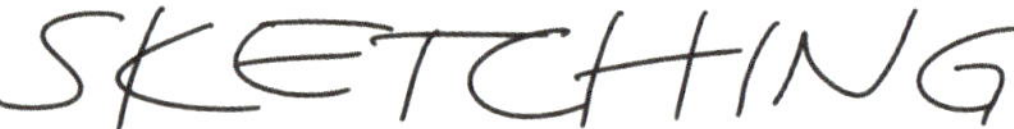

If I am labeling a natural landscape or
an expansive city skyline, widely spaced
lettering is appropriate:

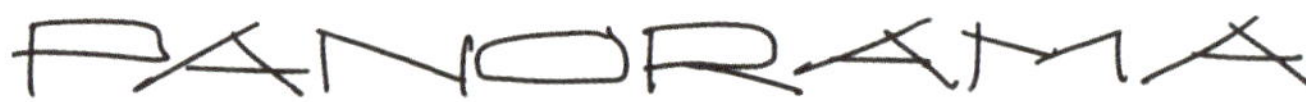

When drawing in vertical format or
portraying vertical subjects (tall trees,
rock faces, skyscrapers), I choose a
narrow block lettering:

For organic shapes, figures, and faces, I use
cursive to emphasize their natural essence:

To highlight certain words or make
lettering look more representative,
I use a widely spaced style:

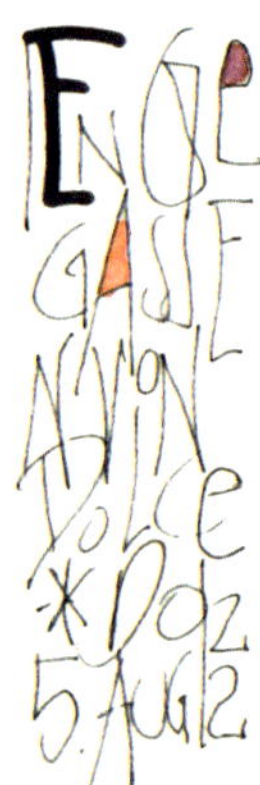

If I want to emphasize the narrative
aspect of a sketch, I like to combine
upper- and lowercase letters, word
breaks, and different stroke widths
within a text block:

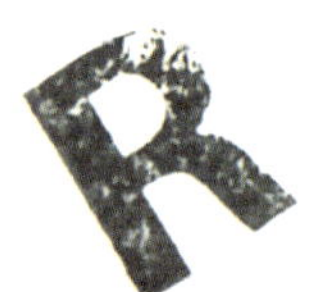

Tip: Dab a little paint inside the
letters. But avoid overly decorative lettering, as this will obscure
your sketch.

*Collage, stamps, labels:
Lettering made from
found objects tells its
own stories.*

Calligraphy or Your Own Handwriting?

The question is misleading. It should be: Is my handwriting suitable for a sketchbook? I think so. For one thing, legibility isn't that important (sketches are meant to be "read" as images, not as text). For another, with a little practice, you can quickly develop your own set of letters for different drawing situations: bold or narrow, formal or playful, block or cursive.

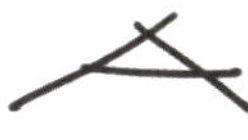

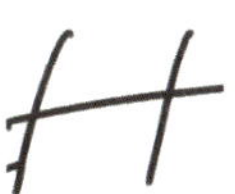

Checklist for Your Own Sketch Handwriting:

1. Write quickly rather than neatly. This will give you a confident stroke.
2. Block capitals look more neutral than cursive.
3. Allow the ends of block letters to overlap.
4. Add dynamics: Angle vertical lines and raise horizontal lines slightly.
5. Keep letterspacing small for a closed typeface.
6. Add notes to sketches as often as possible. This makes writing a natural part of the design.

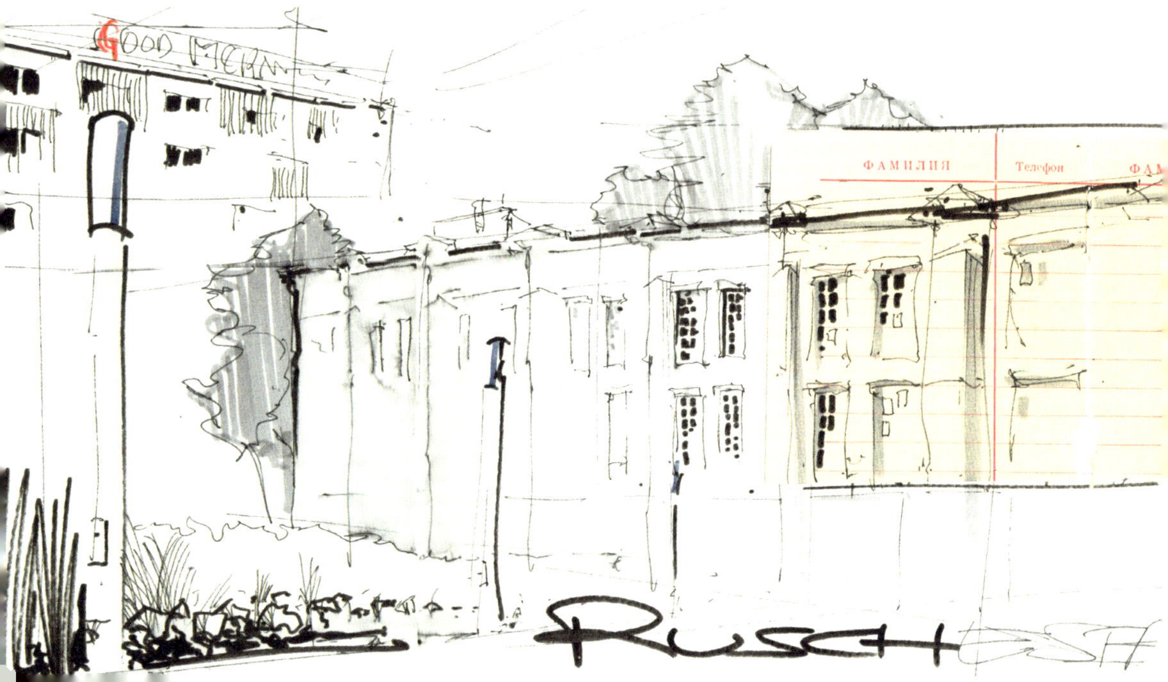

Detour: Modern Cities

I don't need to beat the drum for sketching outdoors in cities. Thanks to the growing urban sketching movement (urbansketchers .org), more and more creative illustrators are venturing outdoors. Architecture has been dusted off as a subject for drawings, and loosely sketched cityscapes show the world on the street.

Uniform retail outlets and identical office architecture make city centers today look increasingly similar, but when you draw on location, you'll find plenty of differences among cities around the world. It's interesting to identify these differences and record them in your sketchbook: the red buses, the cast-iron bollards, the blue subway cars.

Architecture presents itself differently everywhere. Vertical, horizontal, and diagonal lines create typical city skylines. New York is not the same as Berlin, which is not the same as London.

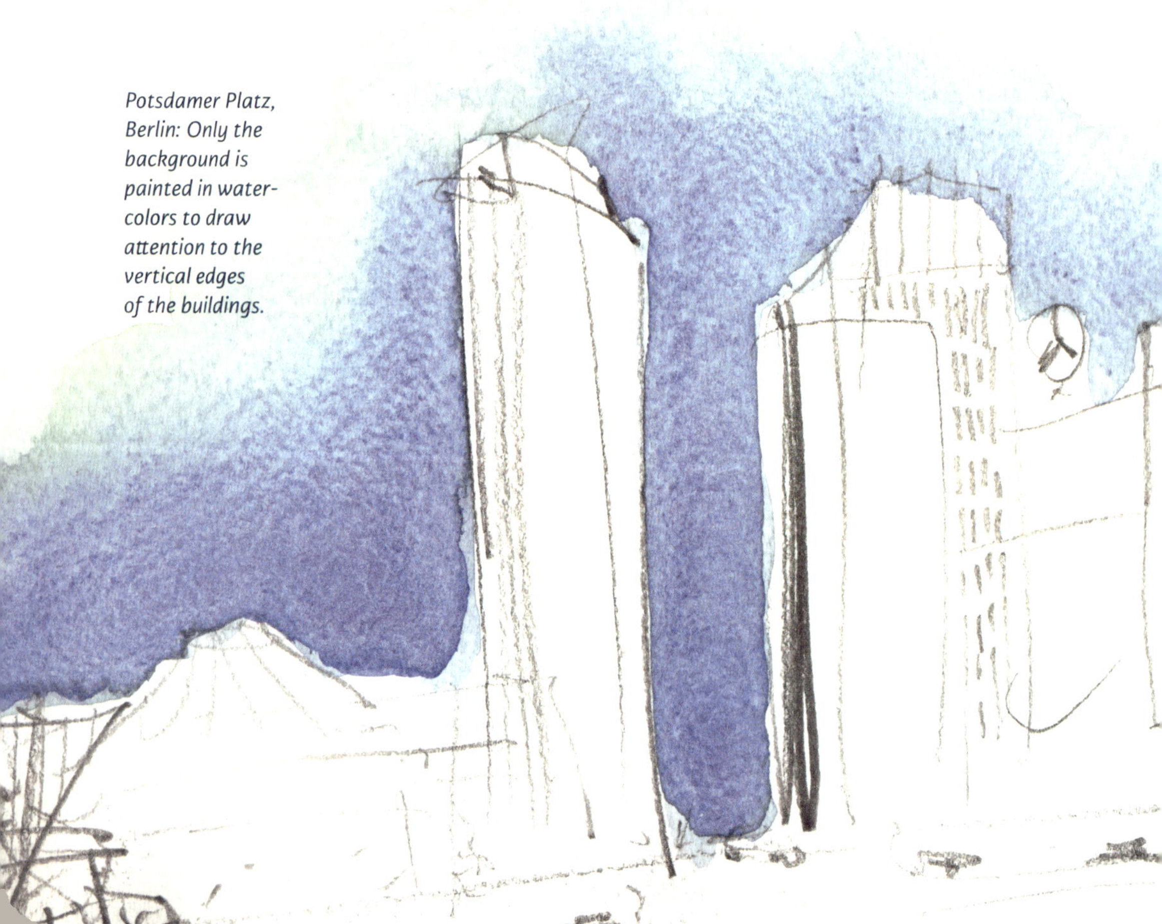

Potsdamer Platz, Berlin: Only the background is painted in water-colors to draw attention to the vertical edges of the buildings.

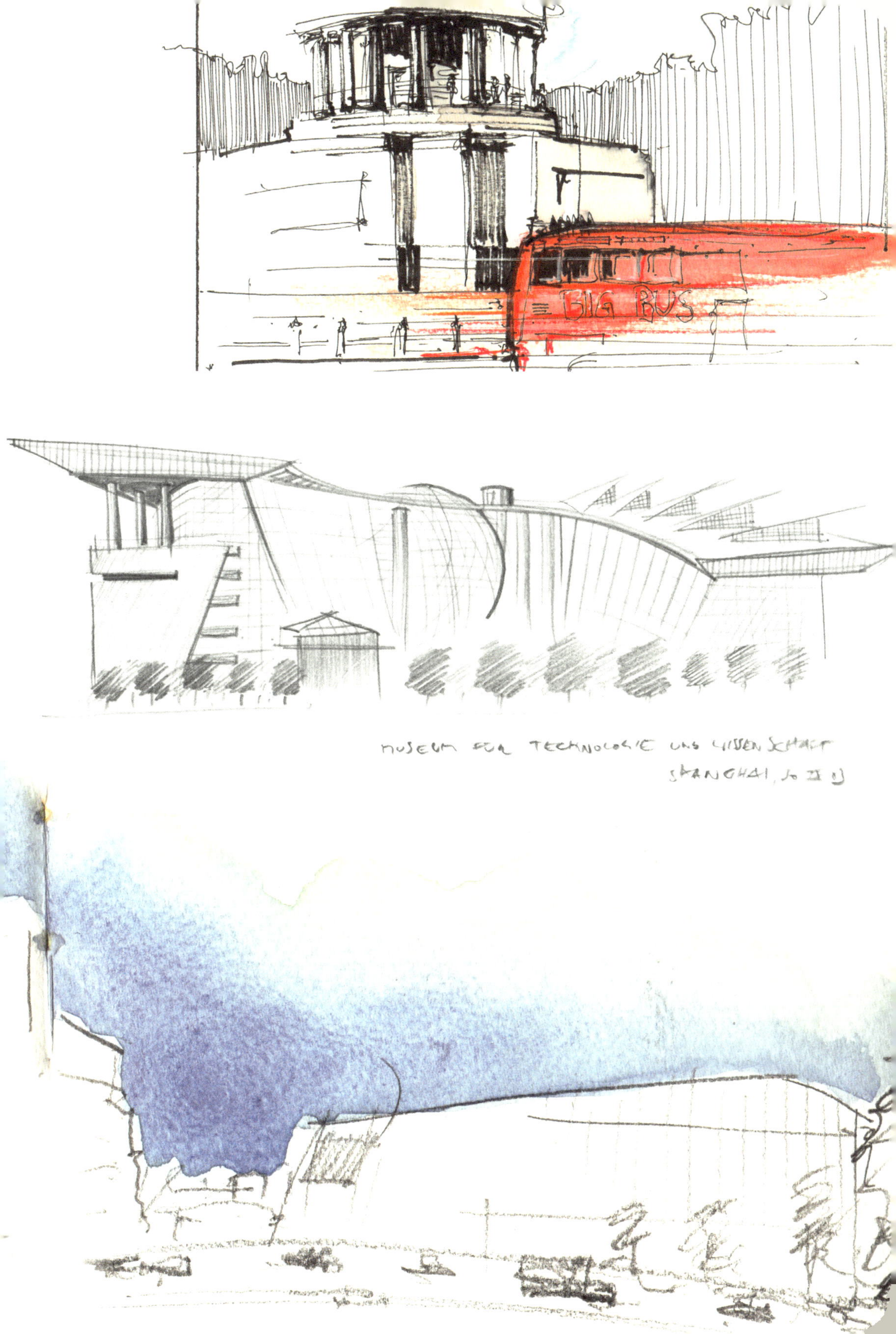
BIG BUS
MUSEUM FÜR TECHNOLOGIE UND WISSENSCHAFT
SHANGHAI, 10 II U

Tiny or Enormous

Cities grow into megacities. Sketches can
convey the feeling of being lost in a big city.
If you want to emphasize the dimensions
of a city, make people, cars, and trees as
small as possible in relation to buildings.

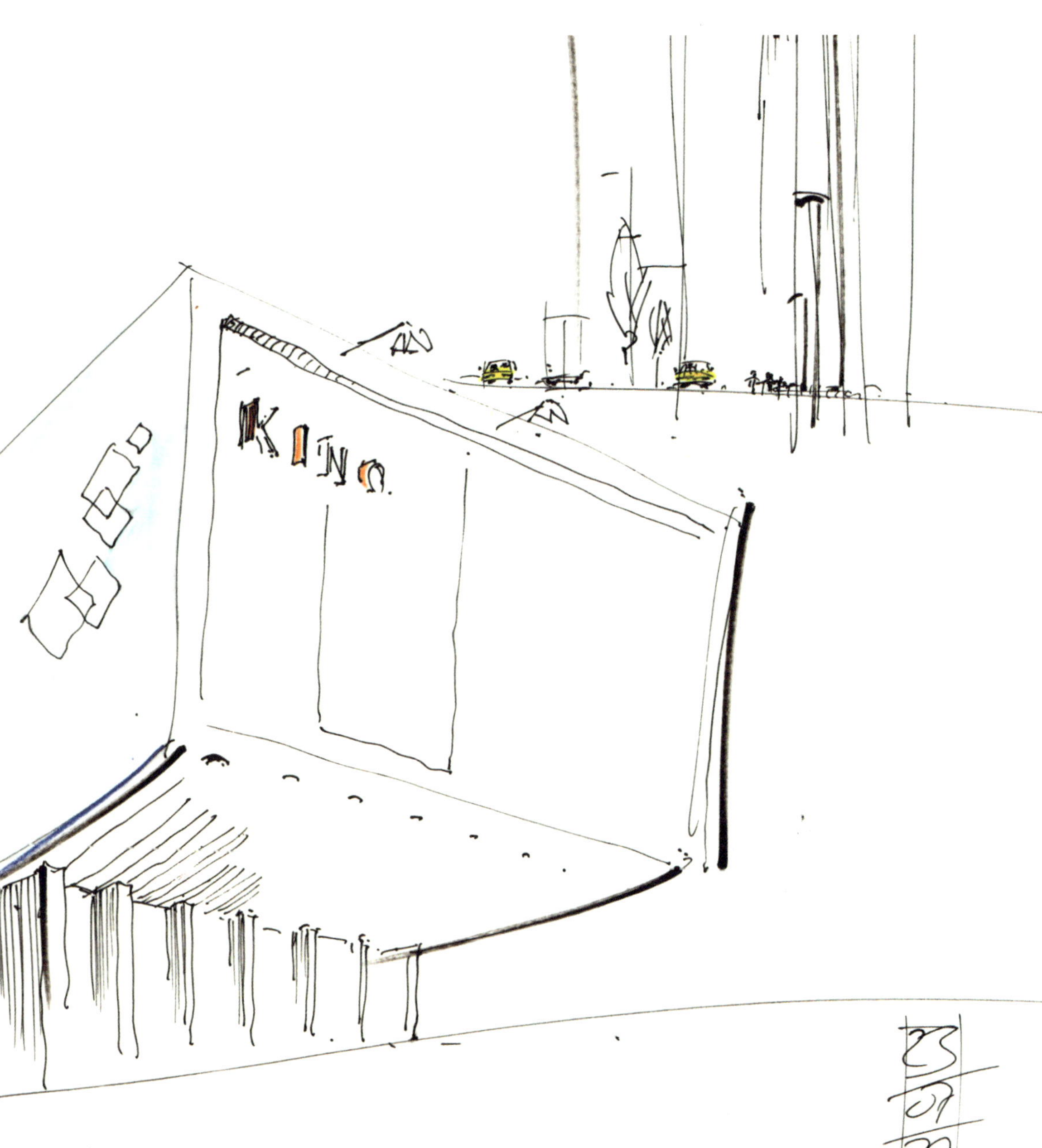

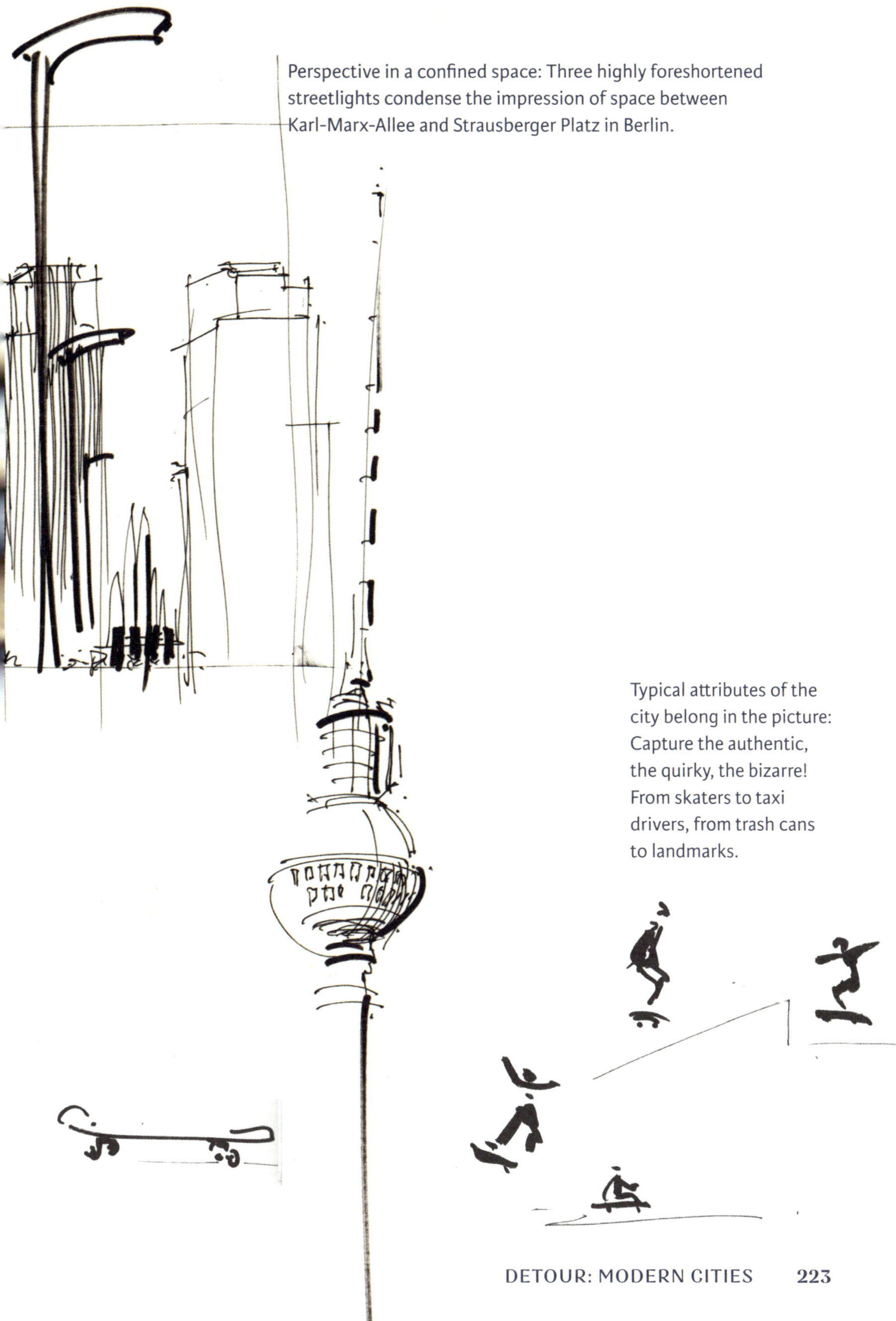

Perspective in a confined space: Three highly foreshortened streetlights condense the impression of space between Karl-Marx-Allee and Strausberger Platz in Berlin.

Typical attributes of the city belong in the picture: Capture the authentic, the quirky, the bizarre! From skaters to taxi drivers, from trash cans to landmarks.

An Oyster in the Middle of Berlin

The Congress Hall (now the Haus der Kulturen der
Welt) is a landmark of the German capital and a popular subject for sketchbooks. Berliners affectionately
call it the "Pregnant Oyster." Steel meets glass, wood
meets concrete, architecture meets nature. A boldly
constructed arched roof is reflected in the water.

I created the drawing using felt-tip pen and
watercolors. The warm yellow tone of the facade
contrasts with the cool blue-green of the background.
Vegetation and sky merge seamlessly and are only
hinted at to emphasize the details of the building.

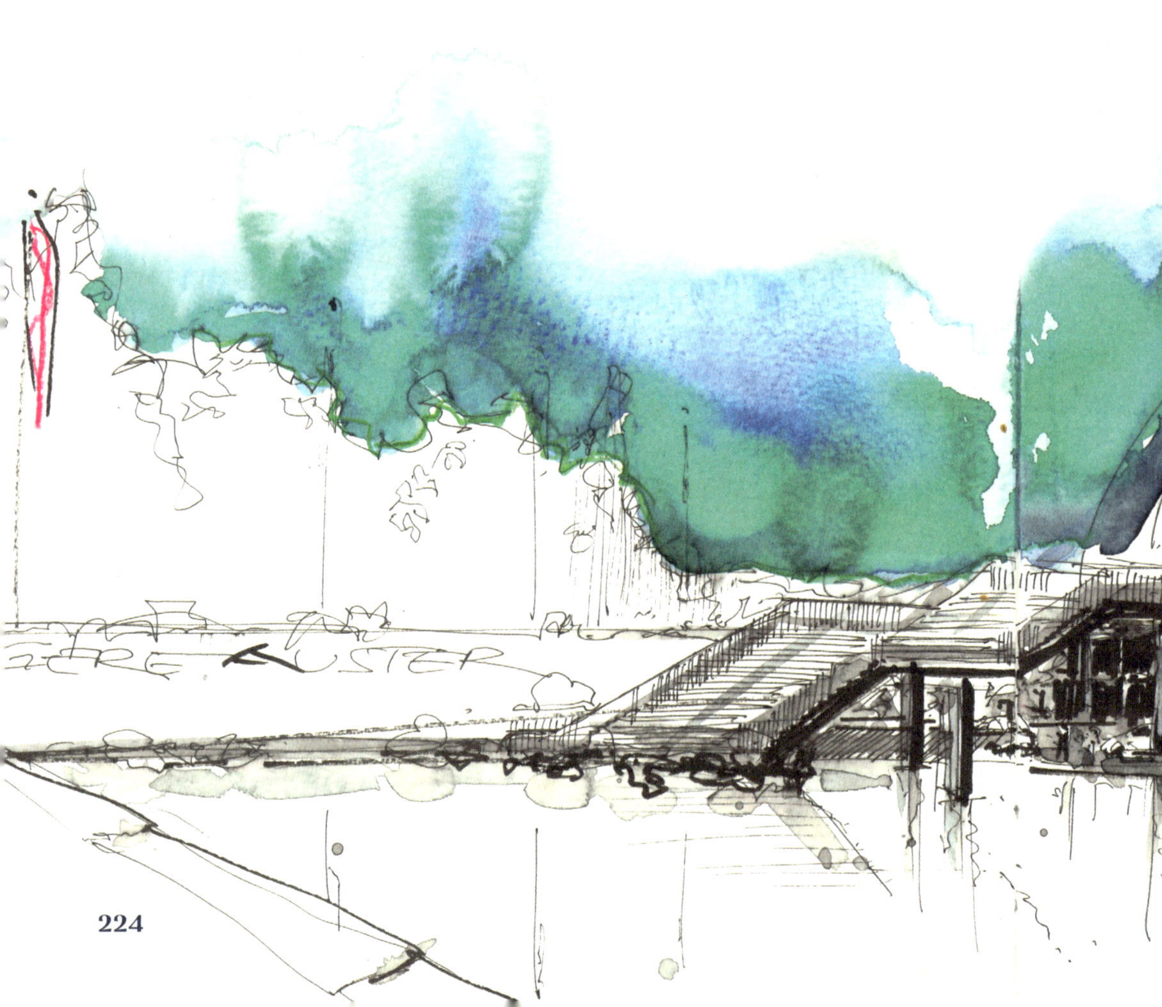

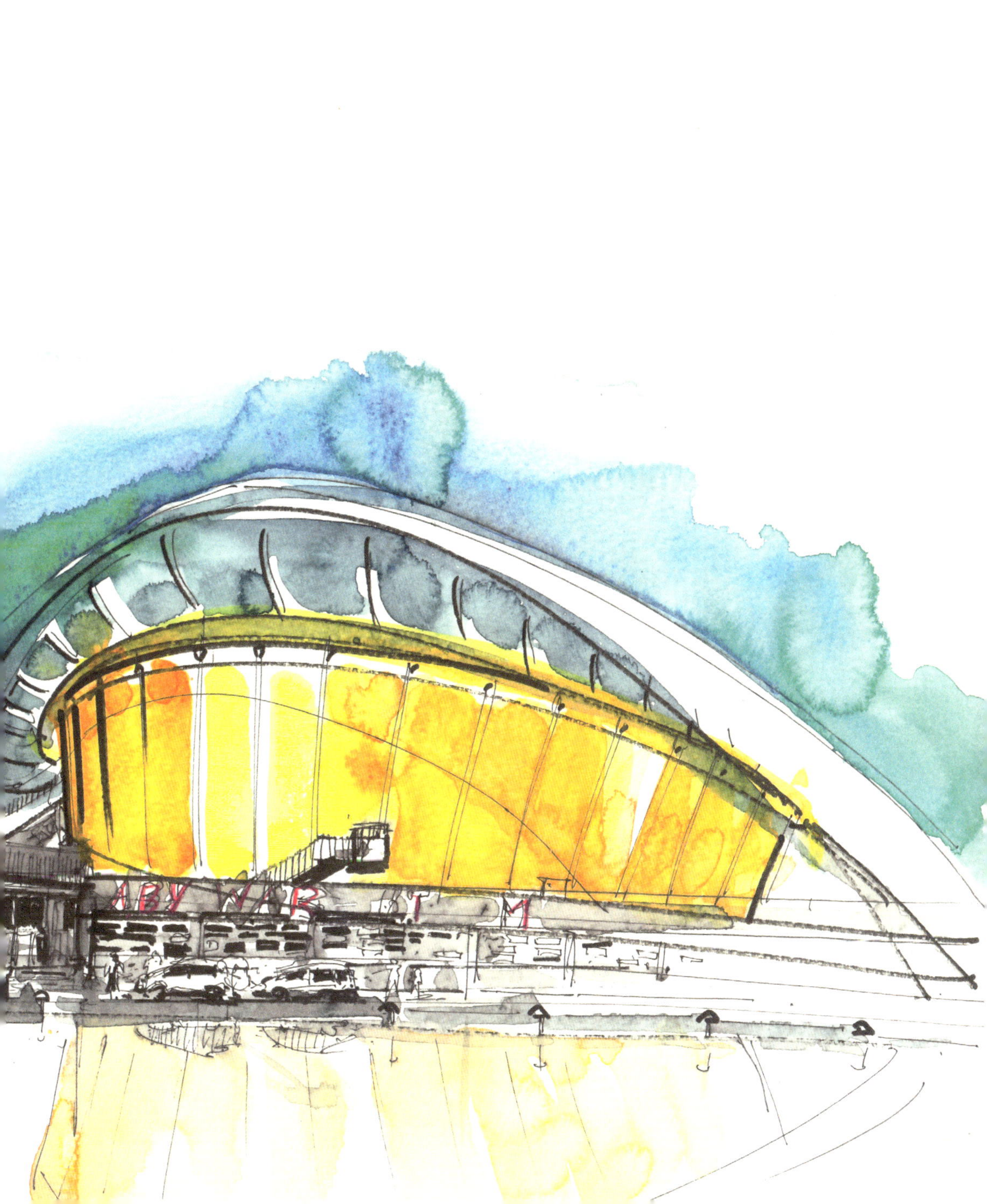
ABY WAR   T M

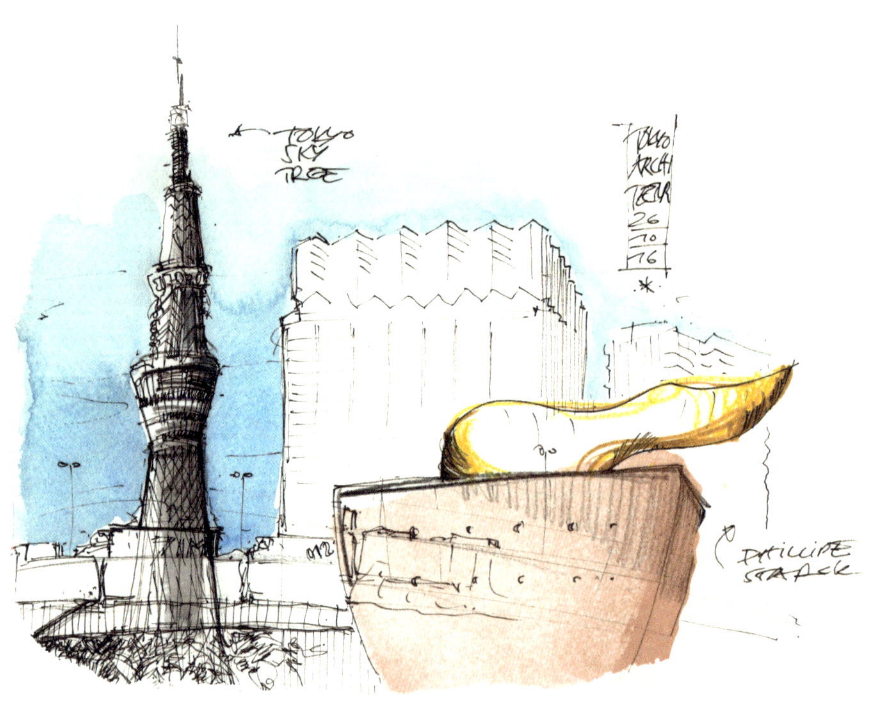

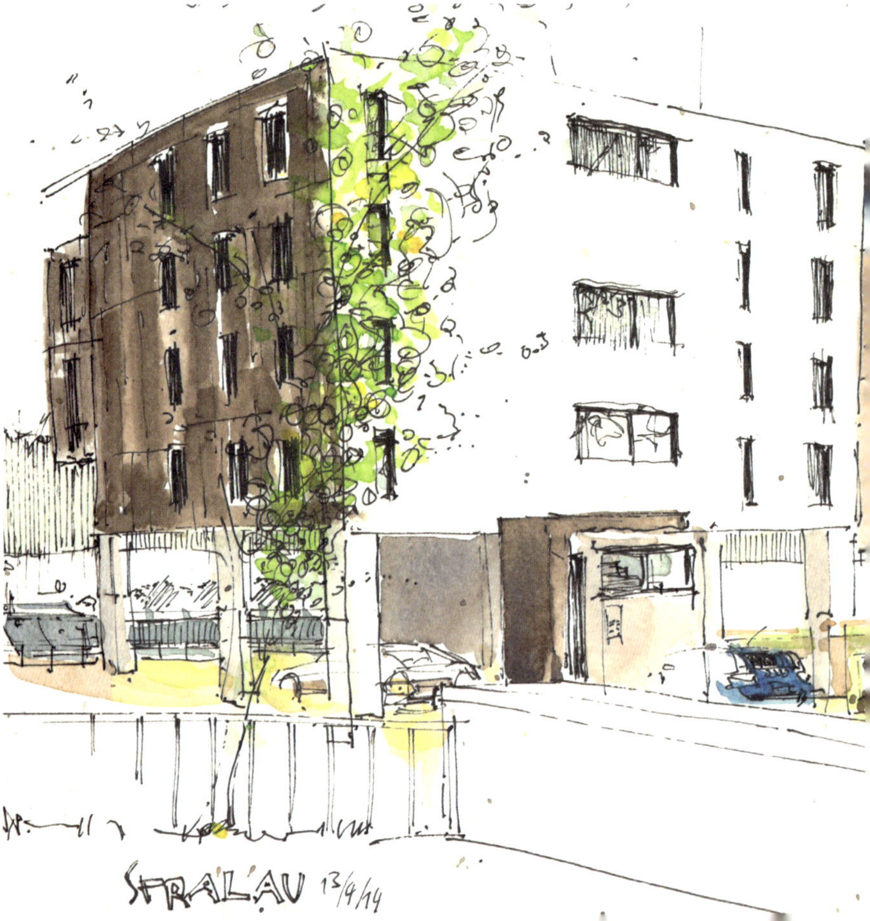

Tip: Leave the drawing "unfinished." If only some details are completed, the charm of a sketch remains intact.

Boxes, Prisms, and Cylinders

When you're drawing, buildings can also be seen as boxes, which greatly simplifies depicting complex shapes and groups. First, transfer the overall outline, for example a cube, onto paper. Mentally divide this outline into further basic geometric shapes. Arrange these "building blocks" one after the other in your sketch. Pay attention to proportion and perspective. Then add details.

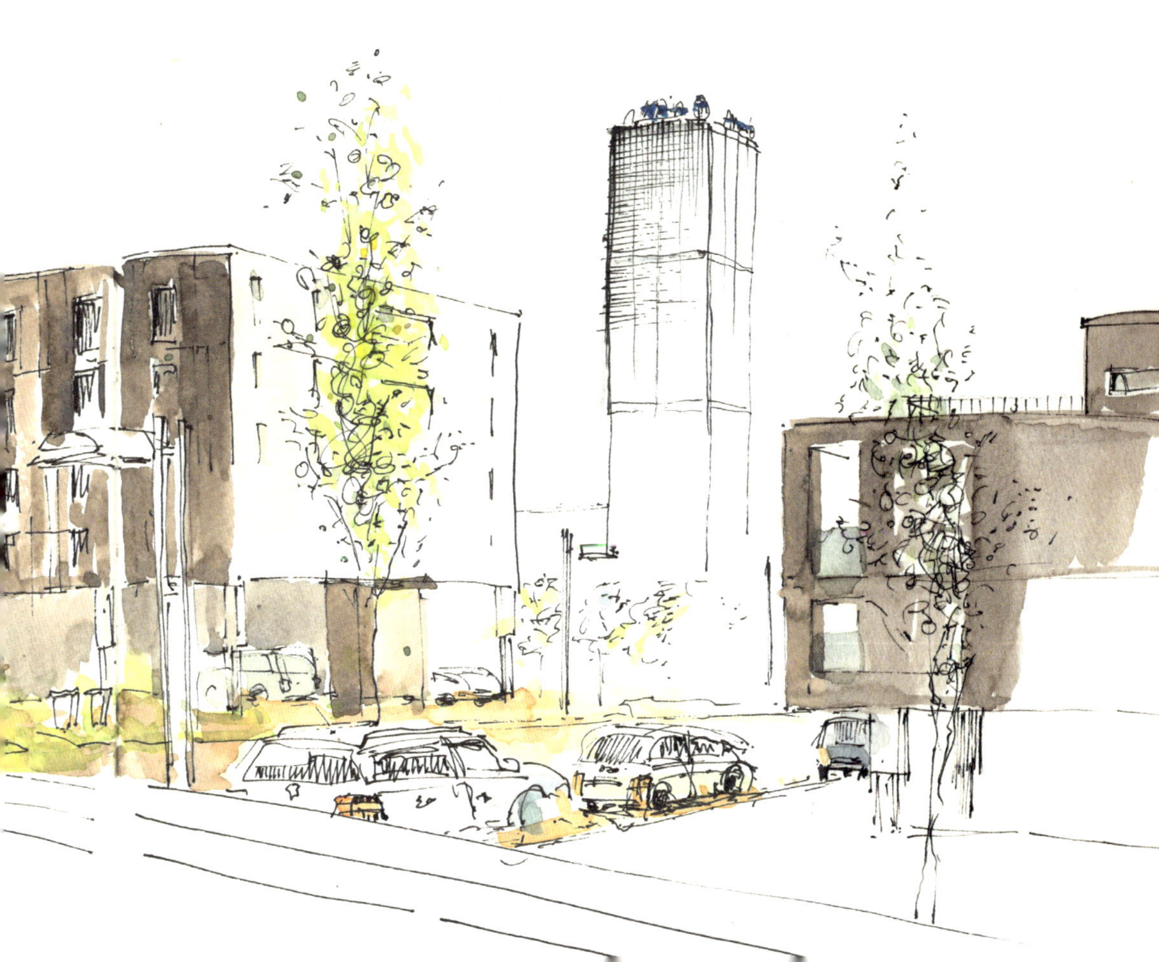

Nighttime

Nighttime pictures of cities are like reverse images. Everything that is bright during the day (usually the sky) becomes dark, and walls and streets that are gray by day turn into illuminated facades and carpets of light. You can easily see this change by scanning a picture taken during the day and then reversing light and dark on your computer.

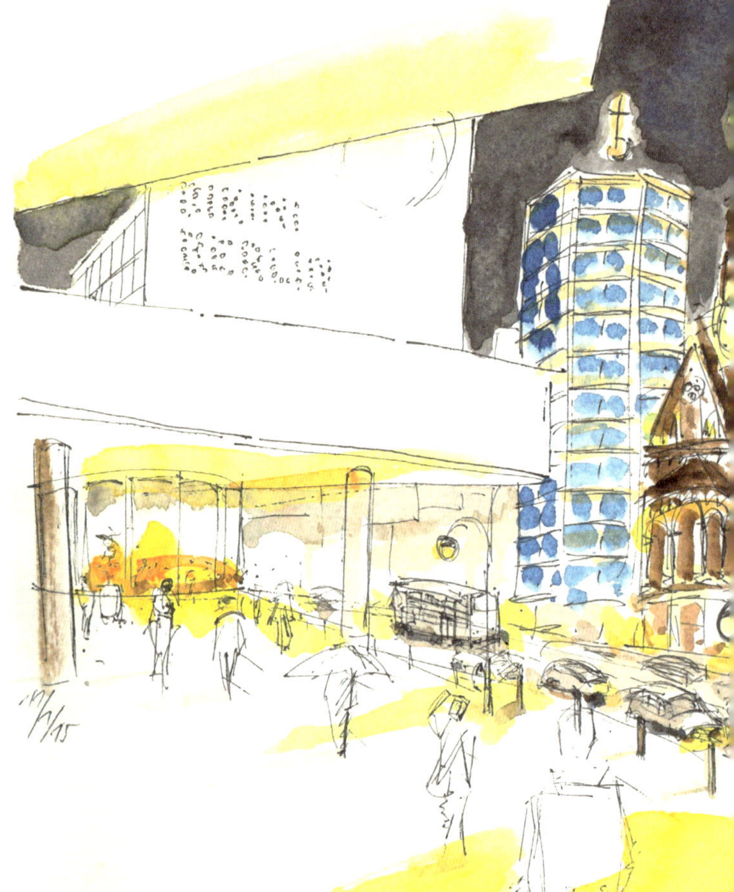

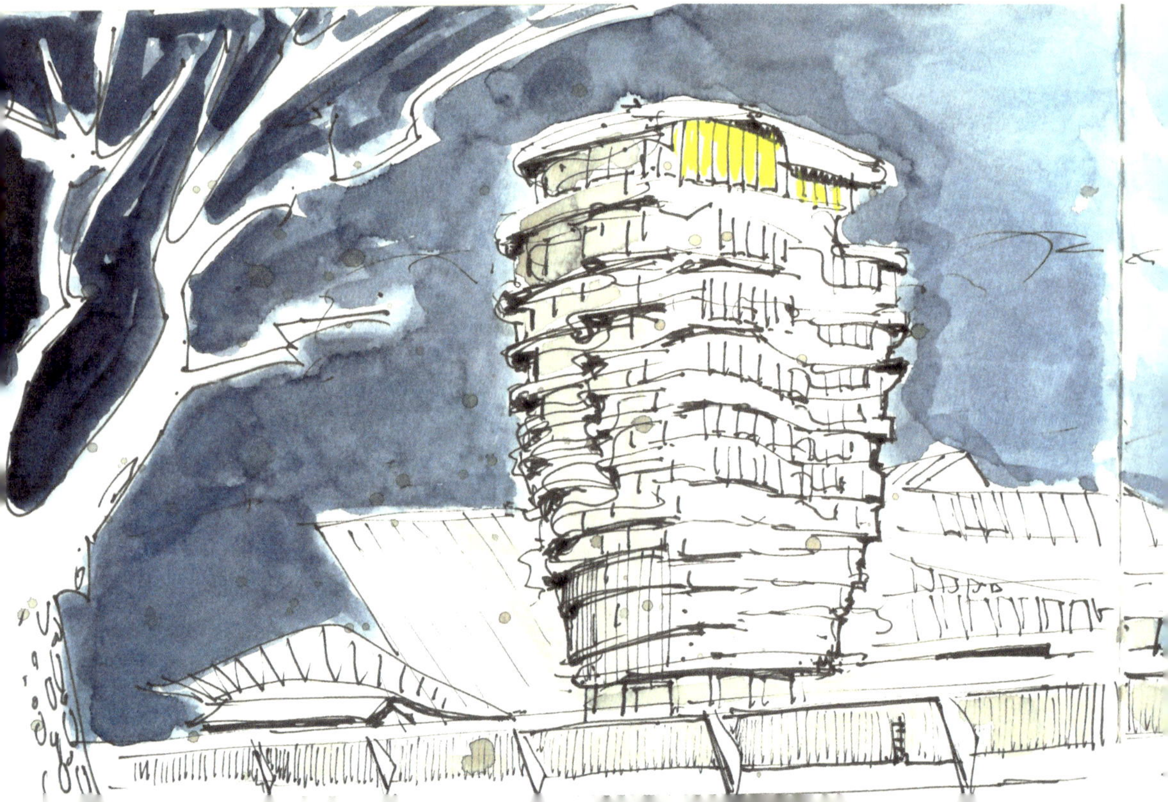

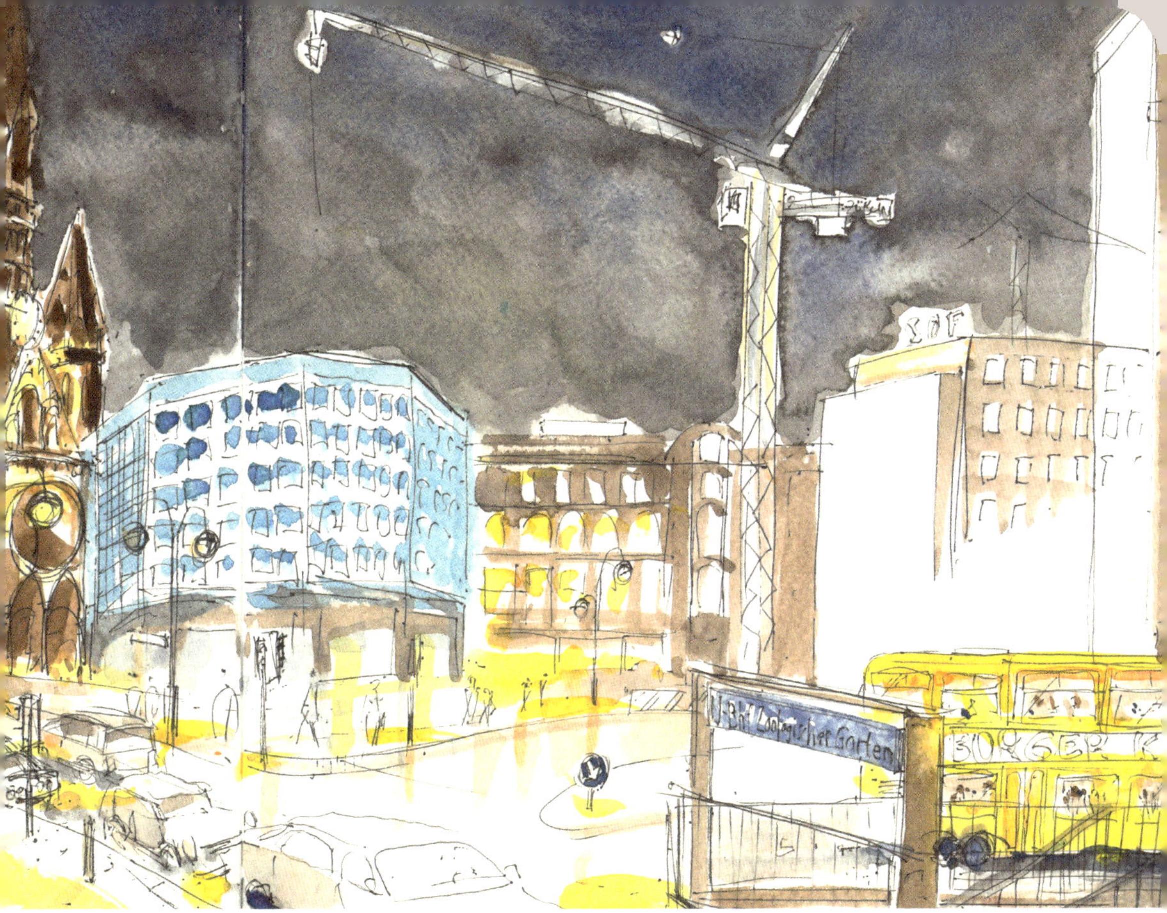

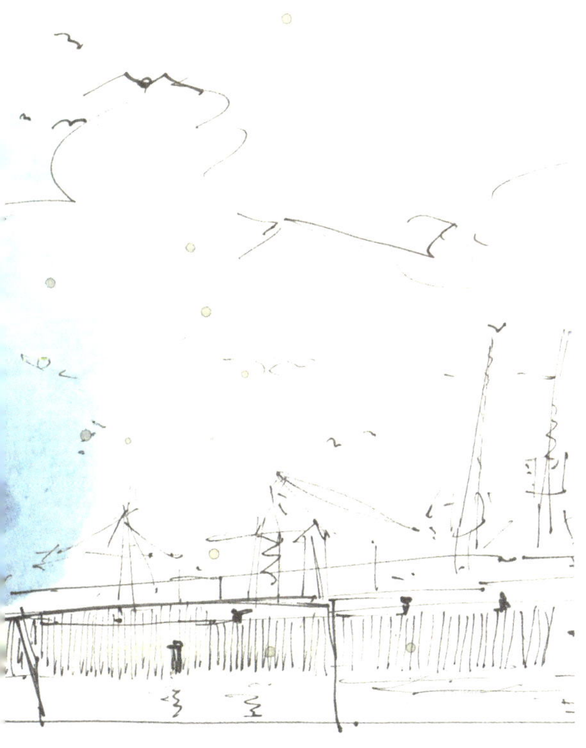

Last One Out, Turn Off the Lights

In this watercolor painting, the background of the picture is filled in with a dark color, like indigo blue. Trees, buildings, and street furniture are left white and only colored in a few places. Now the window rule is reversed: The openings in the facade remain white, with a single yellow light shining onto the street.

Knowing When to Stop

Sometimes in my workshops, I'll see a great piece of work on the verge of being ruined and have to burst out, "Stop!"

Put the pen down! Stop coloring! No more details!

Knowing the right moment to declare a picture finished is an art in itself. So many questions: Did I miss anything? Are the colors just right? Is everything balanced? Are there enough details? Or have I gone too far?

Sketching outdoors is good training for decision-making. Compared to working in a studio, there's little time for doubt and analysis. Subjects change quickly, sketches remain unfinished, and the journey continues. Drawings that are ended abruptly often turn out to be "complete" in retrospect. This is because their sparsity captures the moment best.

So go ahead! Stop drawing and show off what you've done: *This is my picture!*

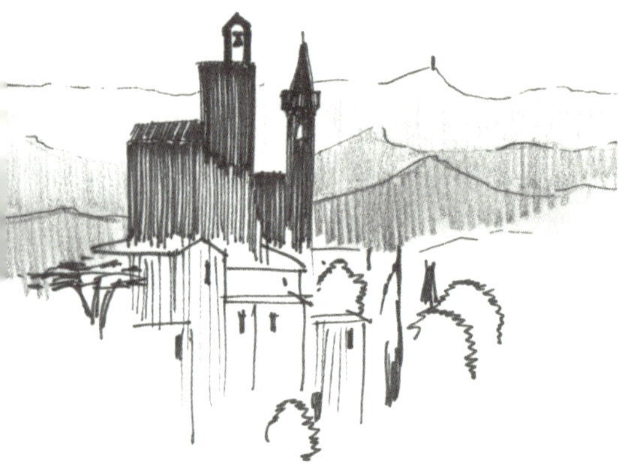

A few lines—lots to see: These minimal fiber-tip pen sketches leave plenty of room for interpretation, whether they depict objects, people, nature, or cities.

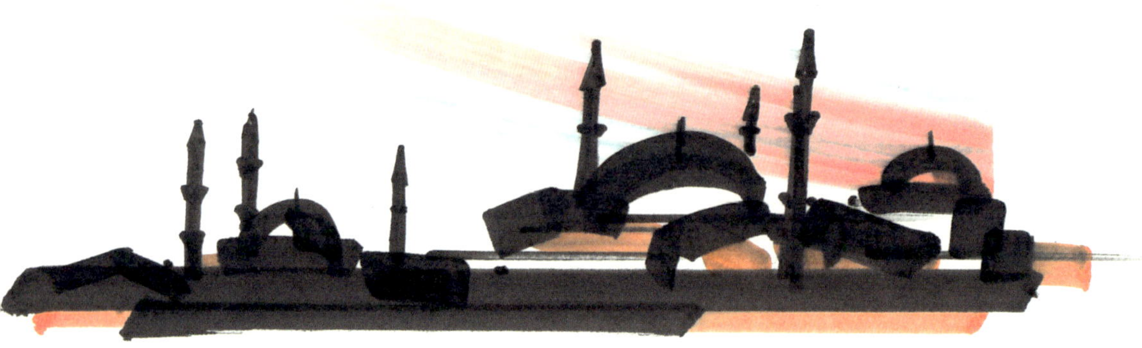

Seven Tips to Keep you from Drawing too Much

1. Reduce or omit typical repetitive elements (roof tiles, windows, leaves).
2. Open up outlines (edges of buildings and objects, contours of bodies and faces).
3. Only work out details in the focal point of the image; suggest the rest.
4. Allow for white space (emphasizes the condensed parts of the image).
5. Color important elements; leave unimportant elements black and white.
6. Limit yourself to one or two colors.
7. Don't paint over watercolor areas multiple times (colors will become dull).

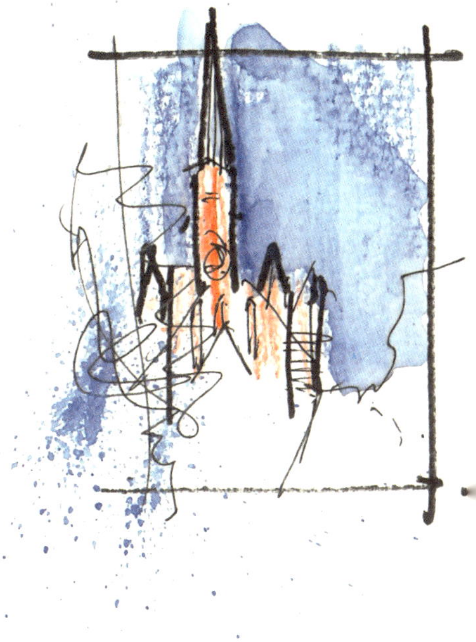

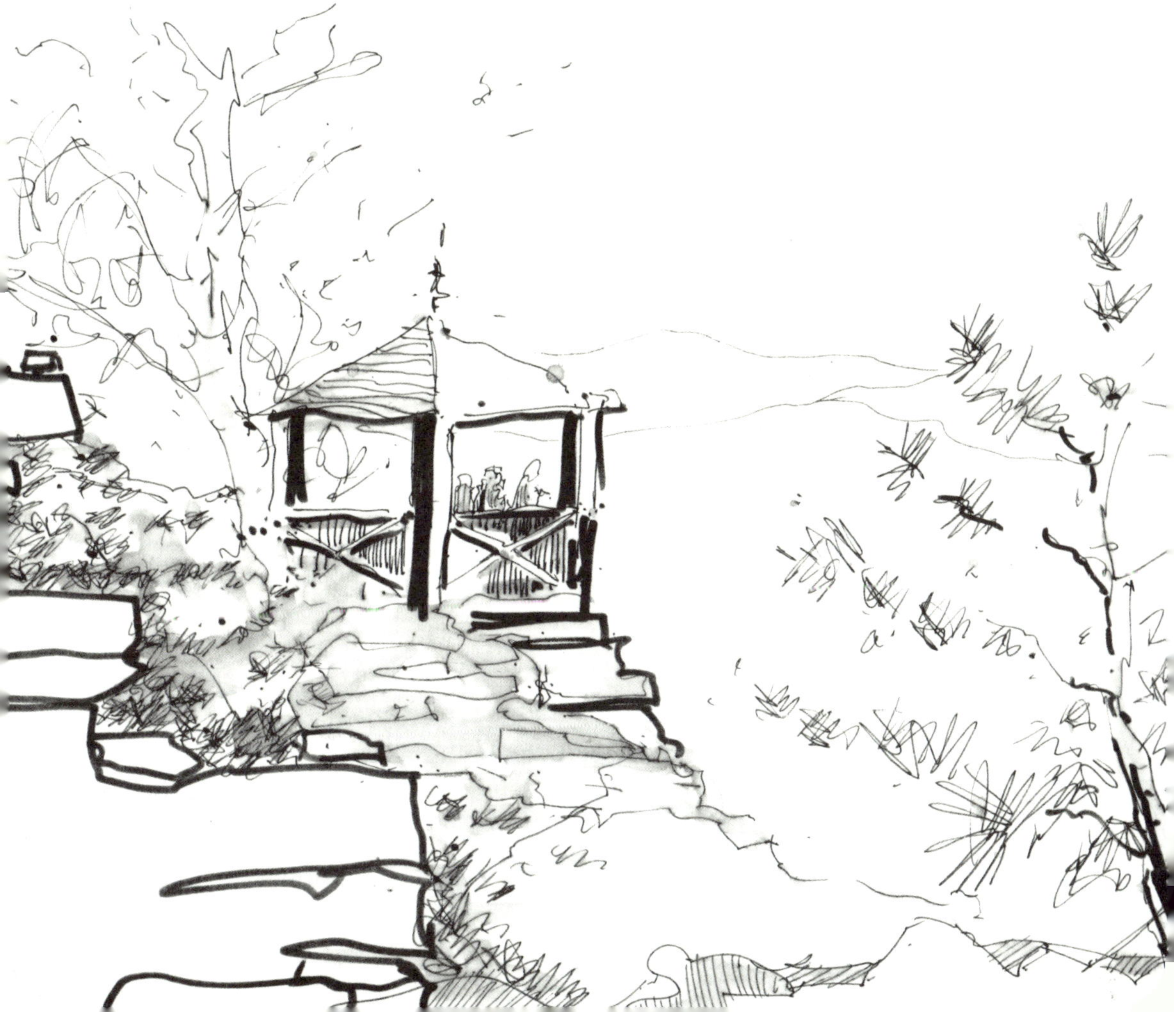

Digital Sketching 7

As a champion of sketching by hand, I had to really step out of my comfort zone when switching from my favorite drawing pen to a pen without ink and when trading my familiar sketchbook paper for the glass surface of a tablet.

Fortunately, I didn't step out alone. I had accompanied architects on lots of sketching tours with pen, paper, and picnic blanket. Now they wanted to learn about the world of digital sketching. Instead of slick CAD technology, quick scribbles were in demand on the construction site. They're easy to create, and even easier to share. And yet digital sketches bear an artistic signature, a personal character that often gives clients that decisive nudge to approve a design.

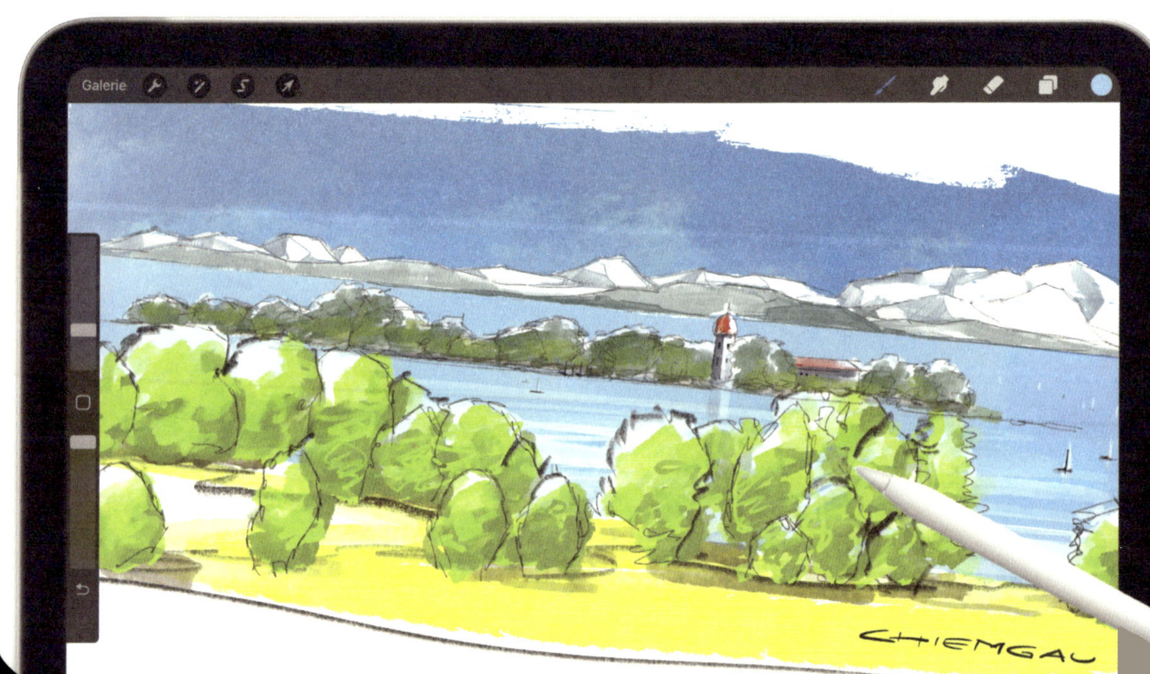

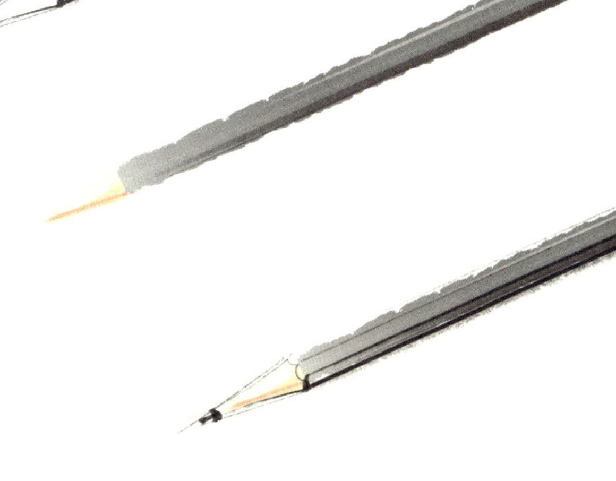

Tablets and other devices are the perfect tools for high-impact presentations and quick sketches. A variety of digital brushes faithfully reproduce surfaces and materials. Practical tools, layer effects, and lots of editing options make drawing much easier. On the following pages, you'll find my tips for digital illustration.

As it happens, I created the illustrations of the drawing tools and many of the practice sketches in this book digitally.

Digital has the advantage of individual layers that allow you to complete the line drawings and coloring separately.

Tip: In my opinion, its wide range of artistic tools makes the subscription-free Procreate app one of the best apps for illustrating and sketching. You'll need a tablet with a display size of at least 10.2 inches.

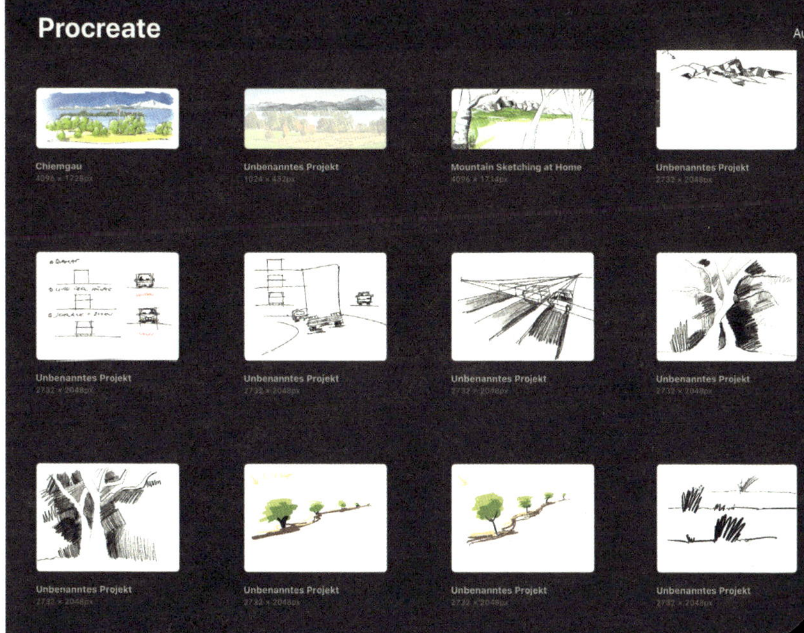

Warm-Up: Draw an Object

As with analog drawing, regular practice is the key to mastery here. To get comfortable with the new technique, choose a simple object as a model, like my water brush pens shown here. You can quickly create contours, materiality, light, and shadow and become familiar with the characteristics of digital brushes in no time.

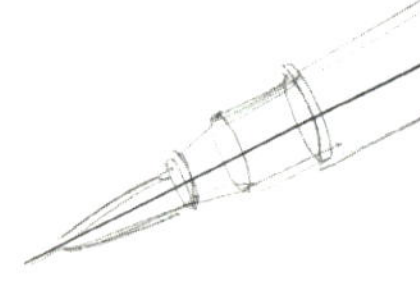

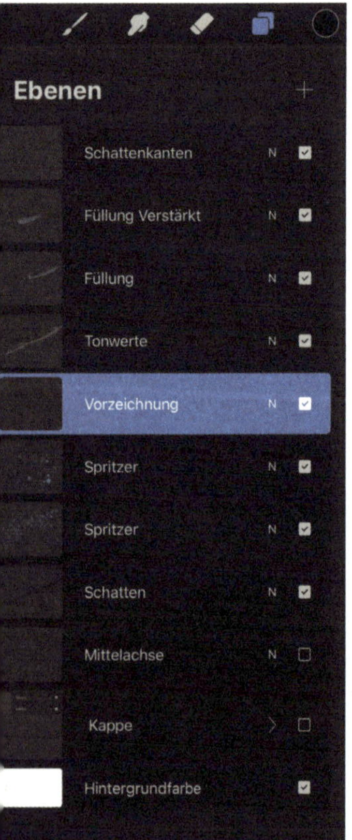

Step-by-Step Exercise: Drawing Tools

1. Create the center axis and preliminary sketch (brush: HB pencil).
2. Create tonal values in grayscale (brush: Gloaming).
3. Suggest water filling (brush: Gloaming).
4. Enhance shadow edges (brush: Syrup).
5. Draw drop shadows (brush: Gloaming).
6. Add splashes (brush: Spritzer).

Layer arrangement: Drawing elements created separately can be modified, duplicated, shown, and hidden as desired.

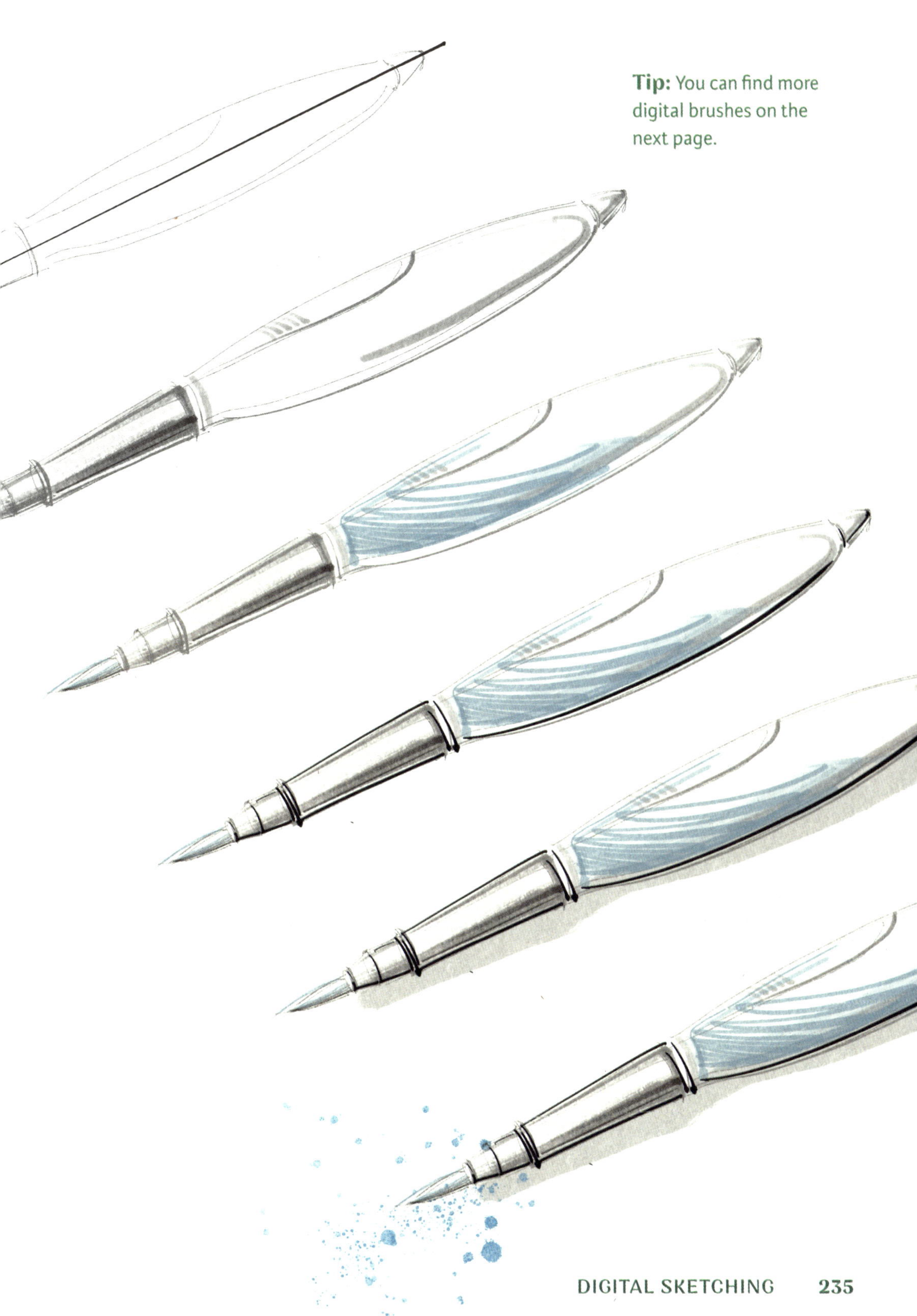

Tip: You can find more digital brushes on the next page.

Paintbrush Paradise

In technical jargon, not only brushes with bristles are considered brushes, but also all pens, painting knives, and spray cans. It feels like there are thousands of brushes available for digital drawing. Since I was very critical of these "fake drawing tools" when I first started using my tablet, I initially went in search of my favorites. I found them, and respect for the programmers of my new tools. Here I show "familiar" tools like pencils and fineliners, their stroke patterns, and the brush names in the Procreate app.

Tip: You can adjust the brush size and opacity using these sliders.

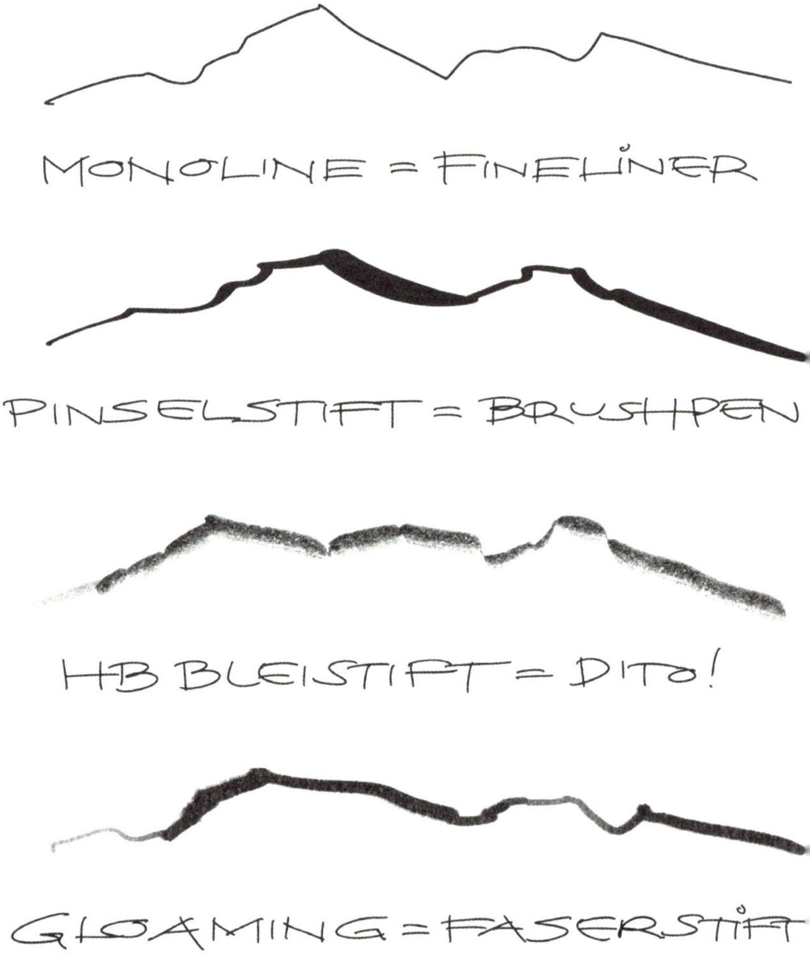

MONOLINE = FINELINER

PINSELSTIFT = BRUSHPEN

HB BLEISTIFT = DITO!

GLOAMING = FASERSTIFT

A selection of flat brushes that I use for landscapes: Whether for lines or larger areas, each brush can be used both to add and remove material (pixels), as when erasing. You can see how to use this technique to create effective backgrounds on the following pages.

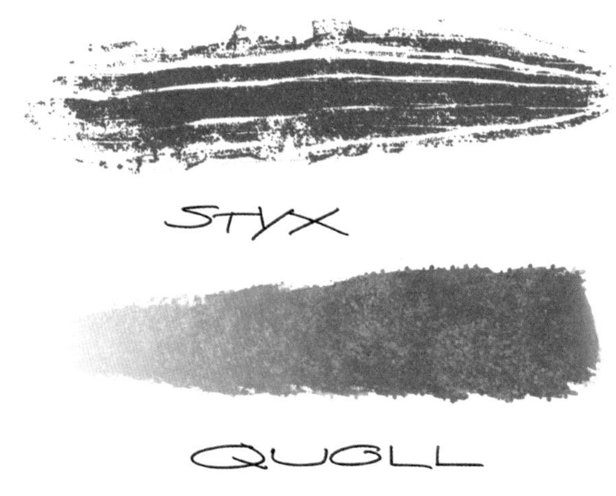

STYX

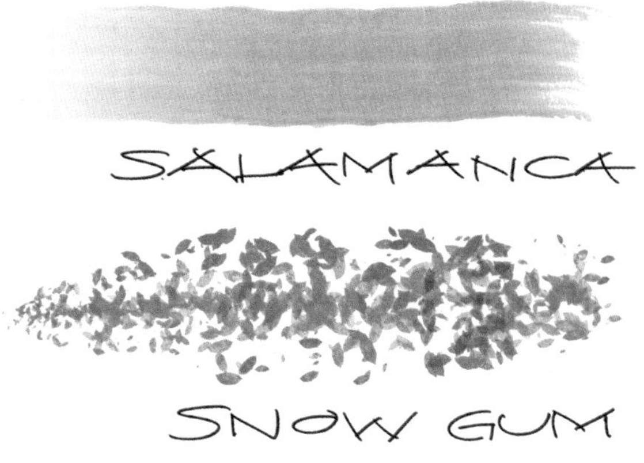

QUOLL
SALAMANCA
SNOW GUM

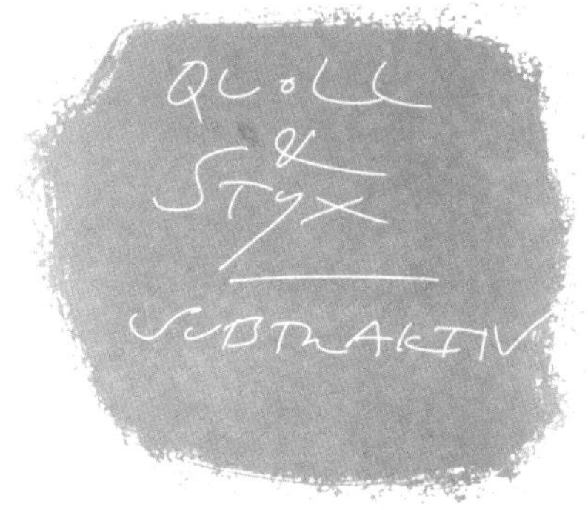

QUOLL
&
STYX
SUBTRAKTIV

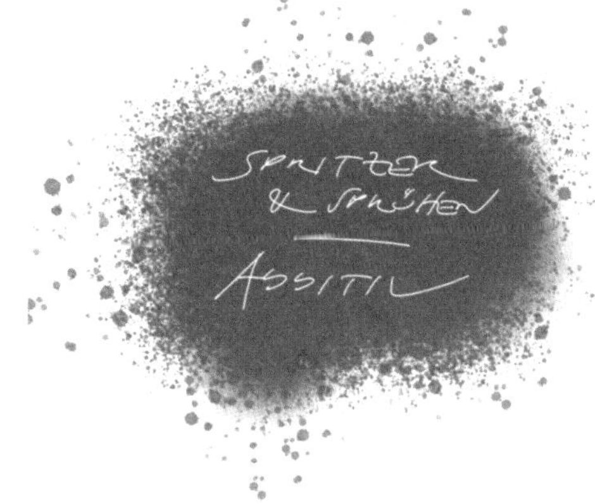

SPRITZER
& SPRÜHEN
ADDITIV

With the monoline brush, you can quickly create the contours of a few mountains. Flat brushes like the Quoll and Salamanca create effective backgrounds. In a further step, you can use the Styx brush to "erase" image edges with a silkscreen effect.

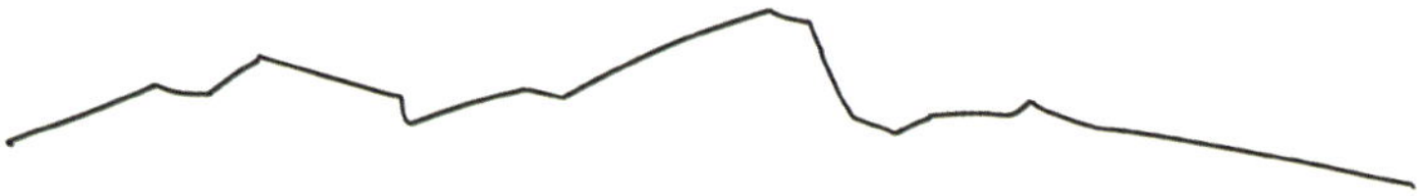

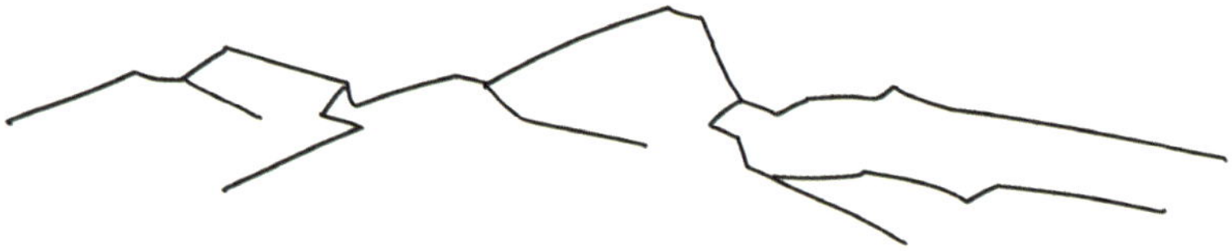

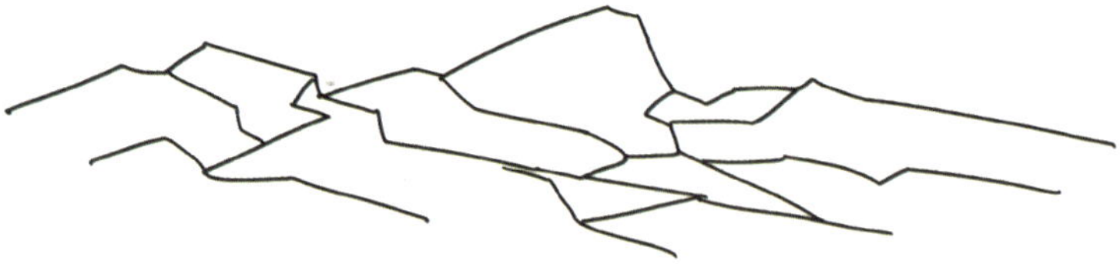

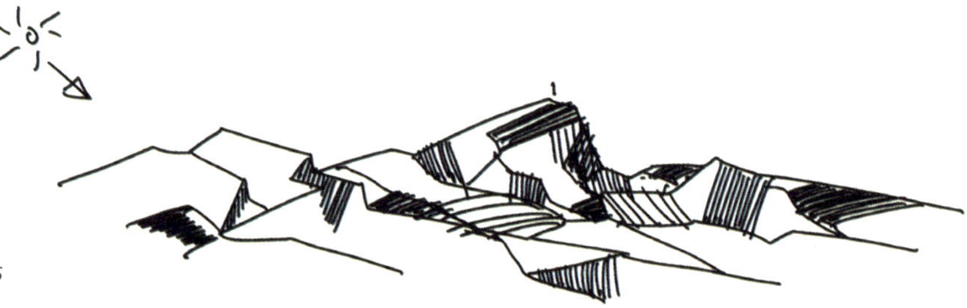

Sunlight from the left casts shadows on the right side of the mountain. Hatching emphasizes the dark mountain slopes.

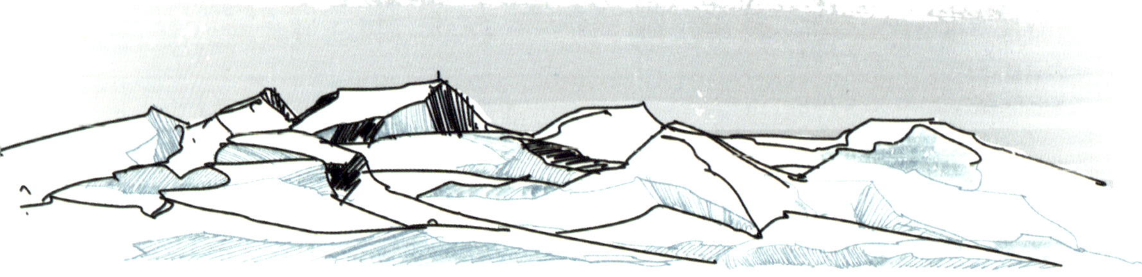

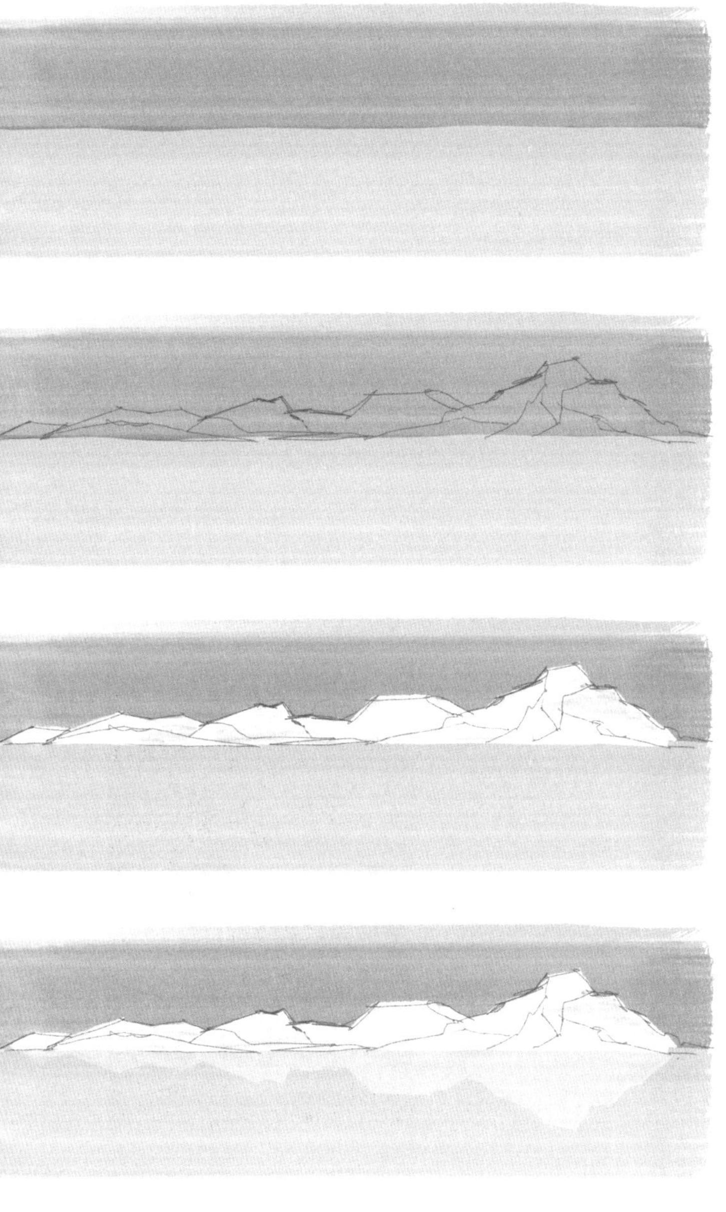

Exercise: Mountain Silhouette with Lake

1. Create the background.
2. Draw in the outlines.
3. Make the mountain areas light in color.
4. Reflect the mountain areas transparently in the lake.
5. Add hatching and reinforce the outlines.

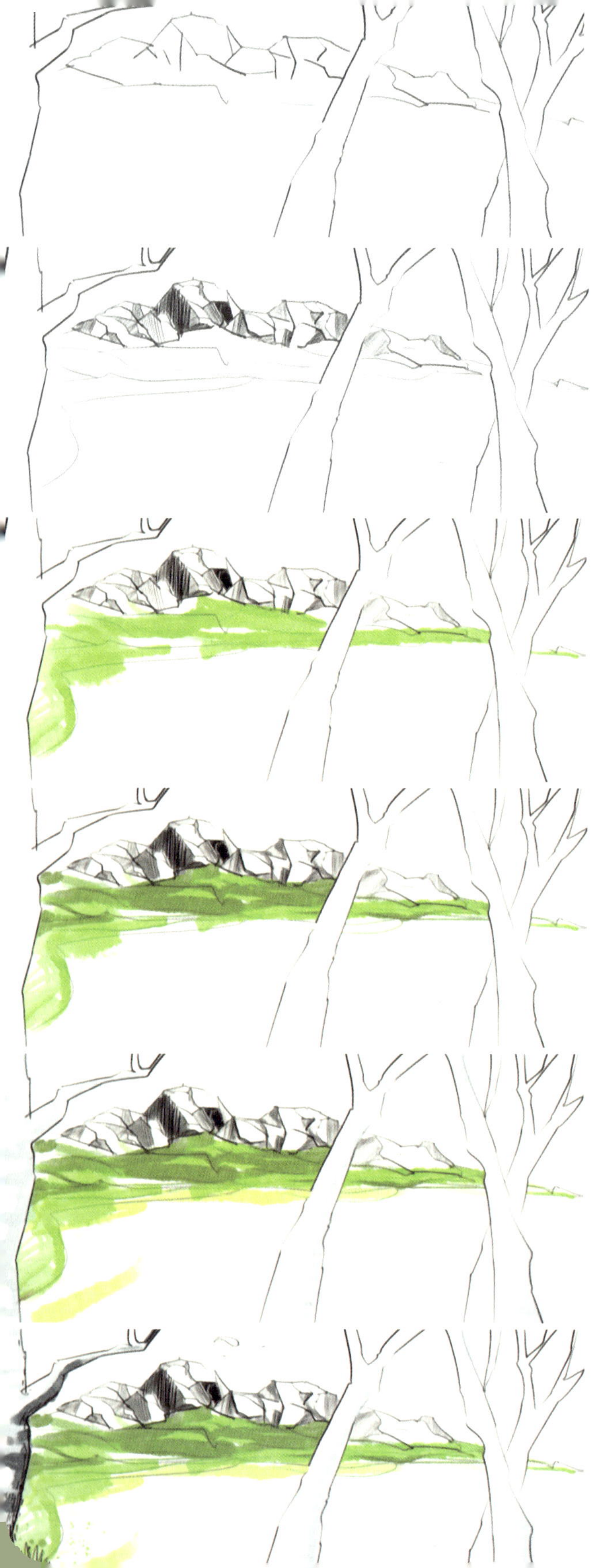

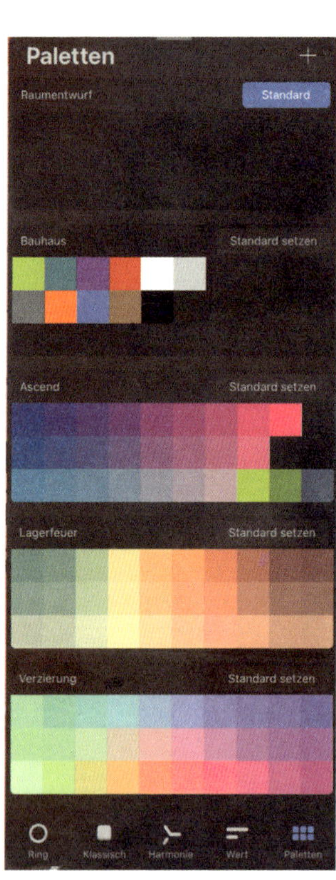

Colors at your fingertips: You can create palettes using the color picker, from image templates, or directly from your tablet's camera.

Hard to Tell Apart

With a little practice, you can try out other outdoor subjects like vegetation, weather, and clouds. Digital brushes have their own painterly expression, and each pen and brush in the app has its own style. Depending on the angle and pressure of the pen on the tablet surface, you can achieve finely differentiated results. You can create sets of your favorite brushes.

Working with colors is also easy in Procreate. Personal color palettes can be quickly created, just like on watercolor paper, and finished color harmonies can be accessed in the app.

The market has long since responded to the lack of haptics on tablet surfaces: Protective films for tablets bring back the "feel of paper." And the works themselves? Whenever I hold a well-made digital illustration in my hands, it's almost impossible to distinguish a tablet sketch from its analog counterpart on paper.

Have I set myself up for failure at the end of this book? Don't our pencils and sketchbooks already seem antiquated compared to tablets and pens? For me, it's not an either/or situation: Both techniques require the mind and hand of the artist. Sketching on a tablet is digital art, but ultimately, it's still created by hand.

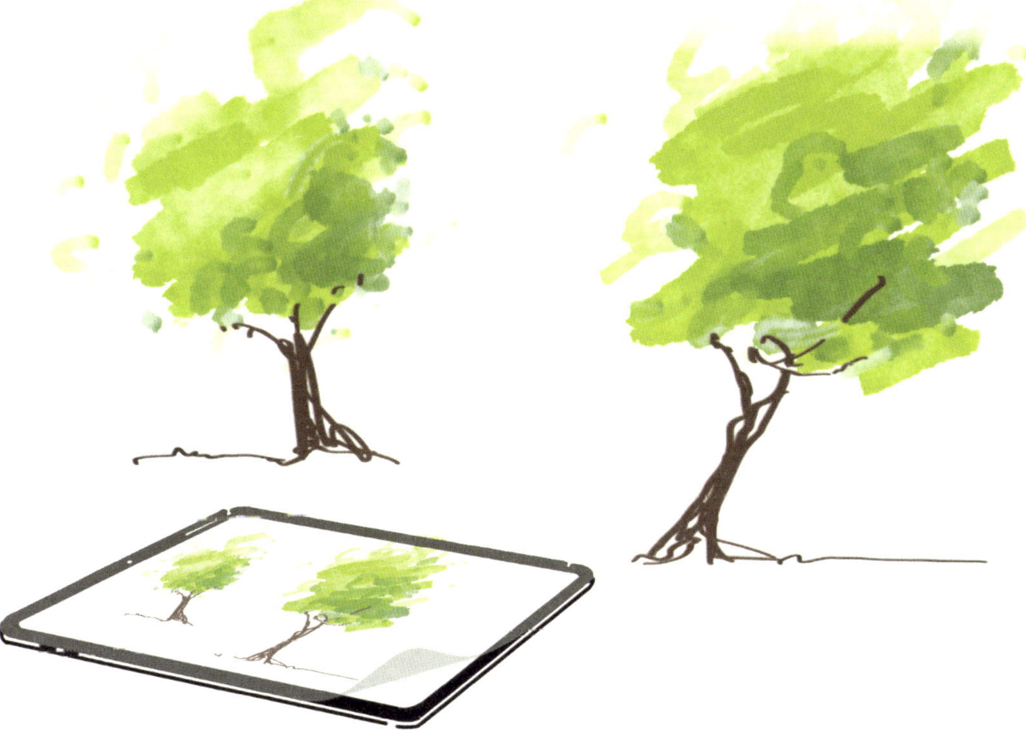

Just like paper: Protective films, like those from Swiss manufacturer Paperlike, offer the tactile feel of paper.

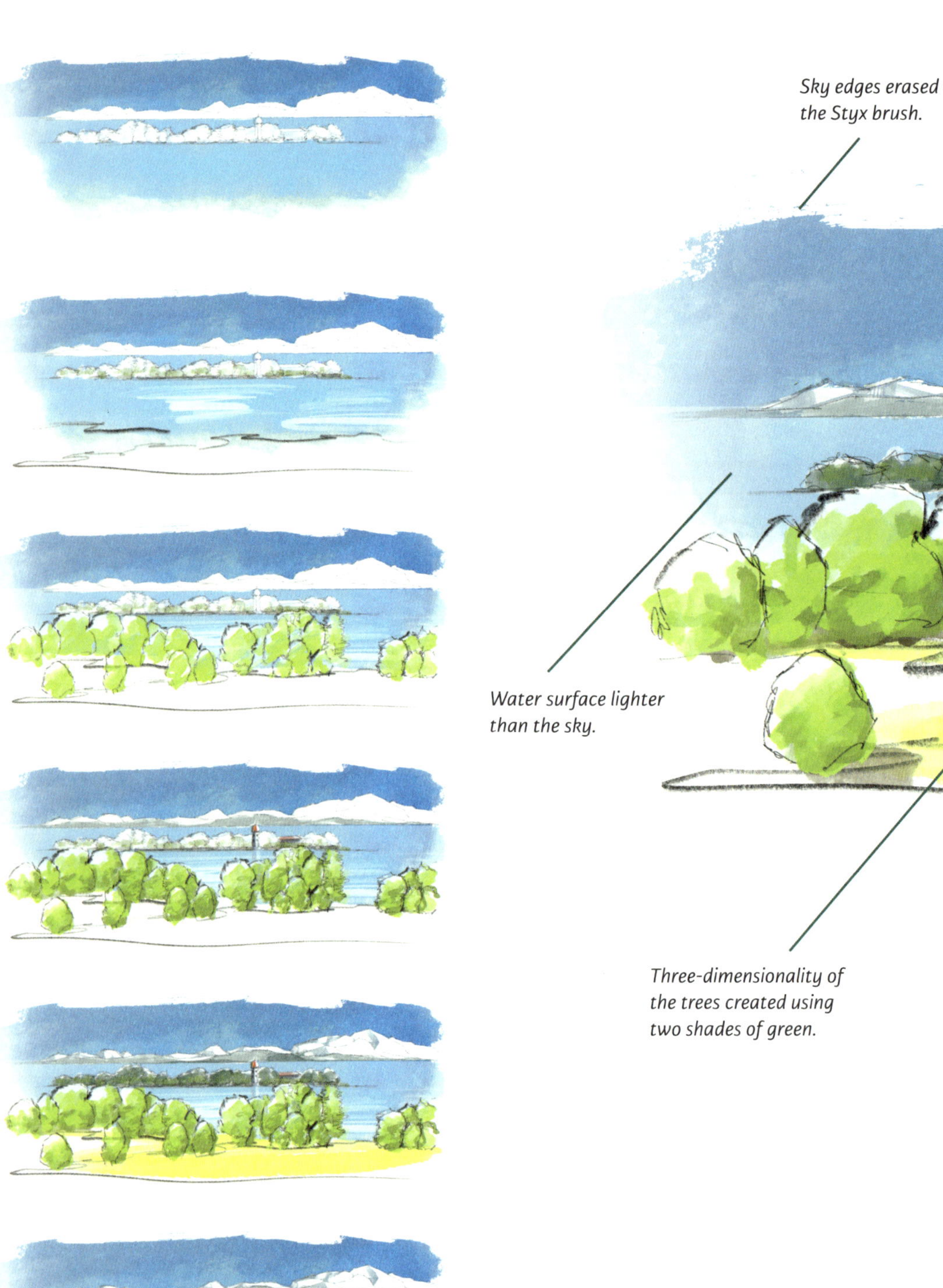

Sky edges erased with
the Styx brush.

Water surface lighter
than the sky.

Three-dimensionality of
the trees created using
two shades of green.

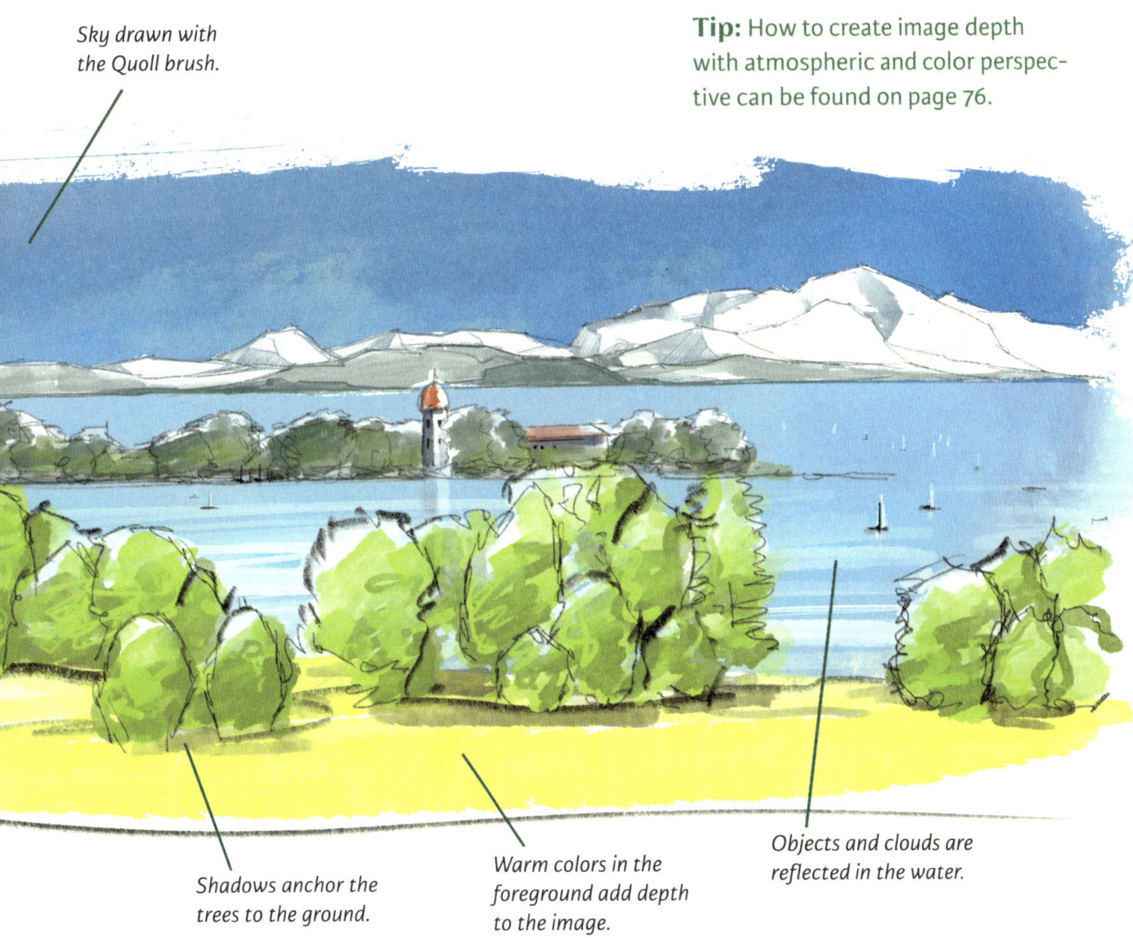

Exercise: Foreground, Middle Ground, and Background

The depth of a landscape drawing is created by layering three clearly separated planes: foreground, middle ground, and background. In the foreground, landscape details are clearly visible; individual trees, grass, and paths are rich in contrast and warm colors.

In the middle ground, the level of detail decreases: Trees merge into groups of trees, buildings are still recognizable but with fewer details. At the same time, the proportion of warm colors in the image decreases, and natural tones become "bluer."

Cool colors dominate the background of the image. The shapes of the landscape are reduced to areas and lines. Due to the great distance, no details can be discerned.

My Materials and Tools

Clockwise: 2B pencil with eraser cap (e.g., Faber-Castell); waterproof fineliner pen, thin (e.g., Pilot gel pen G-Tec C4 0.2) and thick (e.g., Copic Multiliner 1.0); colored pencils and watercolor pencils; fiber-tip pens with brush tip (e.g., Faber-Castell Pitt Artist Pen); Japanese ink pen; round and flat watercolor brushes (e.g., da Vinci sizes 4–12); water brush pens; water-color sketchbook with fine grained paper, minimum 200 gsm (e.g., Hahne-mühle Watercolour A5/A4—landscape and portrait formats); small watercolor set (e.g., Horadam paints from Schmincke)

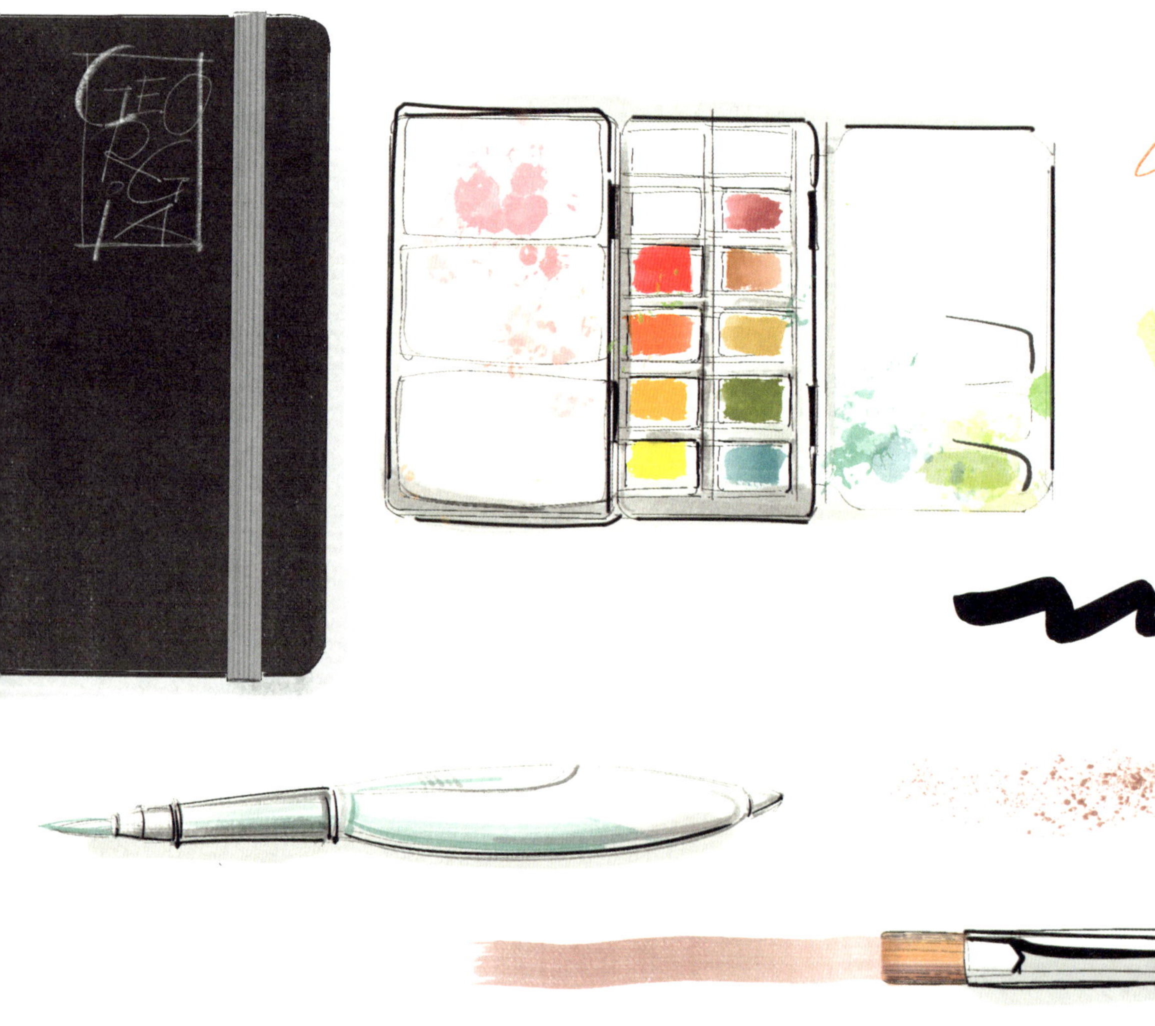

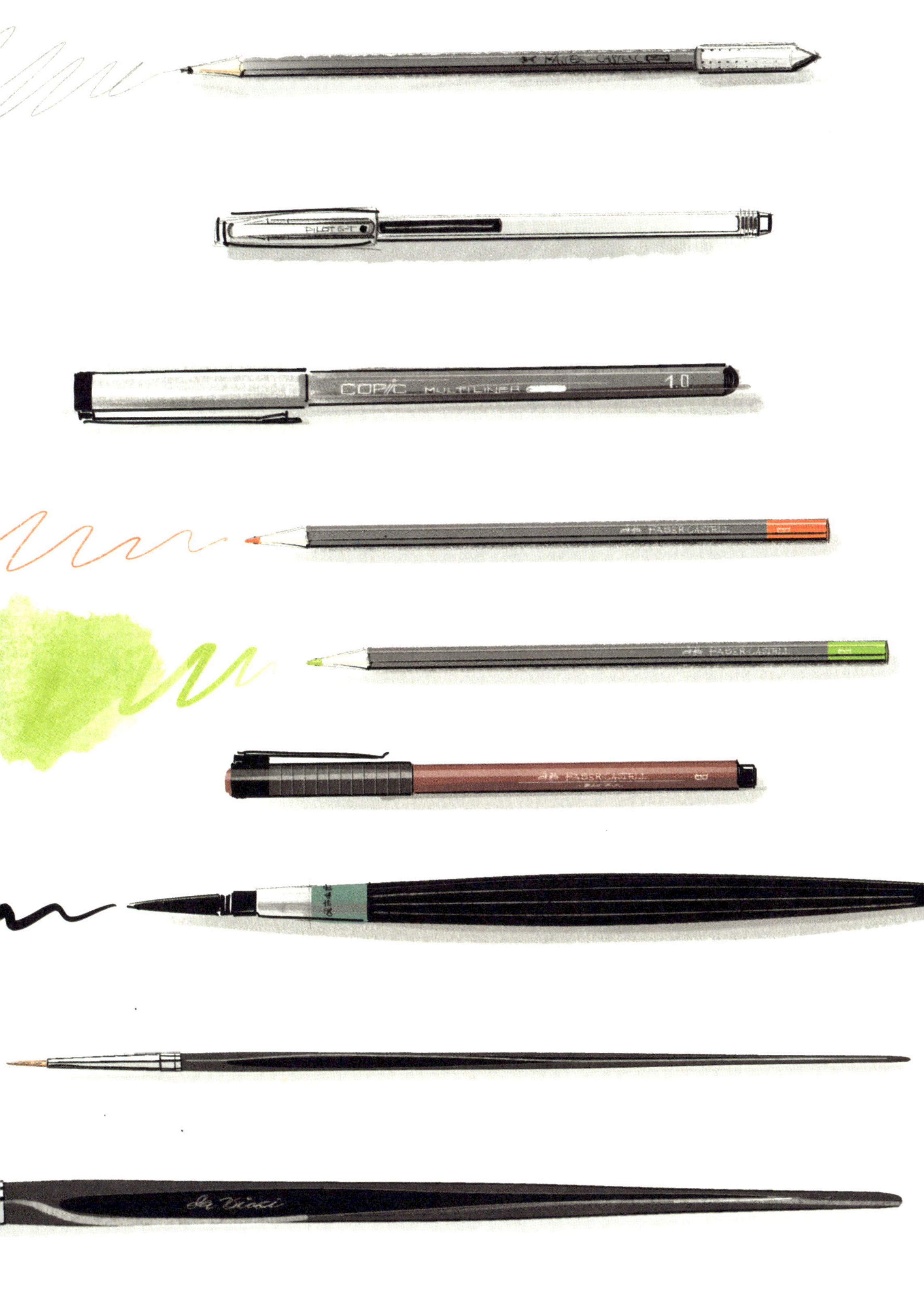

Stick With It and Stay Outdoors

My book lured you out into the open and encouraged you to draw freehand. Now what? Have you only just begun sketching? Do you still have blank pages? You're still drawing? That's wonderful. Then I've achieved my goal: You're sticking with it. You're going out regularly to sketch. You're stopping to capture landscapes, travels, outdoor moments. Your most important tool is always with you: your drawing hand. Use it freely and openly—whether it's moving a pencil across paper or a stylus on a tablet. And if you get stuck, let's go outside together. In my courses, workshops, and sketching trips, I share calm, happy moments of sketching, whether with newcomers, returners, or experts. You can find all the information, dates, and links on my website. I hope you have inspiring experiences, fresh ideas, and, above all, lots of fun sketching.

Tilo Schneider

www.illude.de
kontakt@illude.de

About the Author

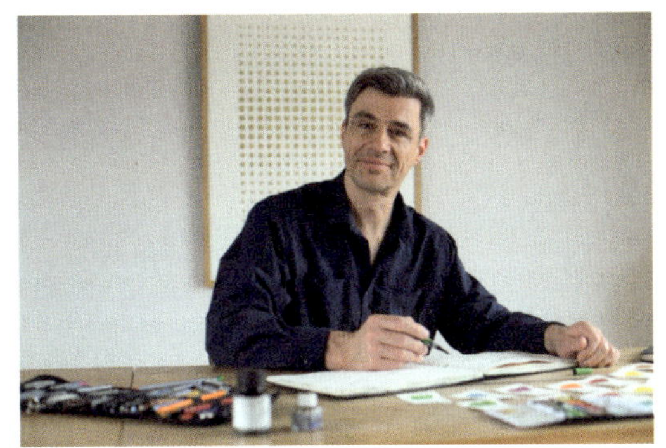

Tilo Schneider is a freelance designer, illustrator, and sketching instructor. For his courses and workshops, he collaborates with various renowned institutes, publishers, companies, and associations. On their behalf, he teaches architects, designers, and hobbyists throughout Germany. He passes on his passion for drawing, building on his many years of experience.

After completing his carpentry apprenticeship, he studied product design at the Schwäbisch Gmünd University of Art and Design. He went on to work in Amsterdam, Vienna, and Munich and set up his own design studio (vierzudrei.de). As cofounder of the Academy for Illustration and Design Berlin, he initiated a pre-study year for design in 2012, which still prepares young designers for their creative studies today. Bavarian by choice, he now lives in Chiemgau, Germany, from where he explores mountains, lakes, and cities on foot and with his drawing pen.

Acknowledgments

I would like to thank Karin and Bertram Schmidt-Friderichs for their meticulous editing, their ever-appreciative collaboration on equal footing, and their insight into the art of creating good books. I would like to thank the publishing team in Mainz for their warm support in all phases of the book project. My special thanks go to Nathalie Hummel (die-hummel.de) for her professional writing support. And finally, my thanks go to everyone who has inspired, supported, and accompanied me on the way to these 248 pages, on my sketching journeys, and in the further development of my workshops: Anne, Denis, Doris, Sepp, Stefan, and every one of my course participants. And Marlene and Jo—on their way into the great outdoors.

Library of Congress Cataloging-in-Publication Data available.

ISBN 978-1-7972-4101-2

Manufactured in Turkey.

Typesetting by Frank Brayton.

10 9 8 7 6 5 4 3 2 1

Chronicle books and gifts are available at special quantity discounts to corporations, professional associations, literacy programs, and other organizations. For details and discount information, please contact our premiums department at corporatesales@chroniclebooks.com or at 1-800-759-0190.

Chronicle Books LLC
680 Second Street
San Francisco, California 94107
chroniclebooks.com

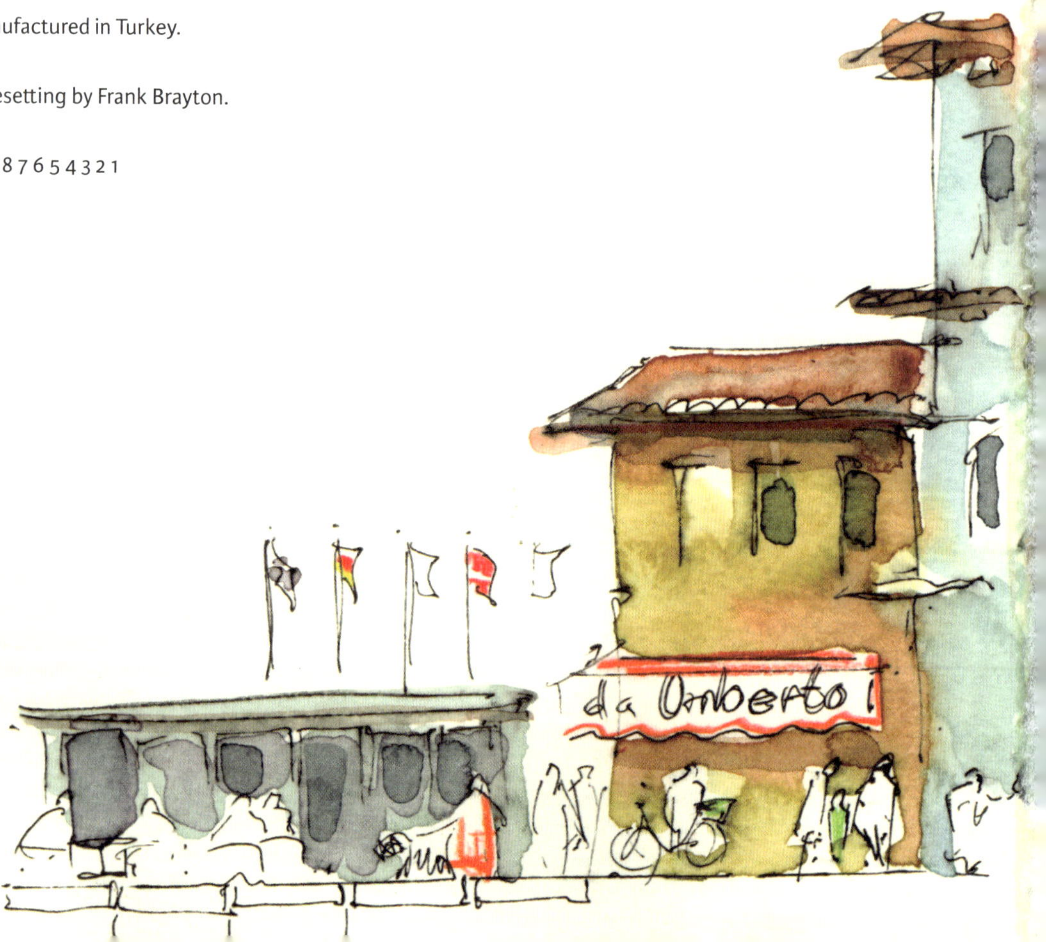

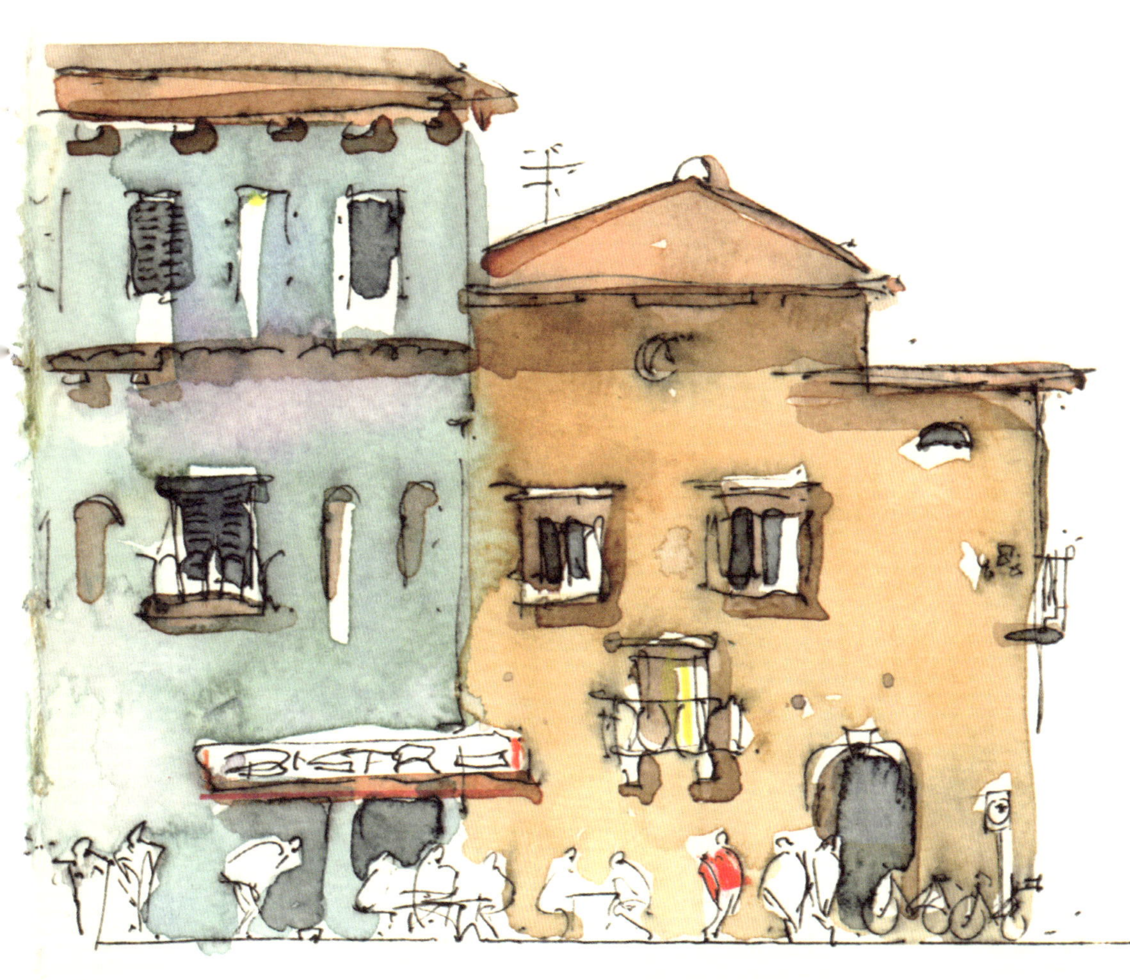
BISTRO

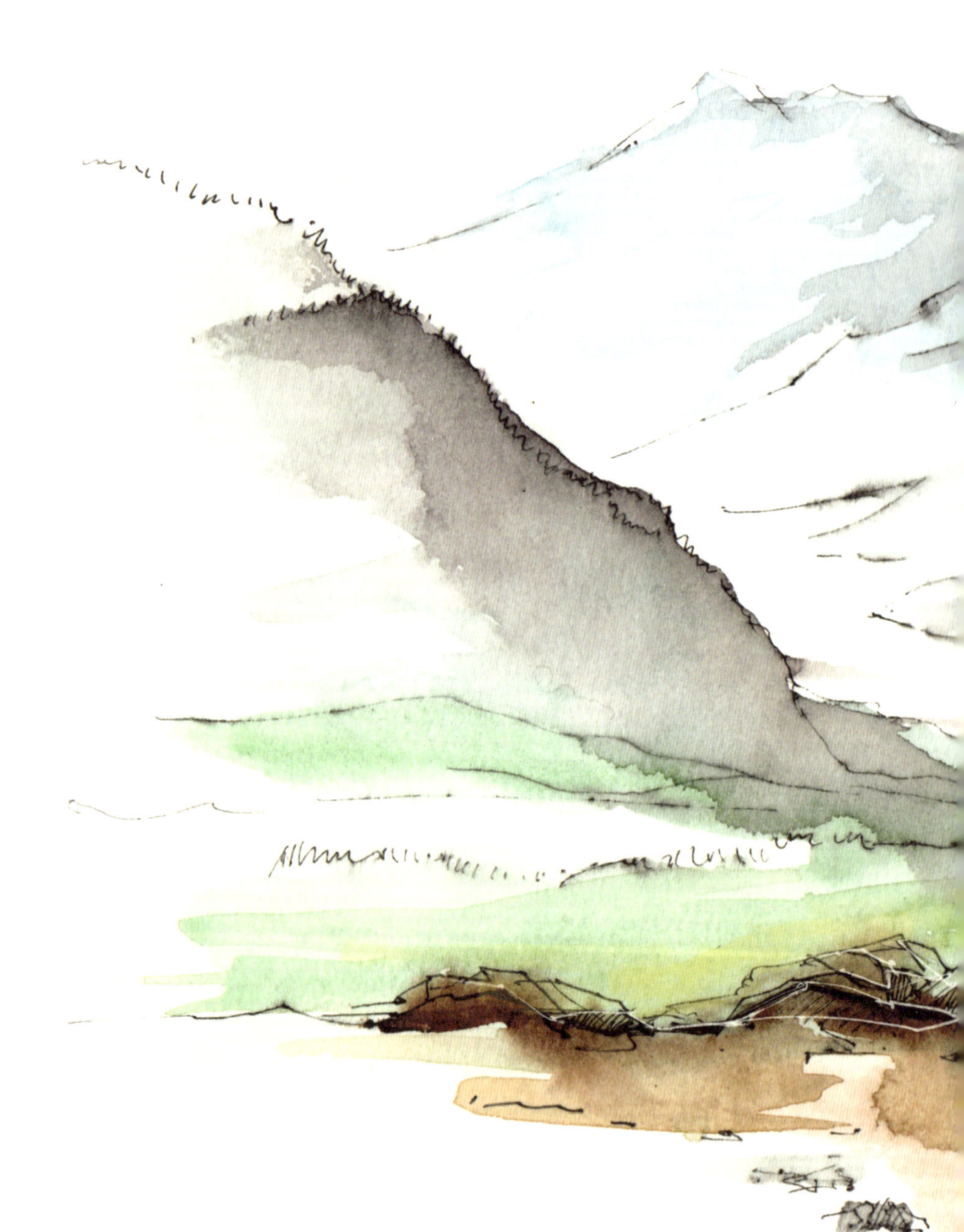